MW01470763

TENNESSEE
GOVERNMENT
AND POLITICS

TENNESSEE
GOVERNMENT
AND POLITICS

DEMOCRACY IN THE VOLUNTEER STATE

EDITED BY

John R. Vile and Mark Byrnes

Vanderbilt University Press
Nashville and London

First edition 1998
98 99 00 01 02 5 4 3 2 1

This publication is made from paper that meets
the minimum requirements of ANSI/NISO Z39.48 (R 1997)
Permanence of Paper for Printed Library Materials ∞

Library of Congress Cataloging-in-Publication Data

Tennessee government and politics : democracy in the volunteer
state / edited by John R. Vile and Mark Byrnes. -- 1st ed.
    p. cm.
Includes bibliographical references and index.
ISBN 0-8265-1309-3 (cloth)
ISBN 0-8265-1318-2 (pbk.)
1. Tennessee--Politics and government. I. Vile, John R. II.
Byrnes, Mark E.
JK5216 .T46 1998
320.9768--ddc21
                             98-8946
                              CIP

Manufactured in the United States of America

to our political science colleagues, past and present,
at Middle Tennessee State University
and throughout the state

CONTENTS

Foreword

"As I travel around the country," said Tennessee Senator Bill Frist in late 1997, "people ask me, 'What's in the water in Tennessee these days, with so many presidential contenders?'" Frist and his interlocutors were referring to Vice President Al Gore, Jr., the leading candidate for the 2000 Democratic presidential nomination, and to two Republicans, Sen. Fred Thompson and former Gov. Lamar Alexander, who were being mentioned as serious contenders for their party's nomination. They may not have known it, but the question of Tennesseans' prominence in national politics is not a new one. In the 1980s, for example, Sen. Howard Baker was the Republican Senate leader, and former Sen. Bill Brock rebuilt the national party as chair of the Republican National Committee. In 1956, three Tennesseans—Gov. Frank Clement and Sens. Al Gore, Sr., and Estes Kefauver—were leading figures at the Democratic National Convention. (Kefauver emerged from the convention as the party's vice presidential candidate, having won the nomination in an open contest with Sen. John F. Kennedy of Massachusetts.) During the nineteenth century, three presidents were Tennesseans: Andrew Jackson, whose name marks the era during and after which he served, James K. Polk, generally regarded by historians as having been a "near-great" president, and the less successful Andrew Johnson, who barely survived the only presidential impeachment trial in American history.

The three stars on Tennessee's flag do not represent its three presidents; but they do represent the political and geographical characteristics of the state—namely, Tennessee's three grand divisions—that have proven most productive of national political leaders. Mountainous East Tennessee has, for more than a century, been one of the most consistently Republican regions in the nation. Middle Tennessee, the hilly farm country that lies between the Appalachians and the Tennessee River, has been almost as strongly Democratic. The flat cotton lands along the Mississippi River that constitute West Tennessee have been transformed politically in recent years from one-party Democratic to what might be called two-party Republican. Arguably, therefore, anyone who can compete politically in as diverse and far-flung a state as Tennessee has been trained and tested in the sort of skill and suppleness required of a presidential candidate in an even more diverse and far-flung nation.

The political consequences of Tennessee's diversity extend beyond its leaders to its voters. Throughout the twentieth century, elections in Tennessee have been the most competitive in the South. During the century's first sixty years, Tennessee's competitive character made it the least Democratic state in the solidly Democratic South. Since then, Tennessee has been the least Republican state in the generally Republican South. In both eras, Tennessee's voters have behaved more like the rest of the country than those of any other Southern state, backing the winning candidate for president in twenty of twenty-five elections.

In the sixteen presidential elections that took place between 1900 and 1960, Tennessee voted Republican five times: for Warren G. Harding in 1920 (the only one of the eleven states of the old Confederacy to do so), for Herbert Hoover in 1928, for Dwight D. Eisenhower in 1952 and 1956, and for Richard Nixon in 1960. No other Southern state matched Tennessee in its willingness to depart from the national Democratic party; only Florida came close. During that period, Tennessee's two Republican members of the House of Representatives were often the only two Southern Republicans in Congress. By national standards, Tennessee was a Democratic state (only one Republican, gubernatorial candidate Alfred A. Taylor in 1920, was to win a statewide election until Baker was elected to the Senate in 1966), but on a regional scale it stood out more for its occasional heterodoxy than for its usual orthodoxy.

Since 1960, as the South has gradually become the nation's most Republican region, Tennessee has continued to stand out politically, but for a different reason. In the nine presidential elections that took place from 1964 to 1996, Tennessee was, along with Arkansas, the only Southern state to support the Democratic candidate for president as many as four times: Lyndon B. Johnson in 1964, Jimmy Carter in 1976, and Bill Clinton, whose running mate was Gore, in 1992 and 1996. Tennessee's presidential-voting pattern seems all the more strange (that is, unless one regards the state's political strangeness as its theme) in view of the success that late-twentieth-century Republicans have had in state and congressional politics. In 1970, when Brock was elected to sit alongside Baker in the Senate, Tennessee became the first Southern state since Reconstruction to have two Republican senators; it also had a Republican governor and a near-majority of Republicans (four of nine) in the House of Representatives. This level of Republican dominance was not exceeded until 1994, when Tennessee's two Republican senators and governor were joined by a majority of five in the nine-member House delegation. But by then, of course, Republican hegemony in the South had become the rule rather than the exception.

One other aspect of Tennessee politics cries out for mention, even in an essay as brief as this one: the state's traditional character. Tennesseans do not always see this quality in themselves, but outsiders, notably the Japanese, often do. (Only California exceeds Tennessee in its concentration of Japanese-owned businesses, and Tennessee's traditional culture explains much of the state's attractiveness to Asian investors.) Politically, tradition manifests itself in a variety of ways. For example, Tennesseans have voted to return every incumbent running for the U.S. House since 1974, when Harold Ford of Memphis defeated Republican representative Dan Kuykendall to become the state's first African American member of Congress in modern times. Similarly, although Al Gore, Jr., is no longer a member of the House, and neither is Jim Cooper (the son of former Gov. Prentice Cooper who initially won his seat in 1982 by defeating Howard Baker's daughter Cissy), fully one-third of the state's nine House members in the 105th Congress are the sons of prominent politicians: Bob

Clement, Harold Ford, Jr., and Jimmy Duncan. The latter two inherited their fathers' seats.

I hope I have persuaded the reader that Tennessee is, at the least, an intriguing state and, perhaps, an exceptional example of those qualities that make the study of government and politics so fascinating. But if I have not, I need not worry: the excellent team of authors that John R. Vile and Mark Byrnes have recruited to write the essays that constitute this book have made that case better than I or anyone else could.

Michael Nelson, Rhodes College

Acknowledgments

We wish to acknowledge and thank the many people who have helped us produce this book. First and foremost, we thank our contributors, who have shown extraordinary dedication and patience throughout this endeavor, including the long and often painful revision process. We are also grateful to the officers and members of the Tennessee Political Science Association (TPSA) for their support of this project and for devoting one of the association's annual meetings exclusively to Tennessee politics and government.

We especially thank the following individuals, who helped with the TPSA meeting related to this project, submitted proposals and manuscripts for consideration, advised us about individual chapters, or helped us in other ways: Professor Craig Bledsoe, David Lipscomb University; Professor Douglas Carlisle, the University of Tennessee at Knoxville; Professor Donald Cheatham, Motlow State Community College; Professor Robert Corlew, Middle Tennessee State University; Professor Mark Daniels, the University of Memphis; Professor Harry Fuchs, Tennessee State University; Professor Ken Holland, the University of Memphis; Mr. Tom Humphrey, the Memphis Commercial Appeal; Professor Robert Keele, the University of the South; Professor Reuben Kyle, Middle Tennessee State University; Professor Larry Hall, Belmont University; Professor Coleman McGinnis, Tennessee State University; Professor Michael Montgomery, the University of South Carolina; Professor Lewis Moore, Columbia State Community College; Professor Ted Mosch, the University of Tennessee at Martin; Professor Michael Nelson, Rhodes College; Professor Thomas Nolan, Middle Tennessee State University; Professor Dwight Tays, David Lipscomb University; Professor Vernon Warren, Austin Peay State University; Professor Sharon Whitney, Tennessee Technological University; and Professor Steven Williams, Tennessee Technological University.

We owe special thanks to the Research Committee at Middle Tennessee State University for supporting our work on this book. We are also grateful to our supportive dean, Dr. John McDaniel, and to our equally supportive colleagues in the Department of Political Science, several of whom have contributed essays to this volume. In addition, we thank Paul Lawrence and Jason Reid for their computer assistance, and we thank Marilyn Davis and Clare Christian for helping us in a variety of ways.

We are grateful to those teachers and professors who use this book in their courses, to librarians who have ordered the volume for their collections, and to those students and citizens who consult our work to learn more about their state government. We hope that you find this book useful, and we solicit your suggestions for improving any future editions.

Finally, we wish to thank the capable staff of Vanderbilt University Press. Early in the process they offered valuable encouragement, and they have worked with us to improve the final result.

Introduction

Writing in 1787 in defense of the proposed U.S. Constitution, Alexander Hamilton noted in *Federalist* No. 17 that human nature was such that "its affections are commonly weak in proportion to the distance or diffusiveness of the object." He predicted, accordingly, that "the people of each State would be apt to feel a stronger bias towards their governments than towards the government of the Union."[1] Anti-Federalist opponents of the Constitution disputed this assertion when it was made, and even more people might do so today. Especially since the Civil War, political writers have typically highlighted the importance of national loyalties over states' rights, and, with the advent of the New Deal, the national government has taken over so many responsibilities (including generating electric power in Tennessee) that its effects are hardly remote from most people.

In recent years, however, many people have begun to reexamine the idea of federalism and the current division of powers between the nation and the states. Whether or not twentieth-century Americans have struck an appropriate balance of power between these two levels of government, many individuals clearly remain attached by bonds of affection, loyalty, and interest to their individual states. States continue to play a vital role in the lives of their citizens. Most Tennesseans are educated in schools financed mostly by state and local governments; Tennesseans still get their driving, hunting, and fishing licenses from the state; many are employed by state and local governments; all depend in varying degrees on a diverse array of state and local services; and all bear the cost of state and local government every time they make a purchase at a store and pay sales tax or pay their yearly county and/or city property taxes. Many Tennesseans know one or more of their representatives to the state legislature, and many are neighbors to members of their city council, mayors, and other officials of city and county governments.

The importance of Tennessee government means that its citizens would benefit from understanding it. Regrettably, many citizens know far too little about state government. Although high schools have recently devoted somewhat greater attention to social studies, most students in Tennessee schools get their last significant exposure to Tennessee government as part of a history course that they take in the seventh grade. Similarly, even students who major in political science in college may never take a course in Tennessee politics; some even miss the more generic course on state and local politics that is a fairly standard curricular offering. Moreover, although there are numerous books on Tennessee cultural and natural history, citizens in Tennessee and interested scholars in other states have little in the way of current books to explain Tennessee politics.

More than twenty-five years ago, a group of political scientists from across Tennessee formed the Tennessee Political Science Association (TPSA). A central goal of the association has been to educate Tennesseans about their state government by encouraging social studies education within the public schools and by conducting other activities to help educate the general public. In 1985 the TPSA published a collection of articles on Tennessee politics and government called *The Volunteer State: Readings in Tennessee Politics.*[2]

For several years, the TPSA has considered launching another such volume. The increasing need for an updated book to use in classes and as a general reference, as well as the recent celebrations of two historic events, recently led members to consider this project with renewed seriousness. In 1995 historical reenactments held in the state capitol reminded citizens that Tennessee's ratification of the Nineteenth Amendment, granting suffrage to American women, was critical in its adoption. The following year's anniversary generated even more attention: 1996 marked Tennessee's bicentennial as a state. Given that Thomas Jefferson reputedly described Tennessee's Constitution as the "most republican [representative] and least imperfect,"[3] it seems fitting that this celebration should result not simply in a bicentennial mall in Nashville (where the magnificent Parthenon, with its reminders of Athenian democracy, still commemorates the state's first one-hundred years) but also in a serious exposition and reflection on state government. That is this book's primary purpose.

This volume represents a collective effort. Members of TPSA have written most of these essays. Other contributors include professors from related disciplines, a journalist, and a former elected official. Although both editors and a number of the authors are members of the faculty of Middle Tennessee State University, the volume's other contributors represent a variety of college and university faculties within the state, both public and private.

This book has four main divisions. The first and shortest examines the foundations of Tennessee government. The second looks at the state's major governmental institutions, focusing on the three branches of state government and surveying the variety of local governmental structures. The third section analyzes patterns and continuities in the operations of Tennessee politics. The fourth examines several prominent public policy issues.

FOUNDATIONS

Tennessee's history dates back to the time when, as the western part of North Carolina, it represented a portion of the American western frontier. Later, the Civil War profoundly shaped the politics of the state. In his essay, prominent journalist M. Lee Smith describes how much of Tennessee's recent political history can be explained by this event. The war accentuated the geographical divisions that had previously divided the state into slaveholding and nonslaveholding regions, and, through much of the twentieth century, prominent politicians arrived at an arrangement between the Republican dominated East and the

Democratically dominated Middle and West. Curiously, such sharp partisan divisions have often been muted in national elections when Tennesseans have joined an increasing number of other Americans in splitting their votes between the two major parties. Smith's analysis of recent state trends raises questions about whether the traditional influences of Tennessee regions and partisan identifications will continue into the twenty-first century.

Although some democratic nations function successfully without a written constitution (Great Britain and Israel, for example), Americans have typically associated republican, or representative, government with such a constitution. Indeed, every state in the Union has its own constitution. Professor Lewis Laska, who has authored a full-length book on the subject, shows that the present Tennessee Constitution, written in 1870, incorporated aspects of several earlier constitutions, including some written even before Tennessee achieved statehood. Remarkably, this 1870 document remained unamended until 1953 but has been changed several times since. Laska shows that many of the individual rights guaranteed by the national Constitution are also protected by the state's, with the judicial branch playing an especially important role in the defense of such liberties. Similarly, the state Constitution outlines the powers of each of the three branches of government. Although Tennessee's Constitution is quite difficult to amend, it contains a number of provisions that seem antiquated and that may well require future alteration.

INSTITUTIONS

The second part of this book begins by examining each of the three branches of Tennessee government. Professors Thomas Ungs and Frank Essex discuss what they call the "institutionalization" of the Tennessee legislature. Noting that Tennessee government was largely dominated by the governor from the 1920s to the mid 1960s, the authors show how the Tennessee legislature has matured over the last thirty years or so: an increased number of incumbents have sought reelection, incumbency rates have consequently risen, party competition has increased, the legislature has hired more staff and increased the volume of legislation it produces, and legislators increasingly view themselves as professionals. In addition, the power of standing legislative committees has increased, and some legislators have attained the kind of visibility that previously only state governors could garner. Finally, the Tennessee General Assembly is no longer a political backwater but behaves more and more as a truly equal branch of government.

In discussing the governor's office, Professor David Carleton emphasizes its roots in history. The governorship received a special boost with the election of Austin Peay in 1923 and with his successful reorganization of executive offices. Like Ungs and Essex, Carleton recognizes that recent years have witnessed the balancing of gubernatorial power by an increasingly professionalized and powerful legislature. Because the governor is a single individual, the power that any one governor exercises may vary more dramatically than that of the legislature; an astute governor, like an astute president, soon recognizes that his office combines formal powers with the opportunity for exercising less tangible, and highly variable, leadership skills. Like presidents, governors still have many opportunities to act on behalf of the common good.

Professor Thomas Van Dervort discusses the judicial branch. The author of a text on the American judiciary, Van Dervort highlights those elements that are unique to the Tennessee judiciary (for example, a state attorney general appointed by the Supreme Court rather than elected by the people) and those that it shares with other states. In addition to describing each level of the Tennessee judicial system and its responsibilities, Van Dervort also shows how Tennessee has adopted through legislative means a number of reforms that it was unable to adopt by constitutional conventions. These include a system of judicial oversight and discipline, a "merit" system of judicial selection, judicial redistricting, and a public defender system.

Professor David Kanervo's essay on local government is a reminder that many citizens are more likely to come into direct contact with county and city officials than with state government officeholders. He notes that Tennessee has 925 local governments, divided into four types—counties, municipalities, school districts, and special districts. These forms in turn have their own variations; for example, some cities utilize a mayor-council system of government while others rely on a council-manager form. Tennessee's increasing urbanization is illustrated by the fact that over 30 percent of its population is now concentrated in the five largest cities. Each city has its own history and ambiance, and each has been influenced by its unique mix of individual leadership, partisan politics, geographical landscape, climatic influences, racial and ethnic balances, and social and economic factors.

POLITICS

No clear division, of course, can be drawn between government and politics. Nevertheless, the chapters of section two focus on institutions and structures while the chapters of section three examine patterns in the political behavior of the participants.

The most widespread and broadly influential political act is voting. Political scientists have long recognized that groups with higher voting rates can exercise disproportionate political influence. In their essay on "Turnout and Partisanship in Tennessee Elections," Professors Lilliard Richardson and Grant Neeley note that, like other Southern states, Tennessee has historically had a low voting turnout. Only in recent years has turnout in Tennessee begun to approach that of the rest of the nation. The national "motor voter" law as well as Tennessee's new system of early voting could both accelerate this trend. As several other authors in this book point out, shifting party allegiances in the state can also affect this trend and, therefore, warrant continuing scrutiny. Richardson and Neeley note that voting patterns in West Tennessee deserve special attention.

For many years, in Tennessee and surrounding states, only white males could actively participate in politics. Two essays demonstrate the important role that women and African Americans now play in the state. However, in her essay, Professor Anne Sloan suggests that a gap separates the self-congratulating rhetoric that accompanied the seventy-fifth anniversary of Tennessee's ratification of the Nineteenth Amendment and the reality of women's position in modern Tennessee politics. Many of the gains women have achieved in Tennessee have come through congressional legislation and federal court decisions rather than through state action. Moreover, relative to their numbers in the state and to their counterparts in many other states, women are significantly underrepresented both in the state legislature and in other state-wide offices. No woman has ever held the governorship, and few have held other state-wide offices.

The essay by Professor Marcus Pohlmann, who with Michael Kirby recently published a book on the subject, focuses on the role of African Americans in Memphis and serves as an interesting case study in local government. Although the population of African Americans extends across the state, their numbers make them an especially powerful force in Memphis. For years, African Americans were essentially frozen out of Memphis politics, but, in recent years, they have even succeeded in electing a mayor. Pohlmann shows that this election was built on generations of prior African American organizational activity and that, in his reelection, Mayor W. W. Herenton was able to attract substantial numbers of white voters. Whether increased representation results in substantial economic gains for African Americans may well affect the sense of political efficacy among African-Americans not only in Memphis but elsewhere in the state as well.

Drawing from his experience as a former U.S. Representative from Middle Tennessee, Jim Cooper notes that Tennessee's special partisan blend has generally produced moderate politicians who have usually worked well together as a congressional delegation on behalf of state interests and who have often made attractive leadership candidates in both major parties. Cooper also describes the pressure on members of Congress—Tennessee's and other states'—to maintain ties with their districts and to devote much of their time and effort to taking care of constituent needs and bringing home the bacon to their districts.

Rounding out the section on Tennessee politics and providing a transition to issues of public policy is the essay by John Scheb, William Lyons, and Grant Neeley on Tennessee public opinion. As in other states, public opinion in Tennessee is not distributed uniformly but can vary dramatically from one social, ethnic, and economic group to another. Scheb, Lyons, and Neeley focus on matters of voter identification and specific issues. Like other authors in this volume, Scheb, Lyons, and Neeley note the rise in Republican partisan identification in the state. This development has corresponded with an increasing number of voters who identify themselves as conservative and with a decrease in the number of those who think of themselves as liberal. As to issues, the authors note that, as of 1998, public support for a state lottery has not been translated into effective legislative or constitutional action. However, public sentiment has long stymied moves for an income tax, even when that issue was promoted by a popular governor, Democrat Ned McWherter. Although many Tennesseans appear to support the view that abortion should be more difficult to obtain, many others support abortion rights as outlined by the U.S. Supreme Court's decision in *Roe v. Wade*.

POLICY

Given the potential volatility of public opinion, public policy issues are often the most difficult to assess; an issue that dominates one election may fade before the next. Because of their wide scope and their potential costs, however, a number of issues that have been important in the past few decades appear likely to remain at the center of public debate in the near future. Accordingly, the last section of this book focuses on developments and debates over education, prison reform, and budgeting. Recognizing that Tennessee is increasingly influenced by developments not only in the rest of the nation but throughout the world, the concluding essay focuses on the impact of foreign investment in the state.

Professors Nancy Keese and Jim Huffman examine recent trends in Tennessee education, noting that governors tend to focus either on elementary and secondary education or on higher education. Like other areas of public policy, educational policy making continues to be dogged by legal challenges. In recent years, the decisions desegregating Tennessee education, as well as the decision mandating greater equality in funding between rural and urban districts, have proved to be especially critical.

Nowhere has the influence of judicial activism been more evident than in the area of prison reform. In his essay, Professor Richard Chesteen, a professor and leader in county government who ran for the Democratic gubernatorial nomination in 1994, examines twenty years of prison reform, initiated largely by a federal court decision. Prison populations rose dramatically during this time, both because of increases in criminal activity and because of demands for harsher penalties. During this same period, state officials found themselves increasingly bound by federal standards of due process and equal protection. Chesteen shows that almost every recent administration has found the issue of prisons to be more complex and expensive than it anticipated and that the solution to the crime problem might be considerably more complex than simply building new penitentiaries.

Because of the appropriations demanded by education and prisons, as well as by health care, welfare, road building, and numerous other programs not directly covered in this book, the essay on Tennessee budgeting and finance is especially important. Tennesseans have yet to adopt a state income tax, and revenues from federal grants, now accounting for about a third of the state budget, do not appear likely to increase in the near future. The resulting reliance on sales taxes (at the state level) and property taxes and user fees (at the local level) continue to shape and constrain governmental choices over a wide range of issues. Such constraints are the subject of economists Kelly Edmiston and Matthew Murray's essay. They point out that Tennessee's budget, like its tax rate, lags behind that of other states. Although Edmiston and Murray write as economists, the political implications of the search for additional, fairer, and more elastic revenue sources will continue to shape state politics into the foreseeable future.

In the book's final essay, Steven Livingston documents the state's successes from the early 1970s to the present in attracting foreign industrial investment. Interestingly, although Livingston credits state leaders with some of these accomplishments, he notes that Tennessee's successes mirror those of other Southern states. This suggests that geographical and cultural factors may have been as important in attracting industrial advancement as political policies. If foreign investing trends persist, Tennessee will continue to find its fate shaped not only by regional and national trends, but by worldwide economic developments.

THE READER AS PARTICIPANT CITIZEN

The editors of this book designed it to explain the basic operations of Tennessee government and to explicate some of the primary choices and challenges that the state faces. Tennessee's government can reflect the wishes of its people only to the extent that its citizens demonstrate the loyalty and affection that Alexander Hamilton and other founders once predicted, and only to the extent that the people continue to participate in the political process. The contributors hope that this volume will not only inform but that it will also encourage many students to contribute to the state through participation in state and local government and through public service.

Part I
FOUNDATIONS

CHAPTER 1

Tennessee's Postbellum Political History:
Voting Patterns and Party Identification
—M. Lee Smith

To understand Tennessee politics today, it helps to know a bit about Tennessee political history from the time of the Civil War. Without any question, the Civil War was the event that most shaped Volunteer State politics for about a century. Only in the last thirty-five years has the long influence of the Civil War on state voting patterns and party identification begun to wane.

The state of Tennessee is a narrow strip of real estate running from mountainous East Tennessee to the flat cotton land of West Tennessee along the Mississippi River. In between are the rolling hills of Middle Tennessee, sometimes affectionately referred to as the "dimple of the universe." Unlike Middle and West Tennessee and most of the South, slavery and the plantation system never prospered in the hills of East Tennessee. As a result, residents of East Tennessee remained pro-Union in sentiment and prior to the Civil War twice voted against secession. But voters in Middle and West Tennessee, where slavery flourished, eventually voted in large numbers to take the state out of the Union. The only exception to this voting pattern was in a few counties of the Highland Rim along the western leg of the Tennessee River, which had almost no slavery and which voted against secession.

After the war the same political cleavage continued. East Tennessee became the Republican area of the state. The Democrats ruled in Middle and West Tennessee except for those same few counties along the western leg of the Tennessee River. They became Republican.

This split between East Tennessee, on the one hand, and Middle and West Tennessee, on the other, proved remarkably durable. Between Reconstruction and the 1960s, political allegiances growing out of the Civil War were forsaken only in rare instances. The Republicans did elect a governor in 1920, the year of the Warren Harding Republican presidential landslide. And Tennessee Protestants rejected Catholic Al Smith, the Democratic nominee for president in 1928.

1

But in most elections for almost a full century after the Civil War, no matter how many votes the Republicans could muster in East Tennessee, the GOP failed to win statewide elections because Middle and West Tennessee remained strongly Democratic. And during the Great Depression when Franklin Roosevelt was president, Congress established the Tennessee Valley Authority (TVA), bringing electric power to the economically depressed hills and valleys of East Tennessee. Nevertheless, even the enormous economic benefit gained under a Democratic president and Congress could not alter the region's traditional Republicanism. Stated simply, in Tennessee, as in most of the rest of the South, the Democrats dominated statewide politics. Winning the Democratic nomination for governor or senator was tantamount to winning the office.

Throughout this long period the Republicans had the votes by inheritance in East Tennessee as did the Democrats in Middle and West Tennessee. But in the second quarter of the 1900s, leaders of the two parties began to encourage the inevitable breakdown of the old political allegiances—or at least so the story goes.

In East Tennessee, Republican B. Carroll Reece of Johnson City won the first district congressional seat in 1920. The well-educated Reece was an economist, a banker, and a publisher. The congressman subsequently became the unquestioned leader of the Republican machinery in East Tennessee, which he continued to control for forty years. During much of this same period Memphis Democratic political boss Ed Crump, the dominant personality in statewide politics, ruled Memphis and Shelby County with an iron hand.

The generally held view was that Crump and Reece "had an arrangement." The "arrangement" was that Crump would give Reece and the Republican machinery a free hand to run East Tennessee if the Republicans would leave the balance of the state and statewide elections to Crump and his organization. Indeed, Reece may have contemplated Republican victory in statewide races with trepidation. Election of a Republican governor or senator would have preempted his leadership of the GOP and infringed upon his control of federal patronage.[1]

Finally, in 1948, Reece forsook his relationship with the Democrats and ran for the U.S. Senate. His gubernatorial running mate was none other than Roy Acuff, the "King of Country Music." The two GOP candidates attracted large crowds as they traveled the state. Reece hoped that a national swing to Republicanism that year would give Acuff and him a chance to win. But President Harry Truman upset that equation nationally with his come from behind victory. In Tennessee, Acuff and Reece lost to Democrats Gordon Browning and Estes Kefauver, both of whom had earlier beaten the Crump machine to win their party nominations.

Reece subsequently won back his first district congressional seat, remaining in office throughout the 1950s until his death in 1961. During that period the "arrangement" was in effect once again, this time between East Tennessee Republicans and Democratic Governors Frank Clement and Buford Ellington. Whether the understanding existed by express agreement or tacit understanding, the results were the same. The Democrats for the most part stayed out of the first and second congressional districts, and the Republicans left the balance of the state and statewide elections to the Democrats.

Finally in 1962 after the death of Reece, the Republicans made a serious effort to win a major office outside the first and second congressional districts. That year Bill Brock of Chattanooga, a young, conservative businessman, capitalized on a split in the Democratic ranks to win the third district congressional seat. After capturing the office, Brock moved rapidly to solidify his base in the third district. He won three more terms in the House before running successfully for the Senate.

By the mid-1960s, the civil rights movement was at peak force across the South. The national Democratic Party led by President Lyndon Johnson championed the cause of black Southerners. And black voters—who had begun moving toward a Democratic orientation thirty years earlier during the Roosevelt era—became solidly entrenched in the Democratic Party. When he signed the Civil Rights Act of 1964, Johnson told an aide, "I think we just delivered the South to the Republican party for a long time to come."[2]

Johnson's comment proved prophetic, at least among some conservative white voters in Tennessee, especially in West Tennessee, where the racial issue sharply polarized the electorate. These voters began moving into Republican columns at election time. The movement of these voters proved both rapid and substantial, especially in big Shelby County, where Memphis is located. In the 1960 presidential election, Republican Richard Nixon carried the Volunteer State, winning 556,000 votes statewide, of which 87,000 came from Shelby County. Four years later Republican Barry Goldwater failed to carry the state against Democrat Lyndon Johnson. Goldwater won only 509,000 votes statewide but 101,000 of them came from Shelby County. In other words, Goldwater polled 14,000 more votes than Nixon in Shelby County but received 61,000 fewer votes than Nixon in the balance of the state. Today the heavily populated area of white suburban Shelby County consistently votes Republican by lopsided margins of four or five to one while the predominantly black inner city area of Memphis is heavily Democratic.

In rural West Tennessee, unlike suburban Shelby County, conservative white voters have never completely forsaken their Democratic heritage. But conservative whites in rural West Tennessee vote Republican in some statewide elections and even more frequently in national elections. During the last three decades that area has demonstrated a large swing vote.

In national elections the Republicans began winning in Tennessee as early as 1952, when GOP nominee Dwight Eisenhower carried the state over Adlai Stevenson. The Republican nominee for president has carried Tennessee in eight of twelve presidential elections in the second half of the twentieth century, losing only in 1964 when Republican nominee Barry Goldwater came to the state promising to sell TVA to private industry, in 1976 when Jimmy Carter from neighboring Georgia carried the state in the aftermath of Richard Nixon's

Watergate scandal, and in 1992 and again in 1996 when Bill Clinton had Tennessee favorite son Al Gore as his runningmate.

Tennessee has had a lot of presidential Republicans—voters who cast ballots for Republican nominees for president but who vote Democratic in some state and most local elections. These ticket-splitters are mostly conservative voters who are out of sorts with the liberal tilt of the national Democratic Party but who find acceptable the more conservative Democratic candidates running at the state and local levels.

Scholars who have studied the politics of the South, including Tennessee, are in general agreement that Republican growth among white Southerners over the last three decades is at least partially attributable to white Southerners' more conservative positions on race issues.[3] Some of these scholars have also concluded that economic issues have been a major contributing factor.[4]

The first serious Republican effort to win statewide elections occurred in 1964. That year Memphis salesman Dan Kuykendall took on Democratic Sen. Albert Gore, Sr., and a young East Tennessee attorney named Howard Baker, Jr., and Democratic U.S. Rep. Ross Bass of Pulaski vied to fill the remaining two years of the term of Sen. Estes Kefauver, who had died in office. Kuykendall and Baker ran on the ticket with Republican presidential candidate Barry Goldwater, who advocated the sale of TVA to private industry while campaigning in Knoxville. Although Kuykendall and Baker both lost in the midst of Lyndon Johnson's landslide victory over Goldwater in Tennessee and across the nation, the two GOP Senate nominees ran substantially better than Goldwater and came surprisingly close to winning their races. Two years later Baker again ran for the Senate and won. By 1972, the Republicans had captured the office of governor, both U.S. Senate seats, five of eight congressional seats, and substantial numbers, although not a majority, in both houses of the General Assembly.

During the period from 1966 through 1982, Tennessee had eleven elections for governor and senator. The Republicans won seven of those elections and the Democrats only four. Despite these successes, however, the Republican Party was not the majority part of Tennessee voters. Of the seven Republican victories for governor and senator in the 1966 through 1982 time frame, three were by incumbents winning re-election, including Sen. Howard Baker in 1972 and 1978 and Gov. Lamar Alexander in 1982. Incumbents, including both Democrats and Republicans, have numerous advantages when seeking re-election. This is especially so for incumbents such as Baker and Alexander who worked hard at avoiding political polarization with major segments of the Tennessee electorate. In each of the other four elections won by the GOP, the Democrats were sharply divided among themselves, and the Democratic nominee carried heavy political baggage.

- In 1966 when Baker defeated Democrat Frank Clement, Clement was a shop-worn governor who had emerged from a bitter Democratic primary with incumbent Sen. Ross Bass of Pulaski. The wounds from that primary never healed. Many of the Bass Democrats could not bring themselves to support Clement.

- In the 1970 gubernatorial election, Republican Winfield Dunn defeated Democrat John J. Hooker, Jr. Hooker had business problems that plagued him every step of the way, and his outspoken liberalism made him unacceptable to conservative Democrats and independents.
- In the 1970 Senate election, Republican Bill Brock defeated Democrat Albert Gore, Sr., who had become sharply polarized with many conservative Democrats and independents on an array of emotional issues, including the ongoing Vietnam War, which Gore opposed.
- And in the 1978 gubernatorial election, Alexander defeated Democrat Jake Butcher, who suffered fallout from the shoddy administration of Gov. Ray Blanton. Butcher was regarded as a wheeler-dealer banker, and he had won the Democratic nomination over Bob Clement in a divisive primary.

In each of these four Republican victories, the Democrats lost the elections much more than the Republicans won them.

In the mid-1970s the Democrats began to learn that they could still win statewide elections but that to do so they had to avoid divisive Democratic primary elections and nominate candidates who were not carrying political baggage. This occurred first in 1976 when Nashville attorney James R. Sasser won a relatively quiet Democratic primary and went on to oust incumbent Republican Sen. Bill Brock in the general election. Sasser would win re-election in 1982 and again in 1988. In 1984, Democratic U.S. Rep. Albert Gore, Jr., won the state's other U.S. Senate seat over Republican Victor Ashe. Gore won easy re-election six years later. In the 1986 gubernatorial election, veteran Democratic House Speaker Ned McWherter, a successful businessman, defeated former Republican Gov. Winfield Dunn, surprising many Repuablican analysts. With the McWherter victory, the Democrats in 1987 held the governor's office, both U.S. Senate seats, six of nine congressional seats, and lopsided majorities in both houses of the General Assembly. McWherter won re-election with ease in 1990. After losing seven of eleven statewide elections from 1966 through 1982, the Democrats won all five statewide elections in the four election cycles from 1984 through 1990. Despite the growth of Republicanism in the mid-1960s, the Democrats were still the majority party in the state.

Then came 1994, one of the most important election years in Volunteer State history. With McWherter ineligible under the state Constitution to run for a third consecutive term, the state had an open race for governor. Also on the ballot were not one but two U.S. Senate elections, including a special election to fill the remaining two years of the second term to which Albert Gore, Jr., had been elected before resigning to take office as vice president.

Benefiting enormously from strong anti-Washington, anti-Congress, anti-Bill Clinton sentiment evident across most of the nation but especially in the

South, including Tennessee, Republicans swept the three statewide elections by sizable margins. Republican U.S. Rep. Don Sundquist of Memphis defeated Nashville Mayor Phil Bredesen in the battle for governor. Heart surgeon Bill Frist of Nashville, a political neophyte, came out of nowhere to oust Democratic Sen. Jim Sasser in his bid for a fourth term. And attorney, actor, and lobbyist Fred Thompson, who toured the state in a red pick-up truck and flannel shirt, crushed well-regarded Democratic U.S. Rep. Jim Cooper of Shelbyville in the contest for the Gore seat.

In 1994 congressional elections, the Republicans also picked up two seats previously held by Democrats. That gave the Republicans a five-four majority in the state's U.S. House delegation. The electorate in Tennessee and nationally had clearly tilted in a more conservative direction. Polls taken nationally and in Tennessee during and shortly after the 1994 election indicated a much higher percentage of voters identified themselves as Republicans.

The 1994 election results forced Clinton to move to the political center and to articulate a number of more conservative themes. As a result, he and Gore prevailed nationally and in Tennessee in 1996 to win a second term over Bob Dole and Jack Kemp, a Republican ticket generally viewed as lackluster.

While Clinton and Gore eked out a narrow Tennessee win at the top of the ticket, Senator Fred Thompson won a second consecutive landslide for the U.S. Senate, this time over attorney Houston Gordon of Covington. Thompson's big win—coupled with his relaxed style and skill as a communicator—immediately made the senator a subject of speculation for the Republican presidential nomination in the year 2000. Meanwhile, Gore continued as an all-but-certain frontrunner for the Democratic nomination, and Alexander, who sought his party's nod unsuccessfully in 1996, made clear his intention to run again in 2000.

What now is the future for party politics in the Volunteer State? The Republicans are gaining strength in the so-called bedroom counties around Nashville and Davidson County. Most likely, the Republicans will continue to carry the state in most presidential elections when factors are relatively equal. The Democrats had difficulty finding a high-profile candidate to run against Suindquist in 1998, leaving the Republican incumbent all but certain to win a second term. Frist and especially Thompson appear relatively safe for now. And the parties may be close to evenly matched in a statewide election for an open seat for governor or senator.

CHAPTER 2

The Tennessee Constitution

—Lewis L. Laska

The Tennessee Constitution has been influenced by war and its aftermath, by public and judicial indifference, by double-digit inflation, and by single-minded reformers, but it has served the noble experiment of democracy reasonably well for over two centuries. The present Constitution was written in 1870, although it has been amended several times since 1953. Despite the constitution's many antiquated provisions, Tennesseans have a strong history of constitutional innovation: they were among the first to require the written ballot, to eliminate property qualifications for voting, to abolish slavery in a Southern state, and to allow for metropolitan government.

A CONSTITUTIONAL OVERVIEW

Pre-statehood Constitutional Government

The constitution that governs Tennessee today is the product of many agreements and constitutions, beginning as early as 1772.[1] In that year William Bean, reputed to be the first permanent white settler in Tennessee, and his neighbors along the Watauga River drafted and signed the Watauga Association Compact.[2] Theodore Roosevelt cited this Compact as the first written constitution adopted by American-born freemen.[3] In 1780, James Robertson and John Donelson led a party of settlers farther west, to where Nashville is today, and established self-government under the Cumberland Compact.

During the period 1784–1788, a group in the mountainous western portion of North Carolina, in what is now East Tennessee, attempted to operate independently of North Carolina. Tennessee might well have been named Franklin (or Frankland) if their efforts had succeeded. They adopted a constitution and even petitioned Congress for admission to the Union.[4] This movement encouraged North Carolina to give the land that was to become Tennessee to the United States government at the time the United States was adopting its new Constitution in 1789. The land then became "The Territory of the United States South of the River Ohio." President Washington appointed William Blount as Territorial Governor in 1790.

The 1796 Constitution

Blount, whose power as territorial governor had been relatively untrammeled, reluctantly led in establishing a representative form of government in 1794 and in November 1795 called for the election of delegates to a constitutional convention. The convention met on January 11, 1796, in Knoxville. The fifty-five delegates were already leaders, and several literally left their names on the map of Tennessee in the form of city and county names: Andrew Jackson, James Robertson, William Cocke, William Blount, Landon Carter, Joseph Anderson, Joseph McMinn, and W. C. C. Claiborne. The Constitution of 1796 was essentially like North Carolina's Constitution of 1776 and was partly influenced by the Pennsylvania Constitution of 1790.

The 1796 Constitution established a two-house legislature and vested executive power in a governor elected directly by the people, a practice followed at the time by only four other states. The judicial power under this Constitution was exercised by courts, but the legislature established the courts and the method for selecting judges. This Constitution did not make land ownership a condition for voting, as was common at the time. All freemen, including blacks, age twenty-one or older, who owned property *or* resided in the county six months, could vote. The 1796 Constitution included a Declaration of Rights, Article ii, which contained a statement making the declaration an integral part of the Constitution. These rights included the freedoms of speech and of press, of assembly, of free and equal elections, of jury trial, and of free navigation of the Mississippi River. Religious tests as a qualification for public office were forbidden. The day the convention adjourned, it sent a delegation to U.S. Secretary of State Timothy Pickering to deliver a copy of the new Constitution and petition for statehood. Tennessee soon became the first state admitted to the union after being a territory. Many new states would follow this same procedure, which, in time, became known as the "Tennessee Plan."

THE 1835 CONSTITUTION[5]

The 1796 Constitution was deemed superior to most in existence at the time. Thomas Jefferson supposedly called it "the least imperfect and most republican of the state constitutions."[6] But the state's population grew six fold from 1800 to 1830, and taxation inequities between town and rural acreage created economic and political pressure. So in 1834 a constitutional convention was held to correct the problems. Braving a cholera epidemic, the sixty delegates met in Nashville and were led by soon-to-be-governor Newton Cannon. They changed the taxation provision to allow taxation of land, bank stock, slaves, and other property the legislature might deem appropriate, all according to value. No one type of property would be taxed at a higher rate than any other property of equal value. The convention also provided for taxation of merchants, peddlers, and such privileges as the legislature would deem appropriate.

Excessive legislative tinkering with the judiciary had caused near chaos in the judicial system through frequent modifications, the threat of politically motivated impeachment of judges, and legislative reversals of court decisions through private acts, some of which even remitted criminal fines. The 1835 Constitution established the judiciary as an independent branch of government, with a three-member supreme court, lower courts to be established by the legislature, and justices of the peace. Terms were set for the supreme court and lower court judges, as well as state's attorneys. Justices of the peace in each county still served as combined judicial, legislative, and executive officers, but they were now elected instead of appointed by the General Assembly. Jacksonian democracy became the new order with popular election of the sheriff, trustee, and register of deeds in each county.

The changes in the judiciary and the election of more local officials increased democracy under the 1835 Constitution, but only for white male citizens. Free black men lost the rights to vote and bear arms.[7] The property qualification for voters and officeholders was dropped, however, leaving only residence and age requirements. Although the subject of slavery was raised at the convention, proposals to abolish slavery were tabled. The convention adopted a resolution declaring that slavery was an evil but one which should not be ended prematurely.[8]

New provisions contained in the 1835 Constitution included a prohibition against lotteries and the requirement of a uniform maximum interest rate. This Constitution also established a perpetual fund for the support of public schools.[9] The 1835 Constitution was not amended until 1853, when the popular election of supreme court and lower court judges, as well as the state attorney general and local state's attorneys, was established. The first amendment without a constitutional convention was heartily approved in a referendum.

THE CIVIL WAR

After vacillating, Tennessee seceded from the Union in June 1861 but was largely occupied by Union forces and administered by Andrew Johnson, appointed military governor in March 1862. After Johnson was elected vice president in 1864, he issued a call for another state convention, hoping to form a government that could send senators to Washington, where Tennessee was then unrepresented. The delegates constituted a body in marked contrast to earlier conventions. Many who came to Nashville in January 1865 were Tennessee Union soldiers. Others were self-appointed rather than chosen by county party caucuses. Johnson—not yet inaugurated as vice president—presided over the convention, originally meant to nominate candidates for a bona fide convention rather than to deliberate, and defended its actions under the Declaration of Rights, which granted the people the right to alter the government as desired. Johnson wanted to reestablish civil government in Tennessee before he left for Washington.

The proposed constitutional amendments abolished slavery and prohibited the laws that had accompanied it. The schedule attached to these amendments, unlike previous schedules that were limited to enabling and transition matters associated with the amendments, contained substantive matters relating to the law. Secession and actions and debts of the secession legislature were declared null and void.[10] Voting qualifications were delegated to the first General Assembly meeting under the revised Constitution.

Only those taking a strict oath were allowed to vote in the constitutional referendum and a separate general election, held ten days later, for governor and legislators. The oath required allegiance to the United States and a declared desire for the overthrow of the Confederate States. Although voting turnout was low, the referendum was unquestionably approved, and the legislature was seated less than two weeks before Vice President Johnson's inauguration.

The legislature elected just after the 1865 convention did not bring good government. The legislature passed laws restricting suffrage and allowing Governor William Brownlow to remove suspected Confederate sympathizers from voter registration lists. Financial mismanagement, corruption, and oppression of ex-Confederates by the Brownlow regime ultimately led to a call for a constitutional convention when Brownlow left the governor's post to become a U.S. senator.

THE 1870 CONSTITUTION

The Constitution of 1870, which still governs Tennessee, began with elections for constitutional convention delegates; these were probably the most democratic elections held in the state to that time. Voting was open to all male citizens at least twenty-one years of age, blacks included. Eighteen of the seventy-five delegates had attended college, forty were lawyers, two would become governor, and several became judges. Nine had fought for the Confederacy. They came to Nashville to make changes that would prevent the types of abuses and minority rule that had occurred under Brownlow. There were restraints on the convention, however. The federal government was still asserting its control throughout the South, and the threat of federal intervention was constant. Delegate A. O. P. Nicholson, a future state supreme court justice, cautioned delegates, "Let us be careful; let us do no more than is absolutely necessary. In ten years from now all this must be done again."[11]

The 1870 Constitution provided for suffrage based only on residence and age but required that any poll tax[12] assessed by the General Assembly be paid. Making poll tax payment a prerequisite to voting satisfied convention delegates that the poor and black, who were considered ill-informed and easily manipulated, would not have political power at the voting booth. The 1870 document also established that voting rights could not be denied to any person entitled to vote except after conviction for an infamous crime.

The governor's power was a primary concern during the 1870 convention. Alterations in the Constitution prevented a recurrence of the perceived evils of the Brownlow era. For instance, the new Constitution required a declaration from the General Assembly before the governor could muster the militia. The Brownlow tactic of appointing local officials and judges, who were supposed to be elected, was specifically prohibited. The governor was, nevertheless, given a limited veto power.

The General Assembly was not exempt from the convention delegates' pen. The legislature's ability to lend money, issue bonds, or invest was restricted. These provisions stemmed from the overwhelming debt that the state had accumulated during the Brownlow era. The expense associated with the General Assembly itself was also addressed by sections that limited the length of legislative sessions, the number of days legislators could be paid, and the legislators' ability to raise their four dollars a day in-session pay. With a view toward restricting grants to specific corporations, especially railroads, the Convention outlawed such special legislation.

The 1870 convention also altered the judiciary. Circuit and chancery courts were expressly mentioned. The Supreme Court was enlarged to five members, with no more than two residing in any one of the three grand divisions of the state. Residency requirements were also added for all judges.

AMENDMENTS AFTER 1870

Although the 1870 convention delegates viewed their work as temporary, their Constitution remained unaltered until 1953, at which time it was the oldest unamended constitution in the nation. Several attempts to amend the Constitution had failed to pass the required two successive General Assemblies or to receive the necessary popular vote. Attempts to call a constitutional convention had been stymied by fears that a convention would run wild. After the Tennessee Supreme Court ruled that a limited constitutional convention could be called to consider only those matters designated by the legislature, a convention was approved. It met in 1953, and the amendments were approved in November of that year.

The 1953 amendments were long overdue. The constitutional amendment process was changed, although the changes did not make amendments much easier. Other changes included higher pay for legislators, the increase in the governor's term to four years and modification in the governor's veto power, and removal of the poll tax as a voting requirement. Local governments were given more control over their affairs, and approval was also extended to the metropolitan form of local government. In 1959 a convention proposal to extend the term for trustees was adopted. That same convention refused to change the sheriff's term or to lower the voting age.

By 1965, the apportionment of the house and senate districts had become a matter of national attention. The U.S. Supreme Court had found that the General Assembly's failure to reapportion for more than sixty years was a justiciable issue entitling the plaintiff-citizens to judicial relief under the equal protection provision.[13] The constitutional convention of 1965 was limited to apportionment issues. Apportionment of both houses of the General Assembly would now be based on population. Senators' terms were increased to four years and staggered. Other amendments provided for legislative salaries, set the time for legislative sessions to convene, and gave county legislative bodies power to fill vacant General Assembly seats.

A 1971 convention met to decide what property-value assessment rates should be set for four specified types of property (public utility, industrial and commercial, residential, and agricultural), because a federal court had ruled that the taxation of railroad property at an excessive rate was unconstitutional. The convention call had outlined ranges—for example, utility property was to be assessed at between 45 to 55 percent. The convention subsequently established 55, 40, 25, and 20 percent rates for the respective classes of property. Later, for future conventions, the courts found this micro-management of convention decision unconstitutional because it made conventions mere legislative puppets.[14] The convention also established a personal property tax exemption of $7,500 and allowed for legislative tax relief to the elderly and needy.

The 1977 Limited Constitutional Convention was the state's most controversial, expensive, and lengthy—which may help explain why a constitutional convention has not been held since.[15] Financial institutions pushed for the convention, maintaining that the maximum legal rate of interest set in the Constitution at 10 percent was stalling the ability to lend money for local needs at a time when double-digit inflation was pushing interest rates well over this rate.

This convention presented the voters with thirteen proposals. These included provisions requiring more fiscal responsibility by the state legislature, giving power to the legislature to set the maximum legal interest rate, changing the form of county government and the length of office for many county elected officials, streamlining some of the General Assembly's procedures, and allowing the governor two successive four-year terms. Other matters included eliminating the ban on interracial marriages, lowering the voting age to eighteen, and abolishing segregated schools. Voters ratified these proposals but, as discussed by Thomas Van Dervort elsewhere in this book, rejected a lengthy proposal to reform the judiciary.

Another amendment was made in 1982, when two successive General Assemblies passed a proposal that was overwhelmingly approved by the voters. This amendment changed the tax provision by allowing for more liberal property tax relief for elderly low-income taxpayers.

Further attempts to amend the Constitution have failed. The expense of a constitutional convention has limited its desirability. Issues concerning taxes, judicial reform, and lotteries, which have resulted in suggestions for amendment, have been too controversial to enable successive General Assemblies to pass any recommendations for change.

THE SHAPE OF THE TENNESSEE CONSTITUTION

THE PEOPLES' RIGHTS

A constitution is designed both to establish a responsive government and to prevent that government from unreasonably violating individual rights, a strength of the Tennessee Constitution since its 1796 article of Declaration of Rights. This article of the Constitution includes items also found in the U. S. Bill of Rights—the freedom of worship and of due process, the right to bear arms, the freedom from forced quartering of soldiers, the demand for humane treatment of prisoners, the proscription against unreasonable search and seizure, the right to jury trial, and the freedom of speech and of the press. The language of these sections requires application to distinct facts. Thus, constitutional guarantees mean not simply what the Constitution says but what the Tennessee Supreme Court says they mean. Tennessee constitutional law thus consists of both the state Constitution and the decisions the court has made interpreting it.

In some cases, citizens enjoy a wider range of specified rights under the Tennessee Constitution than under the U.S. Constitution.[16] These matters are decided on a case-by-case basis. Because the Tennessee Supreme Court has said that rights are co-equal, expanded protections announced by the United States Supreme Court have enlarged those of the Tennessee Constitution too, but when the United States Supreme Court reduces the scope of federal rights, the Tennessee Court does not always interpret the state Constitution in a similarly restrictive fashion. Thus, when in 1983 the United States Supreme Court adopted a new "looser," pro-prosecution, standard for determining the validity of information from confidential informants, effectively overruling prior "strict" rules established in 1964 and 1969,[17] the Tennessee Supreme Court stayed with the old rule, which offered defendants more protection. The Court relied in part on language in the Tennessee Constitution not found in the federal charter.[18]

Freedom of Speech
Freedom of speech has at least co-equal status and may enjoy broader protection under the Tennessee Constitution than is provided by the First Amendment.[19] An unusual aspect of freedom of speech protection in Tennessee is that a person may use loud profanity and insulting language when being questioned by a police officer but once the words become threatening, or "fighting words," they provide the basis for a criminal charge of disorderly conduct.[20]

Speech freedom is not unlimited. Tennesseans have no constitutional free-speech right to examine public records.[21] Public school teachers have no free-speech protection when complaining to the public about unfair treatment or working conditions when that speech is largely concerned with personal issues and does not mainly relate to student welfare or bettering the school system.[22] College students have the right to bring controversial outside speakers to campus,[23] but when college students' protests become so raucous that they disrupt school activities, those students can be expelled.[24]

Homosexual college students have the right to express their opinions, but so does the Ku Klux Klan, even if the latter's language is racially antagonistic, but short of presenting a clear and present danger of violence.[25] It is uncertain whether an African American high school band student can be dismissed from a band for publicly refusing to play "Dixie," because the student who brought the complaint switched high schools and the case was declared moot.[26]

Freedom of Religion
The freedom of worship may enjoy greater protection under the Tennessee Constitution than under the First Amendment, although religious snake-handling, because it involves immediate potential harm to others, may be restricted.[27] Like-

wise, the state may require proof of a social security number as a prerequisite to receiving a driver's license, despite religiously based objections.[28] Conversely, city ordinances may prohibit the sale of beer on Sunday.[29] Constitutional provisions are mixed regarding whether state employees can invoke religion while performing their duties: a city social worker may be barred from talking about religion with clients, but a prosecutor may hold and quote from the Bible in closing arguments in a criminal case.[30]

The Law of the Land: Due Process and Equal Protection

That no man shall be taken or imprisoned, or disseized of his freehold, liberties or privileges, or outlawed, or exiled, or in any manner destroyed or deprived of his life, liberty or property, but by the judgment of his peers or the law of the land.

This language comes directly from the Magna Carta, and the phrase "law of the land" is synonymous with the "due process of law" clause of the Fourteenth Amendment.[31] Due process means fundamental fairness and decency; as such, it depends on the willingness of the courts to cut through habit, custom, and cant to protect the weak from the powerful. For example, it was once considered fair in Tennessee to exclude all African Americans from jury service. Likewise, at one time a misbehaving student could be expelled from a state university without a hearing. Today, a poor person charged with a serious crime is entitled to a lawyer at taxpayers' expense, but the pay may be inadequate (currently, $3,000 in non-capital felony cases). The amount the state will pay for expert witnesses, e.g., forensic experts, is in most cases limited to $5,000.[32]

Due process is required before "property" can be taken away, but the term property is fluid, and due process is triggered only when the state takes property. Thus, the Department of Safety has an approved list of wrecker services that are called when the department investigates a highway accident. When a service is dropped from the list as ineligible, the owner can get a trial to determine eligibility because being on the list constitutes a "property right."[33]

The Rights of the Accused

Generally, Tennessee courts have not extended protections to those accused of crime beyond the federal charter. However, the Tennessee prohibition against ex post facto, or retroactive, laws is more expansive than the similar federal constitutional provision.[34] Although not in the Tennessee Constitution, Tennessee also has the "13th Juror Rule," which provides that a judge may void a jury verdict. This rule is designed to prevent a rush to judgment and to protect innocent defendants accused of hideous crimes. Judges seldom use this power because in most criminal cases that go to trial the evidence is compelling, but on at least two occasions innocent persons have been convicted. Maurice Mays, a black Knoxville police figure, was executed in 1922 for entering a white woman's house and shooting her. Five years later a woman confessed to the crime.[35] In 1975, a Johnson City woman positively identified Douglas Forbes as her rapist. The

Tennessee Supreme Court's review called it a "well nigh perfect trial,"[36] but in 1980 the actual rapist came forward and Forbes was freed from his sixty-year prison sentence.[37]

The matter of police searches and seizures illustrates the rights of the accused. In decisions in 1926 and 1979 police were forbidden from coming onto farmland and looking for contraband, but in 1986 this was changed. Technology and culture had fostered a reconsideration; if marijuana is visible from a helicopter, no search warrant is necessary.[38] Similarly, if a police officer finds a key at a crime scene and suspects it fits an apartment door nearby, a court has ruled that no search warrant is needed before the officer can fit the key into the lock. The expectation of privacy in an exterior house lock is so inconsequential that it does not warrant protection under the Tennessee Constitution,[39] although an officer's right to enter such a house depends on other facts and circumstances. Still, with regard to searches where police without a warrant roam around non-agricultural land near one's house because they "suspect" something, the Tennessee Constitution gives owners more protection than the United States Constitution. Thus, where marijuana plants were found growing seventy-five feet from a defendant's house, a search warrant was necessary, despite the fact that the plants were initially seen by a police helicopter.[40] Unsupervised roadblocks lacking administrative guidelines and approval are not allowed to catch drunk drivers in Tennessee.[41] However, cordless or cellular telephone conversations picked up by police are not protected by the Tennessee Constitution.[42]

Does the Punishment Fit the Crime?

The death penalty does not per se violate that section of the Tennessee Constitution that prohibits "cruel and unusual punishment."[43] Although the condemned are entitled to a "dignified death," no one is quite sure what that means.[44] Prison inmates were whipped until the 1960s, and until 1969 an inmate could be forced to sleep nude on a concrete floor; the Tennessee Constitution provides no greater restriction on harsh punishment than the federal charter.[45] The issue of whether a lengthy prison sentence is cruel and unusual punishment is governed by federal constitutional standards, which the state Constitution follows and apparently does not enlarge.

Equal Rights and the Right of Privacy

The Tennessee Constitution contains no equal rights amendment, but the state supreme court has ruled that requiring a married woman to use her husband's last name for voting is improper in a modern society.[46] Similarly, the biological father of an out-of-wedlock child can block the child's adoption and gain custody under some circumstances.[47] However, different rules for boys' and girls' high school basketball are appropriate, according to 1977 constitutional convention guidelines.[48]

One of the most unusual constitutional cases in Tennessee law involved a dispute over the custody of frozen pre-embryos after a couple divorced. Drawing from other specified rights, the Tennessee Supreme Court said for the first time that the "right of privacy" was constitutionally protected in Tennessee. Under this view, both the right to procreate and to prevent procreation were equally protected.[49] The right to privacy includes parental rights to make child-rearing decisions that do not endanger the welfare of children. Thus, unless the parents are found unfit, a court has no power to order that grandparents have visitation rights.[50] But the right of privacy is not absolute. In an unusual case, the Tennessee Supreme Court said that high school students and teachers have no right to wear beards, because this is an issue of school management and discipline to be determined by the local school board.[51] However, private (in-house) homosexual activity is protected by both the right to privacy and the equal protection provisions of the Tennessee Constitution.[52]

The requirement that a government establish no arbitrary or unreasonable classifications of persons, the "equal protection" guarantee, is found by reading two state constitutional provisions together—the "law of the land," Article I, Section 8, and the requirement that no law be passed benefiting any individual(s), Article XI, Section 8. The classification/equal protection cases turn on whether a rational basis for the difference can be established, rather than on strict fairness. For example, laws that protect doctors from malpractice suits but that do not protect other professionals in the same manner and laws that partially protect hospitals from liability for transfusing impure blood have been upheld as a means of ameliorating the so-called malpractice crisis.[53] Finally, as a related concept, the notion that courts must be "open" means only that unreasonable barriers must not be erected to the bringing of suits. The provision provides little protection. Thus, a state law providing that manufacturers of defective products are immune from suit if the products are beyond a certain age would be constitutional.[54]

Some of the provisions of the Declaration of Rights make sense only in the context of history. A universal favorite is the language that says that "the doctrine of non-resistance against arbitrary power and oppression is absurd, slavish, and destructive of the good and happiness of mankind." The governor and General Assembly who thought it meant that Tennessee could secede from the Union found out differently at Shiloh, Franklin, and Lookout Mountain.

Other, more readily appreciated portions of the Declaration clearly spring from the context of historical events. Article I, Section 29 declares free navigation of the Mississippi as an inherent right of Tennesseans. This was placed in the 1796 Constitution to demonstrate the river's importance in the state's economic life. At the time of its writing, the United States was negotiating with Spain, which controlled New Orleans, regarding navigation of the river. The section providing for safe and comfortable prisons and the humane treatment of prisoners was not included until 1870. During the Civil War many prominent Tennesseans were imprisoned by federal officials, and A. O. P. Nicholson, an influential delegate to the 1870 constitutional convention, had been released only after doctors declared that further confinement would kill him. The provision offers no additional protection beyond that provided by the Eighth Amendment, however.[55] The section giving Tennesseans the right to "keep and bear arms" includes the privilege of "carrying an Army pistol in the open hand."[56]

Sovereign Immunity
Tennessee retains its traditional, and arguably backward, view of sovereign immunity. Under this doctrine no one may sue the state in court for money damages arising from either tort or constitutional violations.[57] The only remedy is to seek recovery from the Claims Commission, where the maximum recovery is $300,000. In rare circumstances, when a state official is found personally liable for violating constitutional rights in federal court under the federal civil rights laws, the state is not financially responsible, though it may voluntarily pay the judgment by way of a settlement. Local governments may be sued for damages in state court, but the case is nonjury and the maximum recovery, depending on the county, is $150,000.

The Legislature

Most authority for the Tennessee legislature is found in Article II. It divides state government into the legislative, executive, and judicial branches and prohibits any person with powers in one branch from exercising powers belonging to another.

The concept of separation of powers is illustrated in a recent divorce case. The trial court ordered the couple to submit to counseling prior to trial. When the husband refused, the case was appealed. The Tennessee Court of Appeals ruled that the grounds and procedures for a divorce were matters for the legislature, and, because the legislature had not authorized mandatory counseling, the court could not order it on its own.[58]

Another case illustrates legislative over-reaching. A statute required that a district attorney had to get approval from the state commissioner of health and environment before he could seek an indictment for polluting waterways. This was found to be an unconstitutional invasion of the power of the judicial branch, of which the district attorney is a member.[59] However, Tennessee law allows forfeiture to local police agencies of autos used in drug-dealing; the commissioner of safety makes such forfeiture decisions. In this case a member of the executive department is permitted to exercise a judicial function because the commissioner's actions may be appealed to a court.[60]

Legislative authority in the state belongs to the General Assembly, which consists of the Senate and House of Representatives. Each house elects a speaker as its leader. Representatives are elected to terms of two years, senators to terms of four. The Constitution specifically states that the House shall seat ninety-nine representatives; it further specifies that the number of senators shall not exceed one-third the number of representatives, and the number thirty-three has been used since 1884. Legislative districts for representatives and senators are apportioned according to the population, but if the U.S. Constitution should ever allow apportionment not based solely on population, one house can be apportioned by other criteria.

Senators and representatives must be qualified voters of the districts they represent, citizens of the United States, three-year residents of the state, and one-year residents of the county represented. Representatives must be at least twenty-one years of age, and senators must be at least thirty. The constitutional wording of "county" in the residential requirements has caused some disputes because of the way apportionment splits counties into separate districts and multiple counties into a single district. The requirement is interpreted as requiring residency in one of the counties of a multi-county district or in any portion of a county that is part of more than one district. The requirement that senators and representatives be qualified voters of the district represented can only be satisfied by their moving into the district, but candidates can meet this requirement any time prior to election day. Elections for state legislators are held on the first Tuesday after the first Monday in November, a date set in 1870 to coincide with federal elections.

The Constitution also schedules when the General Assembly can meet. It must open a short organizational session on the second Tuesday in January after each election for representatives, but it may not pass any final legislation then. If a gubernatorial election has occurred, the governor is inaugurated during the organizational session. The regular session begins on the first Wednesday following the end of the organizational session. A joint resolution of both houses can begin the regular session earlier or set times for adjournment. The General Assembly can be convened by joint resolution, by the governor's power of calling an extraordinary session, or by written request of two-thirds of the members of each house.

The houses of the General Assembly set their own rules, may expel members by two-thirds vote, and can punish disorderly persons who disrupt sessions. If the Senate violates one of its own rules, however, the courts will not become involved unless the Constitution is violated.[61] Members are protected from arrest while going to a session, attending a session, or returning from a session, except for felonies, treason, or breach of the peace. This protection was important when transportation was limited to foot, horse, and wagon; it took days to travel to a session, and political opponents could detain a member on frivolous charges in order to control voting outcomes in the General Assembly. Members are also granted special freedom of speech during sessions, on the floor or in committee meetings, although slander is not protected.

The General Assembly's primary function is to consider and pass legislation. The Constitution sets out the general framework for this, and Tennessee has no provision for initiative or referendum.[62] One of the most significant constitutional requirements for bills was added in 1870, in the wake of abuses during the Brownlow era. Bills must specify which previous laws are affected and be limited to a single subject. The legislature interprets this requirement loosely, considering bills touching a variety of matters to be on "one subject" as long a bill's various components evince a reasonable connection to the subject set out in the caption or title of the bill and as long as the various matters can be construed to have a single purpose or objective. The Constitution prohibits passage of a bill with the same substance as a bill previously voted down by the same session of the legislature. Once a bill is passed and codified in the state law, no challenge to the one-subject rule can be lodged. Bills are passed by a majority vote of total members on the bill's third consideration. Prior to a 1978 amendment each bill had to be read aloud at each of the considerations, and passed bills had to be signed by the speakers in open session, but bills may now be mentioned by number or title only and speakers may sign bills in their offices. A bill becomes law after being signed by the governor, or after ten days if the governor neither signs nor vetoes it.

Spending the Taxpayers' Money

The Constitution limits the General Assembly's power to spend the state's money by requiring that expenses in any given year not exceed revenues and reserves. Concerns that tax revenues were growing faster than personal income and that the legislature was requiring local governments to provide services without providing funding for them precipitated two innovations in the Tennessee Constitution in 1978. A so-called "state spending limitation" mandates that appropriations from state revenues must not exceed "the growth of the state's economy." This so-called "ceiling" on tax-spending was one of the first in the nation but has twice been broken since 1978.[63] Another 1978 innovation addressed the issue of saddling local governments with new unfunded programs, called expenditure mandates or unfunded mandates. This provision voids new programs unless the legislature shares in their cost. The provision has produced a welter of opinions by attorneys general, some difficult to reconcile, but the provision allows legislators to say that they have been successful getting pet programs through the legislature, when such programs actually die for lack of funding.[64]

The Constitution sets forth the general provisions for taxation. The section regarding taxation and valuation of property is so long and specific that courts have generally restricted the General Assembly from taxing anything not specifically mentioned in the Constitution. This section has been the traditional reason for not instituting a personal income tax, only a tax on income from stocks and bonds. Recent years have seen conflicting attorney generals' opinions on this issues. Legal scholars now tend to think that an income tax is constitutional without a constitutional amendment.[65]

The Constitution requires that sessions of each house of the General Assembly and committee meetings be open to the public. There is a provision, invoked when the General Assembly decided to secede from the Union in 1861, that allows for private meetings when "the business shall be such as ought to be kept secret."[66]

THE EXECUTIVE

The executive power of the state is vested in the governor and, by implication, in the governor's appointees. The governor is elected in a state-wide election on a plurality basis. A vote by the General Assembly breaks any tie that may occur.

The General Assembly also officially determines the results of the election and resolves any contests to a gubernatorial election. This has happened once. The 1895 Republican candidate, H. Clay Evans, who had come to Tennessee in 1862 wearing a Union Army uniform, received a 748 vote victory over incumbent Peter Turley, a Democrat and former Confederate officer, according to the first "official" tally. The election contest went to the Democratic-dominated legislature, which threw out thousands of "illegal" ballots and concluded that Turley had won by 2,354 votes.[67]

The governor must be thirty years old, a citizen of the United States, and a resident of the state for seven years. The governor serves for a term of four years and, since 1978, can run for one additional successive term.

The governor is commander-in-chief of the state's militia, the Tennessee National Guard, except when it is called into the service of the United States, as in the 1991 Gulf War. Technically, the militia can be called only by vote of the General Assembly and only during rebellion or invasion. This rule is a classic artifact of Reconstruction; Brownlow had called out the militia at whim, and the 1870 convention delegates meant to stop the practice. Today the provision is ignored. Governors have called out the Guard to handle violent strikes, natural disasters, and urban riots, including those following the 1968 assassination of Dr. Martin Luther King, Jr., in Memphis.

The governor is also the official keeper of the state seal. The office includes a pardoning power but not the power to restore an impeached officer to office. The governor can convene the General Assembly in an extraordinary session, but the proclamation must specify the purpose for the session, and no other matters can be considered. The governor's important power of veto must be exercised within ten days, Sundays excepted, or a bill will become law without the governor's signature. In 1953, the Constitution provided that the governor has a line-item veto power for appropriation bills. A majority vote in each house can override the governor's veto.

THE JUDICIARY

The Constitution mandates a supreme court. The circuit and chancery courts were specifically mentioned in the Constitution in 1870, and some argue that the General Assembly may not abolish them. Attorney general opinions have found that the section merely mandates the General Assembly provide for lower courts that exercise the jurisdiction that circuit and chancery courts exercised when the provision was included.

The Supreme Court of Tennessee consists of five judges. No more than two judges may reside in any one of the three grand geographical divisions of the state. Judges of the Supreme Court are elected by the voters in a state-wide election and must be thirty-five years old and state residents for five years. Supreme Court judges serve an eight-year term. The method of electing the judges is left to the General Assembly. Currently, an appellate court nominating committee presents the governor with the names of three qualified persons. After appointment, judges must stand for election during which the voters vote yes or no on retaining the judge, a method called the Missouri Plan (now the Tennessee Plan). In 1996, Supreme Court Judge Penny White was rejected by the voters after a controversial opinion on a death penalty case became a political issue.

The Supreme Court has the power to issue rules of procedure for civil and criminal cases. This power has been a thorny issue because members of the Tennessee General Assembly think they should have some voice in this matter since such rules can greatly influence the outcome in cases. Court rules are issued by the Supreme Court, but the legislature must approve them, and the Court seldom suggests rules that the legislature will reject.

The Supreme Court exercises jurisdiction over the licensing and disciplining of lawyers. In recent decades the court has set up an agency to disbar attorneys and asserted its inherent power to control lawyers. Thus, the Court invalidated a law permitting a person to take the bar exam an unlimited number of times.[68] Judges of the inferior courts, including circuit and chancery courts, are also elected. Judges of the lower courts must be thirty years old, residents of the state for five years, and residents of the circuit or district from which they are elected for one year. Like Supreme Court judges, they serve eight-year terms. The General Assembly can change the jurisdiction of the inferior courts. It can also remove judges from office by an impeachment proceeding or on a two-thirds vote of each house after ten days notification to the judge.

The Supreme Court appoints the attorney general for an eight-year term, a provision unique to Tennessee. It can also appoint a state's attorney pro tempore if a state's attorney fails to fulfill his or her duties in a case. Other judicial officers included in the Constitution include attorneys for the state, clerk and masters (clerks of chancery courts), and clerks of inferior courts. All of these are elected by the local voters, except for clerks and masters, who are appointed by the chancellor. Trial court clerks serve four-year terms; clerks and master serve six-year terms.

Unlike virtually every other state, the Tennessee attorney general has no independent power to seek prosecutions or supervise local district attorneys; in this sense, Tennessee has no one official top law enforcement officer. The attorney general represents the state in litigation, including all criminal appeals, and the staff spends considerable time drafting legal opinions for state and local government officials.[69]

Several matters dealing with the judicial process are set out in both the article dealing with the judicial system (Article VI) and the Declaration of Rights. A judge may not tell a jury what the facts of a case are but may state what the testimony was and what the law is. Jurors then decide what testimony forms the facts of the case and apply the law, as stated by the judge, to the facts. As mentioned earlier, Tennessee's "13th Juror Rule" provides that if the judge does not agree with the jury, he may throw out the verdict and order a new trial. A judge may neither preside at a trial nor make a decision in a case in which the judge has an interest or if the judge is related to a party by blood or marriage unless all the parties consent. Special judges can be appointed in a case of such a conflict. All indictments for a criminal charge must conclude "against the peace and dignity of the State."[70]

One of the most antiquated sections of the Tennessee Constitution mandates that only juries can impose criminal fines exceeding fifty dollars. This was about two months' pay in 1796 and hardly different in 1870. The rule is riddled with exceptions today. For example, violation of a city ordinance is not deemed a crime,[71] and the word "fine" here does not include all payments made in a matter. A fine must go to the state, not to an individual, and is only assessed in a criminal matter. A defendant can waive this right.[72] If a person is found guilty of a crime for which there is a mandatory, specific fine, the judge can assess it. The appeal of the infamous case of *Scopes v. State*, involving the teaching of evolution in public schools, included this prohibition against judges imposing fines as a matter at issue. The court reversed the conviction because the judge, not the jury, assessed the minimum fine of $100.[73]

LOCAL GOVERNMENT

The Constitution includes provisions involving local governments. The form of county government in Tennessee has undergone vast changes since 1796. The current Constitution provides for election of a legislative body, a county executive, a sheriff, a trustee, a register, a county clerk, and an assessor of property, all for four-year terms. Members of the county legislative body are elected from districts. No legislative body may exceed twenty-five members, and no more than three representatives are to be elected from a single district. The Constitution, however, does allow the General Assembly to provide alternative forms of government when approved by a majority of voters of a county.

The Constitution also allows for "consolidated," or metropolitan, government. This form allows for the consolidation of some, or all, functions of city government with the county government in which it sits. Nashville and Davidson County formed the first metropolitan government under this provision in 1962, becoming one of the first county-wide metropolitan governments in the United States.

Different state laws are needed for larger metropolitan areas than for rural ones or small towns. To accomplish this, many state statutes use population criteria, such as "counties with population of more than 200,000," to define the location of statutory coverage. Most of these laws have been found to have a rational basis, but some have failed this test. For example, a law protecting residential tenants in large counties was approved[74] while a law allowing work release for drunk diving offenders in Davidson and Shelby counties, but not small ones, was struck down.[75]

The desire for special laws applicable only to certain counties and cities generates private acts. These state laws must be approved by the county legislative body after passage. Most are upheld against the claim that they violate the provision of the Constitution mandating only general laws and no laws benefiting an individual. For example, Gatlinburg can charge extra sales tax (mostly paid for by tourists) on retail sales, but Brentwood cannot impose a separate sales tax solely on liquor.[76]

ELECTIONS AND OFFICEHOLDERS

Several sections in the Constitution relate to elections and the qualifications of holders of specific offices, and several apply to officeholders in general. No religious or political test other than an oath to support the constitutions of the United States and of the state of Tennessee can be required to hold an office or public trust. Constitutional provisions forbid priests and ministers from being members of the General Assembly and atheists from holding any civil office. The United States Supreme Court struck down the first prohibition,[77] and the section relating to atheists is deemed to be unenforceable. A quaint constitutional provision prohibits duelists from holding office; the prohibition applies only when the duel, or one of its elements, is committed within the borders of Tennessee.

AMENDMENT OF THE CONSTITUTION

The Constitution may be amended by the legislature or by convention. Both preserve the tradition of the difficult amendment process first established in the 1796 Constitution.

The legislative method starts with the General Assembly. A proposal must be "read three times" before each vote by the General Assembly. Although the full verbatim reading of regular bills is no longer required at each consideration, such a reading is still required for proposed constitutional amendments.[78] After passing a majority vote of one General Assembly, it then moves to the next General Assembly. Six months notice of the proposed amendment is required prior to the election of the second General Assembly that will consider the amendment, and it must muster a two-thirds vote to pass it. If passed, the amendment is then submitted to state voters in a gubernatorial election. If approved by a majority of the voters who cast votes in the governor's race, it then becomes a part of the Constitution. Since many who vote in the governor's race skip the question on proposed amendments, however, this is a very difficult standard to meet. Only one amendment, a relatively uncontroversial tax reform measure in 1982, has been added to the Constitution through the legislative method.

The constitutional convention method of amending the Constitution also begins with the General Assembly, which adopts a bill calling for a convention that uses the same procedures required for passing other bills. After the call is approved by a single session of the General Assembly, the call is submitted to the people for a vote. The call includes the sections or matters to be included for discussion and amendment by the delegates to a convention. If a majority of voters approve, then an election for constitutional convention delegates is held. The number of delegates and requirements have been the same as for members of the House of Representatives, with house district lines applying as well. The call for the convention cannot restrict the actions the convention delegates can take, but can only describe the sections or subject matter to be considered. After a convention has agreed upon a proposed amendment, it is submitted to the people for approval by majority vote. A constitutional convention can be held only once every six years. As explained earlier, Tennessee has used the device of a limited convention; such limited conventions have been held in 1953, 1959, 1965, 1971, and 1977.

Constitutional change remains difficult but not impossible, and this is arguably the way it should be. As U.S. Associate Court Justice Benjamin Cardozo once said, "A constitution states or ought to state, not rules for the passing hour, but principles for an expanding future."[79]

Part II
INSTITUTIONS

CHAPTER 3

The Institutionalization of the
Tennessee Legislature,
1968–1997

—Thomas D. Ungs and Frank Essex

More than a decade ago, scholar Malcolm Jewell called for greater attention to the study of comparative state politics.[1] Jewell pointed especially to Southern politics because it was still in the process of change, an evolution that offered special opportunities for understanding political institutions. He identified Southern legislatures as "specially deserving and growing more powerful vis-à-vis the governor, probably at a more rapid rate than in most states.[2]

This chapter addresses changes in the Tennessee legislature, called the General Assembly, over the past thirty years. Tennessee's General Assembly has been transformed from a governor-dominated legislative system to a more professional, institutionalized assembly that is significantly more independent of executive will and direction. We use the concept of "institutionalization" in this chapter as it has been widely applied to other legislative bodies, especially Congress.

During the twentieth century, Congress has undergone a significant reshaping, including changes in leadership patterns, in the volume and scope of its workload, in the length of tenure of its members, and in the complexity of its organization. The seminal work in the study of this process of institutionalization is Nelson Polsby's analysis of the history and development of the U.S. House of Representatives.[3] More recently, the concept has been applied to state legislatures.[4] In his work on Congress, Roger Davidson defines institutionalization as "the process whereby structures and procedures take shape and become regularized. . . . [T]he institution becomes structured and routinized, responding to widely held expectations about how it should perform."[5] Other students of the legislative process have stressed the relationship between the institutionalized legislative group and the individual legislator.[6]

Such legislator-legislature relationships are directly related to the concept of legislative role within the context of changing legislative institutions. Questions concerning legislative recruitment, the development of "professionalism" in legislatures, the nature of constituency-legislator relationships, party and legislator interrelationships, and "careerism" in state legislatures are essential to the broad understanding of institutional patterns in the nation's state legislatures.

To be sure, all legislatures are institutions with defined functions. In this sense, the Tennessee legislature has always been "institutionalized." It has, for example, operated with rules of procedures, committee structures, and leadership. However, much evidence suggests that the way the legislature has functioned relative to the executive branch, its patterns of turnover of membership, the nature and complexity of its work load, its committee structure, its leadership, and other elements have changed and may still be changing. Alan Rosenthal refers to these changes as the "congressionalization" of state legislatures.[7] We will explore these changes and evaluate how Tennessee legislators assess their role relative to changing institutional patterns.

From 1922 through 1965, the relationship between the legislative and executive branches in Tennessee was almost totally dominated by the governor. Beginning with the administration of Austin Peay in 1923, governors acquired the executive budget and, through reorganization of the administrative branch, were able to exercise effective control over the administration of policy. A series of aggressive governors ultimately reduced the General Assembly to the status of an extension of the executive branch. Governors selected the speakers of both houses of the Assembly, laid out their legislative programs with no fear of disapproval or significant alterations, and punished recalcitrant legislators. The item veto, acquired in 1953, enabled the chief executive to exercise even more stringent control over appropriations.[8]

The rural dominated legislatures of the 1950s and early 1960s began to show independence through changes such as the establishment of a Legislative Council, the improvement in legislator per diem allowances, and a reduced preoccupation with purely private acts (a law applicable only to specific towns or cities). Nevertheless, the Assembly remained a body without independent leadership, adequate staff resources, or even physical facilities to accommodate committee hearings and legislative offices.[9]

Signs of a foundation for the development of a more independent legislature appeared in the early 1960s. The 1962 U.S. Supreme Court decision *Baker v. Carr* sounded the death knell for rural dominance by producing an increase in the number of both urban-based districts (including election of blacks) and Republican legislators. The number of urban-based Republican legislators increased as the result of the redistribution of legislative seats in Republican-dominated East Tennessee. Republicans also gained strength through the redistribution of seats from Democratic rural West Tennessee to more heavily populated East Tennessee. A 1966 constitutional amendment extended the terms of senators from two to four years, permitted annual sessions and annual budgets, allowed for easier revision of legislative salaries, and gave the legislature the power to call special sessions. These structural changes were supplemented with legislative establishment in 1967 of the Fiscal Review Committee, a unit that provided a major source of continuing fiscal information to legislators. By 1975 the legislature had added additional secretarial and other full-time staff and had resolved its space problem through the building of a major office and hearing-room facility.[10]

In 1997 the Assembly created an Office of Legislative Budget Analysis, assigning it a variety of responsibilities related to analysis of areas such as appropriation requests, projected revenues, and proposed capital improvements. This office is also charged with studying the long and short term effects of public-policy decisions and recommending appropriate policy changes. The office's potential as a legislative tool in the state's budget process may be significant, but its ultimate role will clearly depend upon whether it is permitted to evolve as a viable instrument of legislative policy making.

The critical political struggle that altered the pattern of gubernatorial control occurred in 1965 over the selection of a speaker of the Senate. Governor Frank Clement's hand-picked choice for the post, Senator Jared Maddux, was challenged by Senator Frank Gorrell, a candidate backed by a majority of the Democratic caucus. In addition to an intra-party struggle, the selection of a speaker clearly reflected a push for legislative independence.[11]

Political scientists have extensively explored these developments, but no systematic study of their relation to an institutionalized Tennessee legislature has been undertaken. As already noted, the literature is fairly rich regarding studies of the institutionalization of the modern Congress. Until recently, few state legislatures, especially those in the South, followed the national trend. Tennessee's experience over the past two or three decades suggests a pattern of development similar to that of the Congress and other state legislatures.

We have measured patterns of institutionalization in Tennessee in several different ways, each one supplementary to the others. A number of in-depth interviews with legislators, key legislative staff, former legislators, as well as the dean of the press staff covering the General Assembly, provided important background information and critical perspectives on the development of legislative leadership, procedures, and legislative-executive relationships over the past several decades. In addition, we have examined elements related to legislative competition and turnover, the volume of legislation, the growth in legislative budgets, and the expansion of legislative staff resources. We conclude by reporting the results of a 1990 survey of incumbent Tennessee legislators that reveals the extent to which legislators see their role in the context of a professional and firmly institutionalized body.

PATTERNS OF CHANGE, 1968–1997

Professionalization and competence, though not necessarily related, are often identified as measures of institutionalization. Both characteristics are most likely acquired by groups that provide a high level of continuity of membership.

Coleman McGinnis's study of legislative turnover in Tennessee looked closely at the period 1960 to 1984. To place the turnover phenomenon in perspective and to establish a point of comparison, McGinnis reviewed the turnover rate for selected years between 1930 and 1956. At no time during this period did as many as one-half of incumbents seek reelection.

McGinnis's data shows that the number of incumbents seeking reelection increased during the decades of the 1960s, 1970s, and 1980s. To illustrate, during the 1980s 87.1 percent of members of the House and 79.8 percent of senators sought re-election. The incumbent return rate, while relatively high from the 1960s through the 1980s, increased by approximately 10 percent over the previous decade. During the 1980s, an average of 95.4 percent of House members seeking re-election were returned. Senators won re-election an average of 89.5 percent of the time during the same decade. Longer tenure for more legislators translates into a more experienced legislature, and greater experience suggests a greater sense of professionalism. Both are marks of an institutionalized legislature.[12]

Party Competition

A number of scholars have investigated the relationship between a more competitive party system and public policy outcomes. Most agree that party alignment within state legislatures is a variable that needs to be considered in determining levels of institutionalization.[13] Prior to the 1960s, legislatures in traditional one-party Democratic states in the South, including Tennessee, exhibited low levels of institutionalization. In Tennessee, the ratio of Democrats to Republicans in the Senate held at five or six to one through the 85th General Assembly (1967–1968), and at five to one in the House through the 84th (1965–1966). Significant Republican gains in House seats were made in 1966 and in the Senate two years later. By 1970 the Democratic majority in the Senate had been reduced to a margin of twenty-one to twelve. In the House, the two parties held forty-nine seats each, along with a single independent. These changes in party balance occurred simultaneously with a growing assertion of legislative independence from control by the governor.

While both houses were reapportioned in conformance with the Supreme Court's decision in *Baker v Carr* (1962) and each saw an increase in members from metropolitan areas, the urban-based House members were not selected from single-member districts until 1966. Senate districts became single-member constituencies in 1968. As McGinnis has noted, "Such a change always works to the benefit of 'minorities' who may have enough strength concentrated in a geographic area to elect members, but who are unable to control county-wide elections."[14]

Between 1968 and 1997 party competition in the House was generally much closer than in the Senate. Democrats and Republicans held an equal number of seats (forty-nine) in the House during the 1969–1970 session, and Democrats have held sixty-six or fewer seats in each session since, including their fifty-six seats in the 1995–1996 session. The Senate was more Democratic through the 1980s, holding at least twenty of the thirty-three seats from 1975 through 1989. During the 1990s Republicans have challenged more successfully. In fact, two Democratic defections following the 1995 legislative session actually left the Republicans with a one-seat majority for the first time since Reconstruction.

Key persons who were interviewed tended to play down the significance of party influence in the General Assembly. The most long-term observer of Tennessee legislative politics suggested that party affiliation is extremely important in winning election to office but thereafter is clearly obvious only in organizational votes of the two houses. Other interviewees agreed that the greatest differences in legislative politics were not party based. The most salient division was consistently characterized as "liberal versus conservative," especially in fiscal matters. Other important differences were identified as urban-rural, business-labor, or cleavages that reflect East-West Tennessee interests. Also, as would be expected, the Democratic majorities during the years of Republican governors have given greater attention to party efforts to monitor programs. For example, two new oversight committees, Education and Corrections, were established during Governor Alexander's administration (1979–1986) as a means of providing greater Democratic party oversight of these two important areas of state policy.

V. O. Key's 1949 classic study of Southern politics[15] described Tennessee as predominantly Democratic statewide but dominated by Republicans in "Unionist" East Tennessee. Thirty years after Key's analysis, two studies of partisan competition in Tennessee demonstrated the erosion of the state's traditional regional voting blocks, Democratic Middle and West Tennessee, on the one hand, and Republican East Tennessee, on the other. J. Leiper Freeman showed that partisan voting competition in presidential elections had sufficiently "trickled down" to produce general competition in races for both U.S. Senate seats and the governorship.[16] Robert Swansbrough's study of Tennessee electoral politics found that despite the persistence of traditional regional party loyalties, their strength is substantially less, particularly in Democratic West Tennessee.[17]

No one has made systematic measurements of Freeman's "trickle down" effect in partisan contests for state legislative seats. However, some evidence suggests an increase in competitiveness in those races. Prior to the 1960s the Tennessee legislature operated under firm Democratic control. From 1930 through 1959 an average ratio of twenty-eight Democratic to five Republican Senators held firm in each session. Democrats held an average of seventy-nine of ninety-nine House seats during the same period. As previously indicated, turnover in seats was high. Most Democratic incumbents who consistently sought reelection were legislative leaders, the governor's "point men" who did his bidding. Too weak to mount any challenge to Democratic control across the state, Republicans posed no threat to Democratic hegemony. McGinnis found that in legislative elections between 1930 and 1958, Republicans challenged Democrats in only one election year for as many as 20 percent of legislative seats.[18] Over the last thirty years the relative position of the legislative parties has changed, a change reflected in the decline in the size of Democratic majorities.

Another more sophisticated measure of party competition also reflects growing competitiveness in Tennessee elections. An "index of interparty competition," a measure of party competition based on elections for governor and state legislative races developed by Austin Ranney, placed Tennessee in the "modified one-party Democratic" category for the period 1962–1973.[19] Under Ranney's categories, a score between .3500 and .6499 would rank a state as two-party competitive. Using Ranney's index to measure party competition in three separate periods after 1973, the state fell into the competitive two-party category from 1968–1978 (.5371), 1980–1988 (.5345), and 1990–1996 (.5834).

Can the Republican gains in the legislature be linked to the assertion of independence from gubernatorial control? No clear evidence for such a relationship can be identified. Changing partisan balance after the 1960s may have occurred despite the growth of legislative autonomy. The impact of reapportionment and growing Republican electoral strength in large areas of the state, as well as other factors, probably contributed to the achievement of closer partisan balance in the General Assembly. If Republicans could achieve the same degree of success in state legislative elections that they have in contests for presidential and U.S. Senate elections, partisanship would likely become a more significant element in legislative policy making. Highly competitive contests for control of both the governorship and legislature might highlight the need for legislative parties to place greater value on party unity over other influences in legislative voting patterns. To be sure, differences over issues that are not based on party affiliation (urban-rural, East-West, purely local preferences, etc.) will continue to influence legislative behavior. As will be noted in our discussion of member perceptions of the role of party leaders, legislator preferences of "constituency over party" have clearly been the prevailing pattern; thus one can only speculate about the prospects for enhanced party loyalty should statewide electoral trends toward closer partisan balance have a similar impact on legislative elections.

VOLUME AND TYPE OF LEGISLATION AND LEGISLATIVE STAFF RESOURCES

Experienced legislators and long-time observers of the Tennessee legislature interviewed by the authors agreed that over the past several decades legislators focused greater attention on general legislation and less on local or special bills. General bills are those that concern policy on statewide issues while local bills address issues of special concern to a specific city or county.

Our interviewed observers expressed the belief that the reduction in the number of local bills is a natural result of a legislature dominated in the past by the executive and thus less likely to concern itself with general legislation. That is, major policy proposals initiated in the past by the governor's office were rather routinely approved, leaving legislators to focus greater attention on the parochial interests inherent in special bills. Coincidental with the end of gubernatorial dominance, improved legislative staff resources, increased party competition, and more assertive legislative party leadership—all marks of a more institutionalized legislature—was an enhanced legislator interest in general legislative bills. Moreover, our interviewees voiced the opinion that these changes positioned the legislature to write "better quality" legislation as well.

To be sure, if a comparison is made with a long-institutionalized Congress, one might expect more independent Tennessee legislators interested in reelection to mirror the congressional pattern of serving local constituencies.[20] We were nevertheless sufficiently intrigued with the impressions of interviewees to examine the volume and type of legislation in the General Assembly over the period 1968–1995.

The volume of general bills did increase over this period of time. Almost 2,300 general bills were introduced during 1978–1979, the largest number of any period in this study. The following session was also a high volume period, reaching over 2,000. This was followed by a decline in general bills during the three subsequent sessions, but the number rose again in the 1986–1987 Assembly. Even though the average of general bills introduced was slightly higher during the 1970s than during the 1980s, the trend of increasing numbers of general bills seems established.

By comparison, the number of local or special bills declined from 536 to 299 during the period 1968–1995.[21] If measured solely by the volume and type of bills introduced, the impression of our interviewees has been verified. Beyond that we cannot conclude that the changes identified explain a more independent legislature.

Productivity trends cannot address the question of whether the Assembly has produced higher quality legislation. This clearly elusive element depends upon subjective judgments. Nevertheless, experienced legislators and other observers of the legislative process who were interviewed generally agreed that the quality of legislation has improved over the past two decades. They attributed this perceived improvement to more and better legislative staff, a more open and deliberative legislative process, the increasing use of study committees, and decreasing dependence on lobbyists for information. By 1992 legislators in both houses could call upon year-round legislative staff for help and information. In addition, model legislation developed by the Council of State Governments is considered to be of value in some areas of legislation. Overall, these elements are associated with a more professionalized and institutionalized legislature.

Improved staff resources clearly depend on adequate legislative budgets. In the late 1950s the General Assembly's total budget was slightly less than $500,000. By 1980–1981 that figure had risen to $6.7 million, an increase well ahead of the 35 percent increase for all state legislatures over the same period as reported by the Council of State Governments. Legislative branch funding has steadily risen over the succeeding years, with the 1995–1996 budget reaching $18.6 million.

LEGISLATOR PERSPECTIVES

Twenty-five years of developing independence from gubernatorial dominance has been manifest in growing professionalism marked by lower turnover of legislative seats, closer partisan balance, improved salaries and staffing, expanded legislative facilities, and an increase in the number of legislative bills. Is there evidence that legislators describe their role and status within the context of a more professionalized independent law-making body?

To provide a perspective on this question we mailed a survey to all members of the 96th General Assembly (1989–1990). Of the 132 legislators, 67 (50 percent) responded. Respondents included 41 of the 82 Democrats (28 in the House, 13 in the Senate) and 26 of the 50 Republicans (19 in the House, 7 in the Senate). This group had served an average of 9.4 years in the legislature, and 37 held at least one leadership position such as a committee chair or party leader. Measured by party affiliation and legislative branch, our legislators closely paralleled actual divisions in the 96th Assembly. The strong representation of legislators who held one or more leadership positions afforded us the perspective of more experienced and influential legislators.

The survey asked legislators to express their opinions regarding elements of legislative organization, the role of political parties, sources of information, legislative work load, and the influence of the governor. We postulated that legislators who have inherited a long-term trend toward greater independence and who function within an institution enjoying significantly improved physical and financial resources as well as other appearances of a more "professionalized" body would also perceive legislative structure, procedures, and leadership as being more institutionalized and routine. In addition, we speculated that legislators might attribute greater importance to the role of legislative and party leadership relative to both executive influence and individual autonomy in decisions.

ROLE OF THE GOVERNOR

The decline of control by Tennessee governors over the legislative branch probably began during 1967–1968, the final two years of Democratic Governor Buford Ellington's administration. Prior to the assertion of greater independence, governors dominated the legislative process by using a variety of means: patronage, a centralized budget process centered in the executive budget, control over election of speakers, "ripper bills" that threatened or punished recalcitrant legislators, and strong ties with local party leaders and organizations.

By the early 1970s the appearance of a more independent legislature was evident. The General Assembly now played a major role in the budget process; it moved to annual as well as longer legislative sessions; it used its power to override executive vetoes; and it began building power bases of its own through the increasing length of tenure of key legislative leaders. Subsequent improvements in legislative salaries also reflect an institution with enhanced power and independence relative to the executive branch.

To be sure, just as presidents are the symbol of government at the federal level, so governors are the focal point of state government. Tennessee governors consistently win passage of most of their legislative programs, and they continue to set the agenda for action by state government. This success has remained constant even under Republican Governors Lamar Alexander and Don Sundquist. However, in the relationship between the two branches, the governor no longer dominates. In fact, we suggest that, increasingly, the relationship requires the executive to approach the legislature in a spirit of accommodation and partnership.

Table 1 shows legislator responses to questions related to the role of the governor in legislative policy making. Only 51.5 percent of our responding legislators agreed that the governor is "chief legislator." Although the surprisingly modest level of agreement on this item might be a function of understanding the term "chief legislator" as implying dominance, other items in our survey also tend to show a strong sense of legislative independence. Only 38.4 percent saw the governor as an essential "agenda setter" for effective legislative success, and 41.5 percent perceived some legislators as more powerful than the governor in the legislative process. Further, one-half agreed that leadership has "gravitated from the governor to speakers and other party leaders." Recognizing the necessity of providing strong legislative leadership as a buffer to gubernatorial influence, legislators in our sample overwhelmingly (93.9 percent) advocated strong speakers as essential to maintaining legislative independence.

Other responses indicate that the governor's influence on the legislature depends more on good communication, articulation of clear policy positions, the ability to mobilize support, and the recognition of diverse legislative interests. While legislators recognized that a governor's influence is highly significant, 96.8 percent saw that influence as heavily dependent on the ability to mobilize interests; 83.1 percent agreed that effective communication is closely associated with success; and more than three of four asserted that the governor must negotiate with "influential people" to be successful.

Legislators did acknowledge the continuing influence and power of the governor. Nearly 85 percent of respondents agreed that when the governor's position is clear, he usually gets his way, and only 26.5 percent believed that "without doubt" the legislature is "independent of any effort by a governor to control it." Nevertheless, responses to all questions about the role of the governor support the assertion that the relationship between these two branches of Tennessee government has evolved in the last few decades from one of dominance by the governor to one of accommodation, bargaining, and compromise.

This pattern emerges when measured across party affiliation, legislative house, and types of constituency. Despite variation in the strength of responses, the direction is consistent for all groups. Only 27.8 percent of senators agreed

Table 3.1

ROLE AND INFLUENCE OF GOVERNOR
By Party, Legislative Branch, and Constituency
(By Percent)

ITEM	ALL RESPONDENTS Agree or Agree Strongly (N=65)	PARTY Agree or Agree Strongly		LEGISLATIVE BRANCH Agree or Agree Strongly		CONSTITUENCY Agree or Agree Strongly		
		DEM (N=41)	REP (N=24)	HOUSE (N=47)	SENATE (N=18)	RURAL (N=27)	URBAN (N=19)	SUBURB. (N=19)
Governor is "Chief Legislator"	51.5	42.9	68.2	60.9	27.8	51.9	57.9	43.8
Gov's influence greater if he can mobilize interests to support his program	96.8	95.2	100.0	95.7	100.0	96.3	100.0	94.1
Strong speakers are essential to legislature's independence of Governor	93.9	95.2	95.7	95.2	94.4	96.3	100.0	88.2
Some legislators are more powerful than Governor	41.5	40.5	43.5	44.7	33.3	33.3	42.1	52.9
Governor's "personal touch" more important than appeal to party loyalty	87.5	88.1	86.4	87.0	88.9	77.8	89.5	100.0
Diversity of interests among legislators makes Governor's influence more difficult	59.4	63.4	47.8	56.5	66.1	59.3	42.1	35.3
Governor's influence greater if his party controls legislature	91.8	90.5	95.7	91.5	94.4	92.6	94.7	88.2
When Governor's position is clear, he usually gets his way	84.7	75.6	95.8	80.9	88.9	88.9	68.4	88.2
Without doubt, legislature is independent of Governor's efforts to control it	26.5	32.5	16.7	27.7	23.5	26.9	36.8	11.8
Influence of Governor depends on quality and quantity of communication with legislators	83.1	85.4	83.3	89.4	72.2	81.5	89.5	88.2
Without governor as "agenda setter" legislature cannot function well	38.4	36.6	37.5	31.9	50.0	40.7	31.6	41.2
Increasingly, leadership has gravitated from Governor to speakers and party leaders	50.1	58.5	39.1	45.7	66.7	50.0	52.6	52.9

Question: Overall, which of the following statements best characterizes how you view the role and influence of the Governor in the legislature?

that the governor is "chief legislator." The Senate's action over the past decade in selecting the same speaker, John Wilder, illustrates this changed perception of the governor's role. A Democrat, Wilder's reelection to the speakership of the Senate has depended upon votes of minority Republican party members. In the choice of a speaker in 1989, Democratic Governor Ned McWherter failed to intervene despite criticism from Democrats inside and outside the legislature who favored another candidate. As one senator commented to one of the authors, "If he won't use his influence to protect the choice of a majority of his own party's caucus, will he use it at other times?" Undoubtedly, past Tennessee governors would have intervened had the same situation arisen. Wilder's willingness to negotiate with members of both parties in order to retain the speakership reduces a governor's ability to control the votes of his own party as well as those of the opposition party. As we have previously indicated, a governor's legislative success has become more dependent on negotiation with influential legislators than on command of his party's legislators. It should also be noted that a substantial majority of senators (66.7 percent) agreed that "leadership has gravitated from the governor to speakers and other party leaders," while less than half of the representatives agreed. Again, some explanation for this difference may lie in the speakership dispute, but in both cases the data show that legislators increasingly perceive a reduction in the influence of the governor over legislation.

PARTIES IN THE LEGISLATIVE PROCESS

Studies of state legislatures have consistently noted that nominal party membership does not reveal the extent to which partisanship plays an important role in policy making. When John Wahlke and his colleagues sought to measure party influence through their study of legislators in four states, including Tennessee, they concluded that "ambivalence and uncertainty about the meaning of 'party' is a fact of political life, felt by the legislators themselves; it is not just a reflection of the state of political research."[22] Subsequent studies have shown wide variation in the influence of parties in legislatures, ranging from a few states where party discipline is strong to the larger number where parties are more loosely organized and play a reduced role in legislative decisions.[23]

We have previously reviewed changes in party composition, turnover rates, and incumbent success in elections. In our survey of legislators we sought to assess the extent to which partisan awareness might be reflected in a more professional and institutionalized law-making body. It was assumed that a more independent and institutionalized legislature might tend to reflect greater awareness of the need for party cohesion beyond the formal organizational votes critical to the maintenance of majority party control. Given the fact that legislative leadership and committee structure are no longer merely an extension of executive leadership, it might be expected that members would take significant cues from party leadership and might accede to the need to maintain party discipline in important legislative votes. In our survey we sought legislators' opinions on two levels: their views on the importance of party affiliation to "actual" legislative decisions—those of their house or the legislature as a whole—and, secondly, the importance of party to their own decisions.

Our limited data supported the findings of most researchers who have assessed the relative influence of party on legislative decisions. Almost 78 percent of Tennessee legislators support the norm of voting with their party when party differences on major legislation are evident. Nevertheless, 90.3 percent of our respondents reported that they vote their "constituency" when their "party position" is contrary to constituency preferences. What is more, 95.2 percent said they would use their own "best judgment even when party leaders want me to vote their way." We noted no significant variation in responses between senators and representatives or between Democrats and Republicans.

Nearly half (48.4 percent) of lawmakers perceive "strong arm" tactics by party leaders as "very or somewhat important" in legislative decisions but not in their own choices (14.5 percent). Apparently, what they identify in the behavior of others is contrary to what they are willing to admit is proper in their own behavior. While the responses by party and legislative chamber both show some variance, the trend is basically similar for all groups.

The extent to which party membership plays a role in legislative politics cannot be established by our data, but the norms of party loyalty do not appear to apply with similar levels of importance (or unimportance) to what more systematic research has found in other state legislatures. For instance, in response to a question about the importance of pressures by the governor on legislation, 83 percent of representatives and 94 percent of senators agreed that it was "very" or "somewhat" important in their chamber, but only 68.9 percent in the House and 64.7 percent in the Senate admitted that the governor's pressure affected their own decisions. Similarly, 39 percent of Democrats and 48.4 percent of Republicans believed party leaders' "strong arm" tactics were "very" or "somewhat" important in their chamber, but just 17.5 percent and 9.1 percent respectively claimed that such tactics affected their own decisions. Put another way, the trend toward professionalism and greater institutionalization of the legislative role in Tennessee does not seem to have resulted in greater acceptance of the need for legislators to support party over either constituency preferences or individual judgment on legislative issues.

The Flow of Legislation—Standing Committees

A major benchmark of an institutionalized legislature is a high degree of regularization and control of the legislative agenda and the processes by which it is considered. Until 1965 the Tennessee legislature had no standing committees at all. Over the succeeding years, a strong committee structure has developed, as well as a sub-committee system that exercises increasingly important power in the legislative process.

Independence also meant the installation of a new set of "gate keepers" in the flow of legislation. Although the standing committee structure certainly contributes significantly to decentralized legislative power, it may also serve as an instrument of legislative leadership. As one fourteen-year Tennessee legislator commented, "When I came to the legislature I certainly became aware that committees were critical to getting things done. I think they have become even more powerful as a means to move the legislative agenda and to achieve a greater degree of influence by the leadership of both parties." This same view was expressed by a highly respected former legislator who pointed to improved legislative physical facilities (offices and hearing rooms) as "having a dramatic impact . . . a major step toward independence." With improved facilities committee sessions became open to the public and votes were recorded. This "highlighted, to some extent," the need for greater responsibility to party, leadership, and constituency. In short, what had been a more informal and more closed decision process gave way to procedures and expectations more consistent with the development of an institutionalized legislature. A long-time clerk of the Tennessee Senate made an especially strong claim for the impact of the present committee system when he said, "The open hearing is probably the most important single factor in creating legislative independence."

Responses to the six questions in our survey on standing committees clearly show that legislators of both parties and in both houses of the legislature recognized the critical role of these legislative groups. The role of the House Calendar and Rules parallels that of the U.S. House Rules Committee. It controls the flow of bills to the floor. Its membership, relatively large in number, is controlled by the speaker. The degree to which the Republican majority recognizes the committee's function as a gate-keeper for the majority party is revealed by the unanimous agreement of House Republicans in the survey and 93.3 percent of Senate Republicans that the committee exercises "great power over the fate of legislation in the House." Responding House Republicans also unanimously agreed with the statement that Calendar and Rules "is a major instrument of control of agenda of the majority party."

The very high level of agreement (92.1 percent) across party lines and chambers to the statement that "standing committees are increasingly powerful decision making groups in my house" clearly reveals legislators' recognition of how much control standing committees exercise over consideration of bills. However, the extent to which these committees are seen as instruments of the leadership is not clear. Slightly less than one-half of our respondents perceive standing committees as serving more to "decentralize legislative power" rather than as a means to "enhance power and control by leadership." It appears that standing committees of the Tennessee legislature are similar to those of Congress in functioning as "little legislatures," frequently independent of control by party leadership.

Partisanship is not perceived as necessarily the most important element in decisions of standing committees. Only one-third of our sixty-five respondents saw party as "more evident" now than when they entered the legislature. However, almost 60 percent of Republicans found it more important, a response that may indicate greater sensitivity of minority party members to the degree that the Democratic majority and leadership is able to control the content and flow of legislation.

One additional item in our survey lends support to a growing sense of professionalism within the Tennessee Assembly. More than two-thirds of our sample agreed that additional professional full-time staff would enhance the "effectiveness" of standing committees. This may indicate that legislators not only recognize the critical role of committees but that they also see the need to improve committee efficiency by upgrading staff to a level capable of conducting research during and between legislative sessions. To be sure, such additional expertise would further the independence of the legislature from reliance on executive initiative and would also help insulate legislators from reliance on information supplied by lobbyists for interest groups.

Party loyalty and party leadership play a key role in the selection of members of standing committees. Our interviews with legislative leaders confirmed that the speakers in each house exercise strategic and extensive influence over the choice of members for assignment to standing committees. It was also clear that these choices frequently take into consideration the ability, interests (personal and constituency), and expertise of legislators. Our data reveal that legislators, at least to some extent, recognize, on the one hand, the reality of assignment criteria related to party loyalty and loyalty to the speaker. On the other hand, their preferences for committee membership tend to give greater emphasis to the criteria that would increase opportunities to serve their own constituencies, personal preferences, and expertise. Notably, almost 97 percent of the respondents held that the preferences of the legislator and the "ability of individual legislators" should be important in selection to committees. The "need to balance geographical areas" was endorsed by 72.6 percent of all respondents. Little in these preferences run contrary to those elements already identified as supportive of an institutionalized legislature.

The Legislator as Delegate

Although several of the persons interviewed for this study indicated that there appeared to be some signs of development of "full-time legislators," they also found greater value in the concept of the "citizen legislator." To be sure, the great majority of legislators neither depend upon nor prefer to depend on legislative salaries or perquisites to make their living. Nevertheless, the demands on their time appear to be steadily growing. As one legislator put it, "This isn't a two or three month job anymore. Our sessions have gotten longer and I spend an awful lot of time here, even when we are not in session." Workload is clearly increasing, as demonstrated by increased claims on legislator time by committees, constituents, and interest groups. Thomas Dye's finding that constituent interests are most important in the use of any legislator's time[24] is confirmed by the experience of Tennessee legislators. In addition to various constituent services, 60 percent of responding legislators indicated that they devote at least twenty hours per week to legislative business such as committee work and conferences with staff, party leaders, or colleagues.

Fully one-half indicated that they devote between twenty and forty hours per week to legislative business when the legislature is *not* in session. Almost 15 percent reported an out-of-session legislative work week of forty hours or more.

Given these demands, the concept of a "citizen legislature" going to the state capitol for a few weeks each year is more romantic than real. The work load of the legislator of twenty years ago bears little similarity to that of today's member. Greater involvement in the formation of legislation, better staffing, better salaries, stronger legislative leadership, and modern physical facilities, when combined with substantially expanded state budgets and more complex legislation, must clearly contribute to the increasing institutionalization of the role of legislators.

The complexity of the legislative role is also manifested in an expanding set of information sources for the individual legislator. As one of our interviewees described this changing pattern, prior to the 1960s "the legislature met, got the governor's program, passed it, and went home. Whatever consideration had to be given to competing interests about important issues was decided elsewhere, mostly in the governor's office. It's a much different ball game now." One of the survey questions sought to assess the type of information sources ("cues") that a legislator might use in reaching decisions. As would be expected, constituent views are of primary importance, with 72.6 percent of respondents identifying that cue as "very important." But legislators reported the influence of contacts with opinion leaders in their home districts of almost equal importance. Although some cues are more important than others, legislators identified a variety of often cross-pressuring cues—interest groups, legislative leaders, executive branch preferences, legislative colleagues, party leaders, and bureaucrats. It seems clear that legislators must confront the conflicting messages and pressures that are a natural product of a more institutionalized legislative body in a pluralistic political environment.

CONCLUSION

Over the past twenty-five years the Tennessee legislature has moved from the status of an underfunded body of "citizen legislators" that was largely an extension of the executive branch to an independent and more professionalized branch of government. It now selects its own leadership, has a clearly established and powerful committee system, and is composed of a more stable membership. These developments, as well as the increased work load of legislators, suggest that Tennessee may be following the national trend toward full-time state legislatures. Tennessee also shares in the national trend toward development of legislatures that are more highly professionalized units of government, whose officials are better paid, better supported by professional staff, and probably more career oriented than ever before.

Despite repeated calls for greater professionalization of state legislatures, one observer has identified several unintended and undesirable consequences that may stem from such professionalization. Charles Mahtesian compared the performance of the 1996 Tennessee legislature with the more highly professionalized Minnesota legislature.[25] He concluded that during the 1990s the

Tennessee experience has been characterized by "efficient, productive, and thoroughly civilized legislative sessions" while the Minnesota experience has been marked by sharply divisive partisanship and incivility. Extending his observations to five other professionalized legislatures,[26] Mahtesian notes similar patterns—unstable leadership, an increasing number of more sophisticated and narrowly focused interest groups, an absence of comity among members, and strongly polarized partisanship. These features of a "sick legislature" were found to contrast sharply with the bipartisan cooperation, civility, and stable leadership of the Tennessee legislature. Mahtesian notes "some degree of correspondence between professionalism and partisan acrimony," which seems to flow from the presence of "more talented and better informed members . . . who have difficulty avoiding partisan collisions with each other."

Although Tennessee is the only non-fully professionalized legislature in Mahtesian's study, his conclusions suggest that present trends in Tennessee and elsewhere toward increased legislative professionalization should be evaluated over time. Further legislative professionalization may bring disadvantages, as well as benefits, to the Tennessee General Assembly.

CHAPTER 4

The Governorship

—David Carleton

Political power and state leadership in Tennessee rest in the office of the governor. Elected, in the words of the Tennessee Constitution, to exercise the "supreme executive power" of the state, modern Tennessee governors do that and a great deal more. The powers of the governorship extend beyond the formal, constitutional powers of the executive: governors exercise legislative, political, and symbolic leadership as well. Tennesseans expect their governor, more than any other individual or office, to wield power and to lead the state.

The office John Sevier inaugurated on March 30, 1796, as the first governor of Tennessee, exercised fewer functions and powers than the office Don Sundquist assumed on January 21, 1995. The breadth and scope, substance and expectations of the office have changed dramatically. The path taken to the modern governorship, from its early subordination to the legislature to its imperious domination of over those chambers to its current position at the very center of a complex and balanced political process, has tracked broader national trends. In fits and starts, in response to scandals and crises, political machines, and the complexities of modern society and government, the office of the governor has been strengthened all across the United States.

While fully enmeshed in these national trends, the Tennessee governorship has also offered unique features and personalities. First came Sevier, the frontiersman and Indian fighter, elected governor six times, charged with forging state government. Later came the election, personal despondency, and resignation of Sam Houston, prior to still greater glory in Texas. The dual government and military occupation during the Civil War was a uniquely difficult period. Rising from those ashes, former elected and military governor Andrew Johnson later rose to the presidency of the United States. One of the most unusual of all gubernatorial campaigns, the 1896 "War of the Roses," saw Democratic and Republican Parties in Tennessee nominate the brothers Robert and Alf Taylor. In more recent years, Tennesseans have witnessed the disgrace of Ray Blanton, on the one hand, and the national leadership of governors Clement, McWherter, and Alexander, on the other.

The Tennessee governorship, in short, has seen growth and change, success and failure. While the forty-eight individuals who have occupied the office (see table 4.1) have varied with respect to skill, ability, and agenda, the office itself has slowly matured and become firmly established as the central political institution in the state. In this chapter we will examine both the institution and the individuals, discussing in turn the establishment of the modern governorship, the formal powers of the office, the diverse leadership roles now expected of all governors, and the qualifications and characteristics of those who have served.

THE ROAD TO THE MODERN GOVERNORSHIP

The job of governor of Tennessee has become bigger, more complex, more important, more powerful, and more central, both to Tennessee politics and government and to the lives of individual Tennesseans. The governorship in other states has also undergone such transformation, from "figurehead to leader."[1] The history of each state's governorship is unique because of the particular path taken in achieving this transformation. Each state has experienced a unique pace and set of personalities, issues, and concerns that have propelled the governorship to its modern form.

Early in American history, states intentionally sought to create weak governors. In crafting state constitutions, a main motivation was to avoid the control and abuses evidenced by colonial governors and their legislatures under British rule. To forestall the opportunities for such abuses, the first states made the governorship relatively feeble. The legislative branch was designed to be the dominant political institution in the states, providing leadership for and a check on the executive branch.[2] The original Tennessee Constitution of 1796, very strongly influenced by the form and substance of the North Carolina and Pennsylvania constitutions, fully reflected this preference for strong legislatures and weak executives.

The period from 1796 to 1870 was thus one of legislative dominance: the legislature appointed judges and other local government officials; the governor could not veto any legislative acts; legislation could become law without the governor's signature; and governors served for only a two year term.[3] Still, Tennessee governors were drawn from the leading men of the day, and several—most notably, Sevier and Carroll—left real, lasting, and positive marks on the development of the state.

The governorship saw considerable change and contention as a result of the Civil War. Isham Harris (elected 1857) led the state prior to and then into the Confederacy, only to be driven out of Tennessee by Union troops in 1862. Robert Looney Caruthers was elected governor in 1863 but was never inaugurated due to the reality of military government. Former Gov. Andrew Johnson (1853–1857) was appointed military governor of the state (1862–1865), prior to his election as Lincoln's vice-president in 1865.[4] Following this period of uncertainty, the constitutional convention of 1870 stripped the governorship of its power to suspend the writ of habeas corpus, but it also provided for the governor's first veto powers. The governorship, however, was not substantially strengthened until 1923.

Prominent in the 1920s was a movement all across the United States to centralize state functions and to strengthen the office of the governor. Motivated by

Table 4.1

GOVERNORS OF TENNESSEE

Name	Politics	Term of Office
John Sevier	Jeffersonian Republican	3/30/1796 – 9/23/1801*
Archibald Roane	Jeffersonian Republican	9/23/1801 – 9/23/1803
John Sevier	Jeffersonian Republican	9/23/1803 – 9/20/1809
Willie Blount	Jeffersonian Republican	9/20/1809 – 9/27/1815
Joseph McMinn	Jeffersonian Republican	9/27/1815 – 10/1/1821
William Carroll	Jeffersonian Republican	10/1/1821 – 10/1/1826
Sam Houston	Jeffersonian Republican	10/1/1827 – 4/16/1829
William Hall	Jeffersonian Republican	4/16/1829 – 10/1/1829
William Carroll	Jacksonian Democrat	10/1/1829 – 10/12/1835
Newton Cannon	Whig	10/12/1835 – 10/14/1839
James K. Polk	Democrat	10/14/1839 – 10/15/1841
James C. Jones	Whig	10/15/1841 – 10/14/1845
Aaron V. Brown	Democrat	10/14/1845 – 10/17/1847
Neill S. Brown	Whig	10/17/1847 – 10/16/1849
William Trousdale	Democrat	10/16/1849 – 10/16/1851
William B. Campbell	Whig	10/16/1851 – 10/17/1853
Andrew Johnson	Democrat	10/17/1853 – 11/3/1857
Isham G. Harris	Democrat	11/3/1857**
Andrew Johnson	Military Government	3/12/1862 – 3/4/1865
E.H. East	Union Democrat	3/4/1865 – 4/5/1865
William G. Brownlow	Republican	4/5/1865 – 2/25/1869
DeWitt Senter	Republican	2/25/1869 – 10/10/1871
John C. Brown	Democrat	10/10/1871 – 1/18/1875
James D. Porter, Jr.	Democrat	1/18/1875 – 2/16/1879
Albert S. Marks	Democrat	2/16/1879 – 1/17/1881
Alvin Hawkins	Republican	1/17/1881 – 1/15/1883
William B. Bate	Democrat	1/15/1883 – 1/17/1887
Robert L. Taylor	Democrat	1/17/1887 – 1/19/1891
James B. Buchanan	Democrat	1/19/1891 – 1/16/1893
Peter Turney	Democrat	1/16/1893 – 1/21/1897
Robert L. Taylor	Democrat	1/21/1897 – 1/16/1899
Benton McMillin	Democrat	1/16/1899 – 1/19/1903
James B. Frazier	Democrat	1/19/1903 – 3/21/1905
John I. Cox	Democrat	3/21/1905 – 1/17/1907
Malcolm R. Patterson	Democrat	1/17/1907 – 1/26/1911
Ben W. Hooper	Republican	1/26/1911 – 1/17/1915
Tom C. Rye	Democrat	1/17/1915 – 1/15/1919
A.H. Roberts	Democrat	1/15/1919 – 1/15/1921
Alfred A. Taylor	Republican	1/15/1921 – 1/16/1923
Austin Peay	Democrat	1/16/1923 – 10/2/1927
Henry H. Horton	Democrat	10/3/1927 – 1/17/1933
Hill McAlister	Democrat	1/17/1933 – 1/15/1937
Gordon Browning	Democrat	1/15/1937 – 1/16/1939
Prentice Cooper	Democrat	1/16/1939 – 1/16/1945
Jim McCord	Democrat	1/16/1945 – 1/17/1949
Gordon Browning	Democrat	1/17/1949 – 1/15/1953
Frank G. Clement	Democrat	1/15/1953 – 1/19/1959
Buford Ellington	Democrat	1/19/1959 – 1/15/1963
Frank G. Clement	Democrat	1/15/1963 – 1/16/1967
Buford Ellington	Democrat	1/16/1967 – 1/16/1971
Winfield Dunn	Republican	1/16/1971 – 1/18/1975
Ray Blanton	Democrat	1/18/1975 – 1/17/1979
Lamar Alexander	Republican	1/17/1979 – 1/17/1987
Ned McWherter	Democrat	1/17/1987 – 1/21/1995
Don Sundquist	Republican	1/21/1995 – present

* Sevier was inaugurated prior to Tennessee being admitted as the 16th state on June 1, 1796.

** Tennessee seceded as a state on June 24, 1861; Harris served in the Confederacy until 1865.

Sources: Joseph E. Kallenbach and Jassamine S. Kallenbach, American State Governors, *vol. 1 (Dobbs Ferry, N.Y.: Oceana, 1977); Roy R. Glashan,* American Governors and Gubernatorial Elections, 1775–1978 *(Westport, Conn.: Meckler, 1979); Marie Marmo Mullany,* American Governors and Gubernatorial Elections, 1979–1987 *(Westport, Conn.: Meckler, 1988)* Tennessee Blue Book, 1991–1994.

the inefficiency and irrationality of state operations, and, to a degree, by legislative abuses, the movement sought to introduce modern management precepts into state administration. Reformers sought efficiency and effectiveness in rational administrative units and clear lines of authority. Wide-ranging executive departments, answerable in whole or in part directly to the legislature, and a fragmented executive with independent boards, commissions, and agencies were viewed as inherently inefficient. The effort was to streamline functions into a clear hierarchy, with an unambiguous line of authority leading, ultimately, to a single, accountable executive—the governor.

Tennessee was in the forefront of this administrative reform movement, becoming one of the first states to enact wide-ranging reforms. Leadership was provided by Governor Austin Peay (1923–1927), elected in 1923 to the first of three two-year terms. While known popularly as the "Road Building Governor," Peay accomplished a great deal more than six thousand miles of paved roads. His most lasting contribution is found in his establishment of strong gubernatorial leadership. By combining strong personal leadership with meaningful administrative reform, Peay laid the basis for the truly modern Tennessee governorship.

Legislatively, Peay made administrative reorganization of Tennessee state functions his first priority. The Reorganization Act of 1923 consolidated over sixty administrative units—departments, boards, agencies, and commissions— into eight rational, functional departments. The commissioner for each of these eight departments was appointed by and directly answerable to the governor, not the legislature. A centralized executive budget system was created for all departments, rather than the previous "system," wherein each administrative unit oversaw its own budget.[5] Administratively, the new structure was both rational and intelligible, eliminating duplication, ambiguity, and confusion. Politically, the new structure "shifted control of the state government from the hands of the General Assembly to those of the governor."[6]

Personally, Peay was also influential in the example he set for strong, active, forward-looking gubernatorial leadership. With the main controls of state government in his hands, he acted on a broad agenda: road building, much needed at the dawn of the automotive age, from which he acquired his nickname; educational reforms, lengthening the school year, building schools, and literally doubling state expenditures; and conservation, helping to establish, among others, the Great Smoky Mountains National Park.[7] The strength, vigor, and domination Governor Peay brought to the office set a pattern that has influenced most of the governors who have followed.[8]

With the exception of Hill McAlister (1933–1937), all subsequent Tennessee governors have sought—some more successfully than others—to emulate Peay's example of strong, dominating political leadership. McAlister personally believed that the legislature should be the dominant state institution, and, as a result, sought to weaken the office of the governor, supporting a transfer of newly acquired gubernatorial powers back to the legislature.[9] This was only a four year interregnum, however, and the administrations from Gordon Browning's first incumbency (1937–1939) to Frank Clement's second (1963–1967) were marked by clear gubernatorial dominance.[10]

The period from 1937 to the mid 1960s, therefore, saw the state General Assembly largely subservient to the governors. With few notable exceptions, the legislature was entirely supportive of executive programs and priorities. Further, the governors were allowed, in practice, to name the speakers in both houses, as well as the legislative appointments for secretary of state, treasurer, and comptroller.[11] This period also saw the governorship gain a longer, four year term and, for the first time, an item veto for appropriations bills.

The 1960s and early 1970s, by contrast, saw a maturation of the governorship and its place in Tennessee politics. It was a period of reassessment, adjustment, and reassertion of some legislative powers. The General Assembly gradually reclaimed its prerogatives to name its own leadership, as well as the secretary of state, the treasurer, and the comptroller, as provided in the Constitution. It professionalized, taking a more active and critical role in state finance issues and broad policy development.[12] This period saw the final creation of a fully modern state political structure, that is, a strong, central governorship, but with a meaningful legislative check.

The Tennessee governorship has thus made the transition from the office of figurehead to that of leader. As in most states, it began as an institution intentionally subservient to the legislature, only to emerge, along its own path—given the issues confronted and the force of unique personalities—to a position of dominance over the legislature. From its heyday at mid-century, where the governorship stood largely unchallenged, it has evolved and settled into a fully modern conception of a strong, yet accountable, public executive.

THE FORMAL POWERS OF THE MODERN GOVERNORSHIP

The informal powers and duties of the governorship in many ways exceed those formally granted to the office. The Tennessee Constitution, however, does clearly set the foundation upon which the office rests. The Constitution lays out the qualifications for the office, who may serve and who may not. Further, it specifies the formal powers of Tennessee's governors, and, in its more general passages, provides the justification for many of their informal powers and duties as well.

QUALIFICATIONS
State constitutions all limit, in some manner, the pool of citizens from which governors may be chosen. Many states once set extensive qualifying standards, including property ownership or religious affiliation. The number of such restrictive clauses, however, has been significantly reduced over time. Today, Article III, Section 3 of the Tennessee Constitution specifies only that an individual be at least thirty years of age, hold U.S. citizenship, and have been a citizen of Tennessee for at least seven years. The Tennessee Constitution provides only one additional limiting qualification on the governorship. Article III, Section 13 prohibits any sitting

member of the U.S. Congress, or any federal or state officeholder, from simultaneously serving as governor.

These standards of qualification, while limiting in theory, offer little practical impediment to serious candidates for the office. Political reality would demand candidates who are at least thirty years old, are state citizens, and are not encumbered by other political responsibilities. Virtually all politically plausible candidates meet the qualifying thresholds. In Tennessee, as in all states, the informal and unwritten qualifications for the office—with respect to race and gender, marital status, lifestyle and religion, prior political experience, fund-raising ability, and so on—are far more daunting and limiting.[13]

SALARY, TERM, AND RE-ELIGIBILITY

The Tennessee Constitution merely states that the governor "shall, at stated times, receive a compensation for his services" (Article III, Section 7). The basic salary in 1997 is $85,000, with Tennessee governors also enjoying the use of an official residence, domestic employees, expense accounts, and state vehicles.

The constitutional provisions concerning the gubernatorial term and eligibility for reelection have seen several manifestations. The original Constitution of 1796 provided for a two year term, with reelection allowed but with service limited to no more than six of any eight years. Following the national trend toward longer terms of office, the Limited Constitutional Convention of 1953 amended the term from two to four years but, at the same time, precluded any immediate succession. This produced the unique development whereby Frank Clement and Buford Ellington leapfrogged through the governorship: Clement served 1953–1959, Ellington 1959–1963, Clement again 1963–1967, and Ellington again 1967–1971.

Finally, the current provision was established by the Limited Constitutional Convention of 1977, whereby Tennessee governors now serve a four year term, limited to no more than two consecutive terms. While not yet attempted, under the current provision a governor can serve two consecutive terms, sit out one or more terms, and then be selected by voters again.

POWERS AND DUTIES

The Tennessee Constitution includes six sections detailing duties and powers of the governor. Five are quite narrow and specific. Article III, Section 1, however, is broadly drafted and serves as the basis for most gubernatorial actions. It reads, "The supreme executive power of this state shall be vested in a governor." The governor is charged with the execution of all state laws and the administration of all executive departments, agencies, and commissions. This is the central expectation and responsibility of those who assume the governorship, and it is the basis for most of their working authority.

The remaining provisions, by contrast, are far more specific. Article III, Section 5, for instance, establishes the governor as the commander-in-chief of the state militia, army, and navy. Article III, Section 6 grants the governor the power to issue reprieves and pardons for convicted criminals, with the sole exception of impeachments. Article III, Sections 9 and 14 deal with the relationship between the governor and the legislature. Section 9 grants the governor the power to convene the General Assembly for special sessions. Section 14 gives the governor the power to make temporary appointments to offices normally appointed by the General Assembly, if such offices become vacant while the Assembly is in recess.

Article III, Section 18 grants the governor veto powers. The governor may veto whole pieces of legislation or, in the case of spending appropriations, exercise an item veto. That is, the governor may either reduce or eliminate individual appropriations in the legislation, with the remainder of the bill being signed into law. These veto powers are an important political and legislative tool. Yet, they are weaker than those wielded by most governors. A veto by a Tennessee governor is relatively easy to override; Tennessee is one of only six states to require a simple majority vote of elected members of each house.

Finally, with respect to the formal duties and powers of the governor, the Tennessee Constitution does not provide for the statewide election of any other executive or administrative personnel, an important omission. To the extent that other state constitutions provide for the independent statewide election of additional executive positions—such as lieutenant governor, treasurer, and attorney general—they undercut and create competition for the governor's duty and power to execute all laws, to administer the state. Such elected officers have an independent electoral mandate and may or may not share their governor's political views and party affiliation. Tennessee is one of only four states with the governor as the sole statewide elected official. The purity of the Tennessee structure is muddied by the constitutional provision specifying the secretary of state, treasurer, and comptroller as legislative appointees, and the attorney general as a judicial appointee. Prevailing administrative theory would demand that all but the comptroller, who has an explicit responsibility for executive oversight, be administrative appointees of the governor.[14] Beyond this, Tennessee also has a unique structure whereby the speaker of the Senate serves as the lieutenant governor, making the latter a legislative rather than executive position. Overall, however, as the only official with a statewide electoral mandate, the administrative hand of the Tennessee governor is certainly strengthened.

ASSESSING FORMAL POWERS
The formal, legal powers granted to governors have been studied and compared across states and time. Several analysts have scaled and ranked the states according to the strength of the formal powers granted their governors.[15] All have ranked the formal powers of the Tennessee governorship as strong, among the upper half of all states, and as having gained strength over the last half century. A Tennessee governor, as Larry Sabato has pointed out with respect to governors generally,[16] is now firmly "master of his own house"; the formal basis for a strong executive is in place. This says nothing, of course, about how well or to what

extent individual governors make use of these powers, but the potential clearly resides in the office.[17]

THE LEADERSHIP ROLES OF TENNESSEE GOVERNORS

What do Tennesseans expect their governors to do? The answer is neither simple nor static. Former governor Lamar Alexander said that he liked "to think of the governor as Count Basie. . . . When Count Basie was playing the piano, the whole band sounded better. That's true when you have a good governor of a state."[18] The governor is expected not only to wield power and lead the state but to make the state better. Meeting this expectation will vary according to the issues of the day and the personalities of those who serve. It is a complex task, requiring mastery of a variety of leadership roles. Four basic gubernatorial roles can be identified: the governor as public leader, as manager, as chief legislator, and, increasingly, as innovator.

THE GOVERNOR AS PUBLIC LEADER

A governor plays an important public role, serving as the locus of public attention and, hopefully, as a unifying force in the state. Fairly or not, governors are raised to the apex of public attention and are expected to represent the state in deeds, actions, and temperament, both in times of crisis and celebration. It is a role no other official, public or private, can play in a consistent fashion. The governor must take on the traditional American role of "head of state," but, additionally, the governor's role now requires daily interaction with the media.

Communities need symbolic leaders, figures who, by virtue of high-profile office, command respect and unify public focus and concern. The public looks to the governor as a representative and leader of the state as community. This is the case when hundreds of school children write letters not to the leadership of the General Assembly or to a state supreme court justice or to a business leader, but to the governor. It was the case when Govs. Alexander and McWherter traveled overseas, representing Tennessee on trade missions. It was the case when Governor Sundquist toured tornado damaged areas of Nashville and when he assumed leadership of Tennessee's bicentennial celebrations. Independent of program or ideology, the governor is the symbolic leader of Tennessee.

While not in any official job description, Tennessee's governors are always expected to assume this public leadership role. Governors, as a whole, devote a great deal of time to their ceremonial and public roles.[19] The personalities of some governors are well suited for this, while others must struggle to maintain the public persona the office requires. One way or another, governors fulfill this role as an important motivating and unifying factor, because the citizenry expects it and because the governors themselves need to fulfill it to succeed in achieving their goals.

Intimately tied to this role is the interaction of the governor and the media. The political success of governors demands that they be accepting of and adequately skilled in dealing with the media. The extremes can be seen in a comparison of the governorships of Blanton and Alexander, with Blanton in near constant battle with the media and Alexander devoting time and energy to professional media relations. The inability of Governor Blanton successfully, or even adequately, to manage this aspect of his public role clearly hindered his administration.[20] Since Alexander, both Govs. McWherter and Sundquist have recruited and relied on professional media staff to help manage day-to-day press contacts, presentation of message, and general public relations. This is, in the modern era, both an unavoidable and indispensable aspect of the governor's role

THE GOVERNOR AS MANAGER

The governor of Tennessee, as chief executive, assumes a huge managerial or administrative role. He or she sits atop all day-to-day operations of the single largest organization, public or private, in the state. The organizational structure of the State of Tennessee is vast, diverse, and far flung. This makes sound, competent management more difficult, and the governor—who may come to the office with no executive experience, who is suddenly installed at the top of this ongoing enterprise, and who will serve for only a few years—must assume responsibility for all that the public service does and does not accomplish. All governors must be managers, and they increasingly view their management role as their central responsibility.[21]

The organizational or administrative structure of the State of Tennessee is both impressive and challenging. Austin Peay's consolidation and centralization of state operations provided the organizational outline to which the state adheres today. It is a structure intended to provide a clear hierarchy, with unity of command from the governor on down. The structure has nevertheless seen change since the Peay administration. Indeed, as state administrative units have sprung up in response to economic, social, and political demands—"persisting like weeds in a formal garden"[22]—successive governors, including Browning, Ellington, and Dunn, have implemented varying degrees of further administrative reorganization. Overall, Tennessee's administrative structure is unusually clean, parsimonious, and unambiguous.

The administrative organization is certainly larger today than under Peay. The state has added departments and agencies as needs have arisen, and despite repeated reorganizations, the size of the administrative structure has ratcheted upward. In all, as figure 4.1 demonstrates, the administrative structure today encompasses three forms of administrative units: staff, line, and semi-independent departments.

There are four staff departments, which are specialized units providing service, expertise, and oversight for the rest of the administrative structure. Chief among the staff departments is Finance and Administration. The Department of Finance and Administration is the governor's primary administrative arm for both managing the state budget and internal oversight of the state bureaucracy. It plays a powerful role in each administration. Beyond the staff level, there are eighteen line departments, or functional units directly engaged in service delivery to the public. Finally, there are fifteen semi-independent commissions,

Figure 4.1

ADMINISTRATIVE STRUCTURE, STATE OF TENNESSEE

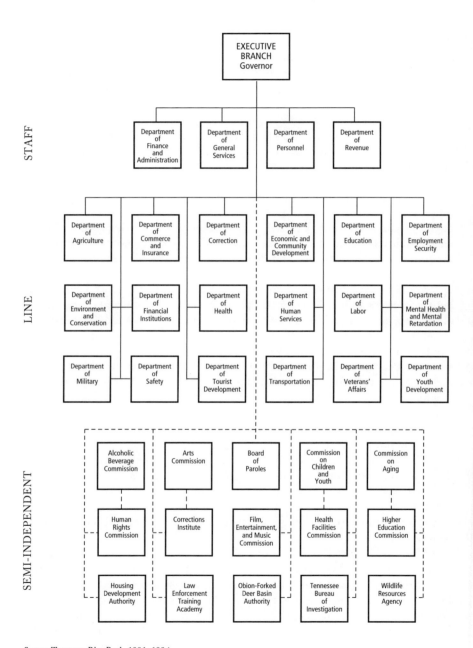

Source: Tennessee Blue Book, 1991–1994.

bureaus, and agencies, with functions ranging from the purely advisory to regulation and direct service delivery. The state employs in excess of 35,000 Tennesseans, operates a budget in excess of 15 billion dollars a year, and is responsible for tremendously diverse functions.

Governors can approach their administrative role as either custodians or managers.[23] The former delegate broadly and act as stewards, only rarely intervening in departmental affairs. The latter take a more hands-on, proactive approach, involving themselves in daily decision making. Either approach can succeed (and fail), with the choice dependent on the unique personality and predilection of individual governors. Whether custodial or managerial in temperament, Tennessee governors have three main mechanisms for managing and steering the ship of state: the governor's office and staff, the governor's appointment power, and the budget process.

The Office of the Governor, the governor's personal staff, is an important gubernatorial tool. Close to the governor, usually personally loyal, these staff members are the heart of any administration. They are a means to develop policy and to coordinate, control, and shape the line departments. The office and staff of the Tennessee governorship has grown significantly, now including legal staff, administrative assistants, legislative liaisons, press and information personnel, and various policy-development and planning personnel.

The power of appointment gives the governor an opportunity to shape and lead each of the several dozen administrative units. Tennessee has developed a thorough civil service system, thereby limiting a governor's reach to the top rungs in each administrative unit. Still, Tennessee has developed the executive service within the civil service structure. The executive service is comprised of top echelon civil service employees, with the governor given broad discretion in their assignment and reassignment. This allows the governor some significant influence within governmental departments without the costs and potential corruption of a patronage-based system.

Finally, the governor can lead and manage the bureaucracy through the budget process. The Tennessee governorship enjoys strong budgetary powers.[24] The governor, by law, must prepare the budget and set the goals, guidelines, and limits for the annual budget. In doing so, the governor guides both a process for broad spending policy as well as oversight to assure bureaucratic control and compliance. The governor has significant budget and finance staff to execute this function professionally,[25] and the power of the purse is taken seriously as a central management tool.

The most visionary of public agendas is meaningless without sound implementation. Thus, again, governors increasingly view their managerial role as the most central. Tennessee governors have a rational structure within which to work, and strong tools to manage that structure—a strengthened staff and appointment and budgetary powers. Good state management, however, is always a challenge, complicated by the size of the organization, the diversity of the functions performed, and the limited experience and tenure of the governors as they assume office.

THE GOVERNOR AS CHIEF LEGISLATOR

Despite a constitutional separation of powers, and a more professional and assertive legislature since the 1960s, Tennessee governors remain the primary initiator of major legislation. On most major public issues, the legislative response is not initiated or generated from within the institution. Rather, the governor proposes an agenda, upon which the legislature then deliberates and acts. The governor sets the agenda and parameters of legislative action. The major actions taken by the Tennessee legislature are almost always tied to gubernatorial action, whether it is the abolition of the Public Service Commission pushed by the Sundquist administration, educational reforms championed by the Alexander and McWherter administrations, statewide kindergarten pursued by the Dunn administration, or mental health reforms urged by the Clement administration. The governor—on major issues—leads the legislature.

Tennessee governors have several tools with which to provide this leadership. Citizens look to the governor as the state's public leader to set the public agenda, and, thus, the governor's priorities carry considerable weight with the legislature. The annual state-of-the-state address provides a uniquely central and powerful forum with which to shape the legislature's agenda for the upcoming year. The governor's command of media attention can be used to bring pressure on the legislature to act. The governor has considerable informational, lobbying, and liaison resources, can call the legislature into special session to deal with any issue, and, in the end, can wield the veto to shape legislative outcomes.

As noted, the Tennessee General Assembly reasserted many of its prerogatives beginning in the late 1960s. During his fourteen years as speaker of the house, Ned McWherter, in particular, believed in and worked to create an independent role for the legislature. Legislative-gubernatorial relations have nevertheless remained both productive and civil. This is due to an environment of "cooperative governance" in Tennessee, the main components of which are a part-time legislature, bipartisanism in fact (with minority members selected to serve as committee chairs, and the Senate speaker elected across party lines), and governors who have led with a soft touch.[26] That is, recent Tennessee governors have provided real leadership to the legislature but have done so largely without heavy handed tactics, such as intense partisan attacks and ultimatums. Gubernatorial leadership has been, as a general rule, far more cooperative, bipartisan, and compromising than is typical in many states.

The Tennessee governorship is aided in this style of legislative leadership by the fact that it stands apart from the other Southern governorships in the strength of its formal or institutional powers. The most recent analysis by Thad Beyle ranks the powers of the Tennessee governor among the nine strongest in the country and certainly the strongest in the South.[27] These strengths aid each Tennessee governor in directing if not controlling major legislative actions. This strong legislative role insures the position of the governor as the central political institution in the state.

THE GOVERNOR AS INNOVATOR

While the aforementioned roles are traditional expectations of governors, the role of the governor as innovator is very recent. Many observers have noted that as the federal government has retreated or retrenched from policy leadership, state governments have moved to the fore.[28] States in all regions of the country have responded with renewed vigor, enterprise, and creativity. State governments are today the most active level of government, true policy entrepreneurs, and governors have led the way.[29]

Recent Tennessee governors have been policy initiators and innovators, with Governors Alexander and McWherter having led the state in creative responses to particularly pressing issues. Alexander and McWherter both exhibited considerable leadership in dealing with issues in education, putting Tennessee among the leaders of all states in designing and implementing meaningful reforms. McWherter, beyond this, led the state to become one of the first to implement a thorough reform of the federal Medicaid system. While a new role for Tennessee governors, the two excelled as innovators. As the federal government sheds or shares additional responsibilities in a variety of policy areas, including welfare and human services, health care, environmental regulation, and others, Governor Sundquist and his immediate successors will almost certainly need to play a prominent role as policy innovator as well.

THOSE WHO HAVE SERVED

Forty-eight individuals have served as governor of Tennessee. The characteristics of those who have served, especially those who have served since Peay ushered in the modern governorship, say a great deal about Tennesseans' demands in their governors and, conversely, the personal attributes an individual must command to be governor.

As discussed earlier, the formal qualifications for governor are not very limiting. The "portrait" outlined in table 2, however, highlights several informal qualifications for the office. These data suggest that the chances for election to the governorship of Tennessee improve if a candidate is male, white, married, Protestant, college educated, a resident of Middle or West Tennessee, and in possession of prior legislative experience. Of these seven characteristics, four of the thirteen modern governors exhibited all seven, another eight exhibited six of the seven, with the remaining governor exhibiting five of the characteristics.

It is important to appreciate that none of these informal qualifications are set in stone. Given the right combination of place and personality, for instance, a woman could certainly be elected governor. The other norms, with respect to race, region, education, experience, and so on, could also be overcome. They do, however, represent a clear pattern. While not immutable, these are characteristics that Tennesseans have been comfortable with and that make it easier to be elected governor.

Table 4.2

PORTRAIT OF THE MODERN TENNESSEE GOVERNOR, 1923–1996

NUMBER OF INDIVIDUAL GOVERNORS: 13

Gender:	Male – 13
	Female – 0
Race/Ethnicity:	White – 13
	African American – 0
	Hispanic - 0
Marital Status:	Married – 11
	Divorced – 1
	Single – 1
College Graduate:	Yes – 11
	No – 2
Residence at Election:	East Tennessee – 0
	Middle Tennessee – 8
	West Tennessee – 5
Prior Elected Office:	State Legislature – 4
	U.S. Congress – 2
	Local Office + State Legislature – 2
	Local Office + U.S. Congress – 1
	State Legislature + U.S. Congress – 1
	None – 3

Sources: *Joseph E. Kallenbach and Jassamine S. Kallenbach,* American State Governors, vol. 1 *(Dobbs Ferry, N.Y.: Oceana, 1977); Roy R. Glashan,* American Governors and Gubernatorial Elections, 1775–1978 *(Westport, Conn.: Meckler, 1979); Robert Sobel and John Raimo (eds.),* Biographical Directory of the Governors of the United States, 1789–1978 *(Westport, Conn.: Meckler, 1978); John Raimo (ed.),* Biographical Directory of the Governors of the United States,1978–1983 *(Westport, Conn.: Meckler, 1989); Marie Marmo Mullany (ed.),* Biographical Directory of the Governors of the United States, 1983–1988 *(Westport, Conn.: Meckler, 1989);* Encyclopedia of Tennessee *(New York: Somerset, 1993); Tennessee Blue Book, 1991–1994.*

CONCLUSION

The Tennessee governorship is today a central and powerful institution. The institution has changed and matured, shaking off its subordination to the legislature, indeed establishing itself as the dominant partner among the two. The time would have come for this transformation, as it has in other states, but for Tennessee the force and personality of Austin Peay was a driving force. His administrations set the foundations for the modern governorship. Both the formal and informal powers of the governorship have been strengthened, so that today the institutional basis is in place for real gubernatorial leadership.

Those who serve, now and in the future, must move and succeed in diverse roles: providing the public leadership citizens both want and need, managing and controlling the public bureaucracy, leading a more assertive legislature, and, in the new era being forged, seeking innovative solutions to pressing concerns. The powers, duties, and expectations of the governorship are all formidable. It is the central political institution in the state, and, as noted at the outset, Tennesseans fully expect their governor to wield power and to lead effectively.

CHAPTER 5

The Changing Court System

—Thomas R. Van Dervort

An understanding of the current Tennessee court system must begin with a review of the substantial reform measures that have been brought about through legislative enactment since 1978. Tennessee's court system has been often criticized as having grown through a process of incremental decisions of local jurisdictions without much planning or rational organization. The resulting "hodgepodge" of courts is confusing to explain and many have criticized its inefficient methods of handling the mounting caseload. The quality of popularly elected judges also has been a major concern of reformers who have sought to modernize the courts of this state.

In 1976, Tennessee voters authorized a call by the state General Assembly for a limited constitutional convention to include proposals for revision of the judicial article. The resulting Proposition 13 ultimately became the first such convention proposal ever to be defeated in Tennessee.

An analysis of the convention's deliberations over the judicial article (Article VI) and the defeat of the convention's Proposition 13 provide an understanding of these complex issues of court reform. Many of the less critical measures proposed by the 1977 Constitutional Convention have since been adopted by state law. These include extension of the modified "Missouri Plan" (voter-approved merit selection of judges) to include the selection of Supreme Court justices, the creation of the Court of the Judiciary to censure judicial abuse of off.ce, a requirement that all judges be licensed to practice law, and creation of a statewide public defender system. The Tennessee Supreme Court has become much more energetic in asserting its authority over the administration of justice throughout the state and has been given extensive authority to assign judges to handle the caseload more efficiently.

THE ISSUES IN THE 1977 CONSTITUTIONAL DEBATE

In May 1977 the delegates to the Tennessee Constitutional Convention came to Middle Tennessee State University to hear various experts on court reform. Attorney Thomas A. DuBose delivered an introductory address explaining the court system and presenting his understanding of the problems the delegates needed to address. These issues were then discussed by: Dr. Frederic S. Le Clercq, director of the most important study of Tennessee courts; Charles D. "Bo" Cole, regional director for the National Center for State Courts; Judge T. Mack Black-burn, first executive secretary of the Tennessee Supreme Court; and Val Sanford, who had served with distinction as Chairman of the Tennessee Law Revision Commission.

These experienced and knowledgeable experts generally agreed that the problems of the Tennessee judicial system were not created by the Constitution but might be successfully corrected by constitutional changes. The major prob-lem was the "hodgepodge" of courts that the legislature had created over time and with overlapping jurisdictions. The extensive practice of "judge shopping" among Tennessee attorneys and the lack of legislative redistricting of the courts had produced gross inequities in judicial workloads.

The experts were concerned about the popular election of judges, a process enshrined in the Constitution, and they thought that extension of the Missouri Plan and the development of adequate provision for tenure, discipline, or removal of judges would provide a reasonable solution. Professor Le Clercq rec-ommended: (1) instituting a constitutionally mandated unified court system, (2) prohibiting the use of "private acts" (a law that applies to only one local area) to change court jurisdiction, (3) state funding of the entire court system, (4) licens-ing of all judges, and (5) selecting judges by a modified Missouri Plan.[1]

The convention delegates were hopelessly confused and divided over how much power the Supreme Court should have to supervise lower courts and cor-rect imbalance in workloads. Instead of following the advice of experts who advocated the general reform pattern suggested in the Model State Constitution, delegates rejected a "unified" court system and compromised for a "uniform" court system that would merely have invested all courts having the same name with the same jurisdiction. A system so unified would have created a trial court for each judicial district and enabled the legislature to add additional trial judges as needed to handle the caseload. The Proposition 13 concept of a "uniform" court system merely attempted to assure that each chancery, circuit, and criminal court within different judicial districts would have, respectively, similar subject matter jurisdictions.

In the confusing redrafting of the judicial article of the state's Constitution, the delegates ultimately deleted the most important provision protecting judicial independence. Since 1834 the Tennessee Constitution had prohibited the legis-lature from changing judges' compensation during the time for which they are elected. Deleting this prohibition would have allowed the legislature to change judicial salaries at will. Proposition 13 also proposed changes in the method of selecting the state attorney general and included provision for a statewide public defender system.

Before the voters rejected Proposition 13 in 1978, the Chief Justice of the Tennessee Supreme Court, Joe Henry, vigorously defended the independence of the judiciary, stating publicly, "It is incredible that in the last three quarters of the twentieth century a constitutional convention would make judges dependent upon the good will of the legislature for their compensation."[2] In the end the judicial article proposal failed because there was no strong lobby in support of it and many discordant voices, primarily those of the Chief Justice and the Tennessee Bar Association, against it.

After convention attempts at court reform failed, the General Assembly, influenced by the Supreme Court and the Tennessee Bar Association, began to modernize the system through existing constitutional authority. Although the Constitution allows for considerable reform, such reform often encounters entrenched opposition by elements that have benefited from the status quo.

CONSTITUTIONAL LIMITATIONS

Article VI of the Tennessee Constitution remains as it was drafted in 1870. It provides few limitations on the legislative authority to create and alter the judicial system. The Supreme Court is the only constitutionally defined court in the present judicial system, and it is therefore the only court that cannot be abolished by the legislature. As Article VI, Section 1 of the Constitution provides, "The judicial power of this State shall be vested in one Supreme Court, and in such Circuit, Chancery and other inferior Courts as the Legislature shall from time to time ordain and establish." Since the circuit and chancery courts are mentioned in the Constitution, their character must be maintained.

The Constitution provides for the election of judges for eight-year terms. However, candidates screened for qualifications and endorsed by the governor may be placed on the ballot for voter approval or rejection, and this method (the Missouri Plan) may be developed by the legislature in such a manner as to constitute election within the meaning of the Constitution.[3] The Constitution also specifies certain minimal age and residency requirements.

The state attorney general is selected by the Supreme Court for eight-year terms, and district attorneys are to be elected to eight-year terms by the qualified voters in each district. There are also minimal qualifications of residence for district attorneys and an unusual provision that allows the court to appoint an attorney pro tempore "where the Attorney for any district fails or refuses to attend and prosecute according to law" (Article VI, Section 5). Section 6 provides that by a two-thirds vote of both houses the legislature can remove judges and attorneys for the state.

Other provisions of Article VI prohibit changes in a judge's pay while serving the term for which elected, require disqualification of judges with conflicts of interest, provide appointment of clerks by the Supreme Court and chancery court for six-year terms, and mandate the election to four-year terms of clerks of inferior courts. The courts have the power to issue writs of certiorari, but the accused may appeal when fines of over $50 are imposed. All other language in Article VI vests the legislature with authority to specify the jurisdiction of the circuit, chancery, and other inferior courts of the state, thus allowing the legislature to abolish or consolidate any of the courts below the Supreme Court that it deems appropriate.[4]

MAJOR LEGISLATIVE CHANGES SINCE 1978

Many legislative enactments have affected the issues raised in the 1977 constitutional debate. Some of these are little noticed because they effect only one district. For example, in District 16, including Rutherford and Cannon counties, the caseload distribution cited by Attorney DuBose in 1976 was severely imbalanced. Over 1,130 civil cases were filed in circuit court, while only 288 cases were filed in chancery court.[5] Shortly after Proposition 13 failed, a "private act" was passed allowing both circuit and chancery courts in the 16th District to have the same jurisdiction over civil, criminal, and equity cases. This act effectively unified the 16th Judicial District, which as of 1996 has three circuit court judges and one chancellor. These four judges may exercise the same jurisdiction at the trial level, and, consequently, the caseload is much more evenly distributed among the trial judges in this district.

The Tennessee Supreme Court's rule-making authority and its supervisory control over inferior courts within the system have also been expanded. This power is restricted by state and federal constitutional limitations and must be approved in part by resolutions of both houses of the General Assembly and published annually in the *Tennessee Code Annotated*. While the grant of general supervisory control over all the inferior courts of the state was given to the Supreme Court in 1970, newer provisions in 1984 and 1993 have provided procedural authority to exercise this control. In addition to other constitutional, statutory, and inherent power, the Supreme Court chooses the administrative director of the courts and directs that officer to take a variety of measures to correct caseload imbalances and to "Take affirmative and appropriate action to correct or alleviate any condition or situation adversely affecting the administration of justice within the state." The Supreme Court may also adopt an annual plan for the orientation and continuing legal education and training of judges. More extensive legislation created the Court of the Judiciary (1979), court redistricting (1984), a statewide public defender system (1989), and expansion of the merit selection, or Missouri Plan, to include the Supreme Court (1994).

The Tennessee Constitution, as interpreted by the state Supreme Court, specifies three ways for the General Assembly to remove a judge. Judges may be removed by the impeachment and removal process defined in Article V or by the removal process provided for in Article VI section 6. Whereas Article V calls for a majority vote of incumbents in the House to impeach and a two-thirds vote to remove in the Senate, Article VI requires a two-thirds vote of both houses. A third option, which does not apply to the Supreme Court, is to abolish the court in question, thus depriving the incumbent judge of the office and salary.[6]

The impeachment process appears more practical than the Article VI removal provision; however, it is more expensive and time consuming. The last judge to be removed by the impeachment process was Criminal Court Judge Raulston Schoolfield, who was removed in 1958 for general misconduct in office, accepting the gift of an automobile, and extensive political activities. This took a special session of the legislature called by Governor Clement at great taxpayer expense.[7] Schoolfield was finally removed after being defeated at the polls. The resulting disbarment of the judge did not disqualify him from future office. He later returned to the bench by popular election as a general sessions judge in Hamilton County. At the time, a degree in law was not required for the position.[8]

In 1974 the legislature established the Judicial Standards Commission to set rules of judicial conduct for judges. This body could investigate and recommend to the General Assembly that judges be "retired or removed," but it had no independent powers. Most delegates at the 1977 Constitutional Convention agreed that a new entity was needed to provide for the swift but fair removal of judges who suffered a "mental or physical disability" or who engaged in misconduct in office. Proposition 13 included provisions for a nine member "Court of Discipline and Removal," appointed by the governor from nominees recommended by the appellate court nominating commission. Although this effort was defeated at the polls, the legislature revived the concept during the year following the defeat of Proposition 13.

THE COURT OF THE JUDICIARY

In 1979, the General Assembly created the Court of the Judiciary in Tennessee to provide a method for inquiring into the physical, mental or moral fitness of judges. Composed of judges, attorneys, and lay members who investigate charges against judges, this court may issue cease and desist orders for minor judicial offenses and may conduct formal hearings for major offenses. After such hearings the court may dismiss the charges, issue a formal reprimand, issue a cease and desist order, suspend the judge from the duties of office with pay for up to thirty days, or recommend removal of the judge from office. The judgment of this court may be appealed to the state Supreme Court.

In cases where the Supreme Court recommends removal from office, the General Assembly has the final authority to decide. The relevant statute provides for review of the evidence by a ten member committee composed of five members of the judiciary committees of both houses, as designated by the respective speakers. This committee must conduct hearings allowing the judge in question to appear and bring evidence in defense. A recommendation for removal by the committee must then be approved by a two-thirds vote of the membership of each house. The legislative intent not to alter the power of impeachment provided in Article V reserves this option as well. The constitutionality of many of the provisions of this act was confirmed in *In re Murphy*.[9]

Changes made by the legislature in 1995 confirm the applicability of this legislation to all judges, including juvenile court and municipal judges. These changes also expanded the number of members of the Court of the Judiciary from fourteen to fifteen and mandated that these members be appointed by the Supreme Court, the Tennessee Bar Association, the governor, and the speakers of the two houses of the General Assembly. The 1995 changes also direct the appointing authorities to select "a body which reflects a diverse mixture with respect to race, including the dominant ethnic minority population, and gender."

The former presiding judge of the Court of the Judiciary, Joe G. Riley, indicates that this court is quite active and serious in its mandate. In 1992, 161 complaints were filed against Tennessee judges. These complaints were almost evenly divided between a group consisting of general sessions, juvenile, and municipal judges, and a second group of circuit judges and chancellors. Most came from disgruntled litigants alleging errors that can more appropriately be addressed on appeal, according to Judge Riley. He indicates that these are routinely dismissed, but meritorious complaints are investigated with the assistance of three judge investigative panels, which may utilize the services of the Tennessee Bureau of Investigation or other agencies. "Of the complaints received in 1992, sanctions were imposed in four cases."[10]

Jerry Scott, chief disciplinary counsel to the Court of the Judiciary, reports that the case load of the Court has been steadily increasing since the 1991–1992 period and reached 200 complaints in the 1994–1995 period. He indicates that they receive about five complaints a week, which are initially investigated by the judges working in panels of three judges each. The panels take cases through two screening stages. During the second stage the accused judge is allowed to appear with counsel and offer rebuttal evidence. Finally, the accused has the opportunity for a full trial before the twelve judges not serving on the initial investigating panel. The trial can be held in the home county of the judge, if demanded. Three disciplinary actions were taken in 1994–1995, all involving cease and desist orders. These actions included two suspensions from office, both involving the same judge, for thirty-day periods.

Three judges, Ira Murphy, Dewey Harper, and David Lanier, have been removed by this process in Tennessee. Dewey Harper resigned after the Supreme Court upheld the recommendation to remove by the Court of the Judiciary. Actions by a two-thirds majority of both houses of the General Assembly removed Ira Murphy and David Lanier. Ira Murphy was a General Sessions Judge from Shelby County. In 1986, the judgment of the Court of the Judiciary recommended Murphy's removal after he was convicted in federal court on felony charges including eleven counts of mail fraud, one count of perjury for lying to a grand jury, and one count of obstructing justice. His appeal to the Tennessee Supreme Court sustained the authority and judgment of the Court of the Judiciary and held that removal proceedings need not be held in abeyance until the judge's appeals in his criminal case in federal court were exhausted.[11]

Dewey Harper was also a general sessions judge, found guilty of soliciting a bribe by asking a party in a legal action before his court to sign over to him a vehicle in exchange for favorable action on a case. The Tennessee Supreme Court upheld the Court of the Judiciary's recommendation that he be removed. Harper then resigned in face of reasonably certain removal by two-thirds of both houses of the General Assembly.

David Lanier, a chancellor in Dyresburg, was the first trial judge to be removed by this process. This action took place after a federal district court found him guilty of felony charges involving extorting sexual favors from employees and parties before his court. He was sentenced to serve twenty-five years for violations under a federal statute enacted after the Civil War. The Court of the Judiciary recommended removal, which was sustained by the Supreme Court and approved by the General Assembly. However, Lanier's conviction was appealed, and the Sixth Circuit Court of Appeals sitting en banc reversed the lower court judgment. The reversal involved the inappropriate application of the statute under which he was convicted, and the case was further appealed to the United States Supreme Court. The Supreme Court subsequently reversed the appeals court, and the twenty-five year sentence was reinstated.

COURT REDISTRICTING

In 1984, the General Assembly attempted "to reorganize the existing trial court system of this state in such a way that its growth occurs in a logical and orderly manner." The act created thirty-one judicial districts for the state, provided for the selection of presiding judges in each district by the judges of that district, and established a formula for determining the need for additional judges, for assistant district attorneys, and for funding increases for public defenders offices.

Presiding judges are selected annually by the judges in that district but are limited to two successive terms. Presiding judges are charged to:

- reduce docket delays and hold congestion to a minimum;
- seek and maintain an equitable distribution of the workload;
- promote the orderly and efficient administration of justice
- and take action to correct or alleviate any caseload imbalance or any condition adversely affecting the administration of justice within the district.

The presiding judge may request assistance from other judges or the Supreme Court.

In 1989, the Judicial Council (an administrative body composed of representatives from all court levels and from all judicial legislative committees) was instructed to submit to the judiciary committees of both houses of the General Assembly a weighted caseload formula for determining the need for additional judges in judicial districts. The Conference of District Attorneys General is also instructed to provide such a formula consistent with the judicial staffing formula. In 1994 the Tennessee General Assembly adopted legislation declaring that new assistant district attorney general positions should be based primarily on population ratios, with secondary consideration given to caseload when uniformly reported caseload statistics become available.

THE PUBLIC DEFENDER SYSTEM

Beginning with the United States Supreme Court decision in *Gideon v. Wainwright* in 1963,[12] which mandated state appointment of counsel for indigent defendants, Tennessee criminal courts had struggled with the appointment of indigent counsel from local bar lists. Subsequently developed U.S. Constitutional standards have established the right to counsel in all criminal cases carrying a potential jail sentence[13] and at all "critical stages" of the process—from custodial interrogation by the police to preliminary hearing, arraignment, trial, and, if necessary, to appeal. State funding for the compensation of private attorneys in indigent cases was often insufficient to fulfill these obligations. For these reasons the Tennessee Bar Association identified establishment of a statewide public defender system as its top legislative priority for 1989.[14]

In 1989 the General Assembly created a statewide public defender system while rewriting the entire criminal code to develop a more rational classification of crimes and punishments. Some districts already had public defender systems, but in 1989 the governor was authorized to appoint a district public defender in each of the thirty-one judicial districts. Election of these officials by the voters in each district for eight-year terms was phased into the system. The act provided for the creation of the offices of district public defender, assistant district defender, and district investigator, including criteria for staffing compensation. It also provided for the determination of indigent status and created a statewide district public defenders' conference headed by the office of executive secretary.

The public defender system, as amended in 1990, 1991, and 1995, now provides that public defenders receive the same pay as district attorneys general.[15] The district public defenders' conference is composed of all district public defenders of the state, with the attorney general of the state included as an ex officio member of the conference to serve as legal advisor. The district public defenders elect an executive secretary for a four-year term to assist in coordinating the efforts of different districts' public defenders and their efforts with other state offices, to prepare budget recommendations and to administer finances of the public defender system.

MERIT SELECTION OF JUDGES: THE TENNESSEE PLAN
Merit selection of judges has long been viewed as the most feasible alternative to direct popular election. The state legislature enacted a modified Missouri Plan selection process in 1971 that applied to all appeals courts, including the state Supreme Court. However, a controversy over its application involving a vacancy on the Supreme Court, due to the death of one of the justices, created a situation during the administration of Governor Dunn that resulted in the repeal of that portion of the act relevant to the Supreme Court.[16].

In a revised judicial article, the experts that addressed the 1977 Tennessee Constitutional Convention recommended the provision of the modified Missouri Plan to prohibit such partisan considerations. Professor Le Clercq argued that partisan elections put judges at odds with the new Code of Judicial Conduct, prohibiting political activity "inappropriate to . . . judicial office."[17] Others opposed popular election but admitted that a constitutional provision extending the modified Missouri Plan concept with an adequate provision for tenure, discipline, or removal of judges would provide a feasible solution to the problems of mixing partisan politics with the judicial function.[18]

The convention delegates were intensely divided over the issue. Many argued in favor of direct popular election and indicated that their constituents also opposed merit selection. The President of the convention, Madisonville attorney J. D. Lee, brought in Arthur M. Bailey of New York, president of the American Trial Lawyers Association, who blasted the modified Missouri Plan as "bar association selection . . . lawyer selection, if you will . . . it becomes the fraternity of the establishmentarian bar."[19] Lewis Laska provides considerable evidence of the debate's intensity, but merit selection for Supreme Court justices finally carried by a 36–46 convention vote. Laska concludes that the vote illustrated how fractured the convention was on the judicial article, with some delegates vowing to work against its ratification.[20] Perhaps the most important concern of those who opposed the Missouri Plan was fear that judges selected in this manner could not be removed.

After the creation and successful operation of the Court of the Judiciary, the General Assembly was finally able to expand the merit selection process in 1994. This was accomplished by the creation of what should be called the Tennessee Plan. It features a unique method of incorporating a judicial evaluation process that will expose the record of appeals court judges to public scrutiny before each election. The Tennessee Municipal League noted that Tennessee will be "the only state with a judicial evaluation program this expansive, and one of only eight states with a program."[21]

The declared legislative purpose and intent of the Tennessee Plan is to

> assist the governor in finding and appointing the best qualified persons available for service on the appellate courts of Tennessee, and to assist the electorate of Tennessee to elect the best qualified persons to the courts; to insulate the judges of the courts from political influence and pressure; to improve the administration of justice; to enhance the prestige of and respect for the courts by eliminating the necessity of political activities by appellate justices and judges; and to make the courts "nonpolitical."[22]

The Judicial Selection Commission is composed of fifteen members. The speakers of both houses appoint seven members each from lists prepared by the Tennessee Bar Association, the Tennessee Trial Lawyers Association, the District Attorneys General Conference, the Tennessee Defense Lawyers Association, and the Tennessee Association of Criminal Defense Lawyers. Each list also includes one nonlawyer selection. The two speakers jointly appoint one nonlawyer member to constitute the total of fifteen members. An intricate procedure of selection from the lists provided to the speakers is designed to provide diversity, and there are numerous stipulations that "persons who approximate the population of the state with respect to race, including the dominant ethnic minority population and gender" must be included. The six-year terms are also staggered to preserve continuity and further isolate the Judicial Selection Commission from politics.[23]

The act not only applies merit selection of judges to the Supreme Court but also to the filling of vacancies that occur among the popularly elected trial court judges of the state. In the past, most such vacancies were filled through gubernatorial appointment. This unrestricted form of political patronage was dramatically altered by the 1994 Tennessee Plan. The Judicial Selection Commission must now review applications and forward three qualified nominees to the governor, who selects one to fill the position until the next general election. The Judicial Selection Commission is required to hold public hearings when a vacancy occurs and is encouraged to seek the most qualified nominees by independent investigation and inquiry. The commission is given sixty days to conduct this investigation and to submit three names to the governor for his consideration. The governor then appoints one of the three to fill the vacancy until the next general election when, in the case of appeals court judges, the judge so appointed will stand for approval or rejection by the voters.

The Judicial Evaluation Commission is composed of twelve members. The Judicial Council appoints six (four state court judges and two nonlawyers); and the two legislative speakers appoint three members each from lists provided by the various attorney associations (including one nonlawyer each). This body also must include diversity with respect to race and gender. This group is to administer a rule adopted by the Supreme Court establishing a judicial evaluation program for appellate court judges to aid the public in evaluating the performance of such judges. A nine-member judicial evaluation guidelines commission also assists the court in this program.

The Supreme Court adopted rule 27 on June 14, 1995, which includes a provision for evaluation of trial court judges for purposes of self-improvement. This part of the evaluation process will not be published and is not required in the legislation. However, the legislative mandate is that the evaluation of all appeals court judges must be published in the major newspapers in each grand division of the state and summarize the results of the examination of each appellate judge. The rule's criteria that are used to evaluate appeals court judges include integrity, knowledge and understanding of the law, ability to communicate, preparation and attentiveness, service to the profession and the public, and effectiveness in working with other judges and court personnel.

THE TENNESSEE COURT STRUCTURE

The National Center for State Courts identifies four types of state court systems based upon the complexity of their organizational structure. These four types are: "consolidated," "complex," "mixed," and "mainly consolidated." The conventional wisdom of state court reform stresses the virtues of consolidation. The two basic dimensions of the "consolidated" category, which the center applied to six states, are uniformity and simplicity of jurisdiction. Uniform jurisdiction means that all trial courts at each level have identical authority to decide cases. Simplicity in jurisdiction means that the allocation of subject-matter jurisdiction does not overlap between levels.

Figure 5.1

TENNESSEE JUDICIAL SYSTEM

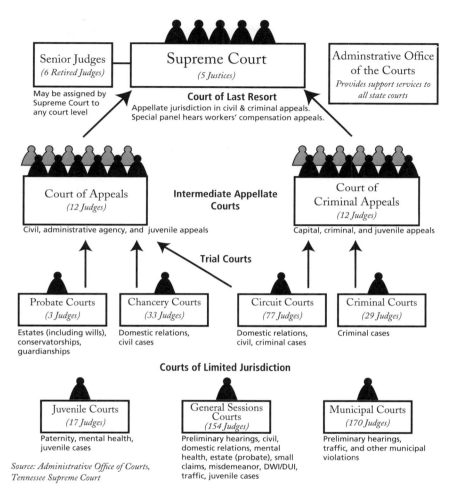

Senior Judges
(6 Retired Judges)

May be assigned by
Supreme Court to
any court level

Supreme Court
(5 Justices)

Court of Last Resort
Appellate jurisdiction in civil & criminal appeals.
Special panel hears workers' compensation appeals.

Adminstrative Office
of the Courts
*Provides support services to
all state courts*

Court of Appeals
(12 Judges)

**Intermediate Appellate
Courts**

Court of
Criminal Appeals
(12 Judges)

Civil, administrative agency, and juvenile appeals

Capital, criminal, and juvenile appeals

Trial Courts

Probate Courts
(3 Judges)

Estates (including wills),
conservatorships,
guardianships

Chancery Courts
(33 Judges)

Domestic relations,
civil cases

Circuit Courts
(77 Judges)

Domestic relations,
civil, criminal cases

Criminal Courts
(29 Judges)

Criminal cases

Courts of Limited Jurisdiction

Juvenile Courts
(17 Judges)

Paternity, mental health,
juvenile cases

General Sessions
Courts
(154 Judges)

Preliminary hearings, civil,
domestic relations, mental
health, estate (probate), small
claims, misdemeanor, DWI/DUI,
traffic, juvenile cases

Municipal Courts
(170 Judges)

Preliminary hearings,
traffic, and other municipal
violations

*Source: Administrative Office of Courts,
Tennessee Supreme Court*

Tennessee was classified as having a "complex court structure" in 1992, along with thirteen other states. Alabama, a state which achieved substantial reform by constitutional revision in the early 1970s, was often viewed as a model by the 1977 Tennessee Constitutional convention. In 1992, the National Center for State Courts placed Alabama in the category of having a "mixed trial court structure" along with fourteen other states. Fifteen states, among them Kentucky, were classified as having a "mainly consolidated court structure."[24]

The diagram provides an overview of the Tennessee Judicial System. This diagram depicts the hierarchy of courts in the state which will be described from the bottom up.[25]

LOCAL COURTS

The local courts at the base of the pyramid of the Tennessee court hierarchy are often called courts of "limited jurisdiction" because they have limited authority and are not trial level courts. These courts are funded by the local city or county, and many of them were established by "private acts" of the state legislature. Popularly elected justices of the peace retained some judicial authority in Tennessee until 1978. These officials were the members of an antiquated body known as the quarterly county court. This body included the "county judge," who also had judicial functions when sitting as the judge of the court of monthly sessions. These officials were replaced by the county commission and the county executive through constitutional revision in 1978. These reforms have done much to reduce the confusion of local judicial authorities that exercise limited jurisdiction.

The general sessions courts, juvenile courts, and municipal courts are now the typical courts of limited jurisdiction in Tennessee; however, there are local variations due, in part, to the extreme differences in the population size of districts and in the subsequent needs among local units of government. Most of the smaller counties do not have juvenile courts, and their functions are performed by the general sessions court. Smaller cities and towns do not have municipal courts, and, again, the general sessions court absorbs these functions. In larger communities, all three of these courts may be present, and caseload expansion has necessitated the authority to add additional judges.

General Sessions Court: Many general sessions courts were created by private legislation and have some variation in jurisdiction; however, the movement to simplify and bring about greater uniformity in these local courts began in 1960, when a general statute established this court as an alternative to the justice of the peace system in all but six counties. By 1982 all ninety-five counties in Tennessee had been brought into this more simplified system through constitutional changes and legislation. By 1994 the number of general sessions judges and municipal court judges with general sessions jurisdiction rose to 154. However, two counties in East Tennessee have different names for their general sessions courts, and the many variations in local jurisdiction and practice require reference to local court rules. General sessions courts have popularly elected judges who serve for eight-year terms.

In 1990 the legislature required that these judges must be attorneys; however, nonattorney incumbent judges were permitted to continue in office until their eight-year terms were completed. In 1980 the Tennessee Supreme Court held that juveniles charged in criminal matters are entitled to a judge licensed to practice law.[26] General sessions judges deal with small claims and misdemeanors and conduct preliminary hearings in felony criminal cases determining probable cause for further prosecution, and many serve as juvenile court judges.

Under the general statute, each general sessions court has jurisdiction extending to $10,000 in all civil cases and $15,000 in counties with a population of over 700,000. The court has unlimited jurisdiction in actions to recover personal property and jurisdiction to award an alternative money judgment not to exceed $25,000. In 1989 the general sessions judges were granted the same power as courts of record to use contempt power to punish violations of protection orders. Appeals from general sessions courts in replevin (recovery of property) cases and forcible entry and detainer cases have to be made within ten days. The general sessions courts are not courts of record in that their judgments may be appealed to the courts of general jurisdiction where the facts of the case must be presented de novo (or repeated for record).

General sessions judges have the power to issue orders of execution of their judgments. They may also issue restraining orders and enforce penalties for the violation of these orders. They have the same jurisdiction as circuit court judges or chancellors to grant fiats, writs, injunctions, and other extraordinary process. Some general sessions courts have the power to issue attachments and impose punishments for contempt of court. However, such contempt punishments are limited to a fine of less than fifty dollars and imprisonment not to exceed ten days.

The general sessions court can hold preliminary hearings on criminal charges. The judge may try the case if the charge is a misdemeanor within the jurisdiction of the sessions court, if the defendant has waived right to indictment, presentment, grand jury investigation, and jury trial, or if a plea of guilty to the misdemeanor charge has been entered. Otherwise, the case is transferred to the court in that county with criminal jurisdiction. General sessions courts do not conduct jury trials in Tennessee.

The general sessions judge has the authority to issue all warrants and to set a bond schedule for the release of bailable prisoners. When trying a criminal case, the judge may impose a fine up to fifty dollars and/or a jail sentence of less than one year, unless the crime involved specifies a longer term to be served in the county jail or workhouse. As in civil cases, disputed judgments may be appealed to a higher trial court with proper jurisdiction.

Local court rules vary the jurisdiction of general sessions courts in individual counties. Some of these courts have jurisdiction over municipal ordinance violations, and some counties have given their general sessions court jurisdiction in probate, juvenile, mental commitment, and domestic relations matters. In most counties, the circuit court clerk acts as clerk of the general sessions court, although some counties employ a full time sessions clerk.

Juvenile Court: Juvenile courts are separate from the general sessions court only in those counties and municipalities, generally the most populous, in which special juvenile courts are provided by law. The proceedings in which this court has exclusive original jurisdiction are those in which a child is alleged to be delinquent, unruly, or dependent and neglected. The juvenile court also has concurrent jurisdiction with the courts of general jurisdiction when a minor is accused of criminal activity. This means that actions may be filed to petition the trial court to treat the individual as an adult or to decide questions of law in dispute.

Much controversy surrounds juvenile courts and procedures today because of the magnitude and seriousness of crimes being committed by minors. U.S. Constitutional case law has extended all the criminal procedural guarantees applicable in adult criminal prosecutions to juveniles, with the major exception of the right to a jury trial. In Tennessee, the state Supreme Court promulgated the Tennessee Rules of Juvenile Procedure in 1984. These rules are designed to provide speedy and inexpensive procedures for the hearing of juvenile cases to assure fairness and equity and to protect the rights and interests of all parties. The rules were designed to promote uniformity in practice and procedure and to provide guidance to judges, referees, attorneys, youth service and probation officers. These proceedings involve the parents as well as the child.

Juvenile judges and referees do not conduct jury trials, but, increasingly, prosecutors are petitioning the general jurisdiction courts to try minors as adults in particularly serious offenses. Some minors are also petitioning the court to be tried as adults in order to secure a jury trial. Tennessee does prohibit the death penalty for persons who were under the age of 18 when the crime was committed.

The Municipal Courts: Municipal courts, called "city recorders" in some areas, have jurisdiction over violation of city ordinances. Generally, a city judge has the authority to assess fines of up to fifty dollars and prison sentences of up to thirty days. In larger cities these courts conduct initial appearance hearings and decide important questions of bail. However, this jurisdiction varies widely from city to city.

STATE TRIAL COURTS OF GENERAL JURISDICTION

The basic trial courts in contested cases are often referred to as courts of general jurisdiction. In Tennessee, the basic court of general jurisdiction is called the circuit court, and it has jurisdiction in all cases where jurisdiction is not conferred on another court in that district. Tennessee is divided into 31 judicial districts, which were redrawn in 1984 when the General Assembly passed the redistricting bill. This legislation had the express purpose of reorganizing the existing trial court system so that the growth of the courts would occur in a logical and orderly manner. Each judicial district contains both circuit and chancery courts. The name *chancery court* was derived from the English court of equity. Such courts deal primarily with equity matters involving specific performance orders and decrees. The circuit courts may handle both civil and criminal matters. The name is derived from the practice of "riding circuit," meaning that they travel from county seat to county seat to hold court. Many judicial districts also have criminal courts. These exist primarily in urban areas where division of labor justifies these special courts. Memphis and Nashville also have probate courts created by private act of the legislature. These courts perform some of the functions that circuit or chancery courts perform in other judicial districts.

The number of trial court judges varies considerably among the judicial districts depending upon the caseload. Each judicial district has a presiding judge, chosen annually by the trial court judges in that district, with the duty to assign cases so as to reduce delays, equitably distribute the workload, and promote the orderly and efficient administration of justice. If so assigned, appointed, or designated, any judge or chancellor may exercise the jurisdiction of any other trial court to facilitate the handling of cases.

The Supreme Court of Tennessee has certain supervisory powers over the circuit, criminal, and chancery courts. These powers include assigning any sitting judge, chancellor, or retired judge to sit as a member of any court; taking affirmative action to correct any caseload imbalance; and alleviating any condition adversely affecting the administration of justice. The Supreme Court may also provide for the orientation and continuing legal education of new trial or appellate judges.

Thus, although the Tennessee judicial system specifies four different types of trial courts of general jurisdiction, current law provides considerable flexibility for balancing the caseload within and between judicial districts. Only two districts have all four named courts, and only thirteen of the thirty-one districts have special criminal courts. A majority (eighteen of thirty-one districts) divide the general trial level jurisdiction between the circuit and chancery courts. Prior to 1984 the chancellor presided as judge with additional administrative functions for that district. This practice has been changed significantly by the newer legislative requirement of electing the presiding judge annually by the trial court judges in the district. The tendency is to add more circuit judges as the case load increases.

As in many other states, all trial court judges of general jurisdiction are popularly elected by the voters of the district to which they are assigned for eight-year terms. All judges at this level must be authorized to practice law in Tennessee, be at least thirty years old, a state resident for five years, and a resident of the district for one year.

Circuit court clerks are popularly elected in each county in Tennessee for four-year terms. These officials are the principal administrative aides to the circuit and most criminal courts. The clerks assist in courtroom administration and records management, organization of the docket, oversight of revenue, maintenance of court minutes, and official communication. The clerk and master (ninety-eight in Tennessee) is the principal administrative aide to the chancery court and is appointed by the chancellor for a six-year term. The clerk of the criminal court is a separate office in the sixth, eleventh, thirteenth, and twentieth judicial districts.

INTERMEDIATE COURTS OF APPEAL

Appellate jurisdiction in Tennessee is exercised by two intermediate courts of appeal, the Court of Appeals and the Criminal Court of Appeals. These courts, together with the state Supreme Court, do not conduct trials, but rather review trial level decisions to correct error and develop the law. They sit in panels of at least three judges. Both intermediate appeals courts and the Supreme Court exercise the functions of error correction and law development; however, the emphasis at the intermediate courts of appeal is on error correction while the Supreme Court puts a greater emphasis on cases bearing on law development. Thus, the Court of Appeals does not have jurisdiction in those cases where the constitutionality of a statute or city ordinance is the determinative question in the litigation, in cases involving the right to hold public office, or in state revenue cases. Such cases go directly to the Supreme Court from the trial court of general jurisdiction.

The Court of Appeals consists of twelve judges evenly drawn from the three grand divisions of the state. They generally sit in panels of three, but may hear certain cases by merging two divisions of the court consisting of eight judges, or en banc, when all twelve judges sit together. Cases are generally heard by three-judge panels in Knoxville, Nashville, and Jackson. Court judgments require a majority vote of those judges participating on the panel.

The jurisdiction of the Court of Appeals was expanded in 1977 to include review of chancery court judgments pertaining to orders of state administrative agencies. The court also has jurisdiction over appeals from juvenile and circuit courts in paternity cases, appeals from circuit and chancery courts involving actions of boards and commissions, and all other noncriminal appeals. Both appeals from final judgments and interlocutory appeals are allowed. Interlocutory appeals (before final judgments are reached) require the permission of the trial court, or an extraordinary appeal may be granted by permission on original application in the appellate court.

Twelve judges now serve on the Criminal Court of Appeals. The General Assembly increased the membership of this court from nine to twelve judges on September 1, 1996. No more than four judges can reside in any one of the state's three grand divisions. The entire membership may participate to review cases of appeal, or members may sit in panels of three or more judges (as is the normal practice). A decision requires the concurrence of a majority of the judges assigned to each panel.

The jurisdiction of the Criminal Court of Appeals extends to the review of final judgments of trial courts in criminal cases, both felony and misdemeanor. Jurisdiction also extends over contempt matters arising from criminal cases, to extradition cases, and to habeas corpus and post-conviction proceedings attacking the validity of a final judgment of conviction or the sentence in a criminal case. Appeal from a final judgment is granted as a matter of right, and interlocutory appeals are by permission from the trial court or by permission of the appellate court in cases of extraordinary appeal.

All judges of the two intermediate courts of appeal in Tennessee are selected by the Tennessee version of the Missouri Plan. When a vacancy occurs in the trial courts or on the courts of appeal, the Judicial Selection Commission receives applications and hears testimony in support of or in objection to the candidates. When the public hearing is concluded, the commission submits three candidates to the governor, who then appoints one of them to fill the vacancy. The appointee serves as judge of the court until the next regular August biennial election. The appointed judge runs unopposed. If the majority of those voting reject the appointed judge, then a vacancy exists and requires a repeat of the process until an acceptable judge is found. All appellate judges must be at least thirty years of age, residents of the state for five years prior to their appointment, and licensed to practice law in Tennessee.

TENNESSEE SUPREME COURT

At the apex of the judicial hierarchy in Tennessee sits the Supreme Court, the court of last resort in all questions of Tennessee law. Only if the ruling of this court involves a controlling question of federal law can the case be appealed to the U.S. Supreme Court. Therefore, for the vast majority of cases, this court has the ultimate authority in deciding questions of law in the state.

The Tennessee Supreme Court is composed of five judges selected, as of 1994, by the same Tennessee Plan used to select intermediate appeals court judges. Members serve for eight-year terms. The state Constitution requires these justices to be at least thirty-five years old, state residents for five years, and authorized to practice law in Tennessee. The Constitution stipulates that no more than two of the Supreme Court justices shall reside in any one of the three grand divisions of the state.

The Supreme Court is vested with constitutional, statutory, and inherent power to supervise the courts and the administration of justice in the state. Until recently, the court rotated the office of chief justice among its members with each serving in the position for approximately nineteen months of the eight-year term. However, a new precedent was established in 1990 whereby the justices now elect their own chief justice for the justice's entire eight-year term. The chief justice exercises a number of constitutional and statutory powers. These include presiding at the trial of any public official who may be impeached under the state Constitution and designating, as needed, special judges, chancellors, and attorneys general to serve circuit, chancery, criminal, or appellate courts. The chief justice may certify the disability of a judge to the governor; the chief justice also chairs the commissions controlling Supreme Court buildings, the Law Library, and the Tennessee Code Commission. The chief justice approves salaries for secretarial assistants of trial judges and chancellors, and in concurrence with the executive secretary sets the compensation for the clerks and stenographers of the Supreme Court justices.

The Tennessee Constitution vests the Supreme Court with appellate jurisdiction; however, the creation of the intermediate courts of appeal has enabled the Supreme Court to use its discretion in deciding whether or not to hear most cases on appeal. Some matters may be appealed directly to the Supreme Court, such as those mentioned earlier and also disciplinary actions involving attorneys, teacher tenure, and death penalty convictions. An appeal by permission may be taken from a final decision of the court of appeals or court of criminal appeals to the Supreme Court on application and in the discretion of the court. Its decisions are made by majority vote among the five justices.

Since the Tennessee Supreme Court sits in Knoxville, Nashville, and Jackson, it appoints one clerk in each of the three grand divisions for a six-year term. The Supreme Court also selects the attorney general of the State of Tennessee, who serves for an eight-year term. No other state selects its attorney general in this manner.

The hierarchy of courts in Tennessee provides adequate protection against arbitrary decisions of trial court judges. Moreover, as Lewis Laska indicates in chapter 2, Tennessee's Constitution provides an extensive set of procedural guarantees, including both federal constitutional guarantees to demand a preliminary hearing before trial and a state constitutional guarantee to an indictment by a grand jury in criminal cases. The Court of the Judiciary, established by legislative act in 1979, provides a means of reprimanding and correcting the abuse of judicial office.

When compared with other states, Tennessee, the seventeenth most populace state, reveals a remarkable contrast between criminal and civil filings. A comparison of criminal filings per one-hundred thousand population reveals a rank of twenty-second among the states.[27] But Tennesseans tend to be far less litigious than most U.S. citizens in civil disputes. Indeed, Tennessee ranks last among the states in civil filings per one-hundred thousand population. In addition, Tennessee has seen a recorded increase in clearance rates concerning disposition of the civil caseload. This indicates that progress is being made in providing timely disposition of cases. The three-year average percentage of disposition of cases increased from 91 percent in 1991 to 94 percent in 1993.[28]

District Attorney

A major feature of the criminal process of litigation is the basic fact that in criminal cases the public prosecutor is the state officer who brings criminal actions against persons accused of crime. The district attorney general has been popularly elected for eight-year terms in Tennessee since 1856. This official is responsible for vigorously prosecuting individuals accused of crimes committed within that district. The same thirty-one judicial districts of Tennessee comprise the prosecutorial districts. The district attorney in each district appoints a staff of assistant district attorneys that is allocated by population and caseload considerations by the legislature. These officials have enormous discretionary authority, particularly not to prosecute (nolle prosequi). They have an ethical responsibility not to prosecute any individual they believe to be innocent of the crime involved. However, the elective nature of the office and the manpower shortage under which most of these offices suffer produce a very high percentage of plea-bargained cases.

According to the 1994 Annual Report of the Tennessee Judiciary, about 96 percent of individuals who are found guilty are convicted through plea bargaining, leaving only 4 percent who are convicted through trials. Still, about 75 percent of all cases involving formal trials did result in convictions. These results are consistent with national trends.[29]

Public Defenders

In 1989, Gov. Ned Ray McWherter initiated the statewide public defender's office by appointing individuals to serve in these positions in each of the thirty-one judicial districts of the state. These positions were then available to qualified individuals who were elected to these posts for eight-year terms in 1992. These popularly elected officials have the duty to provide vigorous defense counsel for indigent defendants in the state and to appoint assistant public defenders as authorized by the General Assembly.

The adversarial system of justice requires adequate and competent counsel to realize its potential for discovery of the truth and effective administration of justice. Lack of adequate staff to handle the mounting caseloads among both prosecutors and defense counsel is generally considered to be one of the most serious problems in our criminal justice systems. However, the complexity of the trial process and extensive procedural guarantees of both the federal and state constitutions make trial procedures risky for prosecutors and defenders alike, contributing to the extensive practice of plea bargaining.

STATE ATTORNEY GENERAL

The Tennessee state attorney general is a unique institution and performs functions considerably different from those of statewide attorneys general in other states. The Tennessee Supreme Court chooses this officer for an eight year term; in most other states the attorney general is popularly elected. Tennessee has had very little scandal or criticism associated with this position, which seems to reflect favorably upon the method. However, the office has no real authority to oversee the local district attorneys and has almost no original prosecutorial functions. The major functions performed by this state agency consist of arguing all cases for the state on appeal before both the state and federal appeals courts. The office also provides advisory opinions to the governor and to the state legislature and performs extensive bill-drafting services for the members of the legislature.

The 1977 Constitutional Convention raised concerns that the Tennessee attorney general lacked independent power to call a grand jury where the local district attorney opposed it. This realization that the state attorney general had no supervisory or parallel power over a local district attorney general contributed to the convention's proposed change to a method of selection by gubernatorial appointment with Senate confirmation, after nomination by an appellate court nominating commission. Under the defeated Proposition 13, the attorney general would have been designated the chief legal officer of the state, and the General Assembly would have been granted authority to designate the duties of the office.[30]

After the successful federal prosecution of major statewide criminal conspiracies in the 1970s, it became evident that Tennessee needed some means of overseeing local district attorneys, or a way of pursuing investigation and grand jury indictments regarding criminal activities that transcend the boundaries of a single judicial district. In 1980, the General Assembly was reluctant to give this new authority to the state attorney general with its independence from the governor and the legislature. Instead, the legislature vested investigative and prosecutorial authority in the Tennessee Bureau of Investigation (TBI), whose director is appointed by the governor from nominees selected by a special nominating commission for a fixed term.

The General Assembly took advantage of that interesting provision of Article VI of the Constitution that allows courts to appoint a district attorney general pro tempore in cases where the district attorney refuses to prosecute. The act provides that the TBI director or designated representative may appear before the grand jury and seek a presentment, and it allows the director to petition for the appointment of a district attorney general pro tempore to prosecute if a presentment is obtained

CONCLUSION

These developments indicate that Tennessee's judicial system has come a long way toward modernizing its institutions to meet the challenges of modern society. However, Tennessee's judicial system is still characterized by a complex court structure with many diverse local variations in jurisdiction. "Judge shopping" is still a prevalent practice by Tennessee lawyers, and too many options exist for filing legal actions in general sessions, chancery, or circuit courts.

The caseload distribution resulting from recent reform measures is greatly improved, and the Tennessee courts are now more efficient. The extension of the merit selection process promises to produce a more highly qualified judiciary in the state, and the mandated evaluation process should provide more adequate information to the electorate for approval or rejection of appeals court judges. Trial court judges will be influenced by this extension of merit selection in that initially they will be appointed by a screening process for merit before a governor may appoint them to fill vacancies. A dynamic structure of the hierarchy of courts provides flexibility through the powers of the Supreme Court to assign judges and institute more uniform rules.

The Court of the Judiciary provides a means of correcting abuses and promotes ethical standards. However, the removal process is still very complicated. These legislative reforms are not the equivalent of the constitutional revision method in that they can be undone by a simple majority of both houses. Nonetheless, these acts have the quality of organic acts that should be more difficult to abolish. These reforms have vested much more administrative oversight over the entire court system in the Tennessee Supreme Court.

The Supreme Court has continued its effort to plan for the future by appointing the Commission on the Future of the Tennessee Judicial System. The charge given to this prestigious thirty-four member group was to develop a vision for a model system of justice that would serve all Tennesseans well into the twenty-first century. This commission was chaired by journalist John Seigenthaler and consisted of an equal number of legal professionals and lay persons from all areas of the state and all major segments of the society. They delivered their report in 1996, after two years of deliberation.[31]

This study considered the broader issues that are beyond the scope of mere court reform. These issues include the problems associated with the proliferation of lawsuits, the fear of crime, controversial jury verdicts, and the high cost of litigation. The commission's report expects these problems to persist on a long-term basis and perceives no quick fixes. Its recommendations include many innovative ideas that may contribute to the development of a more flexible and efficient system. Some of these ideas include more extensive use of alternative dispute settlement techniques, development of an innovative gatekeeper magistrate to facilitate the coordination and management of legal actions, greater consolidation of courts and court districts, and extension of the merit selection plan to include trial court judges.

These futuristic recommendations should be carefully studied and considered. However, the more recent changes that have taken place will first require considerable attention. The first removal of a judge through voter disapproval took place in August of 1996 when Supreme Court Justice Penny White was removed by a popular vote of 55 to 45 percent. Justice White had served only nineteen months of an unexpired term, and she was the first Supreme Court justice to stand for voter approval or disapproval. At the time the process of evaluation to aid voters had not yet been instituted, and the Republicans and conservative activists turned this judicial-retention election into a referendum on the death penalty.[32]

Justice White had been appointed by Democratic Gov. Ned Ray McWherter. The voters' action left the new Republican governor, Don Sundquist, with the opportunity to appoint another justice from three names approved by the Judicial Selection Commission. This early test of judicial reform measures gives indication of a new voter involvement in the process. In this first use of the new system only 19 percent of Tennessee's registered voters, and only about 12 percent of the voting age population, cast ballots in this election. In the next round voters will have the benefit of the evaluation process to aid voters in their choices.

Justice Penny White was the victim of voters' emotional frustration with crime and the lengthy process of appeal in death-penalty cases. She had voted with the unanimous majority of the Supreme Court on technical legal questions concerning the applicability of the death penalty in a controversial case.[33] According to the rules of judicial ethics, Justice White could not explain her actions during this process of voter approval or disapproval, and the voters sent a message that "the people are going to retake the criminal justice system and throw out the soft-on-crime elitists," according to John Davies, president of the Tennessee Conservative Union, the activist organization that launched the campaign to defeat Justice White.[34]

This development raises serious questions about the extent to which voter influence, based upon emotionalism and frustration, should be injected into the judicial system.[35] One of the great issues now confronting the Tennessee judicial system is this challenge to the system as an independent branch of government based upon the rule of law. The balancing effect of the new judicial evaluation process remains to be tested.

CHAPTER 6

Local Government and Politics

—*David W. Kanervo*

L ocal government is an important aspect of politics in Tennessee. Many Tennesseans identify with their county and city of residence as well as with their state, and they participate in local politics because of the importance those governments have for their lives. Citizens are affected every day by the policy decisions that have been made in the chambers, offices, and hallways of local government.

In a nation founded upon the principle of citizen participation in government, local governments provide an important means by which residents can influence the policy decisions that will affect them. Unlike the national and state capitals, which are often distant and frequently out of touch with average citizens, the county courthouses and city halls dispersed throughout the country provide access points to government that are available to virtually everyone. This level of government closest to the people should also be, at least theoretically, the most responsive and accountable to popular wishes.

The four units of local government in Tennessee are counties, municipalities (or cities), school districts, and special districts: 95 counties (only 93 recognized by the Census Bureau), 339 municipalities, 14 special school districts, and 477 special districts for a total of 925 local government units.[1] This total ranks Tennessee thirtieth out of the fifty states in the number of local governments. Each of these types of government provides important services.

COUNTY GOVERNMENTS

Counties are geographic subdivisions of states. Under Tennessee law ninety-five counties have been created (see figure 6.1),[2] though the U.S. Census Bureau recognizes only ninety-three because Davidson county has been merged with Nashville, and Moore County has been consolidated with the City of Lynchburg. The Census Bureau counts these metropolitan governments as municipalities.[3] Most of the counties contain a large amount of rural area; only eight have populations over 100,000 people. The smallest county in population, Pickett, contained only 4,554 people in 1992.[4]

In the South before the Civil War, counties became the important unit of local government because of the rural nature of the states.[5] The chief administrator was a county judge, who also performed some judicial duties. The legislative body was called the quarterly court and quite literally usually met just once each quarter.

By the middle of the twentieth century, the duties of county government required more active public officials. The quarterly court generally began meeting at least once a month, and the county judge became much more of a county executive. These changes in the operation of county government became formalized in state law in 1979 when the Tennessee legislature reestablished the *quarterly court* as the *county legislative body* (frequently called the *county commission*) and the role of the *county judge* was expanded to that of *county executive*.

The creation of the position of county executive in Tennessee was a progressive step not found in a majority of states. Only 24.8 percent of all counties in the U.S. have elected chief executives.[6] Rather, most states have counties that are governed by boards with no formal chief executive. This situation usually leaves those counties with several separately elected administrative officials but with no chief executive to provide leadership and to coordinate the administrative functions of county government.

Counties in Tennessee also possess numerous separately elected officials. The candidates for these positions run on a non-partisan ballot. Sheriffs, county trustees (who serve as treasurers), property tax assessors, registers (of deeds), and county clerks (responsible for official documents) are all officers required under the state constitution. Because these officials are all directly elected by the voters, they each have their own constituency and are not required to cooperate with each other. The county executive is officially the chief executive but has no real authority to impose goals on these other officials. Consequently, conflict is not uncommon among these officeholders. In 1991, the Montgomery County sheriff sued the county executive because the sheriff believed funding for the jail was inadequate. The intrigue that can occur among county officials and the patronage these officeholders can dispense make "court house politics" a lively arena for political activity.

As administrative subdivisions of states, counties perform certain functions that are needed throughout the state, such as conducting elections, registering motor vehicles, and housing prisoners. As population densities have increased in unincorporated areas, counties have also taken on responsibilities frequently associated with municipal governments. They build and maintain roads, provide

Figure 6.1

TENNESSEE'S COUNTIES

for waste disposal, engage in planning and zoning, and financially support hospitals, libraries, emergency services, and elementary and secondary schools. Those counties experiencing the most growth in spending between 1982 and 1987 are located primarily in Middle and West Tennessee.[7]

Revenue to pay for these services comes from local property taxes, the local sales tax, wheel taxes, various fees and user charges, and intergovernmental aid from the state and federal levels. The highest tax rates are found in the most urban counties, while the residents in the rural counties in the state generally have the lowest taxes. The amount of taxes paid per capita tends to be related to the general wealth found in the county. Residents of the poorer counties pay lower taxes. Money to pay for services cannot be raised where it does not exist.

MUNICIPALITIES

Municipalities are corporations created by states to provide general local government and services to the residents who reside within their boundaries. In Tennessee, municipalities are called cities and towns. A minimum population of two hundred people is required before the General Assembly will approve incorporation. A total of 339 municipal governments exist in Tennessee.[8]

Two forms of municipal government are found in Tennessee's cities and towns. The most common is the mayor-council type, which is found in 77 percent of the state's municipalities.[9] Throughout the United States this form of government is found in only 49 percent of all communities.[10] This governmental system depends on a mayor, who serves as chief executive of the government, and a city council elected either from wards or at large, or by a mixture of both. The voters in the community directly elect all of these officials. Mayor-council governments may have either a weak or a strong mayor. The weak mayor has no veto over ordinances passed by the city council, department heads are appointed by city council committees, and the city council may play a major role in formulating the city budget. The strong mayor is much more of a chief executive, enjoying veto power over city ordinances, the power to appoint department heads, and a genuine executive budget, formulated by the mayor and the mayoral staff and then presented to the city council for consideration and modification. This form of the mayor-council system provides the chief executive with more formal authority and, as a result, with more opportunity to provide the leadership expected of a chief executive.

The second type of municipal government in Tennessee, found in 23 percent of communities, is the council-manager form. This is considered a reformed government, because it has been advocated by municipal reformers It is found in 42 percent of the communities in the United States.[11] In this form of government, a city council, usually elected at large from the community rather than from wards, hires a city manager to serve as the chief executive of the city. The city manager is usually a professionally trained administrator with a degree in public administration or a related discipline. The manager is to use his or her expertise to provide the community with efficient day-to-day management of the city's affairs. This system also provides for a mayor, but this is largely a ceremonial position with no real governmental power. The mayor represents the city at public and political functions so that the manager's time can be devoted to administrative activities.

City managers usually have powers similar to those of a strong mayor. They appoint department heads, propose a budget, and suggest public policy, but they have no veto power. City managers are expected to walk a fine line separating the administering and proposing of policies, on one side, and the making of policy, on the other. The distinction is theoretically made between administration and politics, but it is a distinction that does not exist in reality and can put a manager in a tenuous position because of the lack of job security. One important difference from a mayor is that a city manager has no fixed term of office. If a city manager makes a decision that is unpopular with the council or an election brings in a council with a perspective different from the manager's, the manager can be terminated abruptly. Separately elected mayors with fixed terms of office can take controversial positions as they exercise leadership and try to sell their positions to the electorate. City managers do not have that opportunity.

Municipal governments perform a wide variety of services for their residents. They build and maintain streets, provide emergency services, fund local public education, and operate airports, libraries, hospitals, nursing homes; organize, build, and operate gas, water, sewerage, and electric utilities; and construct stadiums, convention centers, and auditoriums.[12] The funds for carrying out these functions come from local property tax, local sales tax, hotel-motel tax, various user charges and fees, and from state and federal aid. In those communities where the property tax is the primary source of revenue for these services, finding a way to maintain a property-tax base while preventing the loss of tax-sensitive industries and recruiting new ones is a major activity and concern.

How such issues are addressed in each municipality is the raw stuff of politics at the local level. Elections in Tennessee's cities are nonpartisan. The candidates offer themselves for public office as individuals, not as members of a political party. Even though party labels are absent from the top of the ballot, local political party organizations may still be active behind the scenes encouraging people to run for office, providing some monetary and personnel support, and trying to mobilize voters behind the candidates they are backing. While political parties may be active beneath the surface, other kinds of local groups encourage people to run, offering their assistance for the upcoming campaign. At the local level it is not unusual for individuals to select themselves as candidates for office and to put together their own personal campaign organization.

PUBLIC SCHOOL SYSTEMS

Two types of school districts exist in the United States, independent and dependent. Independent districts operate as a separate unit of government and possess their own taxing power. Dependent systems do not have the legal authority to raise their own funds and, as a result, are dependent upon a general-purpose unit of government for their revenue. Independent school districts are the most common type; 90.6 percent of all public school systems in the United States fall into this category. Thirteen states have both independent and dependent districts.[13]

Tennessee is one of those thirteen states having both types of school districts. Only 10 percent of the state's 140 districts are considered independent. In Tennessee these independent systems created by the General Assembly are called "special" school districts. Under Tennessee law, residents of a county or city may ask the legislature to create these districts by private act, a law applying to only one jurisdiction. Over the years fourteen special school districts have been created in Carroll (five districts), Gibson (four districts), Henry (one district), Marion (one district), Scott (one district), Williamson (one district), and Wilson (one district) Counties.[14] These special districts receive their funding from property taxes levied on the residents of those districts; however, the tax rate is set for each district by the General Assembly, again through a private act, not by the school district's board.[15]

The remaining 126 public school districts are dependent systems. The overwhelming majority (ninety-three) of these systems are dependent upon the county government for their funding. Local education policy is determined by elected county school boards. The other thirty-three dependent public school systems are municipal systems, receiving their money from the cities in which they exist. In the past their school boards were sometimes appointed by the city council or the mayor, composed of city officials serving in an ex officio capacity, or were elected by the residents of the community. Today all of the school boards are elected.[16] Currently all public school system superintendents are appointed by the school boards, though formerly some of them were elected.

One of the problems dependent school boards face is their lack of authority to raise their own revenue. Those boards are responsible to the citizens in their districts for providing quality education programs and facilities for the children in their jurisdiction, but they may only request the money they need from the county or municipality. Sometimes county commissioners or city council members balk at providing the money because of the subsequent need to raise taxes. Conflict may occur between the school board and the legislative body responsible for providing the funds for education, especially when the school board does not receive the funds it requests and the proposed school system budget must be cut. School board members charge the legislators with not being responsive to the needs of the district's children, and the legislators accuse the school board of wasteful and inefficient spending practices. Having the responsibility for providing public education, but not having the authority to raise the money, can put dependent school system boards in a difficult position.

One measure of how effective school systems are in providing for the education of the children under their jurisdiction is the percentage of adults in the district who are high school graduates. This statistic also indicates the support that the citizens have for education in their community because it shows the desire of students to complete the requirements for a diploma. The higher the percentage of graduates, the more the local community is likely to believe that education is important. The highest percentages of high school graduates are found in those counties containing the five largest cities and in some of their surrounding counties (see figure 6.2).[17] Indeed, the residents of the most urbanized communities in Tennessee have attained higher levels of education than residents of more rural areas because employment in today's technologically sophisticated society requires higher and higher levels of education. School systems in the most urbanized areas are more likely to provide the opportunity for completing the high school degree that the children and their parents want.

Figure 6.2

TENNESSEE'S MAJOR CITIES

SPECIAL DISTRICTS

Typically, these units of local government are created to provide one or a few closely related services over a specified geographic area. In Tennessee some of these special districts are called "authorities." Of the 477 special district governments existing in the state, 440 of them perform only a single function. Supplying water to communities is the most common service provided by special districts in Tennessee, performed by 188 (43 percent) of the single-purpose districts. The second-most-common service (performed by ninety-four districts) is soil and water conservation. Housing authorities are in third place with eighty-nine. Among the other categories of single-purpose special districts are airport authorities, flood control, solid waste management, industrial development, and sewerage districts.[18]

Thirty-seven of Tennessee's special districts were created to perform more than one service. Of those units of government, twenty (54 percent) combine sewerage and water supply service. The others provide various combinations of services.[19]

Each special district is governed by a board that is usually appointed by other public officials, such as the governor, county executives, mayors, or county or city legislative bodies. Some boards also consist of the county executives or mayors whose communities are served by the district. Only a small number of the boards are elected by the voters. Usually the governing boards have the authority to issue bonds, set fees and charges, or levy property taxes to raise the revenue needed for providing their service.

Special districts are an important means for providing services to areas that may not have the financial resources to pay for them on their own. Frequently a geographic area in need of services is some distance from an area also in need but that has the ability to pay for them. Neighborhoods often arise as fairly homogeneous but distinct housing developments. Creating a special district—which encompasses areas needing services but not having the resources to pay for them together with wealthier areas—broadens the financial base so that the cost of the service can be extended to more people in a wider economic range.

One problem with special districts, however, is that they add to governmental fragmentation, especially in metropolitan areas. When a special district is created, it places another layer of government on top of already-existing layers. Citizens in a given community live under the jurisdiction of municipal and county governments and in addition, perhaps, within the authority of these additional units of government with the power to tax them or charge fees. Because units of government tend to pursue their own interests, and because the more government is fragmented the more likely it is that these interests will be uncoordinated, conflict among local governments can occur. This conflict can result in the absence of coordinated efforts to solve local problems and also waste valuable local resources.

A second problem is that special districts are usually not as accountable to constituents as are counties and municipalities, whose officials are, by and large, elected by the people. Because citizens usually do not elect district board members, they cannot gain an awareness of the issues that usually results from a political campaign—for instance, the candidates' voicing of differing points of view concerning the operations of the special districts. Public accountability is reduced because decisions about local services are made by officials who are generally unknown to the citizens and not directly responsible to them. This problem of accountability is exacerbated in metropolitan areas where multiple governments exist and where it is not clear to citizens who is responsible for providing what service. If residents of a community are unhappy with the service they are receiving, they do not know the proper official to contact.

COMMUNITY DIVERSITY AND POLICY MAKING

Tennessee's cities and towns play an important part in the life of the state. From Memphis, with a population of 614,289,[20] to Cottage Grove, and its ninety-four residents,[21] represents a wide variety of community populations and needs. These municipal governments are alike in some ways because they all have charters, governmental structures, and taxing power; provide services to their residents and have conflicts that must be settled through the political process. But they also differ in important ways. One of the significant policy-effecting differences among communities is their contrasting economic bases.[22]

A town's economic base can be defined in terms of its dominant institutions, a college or prison or assembly plant, for instance, or in terms of its employment patterns, determined by how many residents commute to a nearby city, work on farms, provide services to tourists, or work in a local factory. The common stereotype of the small Tennessee town with an agriculturally based economy is giving way to a new reality of diverse economic bases in small towns. High technology, tourism, service occupations, and residential advantages over the problems of larger cities have all contributed to a shift in employment patterns and economic opportunities in many smaller towns, which are attracting a variety of new jobs to their communities.

As it develops, a community's particular economic base influences the characteristics of the town, which, in turn, attract people trying to match their employment skills and lifestyles with the opportunities and services that a community has to offer. One study found that the different socioeconomic characteristics of communities were related to the economic specializations of those communities.[23] The authors of that study concluded that because the socioeconomic characteristics of the communities in the study were different, the problems that existed in those communities would also be different. Economic diversity among communities implies diverse policy-making processes. And the different kinds of problems that occur in towns of differing economic base may also lead to different policies.[24] According to Terry Clark, "distinct employment and population patterns encourage distinct political cultures."[25] Because political culture can influence public policy, this relationship between employment and population patterns and political culture helps to explain why public policy and the policy-making process varies among different types of towns, including those in Tennessee.

There are several categories into which small towns can be placed according to their economic base. Some communities in Tennessee, such as Gatlinburg in East Tennessee, are tourist towns, with much of the employment built on attracting visitors to the community for sightseeing, shopping, and relaxation. An example of a college town would be the East Tennessee town of Tusculum, the home of Tusculum College. Oak Ridge, located just west of Knoxville, because of its nuclear energy research industry, is a community whose economy is based on the existence of a governmental facility. General Motor's Saturn plant has transformed Spring Hill, in Middle Tennessee, into an industrial community. Ripley, in West Tennessee, has an economy tied to agriculture. Finally, the suburbs around Chattanooga, Memphis, and Nashville that supply workers for those major cities can be classified as bedroom communities. Clearly, the smaller towns in Tennessee have a variety of economies. Their economic activity helps to create the environment, or setting, in which their political systems exist. The size of the property tax base, the kind of employment, and the number of jobs provide the financial resources that help to determine the policy alternatives that can be considered by the political leaders in the different communities.

Regardless of the size of the city or town, the importance of economics is a theme that binds the communities together. The desire for a healthy economy and for the jobs that result is important for all municipalities. Communities die when residents must move elsewhere to find employment. Most communities, however, want more than just a satisfactory number of jobs; they want to grow.[26] Increasing job opportunities and growing in population go hand in hand. Both types of growth occur through economic development, which can be defined as the creation, in-migration, and expansion of businesses.

The drive for economic development within a community depends on the encouragement of interest groups and the attitudes of the political leadership. Business groups, such as the Chamber of Commerce, are often strong supporters of growth in communities, to the point that in concert with sympathetic public officials they form what some scholars have called a "growth machine."[27] This pro-growth activity appears to exist in many Tennessee cities of all sizes, as illustrated by the drive for downtown redevelopment and industrial recruitment in the largest cities and in the smaller ones such as Spring Hill and Smyrna.

Business interests are usually among the most important players in local politics. They tend to have the financial resources and the personal contacts that facilitate their input into local political decision making. Not all businesses have exactly the same interests, so it is not accurate to view businesses as a unitary force making the same demands on local governments. The location and the nature of businesses creates different needs for different business owners. Most businesses, however, do tend to favor growth because it means more customers and more profit.

How local governments respond to the desire for growth and to the other community problems depends largely on the political leadership. It is the local leaders, after all, who help to set the agenda the municipal government seeks to address. The personality, energy, and beliefs of the mayors, city managers, and council persons influence the actions that are taken in a community toward the goals that it sets and the problems that it faces. Much depends on how chief executives view their role in the system of local government and on their view of government's role in solving society's ills and in promoting positive change. For example, the vision that Mayor Bredesen has for Nashville as a growing city with a major league sports team, a convention center, and a revitalized downtown has probably been an important factor in helping the city accomplish those goals. In Knoxville, Mayor Ashe appears to have been a major force behind some of the positive changes that have occurred there, such as the river-front redeveopment and city beautification. In cities of any size, leadership can make a difference in the environment of the community.

MAJOR CITIES

All of the diverse collection of cities and towns contribute to the richness of life in Tennessee. But the five largest cities, Memphis, Nashville–Davidson County, Chattanooga, Knoxville, and Clarksville contain 30 percent of the state's population[28] and collectively have an impact that is felt throughout the entire state. Because of the significance these cities have for the political life of the state, it is important to focus briefly on each of them to examine their more noteworthy characteristics.

MEMPHIS

The "Bluff City," named after Memphis, Egypt, is Tennessee's largest city. As Professor Pohlman indicates in chapter 9, a majority of the residents, 55 percent, are African American[29] and a fairly high level of segregation exists in the city's housing patterns.[30] During the decade of the 1980s, the city experienced a 5.6 percent loss in population as middle-class residents moved to the suburbs.[31] This population migration is similar to migrations observed in other metropolitan areas: middle-class whites move to the suburbs away from the increasing minority population in the central city. As minorities obtain the ability to move to the suburbs in sizable numbers, whites move to newer suburbs even farther removed from the central city. This pattern of "concentric ring suburbanization" is characteristic of the Memphis metropolitan area.[32]

Memphis has a poverty rate of 23 percent, which is the fifteenth highest among seventy-seven cities with a population over 200,000.[33] The city's location at the intersection of the Midwest, Southeast, and Southwest has made it a good location for distribution centers and companies, such as FedEx and UPS. These companies provide jobs, but for many of the workers these jobs are menial and low paying.[34]

Because of the majority African American population, race is an important factor in Memphis politics. Until 1991, the city where Dr. Martin Luther King, Jr., was assassinated in 1968 was one of only a few large American cities with a black majority population but without a black mayor and majority black city council.[35] In 1991, Memphis's first black superintendent of schools, Dr. Willie W. Herenton, was elected mayor by a margin of 172 votes. Black majorities were also elected to the city council and the school board for the first time. Mayor Herenton won re-election in 1995 by a large margin.

The ability of African Americans finally to gain political power in Memphis was the result of three factors.[36] First, there was a change in the city's demography. White out-migration to the suburbs resulted in Memphis having a black majority for the first time in 1990. Second, the African American community became mobilized and promoted voter education and registration activities. Before the 1991 election, 5,700 black citizens were added to the roll of registered voters. Third, legal intervention in 1991 by the U.S. Justice Department brought about a change in the way elections were conducted in the city. A suit was brought against the city under the 1965 Voting Rights Act because of its requirement that candidates win election by a majority of votes rather than just a plurality and because of its at-large seats on the city council and school board. The necessity of winning a majority of votes was thrown out by a federal court. That was an important decision because of the difficulty Dr. Herenton would have faced in a run-off election, because of prevailing turnout rates indicating that more whites than blacks would participate in the election. While waiting for a final court decision on the legality of the at-large seats, the U.S. Justice Department accepted the city's proposal to keep the mixture of district and at-large seats. Because the city had a majority African American population, at-large seats were not seen as necessarily disadvantageous to black voters, as the 1991 election results showed.

In addition to race, important concerns in Memphis politics are economic development and crime. City leaders have sought to rejuvenate the community with projects such as the Pyramid, a thirty-two-story structure that houses a sports arena and an observation deck; Mud Island, an entertainment and amusement complex built on an island in the Mississippi River; and the National Civil Rights Museum, constructed on the sight of the Lorraine Motel, where Dr. King was killed. Mayor Herenton began his administration emphasizing downtown development and trying to work with white business leaders.[37]

Like the other larger cities in this state and the nation, Memphis has a high crime rate. The surrounding county of Shelby along with the counties containing Nashville, Knoxville, Chattanooga, and Clarksville all have among the highest crime rates in the state.[38] Memphis's crime rate may help to explain the population loss the city has experienced.

Memphis is a city with a multitude of problems. Drugs, poverty, crime, low educational achievement, and a deteriorating infrastructure[39] plague the city and present its leaders with difficult challenges. Economic development, if it is successful, can help to provide the community with jobs and perhaps the revenue that will enable it to make some inroads into the intractable problems that it faces.

NASHVILLE

Nashville and Davidson County became the first consolidated government in Tennessee in 1963 after the plan was approved in a referendum the previous year. The boundaries of the city were extended to the county borders so that the conflicts that occasionally arose between the two units of government and the duplication of public offices, such as mayor and county executive, would cease. Because the rural portions of Nashville–Davidson County did not need the same level of services as the more densely populated areas, two service districts were created. The general service district covers the rural area in the county while the urban service district includes just the more developed parts of the county. Different tax rates exist for each service district so that the residents in the rural areas are not supporting services they do not receive.

One of the political compromises that occurred when the Metropolitan Charter was drafted was the decision to allow six incorporated communities in Davidson County to continue in existence as governments independent of Nashville–Davidson County. Those communities, Belle Meade, Berry Hill, Goodlettsville, Oak Hill, Forest Hill, and Lakewood, still possess their own local officials, support their own police departments, and engage in their own local planning and zoning. The effect of permitting these small communities to exert their independence is that pockets of divergence from Nashville–Davidson County policies exist and frustrate the desires of those people who dreamed that consolidated government would result in consistent area-wide policies.

Nashville's diversified economy has been healthy in recent years and has served as an attraction to new residents. Between 1980 and 1994, the city experienced a 9 percent population growth rate to a size of 505,000.[40] The Nashville metropolitan region has grown to the extent that it now surpasses the Memphis metropolitan area in population.[41] Its poverty rate of 13 percent[42] ranks the city fifty-seventh among seventy-seven cities with a population of 200,000 or more people. Because Nashville is the state's capital and the home to several universities, hospitals, and corporate headquarters, the city has a somewhat larger white-collar work force than is found in other large and medium-sized cities. Nashville ranks forty-first among cities with populations over 200,000 in the percent of people employed in manufacturing, while at the same time it ranked thirty-third in growth of the labor force during the decade of the 1980s.[43] Much of that job growth occurred in the professional areas of the labor market.

While Nashville is known as "Music City" because of the importance of the music industry to its economy, other important industries are found there also. The health care industry is a major part of the economy of Nashville. Companies based there own or manage half the for-profit hospital beds in the United States. Approximately 50,000 people in Nashville, 10 percent of the local work force, work in health care. During 1992–93, more than sixty companies in the health care business moved to Nashville from other states. In fact, before becoming Nashville's mayor, Phil Bredesen was an executive in the health care business.[44] Other businesses based there are the Bridgestone/Firestone tire company, which moved from Akron, Ohio, Corrections Corporation of America, which brings private-sector management into state and local corrections facilities, and a variety of insurance companies, including American General Life & Accident.

Nashville has been trying for a long time to attract major league sports franchises, NHL hockey, NBA basketball, and NFL football. It appears that Nashville, like many other cities, sees major league teams as adding to the image of the city and making it even more attractive for additional investment by companies not yet located there.[45] In addition, many argue, a sports franchise can help to overcome differences and unify a city. Because many professional sports are well integrated, professional teams can bring people of different races together in support of the home team, thereby reducing racial conflict that can harm the quality of life in cities.[46] After much effort, Nashville now has the Tennessee Oilers football team, which is scheduled to begin playing in Nashville in a new downtown stadium in 1999.

The desire to revitalize the downtown business district has led to the construction of a number of new buildings. Among the major construction projects has been an arena and convention center. The arena was built so that major concerts will have a suitable facility downtown. It is also the home of the Nashville

Kats, an arena-football franchise, and is being used as a lure for an NBA basketball team, which would share the facility with the Nashville Predators hockey team. Like many cities, Nashville seeks to bring trade shows to the city so that their visitors can contribute to the city's economy. While most convention centers lose money, those located in cities that have appeal for tourists do seem to be successful.[47] Nashville is obviously hoping that its tourist attractions will pay off for its convention center.

Nashville's economy is currently booming. But while much of the political focus in the city is on how to keep the "growth machine" running, there are other issues that cannot be ignored. Like most cities of any size, Nashville has a problem with crime, though the rate is lower than for Memphis.[48] Nashville also faces the political problems of racial tension and of managing the difficulties associated with growth, such as the need to expand and maintain the infrastructure and to find additional landfill space.

KNOXVILLE
This East Tennessee city is the third largest in the state and home for 169,311 residents,[49] 15.8 percent of them African American. Between 1980 and 1992, the city lost 4.4 percent of its population.[50] It is also the location of the main campus of the University of Tennessee and the site for the 1982 World's Fair. Producing the Fair was a major undertaking that was supposed to help stimulate the redevelopment of the downtown area. While some projects have had a lasting effect, such as highway construction to ease congestion, a feeling persists that economic development in the city has not been very successful.[51]

Mayor Victor Ashe sought to improve the city's record of economic growth by hiring Knoxville's first economic development director. Ashe also strongly advocated Volunteer Landing, a $42 million waterfront redevelopment project for the downtown. Along with supporting development, Ashe has also tried to beautify the city. He has allocated funds for park improvement and maintenance and appointed the first Greenways Commission in the city to improve the community's walking, biking, and jogging trails.[52] The efforts to improve the quality of life appear to have had some payoff. In 1995, *Money* magazine ranked Knoxville as the 103rd best place to live in the United States, out of the total of 300 cities that were listed. That ranking is the best for any Tennessee city, surpassing Clarksville (109), Nashville (223), Johnson City (234), Memphis (271), and Chattanooga (284).[53]

Effort has also been devoted to combating crime in the city. From 1988 to 1994 the number of police officers on the street increased 32 percent. Ashe wants to do even more and supported a property tax increase, which was enacted, to fund even more police positions. Even though Knoxville is third in the state in size, it ranks sixteenth in crime.[54]

Interest in consolidating Knoxville and Knox County governments persists, but a referendum that would have accomplished that was defeated twice, most recently in 1996. Since the defeat, the city has annexed land as a way of extending services to more urbanized portions of the county. Providing services is at the heart of what cities do. Economic growth throughout the city, not just down-town, is more likely to occur if the basic infrastructure and services important to businesses are in place. Understanding this, Mayor Ashe sees the enhancement of services in fringe areas of the city as a necessity for attracting industry and pro-viding jobs.[55]

CHATTANOOGA

Between 1980 and 1992, Chattanooga lost 9.8 percent of its population. This was the largest loss for any major city in Tennessee during that period of time. The decline left the community with a 1994 population of 152,259,[56] 33.6 per-cent of it African American.[57] The loss of residents seemed to parallel a loss of quality of life for the city. The number of jobs declined because factories laid off workers, the quality of the schools seemed to be falling, and there was crime and racial tension.[58]

In 1984 an organization initiated by the local Chamber of Commerce called Chattanooga Venture was created to bring citizens together to talk about the future of the city. Over 1,700 residents from throughout the city met at a series of community meetings and agreed on a list of forty goals for the city, to be reached by the year 2000.[59] Among the goals decided on was revitalizing the downtown, improving public transportation, creating new jobs, and developing the city into a regional center of culture and tourism. Issues addressed included health care, crime, education, recreation, and the environment.[60]

A number of improvements came to Chattanooga as a result of citizens and government working together. The downtown has seen the restoration of an old theater and the construction of a performance hall and the Tennessee State Aquarium. Recreation areas with bike and pedestrian paths have been created along the Tennessee River, and a historic bridge slated for demolition has been converted into the world's longest footbridge. Chattanooga Venture initiated 223 community improvement projects that created 1,300 new jobs and brought in $739 million in investments.[61]

While the economic development projects have been a significant asset for Chattanooga, they have not solved all the city's problems. Crime and racial divi-sions still remain issues for the community and its leaders to tackle. But, the community has witnessed the efforts of residents who are willing to devote their energy to rebuilding the city. When Chattanooga Venture lost its funding in 1993, a number of local organizations stepped in to provide the leadership need-ed for new projects.[62]

CLARKSVILLE

The fifth largest city, with a population of 92,116,[63] is commonly referred to locally as "the Queen of the Cumberland," in recognition of the river on whose banks the city is constructed. With an African American population of 18.7 per-cent[64] and representatives of many nationalities,[65] Clarksville is a community that celebrates its ethnic diversity. It has also been experiencing rapid growth. Between 1980 and 1992, Clarksville grew 54.1 percent.[66] According to *Nation's*

Building News, it is the second-fastest growing "exurb" in the nation.[67] Labeling Clarksville an exurb means that it is located outside of a major central city's metropolitan area (so it is not a suburb), but that it is at least somewhat tied to a major city's (Nashville's) economy. *Money* magazine rated Clarksville as the fifty-seventh "best place to live," higher than any other Tennessee community, in its 1996 ranking.[68]

The rapid growth has placed a strain on the city's infrastructure and facilities. Streets are crowded with traffic, utilities and city services have required expansion, county schools are overcrowded, and demands on the library required the purchase of a larger building. The growth has been strongly supported by businesses in the community. An Economic Development Council was created in an effort to make industrial recruitment more efficient and effective so that the growth can continue.

Downtown revitalization is seen as a way of encouraging the city's continued growth. The city has joined with Main Street U.S.A., a national organization that helps communities to upgrade their downtown areas and to develop plans for attracting more people to the old business district. In addition to the Main Street efforts, other community leaders are working to develop public areas along the Cumberland River and studying the idea of building a convention center to attract outside groups to the city.

Because Clarksville is the only incorporated city within Montgomery County, there has been interest in the two governments consolidating into one. This idea came to a vote in a public referendum in 1980 but was defeated. The proposal has resurfaced as community leaders have sought a way to make government more efficient in the face of growing service needs and the public's resistance to tax increases. Occasional conflict between the city and county over money has also contributed to the interest in government reorganization. A second referendum on consolidation occurred in 1996. While the issue received majority support in the city, county voters defeated the proposal.

While the city is booming economically, Clarksville is not free of problems. Crime is an issue that citizens want their leaders to address more successfully. Another issue concerns the racial tensions that exist in the community. Despite the efforts to celebrate the city's racial and ethnic diversity, troubling incidents have led to ill feelings. A Human Relations Commission has been appointed by the mayor to recommend ways to prevent racial problems in the future. Finally, the city's rapid growth has caused some citizens to ask for more planning on the part of public officials and community leaders so that development decisions will enhance the quality of life, not detract from it.

CONCLUSION

Local government in Tennessee is an important political arena. In counties, municipalities, school districts, and special districts throughout the state, decisions are made daily about how much money will be allocated to provide a variety of services. In many counties, education is the policy area receiving the bulk of the tax money. Highway construction and law enforcement also require a sizable portion of available funds, as county officials seek to provide their constituents with the services that are demanded and that budgets can afford.

Municipalities provide those services to which most citizens are accustomed. Police and fire protection, street maintenance and lighting, sewage disposal, and recreation are among the most important products of city action. A central concern of municipalities as they ponder which services to fund is what effect their decisions will have on economic development. Promoting jobs, population growth, and tax receipts are important and interlocked priorities for city leaders.

School districts and special districts seek to provide the best service possible with the money they have available. All of these units of government operate side by side or in layers, sometimes working in concert to provide their services and sometimes coming into conflict, as the leaders of each governmental unit pursue the goals that are important to them and to their constituents.

Part III
POLITICS

CHAPTER 7

Turnout and Partisanship in Tennessee Elections
—Lilliard E. Richardson, Jr., and Grant W. Neeley

INTRODUCTION

E
lections play a vital role in American politics. Although citizens can participate in government in several ways, voting is the easiest and perhaps the most important means of influencing government. At all levels of government, elections shape the representation of citizens' views.

Generally, the state is the single most important unit of voting within the federal system. All elections in the United States are either held or sanctioned by states. For example, presidents are elected state-by-state within the electoral college rather than by national popular vote; congressional representation is solely determined by geographic lines that are formed by or within the states; and municipal elections are held according to mandates set forth in state constitutions. Ultimately, the authority for most any election held in the United States is derived from a state or from a combination of states.

One of the most important features of American elections is the tremendous diversity in the political culture of the states. The unique aspects of the South derive in part from its distinct political, economic, and cultural history. For most of the last 125 years, Southerners have been more traditional in their values, more cautious about national political power, and more reliant on family and local community than the rest of the nation. From the end of Reconstruction in 1877 until the civil rights reforms of the 1960s, the South maintained a closed political system. The Democratic Party dominated elections in almost all of the region. In addition, minorities, women, and the poor were effectively excluded from participating in politics for much of this period.

Although Tennessee shares many of the characteristics of Southern political culture, the state has a unique political history that shapes the politics of today. Many observers see Tennessee as being composed of three distinct political regions or grand divisions: East, Middle, and West. As discussed in chapter 1, these regional differences can be attributed to historical, economic, and demographic factors.

East Tennessee is home to what V. O. Key called the "mountain Republicans."[1] During the state's early period, eastern counties relied on small-scale farming and mining never relying on the slave-based economy prevalent in the other regions. Consequently, East Tennesseans overwhelmingly voted against seceding from the Union in 1861 and became known as "Lincoln Republicans." Since then, voters in the eastern counties have supported Republicans for all offices much more frequently than the rest of the state.

The central and western divisions both supported secession from the Union in 1861 and remained loyal to the Democratic Party after Reconstruction. Because of the larger population in these two regions, Democrats enjoyed overwhelming success in statewide elections from the end of Reconstruction until the 1970s. Recently, however, the partisan dynamics of the state have become more complex.

To understand the forces shaping current Tennessee politics, we discuss two fundamental concepts of Tennessee's electoral system: voting turnout and partisanship. These two concepts are easily illustrated by two questions. First, how many people participate in elections in the state? Second, whom do Tennesseans elect to represent them? While we use a historical perspective to inform the analysis, we are generally more interested in the forces shaping politics in Tennessee today.

VOTING TURNOUT

Perhaps the most important feature of any electoral system is the degree to which citizens vote. Generally, voting turnout in America has been much lower than in most other Western democracies.[2] This low turnout is problematic for two reasons: first, some scholars are worried that certain segments of society may not have adequate representation; second, others suspect that low turnout is an indicator of a decline in the public's belief in the political system.

FACTORS AFFECTING VOTING TURNOUT IN TENNESSEE

Scholars who have studied the problem suggest many factors explaining low voting turnout in the United States: the political system, sociodemographic characteristics, and cultural norms.[3] While many of these factors pertain to the nation as a whole, some explanations are specific to regions or even particular states. Voting turnout in Tennessee has been influenced by legal barriers, illegal attempts to restrict voting, registration laws, election laws, and the lack of a viable two-party system.

Historically, the restriction of the franchise, or right to vote, to certain segments of a society has been the greatest factor in low voter participation.[4] In the years following statehood, only white males were allowed to vote in Tennessee, as was the case in the rest of the nation. Black males were not given the right to vote until after the Civil War with the passage of the Fifteenth Amendment. After Reconstruction ended in 1877, many Southern states, including Tennessee, sought to deny blacks the right to vote through various legal measures, and white supremacy groups effectively denied whatever opportunities remained for most black Southerners. The poll tax, used to cripple the voting rights of the poor, was not eliminated in Tennessee until 1953 and not outlawed at the national level until 1964.[5] African Americans did not gain full access to the ballot until the 1960s, when Congress passed a series of reforms designed to ensure the voting rights of all citizens regardless of race. Today, the right to vote is denied only a few groups of Americans: felons, citizens under the age of eighteen, and the mentally incapacitated. Despite the fact that the vast majority of adults are eligible to vote, less than half regularly vote in all elections.

Some barriers to participation are due to government policies not designed to impede voter participation but that nonetheless have that effect. Much of the attention given these barriers focuses on the harmful effect of registration laws and the difficulties associated with casting a ballot.[6] In Tennessee a citizen must register with the county government thirty days prior to an election in order to vote. Because many citizens are not aware of the requirement, do not know where to go to register, or may even be afraid that registration will make them eligible for jury duty, about 30 percent of all Americans are not even registered to vote.[7] In Tennessee about 76 percent of the four million eligible citizens were registered to vote in November, 1996. Consequently, about one million Tennesseans cannot vote, even if motivated to do so.

Even registered voters face many obstacles to participation. For example, in most states a voter must be present on election day to cast a ballot or fill out cumbersome paperwork that must be approved by county officials to vote absentee. The hours available to vote are often limited and restricted to daytime hours, further hindering voting participation. Because voters usually must vote in neighborhood voting sites, some find it difficult to cast a ballot if they commute significant distances to their workplace. In addition, national and most state elections are held on Tuesdays, a working day for most people. Overall, the costs of voting can be quite high and tangible for the average citizen, while the benefits are somewhat abstract.

Barriers to participation in the electoral process are compounded in the American system by the multiplicity of elections in which voters can participate. Turnout in presidential elections has been close to 50 percent of the voting age population (VAP) for the last two decades, but it is much lower for congressional, state, and local elections. Like the rest of the country, Tennessee voters participate at a higher rate in presidential races than in other types of elections, such as those for city, county, and state offices. This difference in turnout rates among the different levels of elections is partly related to the voters' belief in the greater importance of the higher offices. In addition, presidential elections enjoy greater media attention, and candidates spend more money on campaign activities designed to motivate voter participation. Further, many contests for offices at lower levels are characterized by minimal or nonexistent competition. Often, members of Congress and state legislators run unopposed or face poorly funded and badly organized challengers who provide little competition or interest among the constituency.

TURNOUT TRENDS

Turnout in twentieth-century American presidential elections peaked in the 1960 election between Democrat John F. Kennedy and Republican Richard M. Nixon, with 62.8 percent of VAP casting a ballot. As figure 7.1 shows, turnout in presidential elections has declined since 1960. This decline was temporarily halted in 1992 when more than 104 million people voted out of the 189 million eligible to vote. The 55.2 percent turnout rate was the highest since 1972, but this reverse of the downward trend was short-lived. In the 1996 presidential election turnout dropped to the lowest point since 1924.

Figure 7.1

TURNOUT IN PRESIDENTIAL ELECTIONS

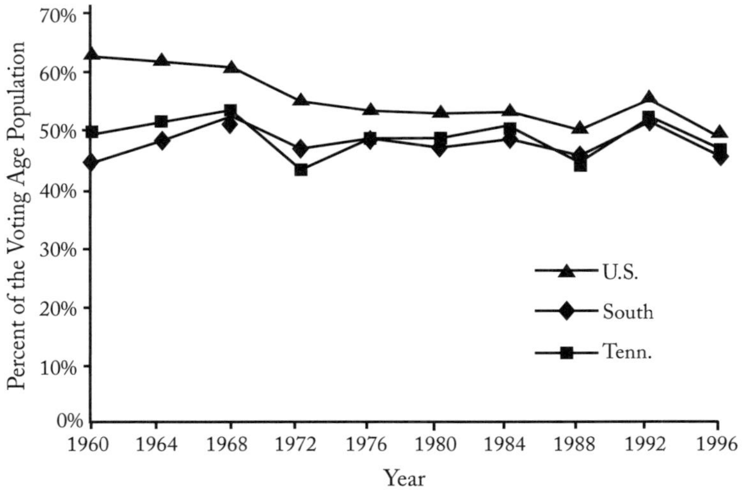

A curious feature of Southern political culture has been voting turnout that is lower than in the rest of the country.[8] As figure 7.1 shows, Southern turnout in presidential elections has been as much as 15 percent lower than the nation as a whole. Three factors help explain this phenomenon. First, barriers to minority participation still existed as late as the 1960s. Second, Democratic dominance of the region greatly reduced the number of competitive races that typically mobilize citizens at a greater rate than one-sided contests. Third, the sociodemographic composition of the South, with generally lower income and education

levels, has contributed to lower turnout. The problem has been even more pronounced in midterm elections for congressional and state offices (when the president is not on the ballot). These elections are likely to be less competitive so
there is less interest in the campaigns, and many voters may not feel that they
have any reason to vote.

In recent years, however, the gap between the national and Southern rates
has narrowed to about 5 percent, on average. This development is at least partly
explained by an increasingly active and successful Republican Party, which has
been able to increase greatly the number of competitive races in the South. For
example, with the exception of the 1976 election of President Carter, the South
has not given a majority of its electoral votes to a Democratic presidential candidate since 1964.

Several other factors have contributed to the narrowing of the turnout gap.
First, almost all Southern states have dramatically reduced the barriers to voting.
In addition, income and education levels have dramatically increased in the
region, and generally wealthier and more educated citizens are more likely to
vote. Also, many areas of the South have experienced an increase in urbanization.
Because of improved transportation systems, greater mass media exposure, and
the expansion of suburban areas, citizens now have greater choices in where and
how they live and more information with which to make choices. Further, the
migration of non-Southerners into the region has changed the South so that it is
more like the rest of the nation in its political culture. Overall, the region is less
dominated by a rural, clannish, traditional society that stifled meaningful participation for many in the past.

Since 1960, turnout in Tennessee has hovered around the 50 percent mark
for most presidential elections, a level closer to the regional turnout rate than to
the rest of the United States. Turnout in Tennessee has been slightly higher than
in the rest of the South in all but two elections: 1972 and 1988. Tennesseeans
appear to have been less than satisfied with the electoral choices they had in each
of those years: Richard Nixon (Rep.) versus George McGovern (Dem.) in 1972
and George Bush (Rep.) versus Michael Dukakis (Dem.) in 1988. This indicates
that many Southern Democrats may have abstained from participating rather
than choosing between a liberal Democrat from the North or Midwest or a
Republican. On the other hand, when given a choice between a moderate Southern Democrat (Bill Clinton), a viable independent (Ross Perot), and a Republican (George Bush), Tennesseeans were more attracted to the polls, as evidenced
by the 1992 turnout rate of 52 percent. In 1996, however, voters in the state did
not participate at such a high level; turnout fell to 47.2 percent. This decline may
have resulted from three factors: weaker support for third-party candidate Ross
Perot; the vigorous health of the economy; and the perceived lack of competitiveness.

As previously discussed, turnout in midterm elections has always been much
lower than in presidential elections. As figure 7.2 shows, national turnout rates
in midterm elections have not even reached 50 percent in any election during the
period studied. Southern turnout has been even worse in that it has rarely

reached even the 30 percent mark. Whereas national turnout in midterm elections has been declining over the last three decades, Southern turnout has been creeping upward. One possible explanation for this increase is the renewed competitiveness of the Republican Party in nonpresidential races in the South. This trend reached new heights in 1994 when the Republicans gained a majority of all congressional seats from Southern states for the first time since Reconstruction.

Figure 7.2

TURNOUT IN MIDTERM CONGRESSIONAL ELECTIONS

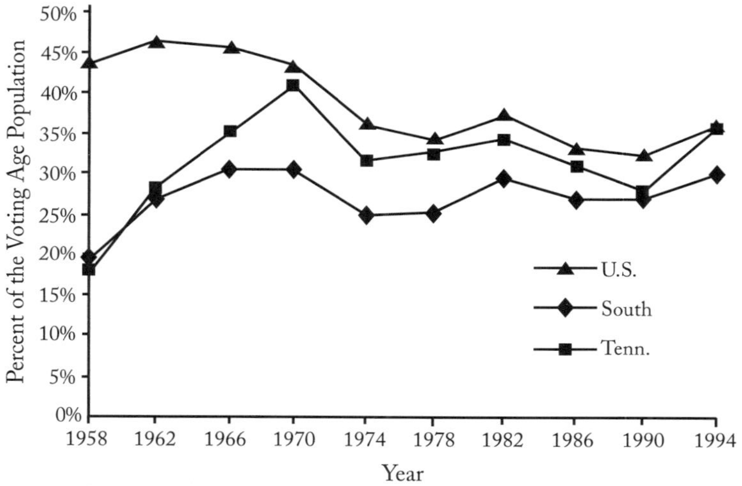

Tennessee turnout has fluctuated somewhat between the low Southern rates and the higher national rates. In the period from 1958 to 1966, Tennessee was similar to the South, but since 1970 the Tennessee trend has generally followed the national pattern. The fluctuation in midterm turnout rates in Tennessee may be largely due to the competitiveness of state elections, which are held at the same time as the midterm congressional elections. For example, in 1990 the incumbent governor, Ned Ray McWherter (Dem.), and the incumbent senator, Al Gore (Dem.), were virtually assured of victory because of the weak opposition they faced, and consequently turnout was much lower than most other recent elections: an anemic 27.9 percent. By comparison, the 1994 election, which featured two competitive races for the U. S. Senate and a highly contested gubernatorial election, had one of the highest turnout rates ever for a midterm election in Tennessee (36.2 percent).

CURRENT ISSUES IN TURNOUT

Recently, several electoral reforms have been suggested to increase turnout by eliminating barriers to participation. One of these reforms, adopted by Tennessee in 1994, is early voting. This program allows voters to cast a ballot during a two week period prior to any state election. As opposed to absentee balloting, which requires an approved excuse to vote earlier than election day, early voting allows everyone the opportunity to vote prior to election day. Besides offering additional days to vote, early voting also allows for evening and weekend hours as well as using nontraditional voting sites that might be more convenient for voters. Because of this convenience, those citizens who previously found it difficult to participate on election day may turn out at higher rates.

Voter response to early voting has been quite positive. Eleven percent of registered voters used early voting in 1994, and about one in five ballots was cast during the early voting period. In the 1996 election 13 percent of registrants voted early, accounting for 21 percent of all ballots cast. Although these participation rates are similar, the greater turnout in presidential elections means that almost 400,000 Tennesseans cast early ballots in 1996, a 60 percent increase over the 1994 number of 250,503.

Another important development affecting turnout has been the passage of the "motor voter" legislation. This federal law requires states to make voter registration more convenient by providing registration applications at various governmental offices rather than just at the office of the county registrar. In Tennessee, these locations include the Department of Safety (where drivers apply for a license), state public assistance agencies, and public libraries. Because many citizens frequent these sites for other purposes, providing registration materials may increase the number of registrants and perhaps increase turnout.

In Tennessee, there was an immediate change in the normal registration trend following implementation of the National Voter Registration Act in January 1995. Even with the purging of inactive voters (as is the case after every statewide election), there was a 2.05 percent increase in registration in the six-month period from December 1994 to June 1995. This increase compares quite favorably with similar post-midterm election registration figures in the 1990s: a 1.64 percent decrease in June 1993 and a .46 percent decrease in June 1991. In the eighteen month period from January 1995 to June 1996, 284,417 Tennesseeans utilized the motor voter registration system. Overall, from November 1994 to November 1996, registration in Tennessee soared from 2,683,422 to 3,055,962, an increase of 14 percent.

PARTISANSHIP IN TENNESSEE

Political parties serve as a mechanism for representing and articulating interests in society by nominating candidates, winning elections, and joining together to form public policy. Since 1860, the political party system in the U.S. has been characterized by two dominant parties: the Democrats and the Republicans. Formed in the 1930s, the New Deal coalition of white Southerners, Jews, urban Catholics, minorities, and unionized workers became the core of the Democratic Party. Generally, the Democrats have believed in governmental intervention in the economy and a more equitable distribution of societal resources. Republicans have been more focused on a belief in a free market economy and more traditional social values and structures.

With the advance of the civil rights movement in the 1960s came the decline of the New Deal coalition. The Democratic Party's support of civil rights reform alienated many Southern whites. In addition, many conservative Southerners were distraught with the Democratic Party's support of a greater federal role in the economy. While Southern whites no longer sided exclusively with the Democratic Party, they did not immediately switch party allegiance to the Republican Party. Until 1994, a majority of Southern congressional seats went to Democrats in both the U.S. House and Senate. Nevertheless, at the presidential level, Southerners left the Democratic tradition decades before. Even in the 1950s, Dwight Eisenhower, the Republican candidate, broke the "Solid South" by winning several Southern states. Since 1964, only President Carter, a Southern governor, was able to forge a Democratic majority in the South. Similarly, Tennessee has supported the Democratic presidential candidate only five of the last thirteen elections, including President Clinton in 1992 and 1996, when former Tennessee Senator Al Gore was on the ticket as a vice presidential candidate.

TRENDS IN PARTISANSHIP

Why do parties matter? The party affiliation of a political candidate can help provide clues about his or her views and beliefs. Many voters use this cue in selecting a candidate for office. Examining the political party affiliation of elected officials provides some information as to the electorate's public policy preferences. One way to understand the wishes of the voters is to look at the partisan composition of the different electoral bodies, such as the U.S. Congress or state legislatures.

One of the recent changes in Tennessee politics has been the rise of the Republican Party in statewide races. The party first asserted its strength in presidential contests. The Republicans gained a majority of votes for a presidential candidate as early as 1952, with President Eisenhower receiving 50.1 percent of the popular vote. Since then, only the Southern Democrats Johnson, Carter, and Clinton have won in Tennessee.

The Republican Party has also made gains in subpresidential elections in Tennessee. Since electing Howard Baker to the U.S. Senate in 1966, the voters have sent a Republican to the Senate in six of the eleven elections, including current Senators Bill Frist and Fred Thompson. In that same time period, the Republicans have also won four out of the eight gubernatorial elections, including Don Sundquist's victory in 1994.

These victories for statewide offices, however, have not been easily converted into electoral success within the Tennessee General Assembly or the Tennessee delegation to the U.S. House of Representatives. The Democrats have controlled a majority of the Tennessee seats in the U.S. House every year since 1953, except for 1973 to 1975 and the two sessions of Congress since 1994 (see figure 7.3). Until 1963, the Tennessee House delegation was similar to the rest of the South with a preponderance of Democrats. From 1963 until 1981, however, Tennessee was more similar to the rest of the nation than the South. Since 1981, the differences between the nation, the South, and Tennessee have been less pronounced. Indeed, the success of the Republicans in Tennessee and the rest of the South helped propel the Republicans into majority status after the 1994 election.

Figure 7.3

PERCENT DEMOCRAT IN THE U.S. HOUSE

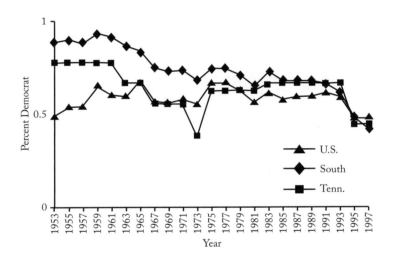

While the Democrats have long maintained control of both chambers of the state legislature, Republicans have enjoyed more success in Tennessee than in much of the South. As figure 7.4 shows, the Tennessee Senate has generally exhibited a pattern more similar to the rest of the nation than to other Southern states. Although the Tennessee Senate has been controlled by the Democrats for decades, the dominance is nowhere near the level exhibited in the typical upper chamber in the South.

It is important to point out, however, that the Democratic grip has weakened in both Tennessee and the South over the last decade. Indeed, the Democrats lost control of the Tennessee Senate during the fall of 1995 when two Democrats switched to the Republican Party. Although this partisan switch did not make much difference from an ideological perspective, it gave the Republicans control of another political institution in Tennessee. The Republican control of the Senate was short-lived, however, with control returning to the

Figure 7.4

PERCENT DEMOCRAT IN THE UPPER STATE HOUSE

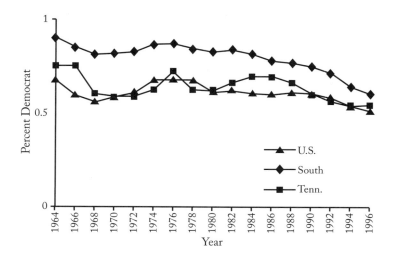

Figure 7.5

PERCENT DEMOCRAT IN THE LOWER STATE HOUSE

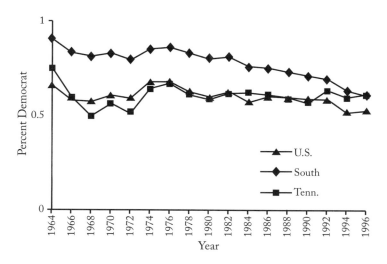

Democrats following the 1996 election in which they captured eighteen of the thirty-three Senate seats.

As one can see in figure 7.5, a similar pattern for Tennessee, the South, and the nation holds for lower state legislative chambers. The South has been far more Democratic than the rest of the nation, including Tennessee, though the Democrats nationwide have been losing lower state house seats. The Tennessee House, however, has been much more competitive than the typical Southern lower chamber since the 1960s, looking much like the rest of the nation. The major event boosting the Democratic profile over the last couple of decades was the influx of new Democrats into the chamber as a result of the Watergate scandal involving Republican Richard Nixon. Like much of the rest of the nation, Democrats gained seats in the Tennessee House in 1974, and since then they have maintained a comfortable majority. After the 1996 election, the Democrats controlled 61 out of the 99 House seats, an increase of two seats over 1994.

REGIONAL DIFFERENCES IN PARTISANSHIP WITHIN TENNESSEE

Regional political cultures within the state have an enormous effect on partisan success rates in Tennessee. Historically, the Democratic Party has dominated statewide elections, but Democrats have not dominated at the local level in all parts of the state. As V. O. Key pointed out, "The peculiar form of the coalitions and combinations that struggle for control of the state grow out of geographical diversity and the powerful influences of long-past events on the voting behavior of its citizens".[9]

While Democrats have typically won statewide offices by dominating Middle and West Tennessee, Republicans have enjoyed great success in electing local officials and state legislators in East Tennessee. Key and others have noted that the roots of these partisan differences emerged in the prevailing economic systems of each region prior to the Civil War. The topography and soil of each region largely determined the agricultural systems that could be used. The mountainous eastern region, with poor soil conditions, could not sustain plantation farming and its system of slave labor. Therefore, the eastern region had few slaves and was pro-Union during the Civil War. It retained its pro-Lincoln stance by supporting the Republican Party after the war.

The impact of terrain and soil conditions has continued to affect the farming economy of all three regions. The western region of Tennessee benefits from the fertile soil and more tillable land of the Mississippi river flood plain, which allows large-scale production agriculture. As a result, the value of farm products sold annually per county in West Tennessee averages $27 million as compared to $15 million per county in Middle Tennessee and $13 million for each eastern county. This type of agriculture currently relies largely on mechanized farming implements, but in the past it required a huge labor force. Until the Civil War, this need was met by the slave economy. This dependence on slave labor explains the overwhelming support for the Confederacy and the vote to secede from the Union in 1861. It also helps to explain the current racial composition of the state: East, 93 percent white; Middle, 87 percent; and West, 65 percent. Given the strong tendency for African Americans to support the Democratic Party, much of the Democrats' support in the western region could be attributed to the large minority population.

Another factor influencing regional political differences has been population growth. Population changes have been unique in each of the grand divisions. West Tennessee has experienced little growth in the twentieth century, and it has even lost population between 1980 and 1990. In comparison, Middle Tennessee has grown by 70 percent since 1900, and the eastern region has expanded by 151 percent during this time. In the 1980s, Middle Tennessee experienced 7 percent growth, and the East grew by 4 percent.

Because of the values, ideologies, and partisan attachments new residents may bring with them, it is also important to look at the source of this growth. According to the 1990 census, Middle Tennessee has experienced a greater in-migration of residents from outside the state than the other two regions. In addition, about 10 percent of Middle Tennessee's residents have moved in from other parts of the state, nearly double the rate of intrastate migration to West Tennessee. Indeed, the Nashville-Davidson County metro area surpassed the Memphis-Shelby County metro area in population during 1995. These recent changes in the demographic composition of the regions may have profound effects on partisanship.

PARTISANSHIP IN RECENT ELECTIONS

As the previous section suggests, regional variation is an important characteristic of Tennessee politics. In addition, the earlier discussion of partisan trends suggests that major changes in electoral competition have taken place over the last few decades. (See chapter 1 for a detailed discussion of the events surrounding several salient campaigns.) While the state as a whole is no longer dominated by the Democratic Party and many Republican candidates have enjoyed statewide success, regional differences persist. In recent elections, Tennessee resembled the rest of the nation in its partisan preferences. The state gave its eleven electors to Democratic presidential candidate Bill Clinton in 1992, and the U.S. House and Senate delegations were dominated by the Democrats. In 1994, however, the state elected a Republican governor, two Republican senators, and five Republicans among the nine U.S. representatives from the state. In 1996, Tennessee supported divided government: Clinton won the state's electoral votes, and the Republicans retained both of Tennessee's U.S. Senate seats and the majority of U.S. House seats.

The 1996 presidential election and the 1994 gubernatorial election illustrate a stark contrast in the ability of each party to garner votes in the different regions of the state. As the maps displayed in figures 7.6 and 7.7 show, there is tremendous variation in the pattern of partisanship across the state. Each of the maps shows the percent of the county vote supporting the Democratic candidate: figure 6 displays the support for the presidential candidate Bill Clinton in 1996, and figure 7 shows the percent of the vote for the gubernatorial candidate Phil Bredesen in 1994.[10]

As the map of the 1996 election shows, Clinton received overwhelming support among those casting a ballot for one of the two major party candidates.

Figure 7.6

PERCENT DEMOCRAT VOTE, 1996

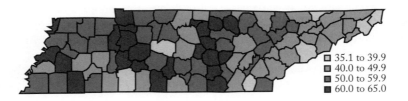

☐ 35.1 to 39.9
☐ 40.0 to 49.9
■ 50.0 to 59.9
■ 60.0 to 65.0

Figure 7.7

PERCENT DEMOCRAT VOTE, 1994

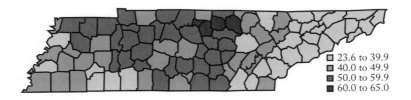

☐ 23.6 to 39.9
☐ 40.0 to 49.9
■ 50.0 to 59.9
■ 60.0 to 65.0

Clinton won a majority of the two-party votes in fifty-seven of the ninety-five Tennessee counties. Of the most heavily Democratic counties (above 60 percent of the two-party vote), five were in the West, none were in the East, and 18 were in the Middle Division. A vast majority of the thirty-eight counties won by the Republican candidate Robert Dole were in the East region. No doubt the Democrats performed particularly well in the 1992 and 1996 election in Tennessee partly because of the presence of Al Gore, a native Tennessean, on the ballot, and Clinton himself is a Southern Democrat. Nevertheless, those elections reflect the current conventional wisdom that East Tennessee is the stronghold of the Republican Party, and Middle Tennessee provides the bulk of the Democratic votes.

While the 1996 contest shows where a successful Democratic candidate can draw support, the 1994 map illustrates the division of party preferences among Tennesseeans in a midterm election. The Republican sweep of the major offices and the pickup of two House seats in 1994 can only be matched by the period from 1973 to 1975, when the Republicans controlled both Senate seats, the Governor's office, and five of the eight U.S. House seats from the state.

Despite this Republican success, figure 7.7 shows that much of the traditional pattern of partisanship persists, albeit in a reduced form for the Democrats. Phil Bredesen, the Nashville mayor and Democratic gubernatorial candidate, was not able to gain a majority of votes in even one East Tennessee county.

The East region was by far the most solid in its support of the Republican gubernatorial candidate, Don Sundquist. As in the 1996 election, the Democrats performed best in the Middle division. The only four counties to give more than 60 percent of the county vote to the Democratic candidate were in middle Tennessee. Further, of the thirty-five counties in which the Democratic candidate won a majority, thirty were in the central region.

The Republican candidate also performed quite well in the western region with five counties providing at least a 60 percent share of the vote and an additional eleven counties giving a majority to the Republican. In viewing the Republican gains in the western region, however, it is important to point out that Don Sundquist represented a congressional district from that region for twelve years. Overall, West Tennessee appears to be the most politically volatile. Given the more enduring party allegiance of voters in the other two divisions, the partisanship of voters in the western region may well be the deciding factor in future statewide elections.

CONCLUSION

The most striking feature of Tennessee elections over the last thirty years has been the rise of the Republican Party. This renewed vitality has had a profound effect not only on the partisan landscape of Tennessee but also on citizens' electoral participation. Increased competition has redefined how elections are conducted and has also led to greater participation by voters who may have previously felt they had no real choices in state elections. Tennessee no longer resembles the closed political system that characterized Southern states in the first half of the twentieth century. Indeed, the contemporary Tennessee electoral system appears more like the rest of the nation in both turnout rates and partisanship.

Without the limitations of a one-party system, political parties have a greater motivation for mobilizing voters, and citizens should find it easier to express their views. Much of the potential for increased turnout lies in the increased opportunities for participation afforded by such reforms as early voting and motor voter laws. These policies can continue to ameliorate barriers to electoral participation by reducing the costs imposed on voters, especially those who may have found those costs insurmountable.

CHAPTER 8

Women in Tennessee Politics

—Anne Sloan

W hen asked about the political status of women in the state shortly after the celebration of the seventy-fifth anniversary of Tennessee's ratification of the Nineteenth Amendment, State Rep. Mike Williams (Dem., Franklin) characterized it as "pretty dismal."[1] Many Tennesseans were self-congratulatory over the anniversary of Tennessee's vote that gave women the franchise. However, as Williams's comment would indicate, Tennessee's overall record on women's rights, their economic status, and their political success leaves little room for congratulations.[2]

Although the legislature did ratify the Nineteenth Amendment on August 23, 1920, antisuffragist forces in the Tennessee House of Representatives just eight days later carried a motion that the House not concur, by a vote of fifty-seven to twenty-four. Because states cannot nullify their ratification of an amendment, the gesture was legally futile; it did, however, set an ominous and lingering political tone. Tennessee was one of the first states to ratify the Equal Rights Amendment in 1972; however, the legislature voted to rescind its ratification in 1974.[3]

Moreover, statutory law in Tennessee has rarely addressed women's rights. The major exception to this was the Married Women's Emancipation Act of 1913, which, in matters involving real and personal property and contracts, gave married women the same rights as unmarried women. The legislature amended this act in 1919 to protect the concept of tenancy-by-the-entirety. (This is a form of joint tenancy that allows the surviving spouse, upon proper vestiture, sole ownership. It excludes such properties from inclusion in the deceased's estate.) Except in these areas, the Tennessee legislature has been virtually silent.[4]

A PATTERN OF FEDERAL JUDICIAL INITIATIVE AND STATE RESPONSE

Tennessee legislators have allowed the federal government to take the lead on most women's rights issues. Much of the progress in women's rights is due to civil rights legislation including: the Civil Rights Act of 1964, the Title IX Education Amendment of 1972, the Civil Rights Restoration Act of 1988, and the Civil Rights Act of 1991. In addition, President John F. Kennedy's creation of the President's Commission on the Status of Women resulted in a report that led to the establishment of a Citizens' Advisory Council to monitor progress and issues in the field of women's rights. Many states soon created similar commissions of their own. In 1964, Governor Frank Clement by executive order created the Governor's Commission on the Status of Women in Tennessee. The commission examined three areas: (1) women and employment policies and practices, (2) the legal treatment of women and their status under Social Security and tax laws, and (3) the education of women.[5] In 1972, the legislature and the governor supported the creation of the Tennessee Commission on the Status of Women,[6] one of the recommendations made by the Governor's Commission in 1964. The 1972 Tennessee Commission was later terminated under the "sunset law," an aspect of the legislature's Entity Review Law of 1977 providing that certain state agencies will eventually expire unless renewed by the legislature.[7]

While the Governor's Commission made a number of recommendations concerning women in Tennessee, including the formation of a continuing committee to work toward necessary legislation such as equal pay for comparable work,[8] changes in women's rights occurred largely because of litigation, not legislative or executive action. In addition, since Tennessee statutory law has rarely addressed the legal and constitutional status of women, most litigation has occurred in federal courts, where such cases as *Reed v. Reed* (1971),[9] *Frontiero v. Richardson* (1973),[10] and *Roe v. Wade* (1973)[11] have set national standards of equal protection and due process.[12]

WOMEN IN THE TENNESSEE SUFFRAGETTE MOVEMENT

During the fight to ratify the Nineteenth Amendment, a number of Tennessee women played major political roles on both sides of the issue. Most prominent among the antisuffragists was Josephine Anderson Pearson, a native of Gallatin, who served as president of the Tennessee State Association Opposed to Women Suffrage (1917–1920) and president of the Southern Women's League for Rejection of the Susan B. Anthony Amendment in 1920.

Tennessee suffragists included Anne Dallas Dudley of Nashville, who organized and served as president of the Nashville Equal Suffrage League from 1911–1915, held the office of president of the Tennessee Equal Suffrage Association, Inc. from 1915–1917, and served as Third Vice President of the National Woman Suffrage Association; Sue Shelton White, born in Hendersonville, who chaired the National Woman's Party (NWP) in Tennessee in 1918, became editor of the NWP's national paper the *Suffragist* in 1919 and helped design the original version of the Equal Rights Amendment submitted to Congress in 1923; and Katherine Burch Warner of Nashville, a prominent club woman and board member, who was selected as president of the Tennessee Women's Suffrage Association in 1918.[13] Regardless of their positions on the suffrage issue, most of the leaders in Tennessee's fight over votes for women were traditional society women. The pro-suffragists were followers of Carrie

Chapman Catt. The exception to this was White, who was allied with the more radical section of the national suffrage movement led by Alice Paul.

WOMEN IN THE TENNESSEE GENERAL ASSEMBLY

Despite the successful efforts of the Tennessee suffragists, political roles for women remained limited. Only five women served in the Tennessee General Assembly between 1921 and 1931—one in the Senate and four in the House. There were gradual, fairly steady increases in the number of women legislators over the next sixty years. From 1931 to 1951, only four women served in the Tennessee General Assembly. The record improved from 1951 to 1971, when a total of twelve women served in the state legislature. Between 1971 and 1991, a total of twenty-one women participated as legislators.[14]

Some of the increase in the number of women legislators might be attributed to the same cause that brought an increase in African American representation. After the court decision in *Baker v. Carr* (1962),[15] Tennessee was forced to redistrict in a way that gave urban and rural areas an equal distribution of seats based on population. The net result was to increase the number of urban seats in the legislature. Because urban areas tend to be more demographically diverse and less bound by tradition, the shift to greater urban representation has produced a concomitant rise in the number of seats held both by women and African Americans. This change seems especially to have benefited African American women.

Figures in the 1990s reflect some marginal improvement in the ability of women to win election to the state legislature (see table 8.1). While the raw numbers look good in comparison with previous General Assemblies, the percentage of women is still low. Indeed, Tennessee still falls below the 1995 national average of about 20.5 percent of state legislative seats held by women.

Table 8.1

WOMEN IN THE TENNESSEE GENERAL ASSEMBLY IN THE 1990S

General Assembly	Senate	House
98th (1993–94)	4 (12%)	15 (15%)
99th (1995–96)	3 (11%)	15 (15%)
100th (1997–98)	3 (11%)	15 (15%)

Tennessee does not fare as badly by comparison to other Southern and border states. Tennessee's percentage is below that of North Carolina, Georgia, and Texas, but it is above that of Kentucky, Virginia, South Carolina, Alabama, Mississippi, Louisiana, Arkansas, and Oklahoma.[16] Still, Tennessee's low ranking holds some rather interesting and possibly negative implications for women. State legislatures are where women historically have had the most political success. Proportionally, on a nationwide basis, more women serve in state legislatures than on county governing bodies or in the U.S. Congress. In 1989, the percentage of women state legislators nationally was 15 percent compared to 5 percent in Congress. That same year, women comprised only 9 percent of county governing boards nationwide.[17] The historically low representation in Tennessee may be one reason why many of the initiatives affecting women in this state have come from court decisions based on civil rights legislation passed by the U.S. Congress.[18]

Low representation may put Tennessee women at a disadvantage.[19] Many of the issues that directly concern women are debated at the state level, and policies that directly bear on women's lives are promulgated by the state legislature. Not surprisingly, a growing body of evidence indicates that women legislators spend more time than their male counterparts promoting women's rights.[20] In addition, some scholars have argued that "the success of the bills affecting women is heavily dependent on the proportion of women actually in the legislative body."[21] Evidence also suggests that, if the percentage of women in a legislative body is below 15 percent, women, like other minority groups, feel constrained in their legislative behavior, focusing on mainstream legislation rather than on initiatives that would be especially beneficial to their minority constituency. Conversely, when women make up what seems to be a critical mass—20 percent or more of the legislative body—women legislators give priority to policy issues and legislation dealing with women, children, and families and have greater success than male colleagues in creating distinctive legislation.[22]

In the 1990s, several women have held leadership positions in the General Assembly. Anna Belle O'Brien (Dem., Crossville) served as chair of the Senate Democratic Caucus; Lois DeBerry (Dem., Memphis) served as speaker pro tem of the House; and Carol Chumney (Dem., Memphis) was majority whip of the House in the 99th General Assembly. That was an increase from the previous Assembly when only Senator O'Brien and Representative DeBerry served in leadership positions. Women did not fare as well in the 100th General Assembly. Only Representative DeBerry retained her position. Senator O'Brien retired and Representative Chumney, although reelected from her district, lost in her bid to become House majority leader. Mary Ann Eckles (Dem., Murfreesboro) also lost her bid to succeed Chumney as majority whip.

In the 98th General Assembly, no women chaired committees in either house. Of the nine standing committees in the Tennessee Senate, two had women as their vice-chairs. Among the twelve standing committees in the Tennessee House, only three women served as vice-chairs. This meant that women made up only 11.9 percent of committee leadership (calculated in terms of chairs and vice-chairs) in the 98th Tennessee Assembly.

In the 99th General Assembly, two women held the position of vice-chair in Senate committees, and two served in that capacity on House committees. Two women legislators also served in lower-level committee leadership positions as secretaries for House committees. Not only are these figures well below the percentage found in state legislatures nationally, where approximately one-third of the committee leadership consists of women,[23] but they also represented a percentage of the leadership that was smaller than the percentage of women in the General Assembly. Recognizing this as a problem, House Speaker Jimmy Naifeh created a new committee, the Children and Family Affairs Committee, for the 100th General Assembly and named Rep. Brenda Turner (Dem., Chattanooga) as chair. While the appointment of a woman as a committee chair is a positive move, the fact that such a move entailed the creation of a new committee, especially one dealing with family and children, means that women are still largely ignored when it comes to the traditionally powerful committees. Overall, women were appointed to ten committee leadership positions.[24]

When committee composition is examined, a rather traditional pattern appears. In the House of Representatives, women have held no more than three positions on any committee. This is not surprising given their small numbers. However, the committees with three women are generally the "women's issues" committees such as Education and General Welfare. It is encouraging that the Judiciary, Commerce, and State and Local Government Committees also listed three women in 1994. Less encouraging is the fact that only one woman served on the Agriculture, Finance and Ways and Means, Government Operations, and Transportation committees. The 99th General Assembly pattern was not dissimilar; however, there were some minor changes. On the positive side, four women sat on the State and Local Government committee. On the negative side was diminished representation on one of the more powerful committees. Only two women (as opposed to five in 1992) served on the Education committee.

The Senate picture is less favorable. Because only four women served in the 98th General Assembly Senate, they were on more than one committee. While it is quite common for all senators to serve on multiple committees, the low number of women in the Senate creates more stresses and probably an increased workload for these women and leaves them as a minority without representation on several powerful committees. Two served on both the Government Operations and the Judiciary committees. One each served on Commerce, Labor, and Agriculture; Education; Environment, Conservation, and Tourism; and the State and Local Government committees. There were no women on the Finance and Ways and Means committee or on the Transportation committee. The 99th General Assembly Senate saw some modest improvement in distribution, despite the loss of one woman senator. The Government Operations committee continued to have two women included in its composition. Carol Rice (Dem., Clarksville) and Anna Belle O'Brien were both on the Transportation Committee while Senator O'Brien and Thelma Harper (Dem., Nashville) were both on the Judiciary Committee. Senator O'Brien also was on the Finance and Ways and Means Committee. Greater representation on the latter three committees, however, meant that no woman sat on the Commerce, Labor and Agriculture, or the Education Committees. This reflects the problem of committee membership for women in the legislature. To achieve representation on powerful committees such as Ways and Means leaves women without representation on other committees. By contrast, not only are males represented on all committees, but they also make up the majority of every committee.

A more encouraging area is the number of women who have served two or more terms. The 1996 election returned Thelma Harper for an additional term in the Senate, and thirteen women incumbents gained reelection in the House. However, two Senators did not return. Anna Belle O'Brien retired at the end of the 99th General Assembly, and Carol Rice was defeated in her bid for a third term by Rosalyn Kurita (Dem., Clarksville). As of the 99th General Assembly, Ms. O'Brien had held her Senate seat for seventeen years and served one term in the Tennessee House before her election as a senator. Thelma Harper was serving her fourth term in the State Senate and Carol Rice her second. Ms. DeBerry was in her twelfth term as a member of the House, and there were eight additional women who were in at least their second term as state representatives.[25]

Several women in the 99th Tennessee General Assembly had served multiple terms. Including Lois DeBerry, seven of the women in the House were serving their fourth term of office. This was also true in the case of several women who served in the 98th General Assembly and who did not return to the 99th. In contrast, for the first thirty years that women were eligible to serve in the General Assembly, from 1921–1951, none served more than two terms.[26] Generally, women have an easier time winning a vacant seat or one previously held by a woman and, like their male colleagues, a difficult time defeating an incumbent. Because the majority of incumbents are male and vacancies are rare, changing the gender composition of the General Assembly is inherently difficult. However, once women are elected, incumbency works in their favor, as it does for most other candidates.

Term longevity is significant for a variety of reasons. The fact that some women have been in the General Assembly for more than a decade has allowed them to move into leadership positions. This trend appears to favor them in appointments to positions of party leadership, especially among the Democrats (Democratic women legislators outnumber their Republican counterparts by more than two to one)[27]; however, it has only recently allowed them to break into the extremely powerful committee chair assignments. In addition, no woman has served as speaker of either the House or Senate. Women also are more likely to be placed on committees that deal with areas that are generally considered to be more in their realm, such as committees on child welfare, social services, and education. This hinders their ability to broaden their policy expertise, which, in turn, may prejudice their chances for election to statewide office. Although this tendency has ameliorated slightly across time, the recent formation of the new committee to "handle legislation on juvenile crime, domestic violence, adoption and child welfare"[28] and the appointment of Representative Turner as its chair seem to reinforce the stereotypical committee assignments of women.

Developing the credentials that make them credible contenders for political office has been one of the chief problems facing Tennessee women seeking office. Historically, women in the Tennessee state legislature, in many instances, established their capabilities through voluntary public service. In comparison to their male counterparts, fewer women had professional degrees, the background of elected office, or private sector experience that made them viable candidates. Most of the career women elected were educators. Many of them also served in appointed positions before seeking an electoral office. Judging by an examination of biographies appearing in recent editions of the *Tennessee Blue Book,* this is beginning to change. Increasingly, women legislators have professional training with advanced degrees and come from business and commerce as well as education.

HOW WOMEN HAVE FARED OUTSIDE
THE GENERAL ASSEMBLY

A brief look outside the legislature gives a slightly different perspective. Women have long been represented by greater numbers in the executive branch of Tennessee government. Many of the governors over the past three decades have appointed women not only to their staffs but also to serve as commissioners of various departments. With the election of Gov. Don Sundquist, two women were appointed to the staff at cabinet rank: Beth Fortune as press secretary and Peaches Simpkins as deputy to the governor. (Simpkins resigned her position in 1996.) The Sundquist administration appointed eight women among the twenty-two commissioners. While the numbers are strong, most of the women commissioners oversee departments that again fall into the "women's issues" category. The exception to this is Ruth Johnson, the commissioner of revenue.[29]

Women have not done well in elections for statewide positions or in congressional districts. The first woman who won statewide election was Jane Eskind, elected to the Public Service Commission in 1980. Later in the 1980s she failed in her bid for a U.S. Senate seat. Martha Craig Daughtrey was appointed to the State Supreme Court in April of 1990 and won election to the court in August of that year. Janice Holder was appointed to the court in 1996. Sara Kyle was elected to the Public Service Commission in 1994; however, in 1995 the Tennessee Assembly voted to dissolve the Public Service Commission, effective June 1996.

As far as congressional districts are concerned, only Marilyn Lloyd in the Third Congressional District has been successful in a bid for election. Earlier congresswomen from Tennessee were appointed to fill the unexpired terms of their husbands. No women other than Representative Lloyd ran in the 1990 races. In 1992, a number of women ran, but, again, only Marilyn Lloyd was elected. Marsha Blackburn, who ran on the Republican ticket in the Sixth District came closest to joining Lloyd in Congress; however, she lost to Bart Gordon by almost 14,000 votes. No women ran in the 1994 or 1996 general congressional elections in Tennessee, although some competed in party primaries.

Tennessee women have also been underrepresented at the state executive level as well. Two women served on the Public Service Commission, considered here as a statewide office, before its dissolution. While there have been women who have sought the governorship, most notably Socialist candidate Kate Ella Bradford Stockton of Fentress County, who ran for that position in 1936,[30] no woman has served as governor or lieutenant governor. Because Tennessee's lieutenant governor is not popularly elected and because the attorney general is selected by the Supreme Court, male gubernatorial candidates have no opportunity to balance the ticket by naming a female running mate for either post. This precludes female Tennessee politicians from emulating Martha Lane Collins of Kentucky, who was first elected as John Y. Brown's lieutenant governor and later elected governor. Women have probably fared best in appointed positions where they have served in various cabinet and staff capacities for at least three decades.

Historically, women have not done well in the executive positions of local government, such as mayor, county executive, or county sheriff (although there are some exceptions[31]); but local elections in the 1990s have seen more women running and winning these positions. Two examples are Gayle Elrod Ray, Sheriff of Davidson County, and Nancy Allen, County Executive for Rutherford County. Their elections marked the first time women have held either position. Part of the increased success of women in local elections may be attributed to increased funding from such organizations as WIN (Women in the Nineties), a non-partisan group dedicated to electing progressive women candidates to local and state offices in Tennessee. This organization played a significant role in Gayle Ray's race for sheriff by urging its membership to donate money through WIN to Ray's campaign fund.

CONCLUSIONS

In general, Rep. Mike Williams was not far off the mark in his appraisal of the political status of women in Tennessee as "pretty dismal." With the major exceptions of the woman's suffrage and equal rights amendments, the legislature has not been particularly sensitive to the needs or desires of a large number of constituents, especially considering that there were efforts to overturn both amendment votes. While the longevity of women in the legislature is improving and slow progress is being made in achievement of leadership positions and committee appointments, the number of women in the Tennessee legislature is below the national average, as is the number of women in leadership positions in the legislature. Tennessee has lagged far behind many other states, including neighboring Kentucky, in the number of women in statewide elected office. However, Tennessee compares well with most of the Southern states in the number of women in the legislature and is certainly on a par with those states when congressional delegations are included. Southern states continue to be more conservative than the rest of the nation concerning the role of women in politics, an attitude shared by some women as well as men. This is reflected in the few Southern women elected in 1992 to Congress. While the number of women in the U.S. House of Representatives rose by nineteen, the number of Southern women in the 103rd Congress remained stagnant.

The political status of women in Tennessee is probably better than it has ever been, but room remains for significant progress. According to a 1996 study by the Institute for Women's Policy Research, Tennessee ranks fiftieth in political participation by women. The state was ranked forty-second in employment and earnings for women, forty-fifth in economic autonomy, and forty-seventh in reproductive rights in the same study. When these composite scores are broken down into their various components, the situation does not look any better. Compared with the other states, Tennessee ranks forty-third in the number of women elected to office, thirty-seventh in the number of women registered to vote, and forty-seventh in voter turnout by women. In each variable category covered in the study, Tennessee ranked in the worst third of states in the U.S. as far as gender issues are concerned, with the exception of women with health insurance. On this variable, Tennessee ranked in the middle third. Tennessee's evaluation based on these criteria is one of the worst in the nation. Tennessee, Mississippi, Kentucky, Arkansas, Alabama, West Virginia, Louisiana, and South Carolina were the lowest ranked states.[32]

Despite the study's overall low-performance evaluation of Tennessee, there is some basis for optimism.

> In the southeastern states, from West Virginia to Tennessee to Florida, women have the least influence and involvement in political matters overall. They do, however, have good numbers of women's institutional resources, a first step perhaps to greater political involvement in other ways in the future.[33]

While low representation of women in elected and appointed positions may partially account for the low ranking of Tennessee in this 1996 study—a finding that reinforces research regarding the correlation between the number of women in lawmaking bodies and the prominence of women's issues in legislation—the problem goes much further. In Tennessee, and the South in general, women not only lag behind in holding office, in income-level, and in reproductive rights; they also lag in such areas as voting registration and turnout. They also tend to be less well educated and more likely to live in poverty. Despite legislation and court decisions that touch on these areas, positive change has been slow, largely because of regional, religious, and sociopsychological mores that have not changed as rapidly in the South as in other regions of the nation. For this reason, the presence of women in politics and their increasing numbers at all levels of state government may well be the most effective demonstration of the changed role of women in Tennessee.

CHAPTER 9

African Americans in Tennessee:
The Case of Memphis

—Marcus D. Pohlmann

At a time when African Americans are playing an increasingly influential role throughout Tennessee, the South, and the nation, no city better epitomizes blacks' political strengths and weaknesses than Memphis, the state's largest city.[1] The city's share of the state's black population has nearly doubled since 1940; and if present trends continue, Memphis will soon contain a majority of Tennessee's African American population.[2]

Chartered as a city in 1849, Memphis soon became a major river port and railway center, with the local economy thriving particularly from cotton and slave trading. Apart from transitory traders, the city's own permanent population soared in the 1850s and 1860s and included a relatively rich ethnic mix of Germans, Italians, and Irish. A limited number of black slaves lived primarily on the outskirts of the city; but given the availability of indigent Irish to do much of the manual labor, the urban demand for slave labor was limited.[3]

As civil war lurked on the horizon, however, Memphis whites supported slavery and even placed restrictions on free blacks (for instance, education was forbidden and a curfew imposed).[4] Nevertheless, the city initially did not endorse secession, although local support for the Confederacy built rapidly once the war began. By 1862, the city had fallen to advancing Union troops. Fortunately for Memphis, the early Union takeover helped the city avoid the kind of wartime destruction that befell cities such as Atlanta; and, along with the entire state of Tennessee, the city was not subject to formal Reconstruction following the war.[5]

Sizable Freedmen's camps quickly sprung up around the outskirts of the city, with large numbers of these former slaves opting to reside in and around Memphis following emancipation. In 1865, for example, the city's black population grew by 500 percent.[6] With the possible exception of New Orleans, Memphis soon had more black residents than any other city in the nation, with Beale Street becoming "the main street of Negro America."[7]

Meanwhile, most of Memphis lacked even the most elementary sanitation facilities. In particular, an area known as Bayou Gayoso drained five thousand acres of an open sewer, receiving deposits from thousands of private privies. This created a fertile breeding ground for mosquitoes carrying yellow fever.[8]

Disaster hit from the late 1870s into the 1880s, as a series of yellow fever epidemics devastated the city. The 1878 epidemic alone produced the highest death rate from an epidemic that any city in the United States had ever seen. Between deaths and departures, Memphis recorded a huge loss of population in the 1880 census. From an estimated 80,000 people before the fever struck, Memphis shrunk to 34,000 residents.[9]

One of the results was a dramatic change in the heterogeneity of the city. With the exception of those Irish immigrants who were too impoverished to flee, virtually all of the members of the white ethnic groups departed. Overall, more than 24,000 people fled, and few ever returned. This exodus left only 6,000 whites. Most blacks were too poor to leave but proved more resistant to the disease; consequently, a much higher proportion of them survived and remained in the city.[10]

In the years between 1880 and 1920, the population increased by approximately 30,000 to 40,000 per decade. The nature of that moderate growth, however, had a lasting impact on the city's political culture. The better-off and more cosmopolitan whites who had fled were replaced by poorer and more parochial whites from the surrounding rural areas of Tennessee, Mississippi, and Arkansas.[11]. Roger Biles indicates that "Memphis developed a personality determined in large measure by its southern location."[12] In the latter nineteenth century, for instance, the Ku Klux Klan was active locally and was even openly involved in electoral politics.[13] By 1900, the city's foreign-born population had declined to 15 percent; while 80 percent of its residents now hailed from the Tennessee and Mississippi countryside.[14]

The period from 1920 to 1970 was marked by the largest population increases in the city's history. Its population increased by approximately one hundred thousand per decade, except during the Depression years. Much of that growth continued to originate from the rural South, and a sizable share of it resulted from the annexation of surrounding areas.[15]

Among other things, this pattern continued to produce a very conservative electorate. In 1968, as a case in point, Democrat Hubert Humphrey received 12 percent of the vote, Republican Richard Nixon 46 percent, and American Independent George Wallace 42 percent. The votes for Wallace, and to a somewhat lesser degree a number of the votes for Nixon, reveal the quite conservative nature of the electorate overall. In addition, Wallace's support cut across all income lines, although it came disproportionately from working-class whites.[16]

BLACKS AND THE LOCAL ECONOMY

Since 1870, Memphis has had a population that has been at least 37 percent African American. This has been true despite black migration out of the area and despite repeated annexations of predominantly white suburbs.[17] This size has made blacks a formidable force in both the city's economy and its politics.

The size and segregation of the city's black population has required the black community to develop its own economic institutions. For example, these circumstances created a need for black doctors, lawyers, and teachers, as well as for black groceries, barber shops, hair salons, funeral parlors, and even banks.[18] Beale Street, the black commercial center in its Jim Crow heyday, was lined with real estate and banking offices, dry goods and clothing stores, theaters, saloons, and gambling joints.[19]

BLACK BUSINESSES

Bert Roddy founded the city's first black grocery chain and attempted to build on W. E. B. DuBois's socialist notion of developing community cooperative businesses.[20] Meanwhile, Robert Church, Sr., was the best known. A former slave, he arrived in Memphis in 1863; by the time of his death in 1912, he had amassed more than a million dollars worth of real estate and other holdings. Most likely the nation's first black millionaire,[21] his Solvent Savings Bank was the first black-owned bank in the city's history; and his donations of Church Park and the adjacent Church Auditorium provided major focal points for black social and cultural life, especially during the Jim Crow period.[22]

More recently, despite desegregation, a number of black businesses have continued to develop and prosper. By the 1980s, Memphis supported more than three thousand black-owned enterprises, with gross receipts of approximately $150 million. Fewer than 1 percent were manufacturers, however, leaving the overwhelming majority operating in the lower-paying commerce and service sectors.[23]

Over time, these businesses provided blacks with goods, services, and jobs that were not always accessible in the city at large. They also generated a number of black leaders who have been quite active in the city's political arena. However, black business success failed to "trickle down" to sizable portions of the African American community as a whole.

BLACK WORK FORCE

The Memphis economy has long been based largely on commerce and services, as opposed to manufacturing. By the mid-1990s, for instance, ten of the metropolitan area's fifteen largest employers were governmental entities. Only eight institutions employed more than five thousand workers. Federal Express was the largest at 18,831; while five of the others were governmental agencies and two were regional hospitals. Of the top 40, employing more than 1,200 workers apiece, only five were manufacturers, the largest with 2,200 employees.[24]

Even in the city's brief period of industrialization, the white community's discriminatory union and employer practices left black men "overwhelmingly concentrated in jobs that entailed hardly any responsibility, skill or prestige, [and] wages and salaries that were at best marginal."[25] Black menial labor was such a bargain that the Tennessee legislature passed "emigrant agent codes" in 1917, making it illegal for outsiders to come into the state to recruit away black workers.[26] Meanwhile, of black women working outside the home, 82 percent were domestics or laundresses while another 10 percent were either seamstresses or in semiskilled employment.[27]

As late as 1950, despite the job experiences that had been accumulated during World War II, black men continued to find employment only as manual laborers or in service positions, and working black women remained largely domestic servants. As a result, black family income was only 44 percent of white family income. The figures would have been worse, but some of the black workers were employed by local branches of federal government agencies and benefited from a somewhat higher than average pay scale.[28]

Even when desegregation efforts and antidiscrimination laws gradually began to dismantle the old Jim Crow system, little would improve for many black Memphians. For one thing, much of the city's job base consisted of low-wage, unskilled positions.[29] In addition, desegregation eliminated the need for many black-owned businesses. The combined results have left Memphis with arguably the poorest black underclass of any large U.S. city. Where blacks made up 58 percent of all Memphis families earning less than $1,000 in 1949, that figure had grown to 71 percent by 1969.[30] Nearly a quarter of the inner-city work force made less than $2.00 per hour that year (as compared to 8.6 percent in Newark, for instance).[31] Not surprisingly, then, nearly 60 percent of the city's African Americans lived below the federal government's poverty level in 1969.[32] By 1990, despite the federal "War on Poverty," some 34 percent were still impoverished. As for the intensity of the poverty, six census tracts had a median household income below $5,500, and three entire zip codes had median household incomes below $6,500.[33] A predictable and troubling result of this pattern of poverty has been a tendency for the black working and lower classes to be suspicious of community leadership, white or black. Among other things, this has generated a certain propensity to shun traditional electoral politics, even when viable black candidates are available.

DIRECT POLITICAL ACTION

A number of Memphis blacks directly resisted the daily degradations of Jim Crow. In 1881, for example, prominent musician and schoolteacher Julia Hooks was arrested for her vociferous protest over not being seated in a theater's white section. In 1905 when Mary Morrison was arrested for resisting street car segregation in 1905, a huge rally followed in Church Park and several thousand dollars were raised for her legal defense.[34] Forms of more direct resistance, including violence, became increasingly common. In 1915 and 1916, for instance, Thomas Brooks killed two white attackers;[35] when white men tried physically to remove Charley Parks and John Knox from their trolley seats, Parks stabbed one,[36] while Knox ended up in a gun battle with another;[37] and a white trolley conductor was stabbed when he tried to collect extra fare from a black rider.[38] Ambush shootings and arson took place on occasion,[39] and, at times, lower-class blacks resorted to "physical means" in order to resist the brutality of local white police officers.[40]

The record of black resistance continued into the modern Civil Rights era. In 1960, a sizable number of student sit-ins occurred, and boycotts were launched against downtown retailers. Harry Holloway estimates more sit-ins and boycotts took place in Memphis than in any other city in the nation.[41] In response, the city's Committee on Community Relations helped usher in gradual desegregation even before the Civil Rights Act of 1964. In addition, public protests against police brutality began in the nineteenth century and continued into the 1990s.[42]

A Memphis labor movement started early in the twentieth century and included many black workers.[43] As an example of its success, the CIO was able to organize Firestone in the 1940s; soon, carpenters, longshoremen, and laundry workers were unionizing as well. At the same time, waiters, busboys, and elevator operators were engaging in wildcat walkouts.[44] More recently, a major sanitation workers' strike occurred in 1968, while the police, firefighters, and teachers walked the picket lines ten years later.

The 1968 strike by black sanitation workers is probably the best known. It began with a sewer worker's grievance over an incident of differential treatment by race. It then accelerated when two blacks were accidentally crushed to death in a garbage compactor. Mayor Henry Loeb's hard-line reaction allowed black leaders to turn the event into a major civil rights struggle. The full-blown strike, ultimately involving 1,100 workers and lasting sixty-five days, was led by AFSCME local no. 1733 and included support from the NAACP, prominent black ministers such as James Lawson and Martin Luther King, Jr., and a group of young "black power" militants calling themselves The Invaders.[45]

Mass violence developed as the sanitation strike progressed. On March 28, for instance, one of the rallies became unruly when windows were smashed and rocks thrown. The police response left one dead and sixty-two injured, and soon four thousand national guardsmen were called in to restore order. Then, following the assassination of Reverend King, the city exploded into days of looting, burning, sniping, and other forms of mass unrest, leaving the city "traumatized and divided."[46]

ELITE RESISTANCE

Among elite blacks, there had long been avenues available for some degree of direct action. Fraternal and benevolent associations arose after emancipation and played active political roles.[47] In the late nineteenth century, educator Ida B. Wells led protests against segregation and lynchings and even proceeded to air these grievances internationally. In particular, she aimed her message at British cotton buyers. "Political leagues" and "civic welfare groups" lobbied on behalf of black interests.[48] And, following the lynching of Ell Persons in 1917, businessmen such as Robert Church, Jr., and Bert Roddy founded the first Memphis branch of the relatively militant NAACP. Subsequently, led by individuals such as Jesse Turner and Maxine Smith, the NAACP would be at the forefront of much of the city's black resistance. Besides leading protests, the association filed federal lawsuits to fight numerous public segregation practices.[49]

Not only did leading activists have to face the majority culture and its laws and restrictions; they also had to face internal struggles among different groups within the civil rights community. As an example of the conflicting pressures faced by elite activists, consider the case of Benjamin Bell. In 1943, Bell was chosen as the chief executive officer of the Community Welfare League (CWL), which had recently become affiliated with the National Urban League (NUL). Attempting to move the local organization more into line with national NUL priorities, he pressed the call for black civil rights in Memphis. This led to a drop in CWL's private contributions, and soon Bell was replaced by the more accomodationist Rev. James McDaniel, whose posture was then criticized by the NUL.[50]

Such economic pressure did not deter subsequent assertions of black power, however. The 1960s, in particular, marked a time when "the politics of moderation was replaced by the politics of race."[51] By the 1970s, John and Harold Ford came to symbolize this militancy as they stood up to the city's white leadership. In 1974, for example, city councilman John Ford was cheered by many in the black community when he publicly told a white fellow council member to "go to hell."[52] Just as dramatic and controversial was an incident on election night 1991. Congressman Harold Ford was applauded when he challenged the election board's tallying of absentee ballots in a fiery televised tirade. In responding to the latter incident, a prominent white leader referred to Ford as "the embodiment of evil."[53]

ELECTORAL POLITICS

More than three hundred "free Negroes" were voting in Memphis as early as 1850, while the state of Tennessee enfranchised all of its black citizens in 1867.[54] By 1875, a coalition of blacks, Irish, and Italians dominated Memphis politics. Led by the likes of militant saloon-keeper Ed Shaw and the more conciliatory Hezekiah Henley, African Americans held seats on both the elected city council and school board, as well as positions such as wharf master and coal inspector.[55]

Shaw, a Republican—as were most Memphis blacks for nearly a century[56]—became the first African American elected in West Tennessee. Yet, within six months of his 1869 election to the Shelby County Board of Commissioners, that body was abolished, and no black would hold local office again until H. S. Prim was elected to the Memphis City Council in 1872.

Then, amid the ravages of the yellow fever epidemic, the city's charter was revoked in 1879, and the city became the Shelby County "taxing district" until 1893. Among other things, this reorganization allowed creation of an entirely new governing structure. One of the nation's first commission forms of government was developed; some of its members were chosen by the governor and local judges, while the rest were elected. This time, however, officials were elected at-large. The result was a commission government comprised exclusively of whites, most of whom were wealthy.[57]

The city's charter was reinstated in 1893, but only after the state had imposed a poll tax restricting black voting participation.[58] Thus, although a few blacks did serve on the Taxing District Commission and later in elected Republican Party positions,[59] no African American would even seek elective city office from 1888 until 1951.

In the interim, three major players in particular—Robert Church Jr., George W. Z. Lee, and O. Z. Evers—continued the struggle to gain political representation. Among other things, Church helped organize and then led the Lincoln Republican League of West Tennessee, a branch of the national Lincoln League. The League was integral in teaching blacks how to register and vote.[60] Lee led a local Lincoln League that also engaged in rallying black Republicans. His group was mostly businessmen and ministers, although as many as 1,600 African Americans would rally in Church Park to nominate a black Republican slate of candidates.[61] Evers, on the other hand, headed a small group of independents, calling themselves the Unity League. Despite their differences, such groups were able to unite behind candidates viewed as most supportive of black interests.[62] Consequently, this loose coalition of black Democrats, black Republicans, and black independents, including liberals and conservatives, led Harry Holloway to characterize black politics in Memphis as "pragmatic" and "independent."[63] As George Lee put it, "Freedom is non-partisan, and the battle for freedom needs to be fought."[64]

THE CRUMP ERA

E. H. "Boss" Crump was clearly the city's most powerful political figure during the first half of the twentieth century. As the Crump machine developed, a selected number of blacks had their poll taxes paid and were marshaled to the polls; in return, the black community received a share of the city's largesse for delivering what became a critical voting bloc.[65] Thus, as early as the 1930s, Memphis blacks did not face the "white primaries" and other voting obstructions that would continue to plague a South mired in Jim Crow laws and traditions. As Paul Lewinsohn put it, "The only place in the South where the Negro had by 1930 made a real breach in the white primary system was Memphis."[66] He attributes this "to the outright strength of the Negro population, under very skillful (Negro) leadership."[67]

Memphis blacks, for example, formed a Colored Citizens Association early in the century and later formed the West Tennessee Civic and Political League. Then, in 1938, the *Memphis World* newspaper sponsored the election of a symbolic "Mayor of Beale Street." Throughout, black leaders such as George Lee, Robert Church, Sr., and Robert Church, Jr., rallied black voters and brokered black political support for patronage benefits. Although the leaders were Republicans, as were many of the businessmen and professionals in the black leadership elite, they were able to work effectively with white political leaders—especially while the large majority of blacks remained loyal to the "Party of Lincoln."[68]

Boss Crump's rewards took many forms. Besides the traditional money, jobs, services, and fixed parking tickets, they included the naming of city monuments for well-known local blacks. Nevertheless, blacks were not allowed to rise to positions of authority within the party structure or the bureaucracy; and, once Crump had fully cemented his position, fewer blacks were registered and fewer rewards were forthcoming.[69]

Before problems with Boss Crump emerged, however, a combination of Crump's efforts and Franklin Roosevelt's emerging New Deal electoral coalition lured many blacks from their traditional allegiances to the Republican Party. At that point, Dr. Joseph E. Walker organized the Shelby County Democratic Club as an independent political base for black Memphians. Although the Democratic Club would remain separate from the Crump machine, Walker worked with Crump until the two had a falling out over the issue of segregation. Such disagreements drove Walker into the camp of a number of white "reformers" who emerged around the successful machine-challenging U.S. Senatorial bid of Estes Kefauver. Meanwhile, the independent nature of the Democratic Club made it difficult to raise money and to provide the patronage necessary to hold the organization together. Yet, the club persisted, and by the 1960s Holloway would describe it as an "effective, aggressive, mass-based organization."[70]

AFTER CRUMP

In 1951, Walker challenged the machine himself by running for the school board. In the course of the campaign, he and George Lee mounted the first of many aggressive voter registration drives within the black community. Although Walker was soundly defeated, he was the first black candidate in decades to seek public office, and black voter registration nearly tripled in 1951 alone. Then, after Crump died in 1954, the poll tax was eliminated, registration drives continued in earnest, and the percentage of registered blacks tripled again over the course of the 1950s, leaving more than 60 percent of the city's African Americans registered by 1960.[71] By 1963, as blacks struggled for the right to vote across the South, black Memphians were already registered at the same rate as white Memphians, participating at quite possibly the highest rate for blacks anywhere in the South.[72]

Meanwhile, a "second reconstruction" was developing. The nation had become more attuned to issues of justice and democracy following World War II, and it had been jolted out of its complacency by civil rights marches and urban unrest. The U.S. Supreme Court responded with decisions such as *Smith v. Allwright* and *Brown v. Board of Education*, while the Congress added the Twenty-fourth Amendment, the 1957 and 1964 Civil Rights Acts, the 1965 Voting Rights Act and the 1968 Fair Housing Act. These national events provided a significant context for emerging racial assertiveness in Memphis.[73]

In addition, local black churches were often at the heart of these developments. While some ministers eschewed politics in favor of reaching quiet accommodation with wealthy whites,[74] others were more political. In 1955, as just one example, dozens of churchmen representing virtually every black denomination came together to form the Ministers and Citizens League. They adopted a $2,000 registration budget, hired three full-time secretaries, and pledged themselves to utilizing other resources at their disposal to increase black voter registration. The black ministers also used the pulpit to preach the need to register, held mass meetings, and even drove unregistered voters to the court house.[75]

That same year, 1955, Walker's Democratic group endorsed the mayoral candidacy of Edmund Orgill, who won in no small part because of black votes. However, the city commission thwarted Orgill's subsequent attempt to name Walker to the city hospital board.[76] Meanwhile, black minister Roy Love ran for the school board. He finished fifth in his race for one of four school board seats; and apparently because of this "close call," the election rules were quickly changed so that candidates would have to run for specific seats instead of allowing the top vote getters to gain the seats that were available. Despite that setback, the *Memphis World* noted that in the 1955 local elections black voters had demonstrated awareness of their power.[77]

When S. A. Wilbun, a black man, ran for the state legislature in 1958, he did well in the black community and still managed to attract a number of white votes. But even more importantly, his campaign manager, Harvard-educated lawyer Russell Sugarmon, Jr., soon succeeded in creating at least a temporary precinct-level political organization for the Shelby County Democratic Club. With the death of J. E. Walker that same year, the organization was now in the hands of aggressive young leaders such as Sugarmon, Benjamin Hooks, and A. W. Willis. They interviewed white candidates prior to endorsing them; and, in the process, they struck bargains on behalf of the black community.[78] At the same time, this renewed assertiveness and the practice of black "single shot" voting in multimember district elections[79] also began to worry many whites.

In 1959, Russell Sugarmon ran for a seat on the city commission and led a field of black candidates, prompting formation of the Citizens' Leadership Council to bring together black Republicans, Democrats, and independents to support Sugarmon and his Volunteer Ticket. Among other things, they raised $20,000 and enlisted some 1,200 precinct workers.[80]

Predictably, this became a very racially divisive election. While prominent African Americans such as Martin Luther King, Jr., and Mahalia Jackson appeared to help rally the black vote, the white Citizens for Progress ran under the banner "Keep Memphis Down in Dixie."[81] Meanwhile, the *Commercial Appeal* editorialized that "at this juncture, it would not be well for the Negro citizens or for community tranquillity to elect a Negro Public Works Commissioner or Judge of the Juvenile Court."[82]

Although all black candidates were defeated, Sugarmon had made a strong run for the city commission; each of the Volunteer candidates finished second, and nearly two-thirds of black voters were now registered. Sugarmon concluded, "We won everything but the election."[83] Sugarmon stood at the end of a long effort. In 1887 Lucius Wallace had been the last black elected in Memphis for nearly three quarters of a century. Then, in 1960, Jesse Turner finally won a seat on the Democratic Executive Committee.

In 1960, Sugarmon's organization displayed its pragmatism and independence by striking a votes-for-patronage deal with a conservative segregationist Democrat, Paul Barrett.[84] In 1963, however, the group openly opposed Sheriff

M. A. Hinds' mayoral bid, claiming Hinds had served under Crump as the "head of the Gestapo to keep the Negroes in their place."[85]

By the mid-1960s, the city of Memphis had a voting age population that was approximately 34 percent black, and two-thirds of them were registered. Odell Horton had received a federal appointment as an assistant U. S. Attorney, and Benjamin Hooks had been appointed to the criminal court bench by the state's governor. Nevertheless, the city commission was comprised of five white men, all elected at-large. No African American had ever even been a viable contender for any one of those positions. As H. T. Lockard put it, "There has been no conscientious effort by the Democrats over the years to cultivate any real working relationship with Negroes who are also Democrats."[86]

In 1964, with the help of a large presidential election turnout, A. W. Willis won a seat in the state legislature and Charles Ware won a constable position— both by plurality votes.[87] Thus, it was not long before a successful effort was launched to create a runoff provision in local elections. Meanwhile, the number of annexations of predominantly white areas continued with vigor. In addition, as Harry Holloway points out, Republican "election challenges" focused on registrations in the black community; and extra field wages would be offered on election day, the field hands then working too late to vote when they returned to town.[88]

PROGRAM OF PROGRESS

By 1965, although for somewhat different reasons, many blacks and whites had become dissatisfied with the commission arrangement. The Program of Progress grew out of this discontent, and it would soon usher in a new governmental structure.

The city proceeded to adopt a mayor-council system of government. In 1967, despite much advice to the contrary, A. W. Willis launched a mayoral bid. His candidacy split the black community, as a variety of more gradualist ministers and community leaders disagreed with the NAACP's inclination to press for the election of a black mayor at that time. In the end, a majority of blacks voted for white liberal William Ingram. Willis failed to make the runoff, and Ingram was then defeated by Henry Loeb.[89] Nevertheless, seven of thirteen council members were now being elected by districts, and African Americans Fred Davis, James Netters, and J. O. Patterson won three of the thirteen city council seats that year.

In 1972, Patterson became Tennessee's first black major-party candidate for the U. S. House of Representatives since Ed Shaw ran as a Republican a century earlier. Then, in 1974, Harold Ford became the first and only black Tennessean ever elected to Congress, defeating four-term incumbent Dan Kuykendall to win a House seat by 774 votes out of the 135,000 votes cast.[90]

After his election, Ford developed the most effective political operation in Memphis. Besides personally paying overdue rents, distributing food at Christmas, contributing to church bazaars, giving graduation presents, and so on, his local congressional staff was also quite proficient at helping constituents through the maze of federal and local bureaucracies. In addition, his congressional seniority and consequent committee assignments put him in a position to bring federal funds to Memphis. The word was that "Harold delivers," and his deliveries were extensively chronicled both in his newsletters and in the *Tri-State Defender*. Such service helped build a core of very loyal supporters.

In addition, the congressman, his staff, and a small group of loyalists regularly composed and distributed a sample ballot endorsing particular candidates. Such endorsements, which often appeared to require a financial contribution to the congressman's campaign fund, are believed to have generated a sizable number of votes for the endorsed candidates.[91] In 1996, his organization appeared to be integral in electing Harold Ford, Jr., a political novice, to succeed his father in the United States Congress.

FACTIONALISM

Despite devices like Ford's sample ballot, black leaders in Memphis, especially in recent years, commonly have disagreed over which mayoral candidate to support. These splits have been based on such factors as partisanship, gender, intergenerational rivalries, and personalities and have weakened the influence of the black community. This has been particularly problematic in a city where whites managed to remain a thin electoral majority, where white allies have been few and far between for black candidates, and where much of the black population has remained exceptionally poor and difficult to mobilize. [92]

An excellent example of this division took place in 1975 and 1979 when W. Otis Higgs, Jr., became the first serious black candidate for mayor, running against incumbent Wyeth Chandler. Higgs, a lifelong Memphian, put together an integrated campaign team and ran on an accomodationist platform stressing economic development, improved race relations, and his own personal attributes.[93] His approach won him unprecedented white support, including between 8 and 11 percent of the white vote over the course of four elections.[94] He also garnered virtually all of the black votes cast. However, at least in part because he was viewed as having crossed the line and become too accommodating to whites, his candidacy simply did not generate enough excitement in the black community. As a result, there was not enough black turnout to overcome Chandler's incumbency, campaign funds, and endorsements, besides the fact that whites held a clear majority of eligible voters. Even at the leadership level, Charles Williams concludes that "various local black leaders could not agree on Higgs' candidacy."[95]

In a 1982 special election after Chandler left office, the long-standing rivalry between the black then-acting Mayor J. O. Patterson and the Ford family hurt the Patterson candidacy. At least in part due to this split, Patterson lost the mayorship to Dick Hackett. In 1983, black candidates Higgs, John Ford, and D'Army Bailey split the African-American vote, despite Harold Ford's black unity efforts and a highly successful voter registration drive.[96] This split helped allow the incumbent, Hackett, to win his first full term. Then, in 1987, black candidates Minerva Johnican and Teddy Withers competed for votes in the black community. Unable to establish their viability, both lost badly to Hackett who garnered 18 percent of the black vote. Meanwhile, John Ford's ballot had endorsed a white Republican.[97]

Following the 1987 election, black union leader James Smith called for a leadership summit. As he stated, "I think the leadership of this community—the black leadership—is going to have to sit down and come up with a consensus candidate."[98]

POLITICAL CHANGE

The traditional political culture in Memphis before 1991 had long allowed the white majority to unify behind white candidates in citywide elections. With the help of laws that this majority had established over time, virtually all victorious candidates continued to be white, even after viable black challengers began to emerge. Racial polarization in mayoral elections, for example, had typically ranged from 90 to 99 percent in both the black and white communities.[99] Before 1991, only two black candidates had won citywide victories, and both of these successes were anomalies. Minerva Johnican won an at-large city council seat in 1983 by creating a coalition with white Republican women as political repayment for helping a Republican woman get elected to the state legislature. Then, in 1990, Earnestine Hunt won a city court position in an off-year election with very low turnout.

Nevertheless, important changes were in the works. A combination of white flight to the suburbs, higher black birth rates, and new annexation laws meant that black eligible voters would outnumber whites by a 50 to 49 percent margin in 1991. In addition, the federal Voting Rights Act was used to prevent the city from employing the runoff in citywide elections.

ELECTORAL CHANGE

Historic changes took place in Memphis as a result of the 1991 election. An African American, Dr. W. W. Herenton, was elected mayor in a hotly contested race that ended more than a century of white conservative control of that office. In addition, two blacks were elected to at-large positions on the city council, one on the school board, and one on the city court. The city's penchant for racially polarized voting would no longer automatically spell defeat of all black candidates.

The 1991 mayoral election still had polarization rates that approached 99 percent. It is worth noting, however, that polarization had been moderating some for the other at-large offices. Polarization averages for all 1983, 1987, and 1991 citywide elections were 61 percent, 62 percent, and 65 percent, with white polarization exceeding black by an average of between 2 and 12 percent. Although polarization did vary considerably by individual office, no office showed the same high level of polarization as was found in the mayoral races.

Thereafter, the 1995 city elections served to validate and extend what had transpired in the seminal election four years earlier. This time, incumbent Mayor Herenton easily won reelection, garnering nearly 75 percent of the vote to defeat relatively token opposition in a very low turnout election. Nevertheless, he managed a white crossover that approached 40 percent, nearly four times the highest any black mayoral candidate had ever attracted. The citywide elections for school board and city court, however, provided less evidence of racial crossover voting. And with at-large elections now eliminated, blacks won seven of the thirteen seats on city council, although the new districts did not allow for much racial crossover, given the city's degree of residential segregation.

CONCLUSION

Despite a host of social, economic, and political obstacles, African Americans have continued to be a sizable and assertive political force in the city of Memphis. Nevertheless, they have had difficulty maintaining internal cohesion; further, unlike minority citizens in most other large U. S. cities, Memphis blacks simply have not had a reliable white liberal contingent with which to align in long-term coalition. Whites, whether liberal or conservative, have been disinclined to support black candidates for citywide office unless those candidates project such a moderate image as to dampen enthusiasm in the African American community.

Had Memphis history developed differently, allowing the city to retain a larger number of more liberal whites, the city's degree of racial separation might not have been nearly as severe. In order to win, white politicians would likely have been more racially neutral, while black candidates could have withstood the defection of the most race-conscious blacks by regularly supplementing their vote totals with a reasonable number of white votes.

Nevertheless, evidence indicates that white liberals, or at least moderates, have been reemerging as the city has diversified over the past quarter century. And, when looking at the level of crossover voting in a number of recent citywide races, this diversification grows evident, finally, in the city's election returns.

Conceivably, a relatively successful Herenton stewardship could help cement and build upon that evolution, as the 1995 election results suggest. Should Mayor Herenton's leadership continue to succeed in developing that coalition, a progressive black-white governing majority might well be able to weather either internal divisions within the black community or further annexations, both of which otherwise could lead to a return of conservative white domination in the city of Memphis.

CHAPTER 10

Speaking for Tennessee in Washington

—*Jim Cooper*

Representing a constituency in the U.S. Congress has always been a daunting task. Not surprisingly, most Tennessee politicians have preferred to run for state or local offices instead of for Congress. Still, some candidates have always come forward to wage campaigns for the honor of representing Tennessee in the national government. Like all states, Tennessee has two U.S. senators; since 1910, its number of U.S. representatives has varied from eight to ten—currently, nine serve in the House of Representatives.

Every year, Tennessee's congressional delegation works part-time in Washington and part-time in Tennessee to cut red tape for their constituents, cut ribbons in local ceremonies to get free publicity, and cut as much of a figure as they can in congressional debates to help both the country and themselves. As those of us who have served in Congress can attest, the job can be exhausting and confusing. Many Tennesseans are not aware of where their representatives work. Constituents complain that representatives spend too long in Washington, and then, when they travel to Washington to lobby their Congressperson, they discover that he or she is usually back home and that they could have saved a trip. Congressional back-and-forth air travel is relentless. The joke is that no one is elected to a seat in Congress but to a seat on American Airlines. And the government keeps the frequent-flier miles.

THE POLITICAL LANDSCAPE

Geography is part of the difficulty of representing Tennessee. Stretching almost five hundred miles from Bristol to Memphis, or, more accurately, from Laurel Bloomery to Mud Island, the state runs from the tallest mountains of the Appalachians to the Mississippi River delta. If the state were hinged on the eastern end and swung north, Tennessee would touch Canada. The state's location makes it a fast-growing industrial and transportation hub within six hundred miles of nearly three-fourths of the U.S. population. But it has also made Tennessee a crossroads and border state that has bred an interesting and popular mix of federal politicians.

Three major physical barriers have trisected the state: the Appalachian Mountains, the Cumberland Plateau, and the widest part of the Tennessee River as it flows north to Kentucky. These natural road blocks have tended to segment the state politically and to shape its political and economic history. A common road sign used to welcome interstate highway travelers to the "three states" of Tennessee. Even local news coverage rarely includes stories focusing on one of the other three "grand divisions" of the state.

From the earliest Tennessee settlement at Trade in Johnson County, from the rise of the Free State of Franklin, and from the Cumberland Gap as a doorway to the West, early settlers brought their belongings, their Bibles, and their political beliefs to a rough frontier. River travel on the Holston, the French Broad, and the Hiwasee led to the mighty Tennessee, and those who could scale the Cumberland Plateau could venture down the Cumberland River itself. Those routes made a difference then and now because settlement patterns have proved remarkably enduring. The ethnic groups were primarily Scotch-Irish, English, or German, but traces of their settlements are still perceptible. Once the pioneers unpacked, they tended to stay for a long, long time.

The descendants of these pioneers still do not like to be told what to do by outsiders. They make up their own minds, control their own local schools and school boards, and usually vote with the political party of their ancestors. Communities and cemeteries have real meaning here, as shown by countless annual church "decoration" days to place flowers on the graves. The Protestant work ethic and religious fundamentalism remain widespread ways of affirming faith in God. Powerful Tennessee church denominations like the Southern Baptists and the Church of Christ have organizational structures that reject distant hierarchies like bishops and ordination, favoring instead the autonomy of local churches and sometimes even self-appointed, or divinely inspired or "called," ministers.

It seems odd to outsiders, but these qualities have attracted more Japanese investment to Tennessee than to almost any other state. Over eighty major Japanese facilities have located here, including the giant Nissan plant at Smyrna and the only Japanese preparatory school in America at Sweetwater. Whether it is the old pioneer work ethic (as demonstrated by the loyal employees at a firm like the Jack Daniel Distillery in Lynchburg) or an oriental work ethic (in factories like Nissan where the boss wears the same work shirt as the "associates" and parks in the same lot), Tennessee employees expect to be treated fairly, almost like family. Former Gov. Lamar Alexander even commissioned a book of photographs o show the many similarities between Tennessee and Japanese culture.

Geology has been another shaping factor in the political and economic history of Tennessee. The thin soil of East Tennessee hills and mountains allowed only a meager living for independent yeoman farmers, whereas the rich, flat bottom land of the rest of the state produced better crops, especially in West Tennessee. East Tennesseans could not afford to own slaves or hire much outside help, whereas the planter culture of West Tennessee depended heavily on slavery. Middle Tennessee had elements of both cultures. The great short story writer Peter Taylor chronicled these differences in social outlook in his numerous works.

Our soil turned bloody during the Civil War, when Tennessee endured more battles than any other state except Virginia. Many East Tennesseans sided with the Union and the new Republican Party, whereas most people in the rest of the state joined the Confederacy and remained Democrats. Although Tennessee's own Gov. Andrew Johnson became President of the United States after Lincoln's assassination, he was an East Tennessean who was extremely unpopular in the state. Only in 1995 was a statue of Johnson erected on the grounds of the state capitol. In his classic 1948 work, *Southern Politics*, V. O. Key was struck by the lasting effect of the Civil War on state politics. He noted that East Tennessee was one of the strongest Republican areas in the entire United States. Also in certain hill counties like Wayne and Henderson in Middle and West Tennessee, the thin soil and yeoman farmer tradition continue to make those counties islands of Republicanism in a sea of traditional Democrats.

Leaders of both national political parties have come from Tennessee, although Democrats have predominated. This mirrors state politics. Andrew Jackson and James K. Polk both served successful terms as president. As already mentioned, Tennessee's Andrew Johnson, a pro-Union Democrat picked as Abraham Lincoln's running mate in 1864, became president after Lincoln's assassination.

Franklin Roosevelt and the New Deal did not fundamentally change East Tennessee allegiances despite the sweeping improvements the New Deal brought to the state. Although remaining Republican in spirit in the 1964 election, voters in the region did not, however, strongly support Barry Goldwater, who, while campaigning for president in Knoxville, hurt his chances even among East Tennessee Republicans when he promised to sell the Tennessee Valley Authority, a Roosevelt innovation. For several years after 1970, the governorship, both U.S. Senate seats, and a majority of the state congressional delegation were Republican. Democrats reclaimed control by 1976. By 1994, Republicans had returned to power.

THE POLITICIANS

How Tennessee's federal officials have handled people with these deep roots is hard to summarize in a few pages. The stability of our population has often meant that Tennessee voters have favored political families whose forebears have served the state well, such as the Gores, the Clements, the Bakers, the Duncans, the Fords, and the Coopers. And state voters have often elected young federal leaders and kept them in Washington as long as they stayed close to the people back home. It is still too early to say whether the recent term limit movement will interfere with this pattern. Tennessee shares these traits with a number of Southern states, but a remarkable moderation in Tennessee politics has drawn a line between us and the Deep South states that has often marked an important national political boundary.

There has been less meanness in Tennessee politics, fewer dirty tricks, less race-baiting, and less negative advertising (until recently) than in most Southern states. The television ads that Republican Congressman Robin Beard ran against Sen. Jim Sasser in 1982 are often cited as the beginning of negative advertising in the state. By straining to link Sasser with Cuba's Fidel Castro, Beard's advertisement offended many Tennessee voters more focused on the effects of recession. The success of negative advertising in the 1994 elections may mean that Tennessee has finally adopted the rough politics of many of its Southern neighbors, however.

The lives of Tennessee senators have been chronicled in *Tennessee Senators*, by the late Kenneth D. McKellar of Memphis, the longest serving U.S. senator in state history. The lives of Tennessee House members are too numerous to tell, but they include a number of figures who captured national attention.

In the early 1800s, William C. C. Claiborne was elected to the U.S. House at the age of twenty-three, below the Constitution's minimum age of 25. Claiborne was still allowed to serve, partly because transportation was so poor that returning to Tennessee and holding a new election would have been too time consuming. President Jefferson needed Claiborne for a few tough votes, and Claiborne was rewarded first with the governorship of the Territory of Mississippi and then with that of the entire Louisiana Purchase.

Davy Crockett was a legendary Member of Congress who served three terms, lost a reelection race in 1835, denounced the body in a still-famous speech, and returned home for more frontier adventures. Denouncing Washington both before and after election to Congress is still a very popular campaign strategy. Voters never seem to tire of it.

James K. Polk may not have been colorful, but he still ranks as one of the most competent officials ever to have served on the federal level. Due partly to the knowledge of Washington he acquired as a congressman and as Speaker of the House, he is the only American president to have honored every single one of his major campaign promises.

Early in the twentieth century, and before the days of no-tax pledges from politicians, Democratic Congressman Cordell Hull sponsored the first federal income tax and later became the longest serving secretary of state in U.S. history. A Tennessee congressman from the Republican Party, B. Carroll Reece, also captured the national limelight early in the century by serving as the national chairman of his party.

By the 1950s, Tennessee had no less than three Democratic contenders for president or vice president: Estes Kefauver (who first popularized the New Hampshire primary), Frank Clement (who gave a famous keynote address at the 1956 Democratic National Convention), and Albert Gore, Sr. (a fiddle-playing populist who was instrumental in creating the nation's interstate highway system). Also in the 1950s, Democratic Senator McKellar was speaker pro tem of the U.S. Senate, and Democratic Rep. Jerry Cooper was Chairman of the House Ways and Means Committee.

In the 1970s, then-Congressman Bill Brock became national chairman of the Republican Party. In the 1980s Republican Sen. Howard Baker was Senate majority leader, ran unsuccessfully for the Republican nomination for president, and served under President Reagan as White House Chief of Staff.

Today, after a career as Tennessee congressman and senator, Al Gore, Jr., is the vice president of the United States. Former Gov. Lamar Alexander ran for the 1996 Republican nomination for president and seems poised to run again in 2000. Although Alexander was never elected to federal office, he has the rare distinction of having worked in all three branches of the federal government: judicial, as a law clerk for Judge Minor Wisdom; executive, as secretary of education under President Bush; and legislative, as a Senate staff aide. Sen. Fred Thompson is a rising star in the Republican Party and has also been mentioned as a possible presidential contender.

A number of retired or defeated Tennessee senators and congressmen either reside permanently in Washington, maintain offices there, or lobby on a regular basis, proving that former politicians can still have major influence on the policies that our elected representatives endorse. Lesser-known but influential Tennesseans have led national trade and professional organizations that have a major lobbying presence in Washington. Their impact on federal legislation should not be underestimated. The same skills that have enabled members of the congressional delegation to rise in the national ranks have also made Tennessee trade association figures very popular.

THE NEW DEAL ERA AND AFTER

Until the New Deal, much of Tennessee's economic potential remained unfulfilled. The magnificent river system of the state both fertilized and flooded hundreds of miles of low-lying land. The terrific energy of the rivers was unharnessed until, after decades of prodding by a visionary Nebraska congressman turned senator, George Norris, Congress created the Tennessee Valley Authority (TVA) as part of President Franklin D. Roosevelt's "New Deal." This huge federal program, in conjunction with the formation of 160 electric distribution cooperatives and municipal power companies, created the largest electric utility in the United States in an area shunned by private power companies.

TVA gave Tennessee, and six other states that border on Tennessee, a chance to swap coal-oil lamps for affordable electric lights and appliances. Low electric rates not only revolutionized the quality of life for countless farm families, but also attracted major industry. For example, Alcoa, Tennessee, was named in honor of the Aluminum Company of America's decision to locate a giant plant there, due to cheap electric rates.

Other New Deal legislation that transformed the state included the creation of the Great Smoky Mountains National Park (with 14 million visitors annually, by far the most-visited national park in America) and the Oak Ridge National Laboratory (created during World War II to develop the first atomic bomb). The electric cooperative movement also encouraged the formation of more local telephone co-ops and agricultural co-ops than existed in most of the rest of the U.S.

Seldom in American history has federal legislation benefited a state so dramatically, but the underlying political sentiments of most East Tennesseans were not changed. John Waters, who served as Sen. Howard Baker's campaign manager and later as TVA Director, exemplifies this attitude. He has said that the three strongest influences in his own life, apart from his family and church, were the TVA, the Great Smoky Mountains National Park, and Social Security—all Democratic programs—and yet he remains a hard-shell Republican.

Electricity and the relocation of plants from the North and Midwest dramatically changed Tennessee. Although our state became officially categorized as industrial in the 1940s due to the number of part-time farmers working in factories, many Tennesseans have an agricultural outlook. For example, Farm Bureau and 4-H programs are stronger in Tennessee than they are almost anywhere else in America. With over three hundred thousand farm-family members, and with county boards of directors comprised of pillars of the community, the Tennessee Farm Bureau is probably still the most potent political lobby in the state legislature and is very powerful with the Tennessee delegation in Washington as well.

With the rural outlook goes the traditional emphasis on church-going. There are more churches per capita in Nashville than almost any other American city, and countless churches dot the countryside. Nashville is the headquarters of the Southern Baptist Convention, perhaps the most powerful religious denomination in America, with 15 million members and 38,000 churches scattered primarily through the Southeastern United States. Other churches or church offices headquartered in Tennessee include the Church of God in Cleveland, the Church of God in Christ in Memphis, and the Methodist Publishing House in Nashville. If the radically decentralized Church of Christ allowed a headquarters anywhere, it would probably be in Nashville, along with one of its leading educational institutions, David Lipscomb University. In addition, numerous other religiously affiliated colleges and universities flourish throughout Tennessee.

Country music also promotes a rural image of Tennessee. The Grand Ole Opry was started in Nashville in 1925 and the Knoxville Barn Dance in 1942. As in so many things, Memphis has its own traditions with the jazz and blues of W. C. Handy, Elvis Presley, and B. B. King.

True to the spirit of "the volunteer state," many Tennesseans served in both world wars, Korea, and Vietnam. Whether as the result of intense patriotism, a distaste for farming, or the attractions of the military career, Tennesseans have enlisted and produced many warriors to follow in the footsteps of Andrew Jackson, hero of the Battle of New Orleans in the War of 1812. Sgt. Alvin C. York, the greatest hero of World War I, is only the most famous. For many years, being state commander of the American Legion was one of the best stepping stones to high political office. Veterans returning from World War II spurred the reform of county-level politics across Tennessee and contributed to the 1948 overthrow of the Boss Crump/Carroll Reece/Burch Biggs political machine, which had been a remarkably enduring alliance of East Tennessee Republicans and Memphis Democrats.

Protest over the war in Vietnam was particularly hard for most Tennesseans to understand since our ancestors had volunteered in record numbers for other questionable conflicts like the Spanish-American War and the Mexican War. Sen. Albert Gore Sr.'s opposition to the Vietnam War was a key issue in his defeat in 1970, even though his son had enlisted and was serving in Vietnam at the time.

The Civil Rights movement has also had an enduring impact on state politics, despite the relatively small African American population of 16 percent statewide. Little violence occurred in the early years under the progressive governorship of Frank Clement and the Senate leadership of Estes Kefauver and Albert Gore, Sr. (the only two Southern senators who refused to sign the 1958 Southern Manifesto). A great moderating influence in the Civil Rights movement both in Tennessee and the South was the staunch nonviolence preached by Rev. James Lawson and the leaders of the "Nashville Movement," which is retold by David Halberstam in his 1998 book, *The Children*. Whether integrating Nashville lunch counters or leading "Freedom Riders" on Southern buses, students such as John Lewis (now a congressman from Atlanta) demonstrated remarkable courage and restraint. The state's legacy of nonviolence was, of course, obscured by the tragic assassination of Martin Luther King, Jr., in Memphis in 1968.

Tennessee congressional Democrats were the early beneficiaries of increased numbers of black voters, because Washington got most of the credit for progress in civil rights, not the governor or local mayors. But the Tennessee Republican Party also subtly used civil rights as a wedge issue with white voters. Busing school children to achieve racial balance in the schools became almost universally unpopular among white voters. In urban areas it was seen as working against the comfortable notion of the neighborhood school. Busing over great distances was something that rural parents were used to in order for their children to attend the single county high school, but they were not accustomed to the thought of doing it for purposes of racial diversity. As Kevin Phillips predicted in *The Emerging Republican Majority* in the late 1960s, civil rights helped make the once-Democratic "solid South" now nearly solidly Republican. In the mid-1980s it was still extremely controversial in many rural parts of Tennessee to support a national holiday in honor of Martin Luther King, Jr.

TENNESSEE POLITICAL TECHNIQUES

How do Tennessee politicians represent such a wide variety of backgrounds and beliefs? Because the political culture of our state is so diverse, and perhaps because Tennessee borders more states than any other (8), Tennessee politicians have had remarkable success at the national level. For a small state, we have had more national figures than would be expected. To state it negatively, little in the way of the generic political and social characteristics of a typical Tennessean's background disqualifies him or her from major national office. For example, our leaders have usually been independent and hard to stereotype, not captured by large urban political machines or national labor unions. Candidates from farther South are more likely to be associated in voters' minds with racial or cultural extremism.

The alternating strength of the Democratic and Republican Parties in Tennessee has encouraged leaders in both parties to be political moderates, and to be somewhat more courteous than in many other Southern states. There have been three changes of party control of the state's congressional delegation since 1970. When riding a political see-saw, a partisan is more likely to abide by the Golden Rule. Members of the Tennessee delegation have numerous opportunities to criticize each other in the press, but seldom do. The delegation has been particularly unified on issues of economic concern to the state. This is in contrast to the bitter infighting found in many other state delegations. Our unity enables the Tennessee delegation to compete effectively with much larger states. For example, as recently as 1930, Tennessee had twelve federal office holders, almost as many as California did with thirteen. Today we are outnumbered by California fifty-six to eleven. But we are usually competing only against a faction of the splintered California delegation.

Patronage and pork have been effective substitutes for ideology in terms of getting votes in state politics. Senator McKellar was reportedly interested in converting all of TVA's jobs into patronage positions. When McKellar was one of the handful of Americans told of the Manhattan Project because of his ability (as chairman of the Senate Appropriations Committee) to obtain secret appropriations, his only question was to ask President Roosevelt where in Tennessee he would like the project to be located. For most of this century, postmasterships in every community were political plums. With the reform of the Postal Service in the 1970s, however, it became illegal for members of Congress even to recommend anyone for a postal position. But Congressman Joe L. Evins became legend anyway for building a new post office in every small community in his vast district, as well as for appointing countless pages to serve a month or so in Washington. Military academy appointments can still be made directly by senators and congressmen (a free four-year university education is still a very powerful political tool), although the academies discourage it. Members often nominate a list of ten for each academy so that the academy can choose the most qualified.

Pork is still quite popular. In 1982, when *Newsweek* listed the top ten pork-barrel projects in the United States, three were in or around Tennessee: the Clinch River Breeder reactor, the Columbia Dam, and the Tennessee-Tombigbee Waterway. The tradition continues. Today a highway tunnel is being constructed next to Cumberland Gap that has already cost over a quarter of a billion dollars. TVA is the only utility in America to get over $100 million in taxpayer-funded appropriations for their "non-power" work. Before TennCare, our congressional delegation fought for years to enable Tennessee to underfund

its Medicaid obligations. Countless other programs may fit in the special regional interest category: until recently, the Great Smoky Mountains National Park
was the only one in American that did not charge entrance fees; and the federal
tobacco program helps Tennessee as one of the top four production states.

In general, the Tennessee delegation has favored bricks-and-mortar projects
as opposed to investing in the work force. This is a shame because Southerners
lag in literacy and other basic job skills. Annual surveys of industry continually
praise Tennessee's roads more than its schools, but the "edifice complex" is so
strong that warnings from business leaders of a shortage of skilled labor go largely unheard.

Constituent service may be the strongest glue binding congressmen to the
voters. Former Congressman John Duncan, who became the ranking member of
the House Ways and Means Committee, was known for personally delivering
Social Security and Veterans Administration checks to needy constituents in
their homes. Former congressman Jimmy Quillen drank coffee every Saturday
morning in Kingsport and spent the rest of the day with an "open door" office
for his constituents. Most every member of the delegation does something similar every time the voting schedule in Washington permits. With convenient air
travel to each of the state's airports, members of Congress are expected home
almost every weekend to attend local parades and dinners. The last congressman
with an aversion to air travel who only returned to Tennessee a few times a year
was Joe Evins, who retired in 1976. He was followed by Al Gore, Jr., who, stung
by the memory of his father's defeat in 1970 for being anti-war and "out of touch
with Tennessee," made a relentless goal of staying close to home. He did not wait
to be invited; he called over one thousand "open meetings" of his own from 1977
to 1983. His successors have felt obligated to try to continue the pace.

BECOMING MORE LIKE OUR SOUTHERN NEIGHBORS

The role of ideology has recently increased in state elections. Republican primary fights, once unheard of, are increasingly common as religious conservatives
battle "business" Republicans. Many voters are divided both on policies and on
the sources of the policies: should answers to social problems be addressed at the
state or federal level? Gun control is usually a hot issue at election time, and federal laws are unpopular even when they imitate successful state reforms. For
example, although for thirty years Tennessee has had a fifteen-day waiting period for handgun purchases, many Tennessee voters have found a federal seven-day
waiting period troublesome. Issues like abortion and school prayer strike strong
chords in Tennessee, which probably has more creationists today than it did in
1925, the year of the Scopes "Monkey" Trial in Dayton, Tennessee. The popular
play based on this trial, *Inherit the Wind*, can still generate a hot debate in rural
Tennessee counties. Not many ministers have been candidates yet (the state constitution used to ban their candidacy), but more and more churches have become
expert at voter registration and poll watching. It is not unusual to have petition

drives against libraries in protest against certain books on their shelves, or petitions against sale of alcoholic beverages. The Tennessee Constitution is one of the strictest in the nation, banning all forms of gambling, even church bingo, despite the proliferation of lotteries and river casinos around the state's borders.

On the Democratic side, labor unions and African Americans have started to demand stricter loyalty from officeholders who have won their support. Issues like striker replacement, health care reform, family and medical leave, and mandatory plant closure notice have been hot-button issues for labor leadership, although many union members may care about gun-control and religious issues more than these workplace issues. Minority issues of preserving affirmative action and set-asides, ending capital punishment, and improving welfare reform can still be litmus tests. All in all, the current political landscape in Tennessee is becoming more fractured and more hotly debated than in the recent past, making our political climate more similar to that of many of our Southern neighbors.

PERSONALITY IS KEY

In Washington, probably the most repeated story about a member of the Tennessee delegation tells of the defeat of the former Ways and Means Chairman, Jerry Cooper, back in the late 1950s. A folksy challenger Robert "Fats" Everett went around the West Tennessee district speaking to farm audiences and asking them which committee Jerry was on in Washington. "Is he on the Agriculture Committee so that he could help the farmer? Is he on the Public Works Committee so that he could build better roads? No! He is on the Ways and Means Committee, which figures out ways and means to get their hand in your pocket to take your tax dollars. And Jerry is so good at it, they've made him chairman of the whole darned committee!" Needless to say, Jerry Cooper was defeated in the next election by Fats, who went on to serve on the Agriculture Committee. In the opinion of the late Speaker Tip O'Neill, no mean story teller himself, Fats was the most engaging member of Congress.

This story tells more than it seems to. In general, the Tennessee delegation has not focused on getting major committee assignments or passing major legislation in Washington but has spent far more time and effort keeping in touch with the folks back home. Constituent service is the daily imperative. Genuine authorship of bills or books is rare. The only major issue-oriented book written by a delegation member is probably Al Gore Jr.'s *Earth in the Balance*.

Several Democratic congressmen have even sacrificed or talked of sacrificing major committee assignments to return home to be mayor, such as Richard Fulton (Ways and Means for Nashville), Bill Boner (Appropriations for Nashville), and Harold Ford (Ways and Means for Memphis). Since Tennessee is a relatively small state, there are no "assigned" spots on any committee for Tennesseans, and it is highly unusual to have more than one Tennessean on a single committee. Committee slots are won by personal lobbying of the party leadership and by supplying regional balance to particular committees.

Personal lobbying has resulted in a number of Tennesseans obtaining party leadership positions in both bodies. Republican Howard Baker became Senate minority leader and then majority leader; Democrat Jim Sasser probably would have been majority leader but for his unexpected defeat in 1994 (he is now the U.S. ambassador to China); Democrat Bart Gordon is on the House leadership ladder, and John Tanner is a leading "Blue Dog," or conservative, Democrat. There are a number of informal groupings of House and Senate members such as the TVA Caucus and the Conservative Democratic Forum in which Tennesseans have played major roles.

CONCLUSION

Members of Congress from Tennessee will tell you that Tennessee voters are some of the most independent, fair-minded, honest, hardworking people on earth and that they expect the same from their elected representatives. Getting the support of Tennesseans is sometimes as tough as riding a Tennessee mule, but no mount is stronger or, when properly communicated with, more reliable. Mules are stubborn at times and they can kick, but you can sure get a lot of work done together.

CHAPTER 11

Trends in Public Opinion,
1989–1996

—John M. Scheb II, William Lyons, and Grant W. Neeley

He who writes of the state, of law, or of politics without first coming to
close quarters with public opinion is simply evading the very central
structure of his study.
—Arthur Bentley, *The Process of Government* (1903)

INTRODUCTION

"Public opinion" consists of the measurable values, beliefs, attitudes, and
opinions of the mass public. Nearly all political scientists, following
Arthur Bentley, recognize the importance of public opinion in politics
and the policy process.[1] While it is true that much of the stuff of public opinion
is unstable or even ephemeral, some elements of public opinion not only endure
but also reveal political preferences and behavior. Certainly, party identification
and ideological self-identification are examples of reasonably stable attitudes that
are linked both to issue positions and to candidate evaluation.[2] Party identification has long been recognized as the main long-term force underlying voters'
positions on policy issues and ultimately influencing their decisions in the voting
booth. Ideological self-identification, while somewhat more changeable than
party identification, is also a relatively stable, enduring political force that is likewise linked to issue positions and voting behavior.[3]

In this chapter, we examine the party identifications and ideological orientations of Tennesseans from 1989 through 1996, as revealed through survey
research. We also look at Tennesseans' positions on several issues of public policy that have been salient in state politics during this period. Our intent is to isolate any trends in the partisan and ideological character of the state while examining citizens' positions on key issues.

The data upon which this chapter is based are derived from the Tennessee
Poll, a statewide survey of adults conducted periodically by the Social Science
Research Institute (SSRI) at the University of Tennessee, Knoxville. The first
Tennessee Poll was taken in April 1989; we have used surveys conducted through
October 1996. During these eight years, SSRI conducted fifteen installments of
the Tennessee Poll, from one to three polls per year, depending on the frequency

of important or controversial issues. In every instance, respondents were interviewed by telephone and selected by random-digit dialing. Sample sizes varied slightly, but with the exception of the 1994 survey (n=694) and the Fall 1996 survey (n=665), the sample size exceeded 800 respondents.[4] In all editions of the Tennessee Poll, the demographics were such that we can be confident that the samples are representative of the adult population of the State.

Over the years the Tennessee Poll has attempted to gauge public opinion on a variety of issues, ranging from people's perceptions of Elvis Presley after his death to their predictions of the outcome of the annual Tennessee-Alabama football game. Many social issues of a more serious nature have been addressed as well, including drug use, teen pregnancy, AIDS, use of the Internet, violence, and pornography. The Tennessee Poll has also assessed public opinion on a fairly large number of public policy issues, including questions involving criminal justice, health care policy, education, and welfare programs. Unfortunately, most of these questions were asked in only one or two polls, reflecting the constantly changing public dialog in the state and national media.

Here we focus on five variables for which we have data over the entire time period: the matters of party identification, ideological self-identification, the state lottery, the state income tax, and abortion. The exact questions taken from the Tennessee Poll are contained in the appendix. Our selection of these questions is not dictated by convenience alone. As suggested above, partisanship and ideology are fundamental to any analysis of public opinion. The lottery, income tax, and abortion issues have been particularly salient in Tennessee politics over the last several years. While far from a complete mapping of the opinion landscape of the state, these data do provide a good sense of the opinion climate. To simplify the presentation as well as smooth out fluctuations due to sampling error, we have averaged the data by year. Thus we will be discussing eight points in time—each of the years from 1989 through 1996.

TRENDS IN PARTISANSHIP

In his 1949 classic *Southern Politics*, V. O. Key remarked that "the forces of history . . . may have destined Republicans to a minority position" in Tennessee politics.[5] While that may have been true for many years after Key made his observation, the level of party competition in Tennessee has increased significantly over the last three decades. Until the early 1960s, Tennessee was a one party state in the tradition of the post–Civil War South. East Tennessee remained solidly Republican while the rest of the state was part of the "solid South" that delivered consistent Democratic victories statewide. This changed in the early sixties with the growth of a less traditional, more ideologically conservative Republican Party in the middle and western parts of the state.

As the national Democratic Party moved to a more liberal position on social issues, especially civil rights, a grassroots conservatism developed in the South and elsewhere. This surge of conservatism helped the Republicans make a strong comeback in the once "solid South." In Tennessee, this new life for the Republicans led to the election of two senators, Howard Baker and Bill Brock, as well as to the first Republican Tennessee governor of the century, Winfield Dunn of Memphis. While the newly rejuvenated Republican Party has greatly invigorated political competition within the state, it has never matched the Democrats in organization or levels of mass voter identification. The East has remained the stronghold of the party, but that strength has not shown the ideological fervor that motivated many of the newer converts. Republicans in East Tennessee follow a tradition of Republicanism dating back to the Civil War. The new Republicans in the Middle and West were more likely to have had Democratic family roots and to find their partisanship grounded in ideological conservatism rather than in family or community tradition.

The two facets of Tennessee Republicanism were very evident in the 1976 Republican presidential primary. Gerald Ford came from the moderate wing of the party. After succeeding Richard Nixon in 1974, he sought the nomination on his own. He was challenged by California Gov. Ronald Reagan, who was the candidate of the more conservative wing of the party. In the Republican primary, Reagan carried Middle and West Tennessee, while Ford won easily in the East. Tennessee had one Republican party, albeit one with a dual personality, but the G.O.P. was finally a force in Tennessee politics.

During the 1980s, the Tennessee G.O.P. enjoyed some statewide success, most notably the election and reelection of Lamar Alexander as governor. Still, the Democrats won both U.S. Senate seats (Gore and Sasser) and continued to dominate the state legislature. However, the 1990s witnessed a dramatic upswing in the Republicans' electoral fortunes. By the end of 1994 the state once again had two Republican senators and a Republican governor. Moreover the Republicans also controlled the state Senate, leaving only the House of Representatives and the soon to be abolished Public Service Commission controlled by the once dominant Democrats. Those developments, however, do not make certain the beginning of a new era of Republican dominance of state politics in Tennessee. In the 1996 elections, the partisan makeup of the U.S. House and Senate delegations remained unchanged, although Democrats won back control of the state Senate.

The Tennessee Poll data on party identification suggest, at least in the near term, close competition and fairly regular swings in power between the parties. In 1981, UT-Chattanooga political scientist Robert Swansborough found that 25 percent of Tennesseans identified with the Republican Party, although he noted that this level was substantially higher than in the South generally.[6] Our data, which reflect the last eight years, indicate that Tennessee now possesses a very competitive partisan environment.[7] On average, over the eight-year period, 30 percent of those surveyed identified themselves as Republicans, as compared with 32 percent as Democrats and 38 percent as independents (see table 1). This level of Republican identification represents a significant increase over the 25 percent level found by Swansborough in 1981, although it is still a long way from

Table 11.1

TRENDS IN TENNESSEE PUBLIC OPINION, 1989–1996

	1989	1990	1991	1992	1993	1994	1995	1996	Avg.
Party Identification									
Democrat	31%	32%	30%	31%	34%	35%	33%	31%	32%
Independent	40%	41%	43%	39%	38%	33%	33%	36%	38%
Republican	30%	27%	27%	30%	28%	32%	34%	33%	30%
Ideology									
Liberal	15%	14%	17%	15%	12%	17%	17%	17%	16%
Moderate	54%	51%	51%	50%	45%	38%	45%	43%	47%
Conservative	31%	35%	32%	35%	43%	45%	38%	40%	37%
State Lottery									
Favor	60%	62%	70%	70%	72%	71%	67%	68%	68%
Not Sure	6%	6%	6%	8%	4%	6%	6%	7%	6%
Oppose	34%	32%	24%	22%	24%	23%	27%	25%	26%
State Income Tax									
Favor	30%	30%	34%	32%	31%	26%	31%	24%	30%
Not Sure	11%	12%	10%	10%	8%	15%	10%	11%	11%
Oppose	59%	58%	56%	58%	61%	59%	59%	65%	59%
Abortion Law									
Easier	5%	7%	9%	7%	10%	n/d	8%	5%	7%
About Right	49%	50%	47%	49%	43%	n/d	46%	50%	48%
Harder	46%	43%	44%	44%	47%	n/d	46%	45%	45%

Note: Data derived from the Tennessee Poll conducted by the Social Science Research Institute at the University of Tennessee, Knoxville, 1989–1996.

a majority. The independents, who number in the plurality, will dictate which party controls government. Thus, divided party government at the state level remains highly likely.

In terms of mass party identification, Tennessee is reasonably consistent with the national picture. Using data collected by the General Social Survey and the National Election Study (see table 2), we estimate that over the 1989–1994 period, 30 percent of Americans identified as Republicans, 37 percent with the Democrats, and 33 percent as independents. Tennessee is therefore indistinguishable from the national environment with respect to the proportion of Republican identifiers. It differs slightly in that Tennesseans are a bit less likely to identify as Democrats and a bit more likely to identify as independents.

Obviously, the elections of Republican Don Sundquist to the governorship and two Republicans, Bill Frist and Fred Thompson, to the U.S. Senate in 1994 (as well as Thompson's re-election in 1996) demonstrate the viability of Republicanism in Tennessee. The resurgence of the Republican Party is certainly not unique to Tennessee, as indicated by the Republican takeover of Congress in 1994. Indeed, the shifting party loyalties of Tennesseans parallel what is happening throughout the South, as whites defect en masse from the Democratic Party. This development is obviously related to race, but it is also related to ideology. In Tennessee, as throughout the South, many whites are apt to eschew a

Table 11.2

NATIONAL TRENDS IN PARTISANSHIP AND IDEOLOGY, 1989–1996

	1989	1990	1991	1992	1993	1994	1995	1996	Avg.
Party Identification									
Democrat	38%	36%	36%	36%	35%	37%	*	42%	37%
Independent	29%	32%	33%	39%	35%	35%	*	28%	33%
Republican	33%	32%	31%	25%	30%	29%	*	30%	30%
Ideology									
Liberal	28%	27%	28%	28%	27%	24%	*	26%	27%
Moderate	39%	36%	40%	31%	37%	36%	*	30%	36%
Conservative	33%	37%	32%	41%	36%	37%	*	44%	37%

Note: Theses data are derived from the General Social Survey, except for 1992 and 1996, which are based on the National Election Studies conducted by the Center for Political Studies at the University of Michigan. The NES data appear to overstate somewhat the proportion of conservatives and understate the proportion of Republicans. This is, no doubt, due to slight differences in instrumentation between the GSS and the NES. Still, the average for the eight-year period provides a reasonable estimate of these parameters during this time-frame.

Democratic Party that they perceive to be too liberal. Indeed, in our aggregated 1989–1996 data, 63 percent of black respondents but only 28 percent of white respondents identified themselves as Democrats (see table 5). Our additional research found that as a group, these white Democrats tend to be less well educated, less affluent, older citizens than whites identifying themselves as Republicans or independents. They are also much more likely to be comfortable with the "liberal" label, which brings us to the next topic—ideology.

TRENDS IN IDEOLOGICAL SELF-IDENTIFICATION

While there are a number of ways to conceptualize ideological variation, the standard device is the liberal-conservative continuum that ranges from "very liberal" or "extremely liberal" on the "far left" to "very conservative" or "extremely conservative" on the "far right."[8] Viewing the liberal-conservative continuum more simply as a trichotomy (i.e., "liberal", "moderate" and "conservative"), our data show that the proportion of liberals in Tennessee has remained fairly stable (and small) over the eight year period (see table 1).[9] On average, only 16 percent of Tennesseans prefer the liberal moniker. This stands in sharp contrast to our national estimate in which 28 percent of Americans are identified as liberals for the entire time-frame. Our data suggest that, as with Democratic identifiers, liberals in Tennessee tend to be less educated and less well-off than other citizens. Interestingly, our data suggest that while blacks are much more likely than whites to call themselves Democrats (63 percent to 28 percent), they are only marginally more likely than whites to self-identify as liberals (23 percent to 14 percent).

The proportion of self-identified conservatives increased substantially throughout the eight-year period. Whereas in 1989 about 31 percent identified as conservatives, in 1994 the number grew dramatically to 45 percent. It then decreased significantly in 1995 to 38 percent, perhaps as a reaction to perceived excesses of the national Republican agenda. In 1996, the proportion of conservatives bounced back to 40 percent. The average for the entire period is 37 percent, which is remarkably close to the national norm (see tables 1 and 2).

The percentage of Tennesseans identifying themselves as moderates dropped significantly from 54 percent in 1989 to 38 percent in 1994. Of course, in that year, Tennesseans gave the Republicans huge electoral victories that helped the GOP take control of Congress. In 1995, Tennesseans appeared to pull back to the center. The proportion of moderates jumped from 38 percent to 45 percent. The proportion of conservatives dropped from 45 percent to 38 percent (the proportion of liberals remained constant at 17 percent). The 1996 data do not reveal statistically significant differences in ideology and partisanship from 1995.

Averaging the data over time makes clear that Tennesseans are more likely than Americans generally to self-define as moderates (compare tables 1 and 2). They are just about as likely as Americans generally to identify themselves as conservatives. But Tennesseans are considerably less likely to adopt the liberal label. Viewing the liberal-moderate-conservative trichotomy as an interval measure, one can clearly say that the central tendency of Tennesseans falls somewhat to the right of Americans generally. It would be fair to characterize the Tennessee political environment as moderately conservative. This label is consistent with the observation that most, if not all, successful statewide Republican candidates, including Lamar Alexander, Don Sundquist, Fred Thompson, and Bill Frist, have avoided making obvious appeals to the far right in their campaigns.

THE STATE LOTTERY ISSUE

In the late 1980s, Tennesseans became interested in the possibility of establishing a state lottery to supplement or replace other sources of state revenue. As adjoining states like Georgia, Kentucky, and Virginia adopted lotteries, concern mounted that Tennessee was losing sales tax revenue as consumers near the borders crossed state lines to buy gasoline and groceries at stores where they could also purchase lottery tickets. Since 1989, the Tennessee Poll has included the following question: "Some have suggested a state lottery for Tennessee. How do you feel? Would you favor or oppose instituting a lottery in Tennessee?" The Tennessee Poll has consistently found high levels of public support for the lottery. On average over the eight-year period, about two-thirds of respondents have indicated support for the concept; about one-quarter have expressed opposition. Opposition to the lottery is most intense among strong conservatives, the elderly, people who live in rural/farming areas, fundamentalist Protestants, and, interestingly, those with the highest levels of education.

Despite strong public backing, there has been little movement in the General Assembly to enact a lottery for Tennessee. Many no doubt wonder how the status quo can remain intact in the face of this much support for a change in policy. Most people are probably unaware that the state Constitution prohibits lotteries and that changing it is extremely difficult. However, in the 1994 legislative session a call for a state constitutional convention was almost approved. The major stumbling block came in the state Senate, where a number of senators based their opposition on their personal values. Most of these senators are unlikely to change their views, regardless of the degree of support for the lottery among their constituents. This reflects the traditional political culture still apparent in Tennessee. The fact that the citizenry tolerates a few senators' ability to prevent a procedure to consider a policy favored by the majority underlines the deference to authority that is part of such a culture.

THE STATE INCOME TAX

In their seminal textbook *Government in Tennessee*, Greene, Grubbs, and Hobday remarked that "if controversies are lacking, a fight can always be stirred up on taxes."[10] A long-standing question in this state has been whether to institute a personal income tax. Greene, et al. thought that "the insatiable demand for governmental expenditure" might lead to the adoption of such a tax, although they admitted that "by all signs it is unwelcome at present."[11] Tennessee relies primarily on a very high sales tax to generate revenue. This system is often criticized as regressive and unstable. At times, such as during Ned McWherter's second term as governor, the issue has actually made it onto the public agenda, but never has an income tax proposal come anywhere close to being enacted.

Governor McWherter had given many people reason to believe that he would aggressively support tax reform once he was elected to his second term. He had noted the unfairness in the highly regressive sales tax and the system's inability to keep pace with economic growth. However, McWherter did not fully utilize his political resources in seeking to bring about tax reform. Some observers believe that the only chance for a general state income tax would be to embed it in broad-based tax reform enthusiastically marketed by a popular political figure. McWherter never vigorously championed his proposals, and the window of political opportunity soon shut tight. In the increasingly antitax 1990s, serious consideration of an income tax by state politicians seems doubtful. In the 1994 election for Governor, both Republican Don Sundquist and Democrat Phil Bredesen took firm stands against the income tax.

While a substantial minority of Tennesseans favor a state income tax, the weight of public opinion is clearly on the other side (see table 1). There appears to be very little prospect for change in the climate of opinion on this issue. Rather, any movement appears to be away from support for the income tax. As a policy issue, a state income tax may not yet be dead and buried, but it is clearly "on life support." Although there is a viable, well-funded organization called Tennesseans for Fair Taxation that is committed to keeping the issue alive, most politicians in the state would be more than happy to "pull the plug."

THE ABORTION ISSUE

Although abortion remains one of the most hotly contested policy issues on the national scene, the debate in Tennessee has not been nearly as contentious. The issue has not figured prominently in campaign rhetoric nor have antiabortion protests in Tennessee been characterized by the violence that other states have witnessed. Still, an examination of Tennesseans' views on this divisive national issue is warranted and revealing.

As table 1 indicates, few Tennesseans want getting an abortion made easier. A substantial minority, approaching a majority, would like to see them made harder to obtain. Does this mean that Tennesseans would support a fundamental change in policy on this issue? To test that hypothesis, we included the following question in the October 1995 survey: "Do you think that the United States Supreme Court should overturn or uphold its 1973 decision in *Roe v. Wade* which effectively legalized abortion in this country?" Although a substantial minority (39 percent) favored overturning *Roe*, a greater percentage (49 percent) preferred that the decision be upheld (12 percent were not sure).[12] Like Americans generally, Tennesseans are troubled by the abortion issue and would like to see the number of abortions reduced, but most of them do not support a fundamental change in public policy in this area.

In many ways Tennessee has been spared the most divisive political battles on the abortion front. While the pro-life movement has become increasingly active in attempting to elect lawmakers with like views, very few have taken office, despite the Republican electoral successes in recent years. Moreover, organizations such as Operation Rescue have not undertaken major efforts within our state. Perhaps the even split in public opinion, in a broader climate of more moderate conservatism, has injected a bit of caution into the thinking of any politician risking alienating opponents on either side of the issue.

IDEOLOGY, PARTISANSHIP AND POLICY ISSUES

In Tennessee, as in national politics, ideology and party identification are definitely related, though they are far from synonymous. In our aggregated data, 49 percent of the self-described liberals interviewed by the Tennessee Poll also described themselves as Democrats (see table 3). More than one-third of the liberals (36 percent) preferred the "Independent" label. Similarly, only 42 percent of conservatives identified themselves as Republicans, with 33 percent of them preferring to cast themselves as independents. Looking at the relationship the other way, only 8 percent of Republicans describe themselves as liberals, whereas 24 percent of Democrats espouse the liberal label. Not surprisingly, independents are most likely to self-define as moderates; moderates are most likely to identify themselves as independents. Ideological moderates are more likely to attach themselves to the Democrats than to the Republicans (32 percent to 24 percent), but independents are twice as likely to self-define as conservatives than as liberals (31 percent to 14 percent).

Table 11.3

ISSUE POSITIONS BY PARTY IDENTIFICATION AND IDEOLOGY (1989–96 aggregated)

	Democrat	Independent	Republican	Liberal	Moderate	Conservative
Party Identification						
Democrat	—	—	—	49%	32%	25%
Independent	—	—	—	36%	45%	33%
Republican	—	—	—	15%	24%	42%
Ideology						
Liberal	24%	14%	8%	—	—	—
Moderate	48%	55%	39%	—	—	—
Conservative	28%	31%	53%	—	—	—
State Lottery						
Favor	64%	64%	57%	73%	66%	54%
Not Sure	6%	5%	5%	4%	5%	5%
Oppose	30%	31%	38%	23%	29%	41%
State Income Tax						
Favor	35%	31%	27%	38%	33%	26%
Not Sure	10%	9%	9%	8%	9%	9%
Oppose	55%	60%	64%	54%	58%	65%
Abortion Law						
Easier	13%	10%	7%	14%	11%	7%
About Right	50%	46%	39%	58%	51%	33%
Harder	38%	44%	54%	28%	39%	60%

Note: Data derived from the Tennessee Poll conducted by the Social Science Research Institute at the University of Tennessee, Knoxville, March 1996.

In terms of policy issues, Republicans and conservatives are much more likely to favor toughening abortion laws. Both groups also manifest greater levels of opposition to the lottery and to the income tax. However, the relationship between ideology and the income tax issue is very weak, suggesting that ideological orientations among Tennesseans today may have more to do with social and moral questions (e.g., gambling and abortion) than with pocketbook issues.

REGIONALISM WITHIN THE STATE

Students of state politics have for many years noted that Tennessee is divided into three grand divisions, each of which is culturally and politically distinctive. Our data suggest that regionalism is becoming less significant as a determinant of public opinion (see table 4). While it remains true that East Tennessee is the most Republican of the three grand divisions, the differences in partisan identification across the state are not that pronounced. The same is true of ideology. The East and Middle regions are identical; the West is slightly more conservative. The three regions are indistinguishable in terms of their collective sentiments regarding the lottery and are only marginally different on the abortion and income tax issues. It appears that the state's political culture, once regarded as tripartite in character, has become largely homogenized.

Table 11.4

PARTY IDENTIFICATION, IDEOLOGY, AND ISSUE POSITIONS BY REGION
(1989–96 aggregated)

	East Tennessee	Middle Tennessee	West Tennessee
Party Identification			
Democrat	27%	36%	37%
Independent	41%	41%	35%
Republican	33%	23%	29%
Ideology			
Liberal	15%	16%	15%
Moderate	49%	49%	46%
Conservative	36%	36%	39%
State Lottery			
Favor	62%	62%	62%
Not Sure	6%	5%	6%
Oppose	33%	33%	33%
State Income Tax			
Favor	29%	32%	30%
Not Sure	10%	10%	11%
Oppose	61%	58%	59%
Abortion Law			
Easier	9%	10%	11%
About Right	43%	48%	44%
Harder	47%	42%	46%

Note: Data derived from the Tennessee Poll conducted by the Social Science Research Institute at the University of Tennessee, Knoxville, March 1996.

RACE, GENDER, AND SOCIOECONOMIC STATUS

Racial differences in American public opinion are well documented. Tennesseans are no exception. There are clear differences between Anglos and African Americans in Tennessee on all the variables included in this study (see table 5). By far the most pronounced racial differences are in the area of partisanship, with blacks more than twice as likely as whites to identify as Democrats and whites more than three times as likely as blacks to self-identify as Republicans. Blacks are also somewhat more likely to see themselves as liberals but, interestingly, almost as likely as whites to self-define as conservatives. On the lottery issue, there are no racial differences. On abortion, blacks are somewhat more likely to favor the pro-choice position. As a group, blacks are significantly more supportive of instituting a state income tax.

Our data also reveal something of a "gender gap" in Tennessee with respect to party identification (see table 5). Women are significantly more likely to embrace the Democrats and slightly less likely to adhere to the Republican Party. In terms of ideology, women as a group are less conservative than are men, but the gap is fairly narrow here (indeed, it is within the margin of error and therefore may be a statistical artifact). On the issues, there are some differences, but none are especially dramatic.

Table 11.5

PARTISANSHIP, IDEOLOGY AND ISSUE POSITIONS BY RACE, GENDER AND SOCIOECONOMIC STATUS, 1989–1996 (aggregated)

	Male	Female	White	Black	Low Income	Middle Income	High Income
Party Identification							
Democrat	28%	36%	28%	63%	39%	29%	25%
Independent	42%	37%	41%	27%	38%	41%	38%
Republican	30%	27%	31%	11%	23%	31%	38%
Ideology							
Liberal	14%	17%	14%	23%	17%	15%	14%
Moderate	47%	49%	49%	42%	46%	51%	49%
Conservative	39%	35%	37%	35%	37%	34%	38%
State Lottery							
Favor	66%	59%	62%	62%	63%	65%	59%
Not Sure	4%	6%	5%	5%	6%	4%	6%
Oppose	30%	35%	33%	33%	32%	31%	35%
State Income Tax							
Favor	31%	30%	29%	41%	31%	31%	31%
Not Sure	7%	13%	10%	11%	13%	7%	7%
Oppose	62%	57%	61%	49%	57%	62%	62%
Abortion Law							
Easier	10%	10%	9%	15%	11%	10%	8%
About Right	47%	43%	45%	44%	38%	48%	51%
Harder	44%	47%	46%	42%	51%	42%	41%

Note: (1) Data derived from the Tennessee Poll conducted by the Social Science Research Institute at the University of Tennessee, Knoxville, 1989–1996. (2) "Low income" includes respondents whose annual household income is less than $15,000; "middle income" includes respondents whose annual household income is between $15,000 and $50,000; "high income" includes respondents whose annual household income exceeds $50,000.

Finally, we come to socioeconomic status (see table 5). As we noted earlier, there is a relationship between income and party identification. In keeping with conventional wisdom, Democrats are, on average, less well off than Republicans. This difference in partisanship does not translate into dramatic ideological differences across income levels, however. Low-income, middle income, and high income Tennesseans do not differ very much when it comes to the three issues either. Of course, one might posit other issues beyond the scope of this study on which dramatic differences would emerge.

CONCLUSION

Tennessee politics has become more competitive over the last half century. Public opinion data collected over the last eight years paint a picture of a state whose electorate may be flirting with a switch to a period of Republican dominance. But, as of 1996, the Democrats remain competitive.

Tennesseans have cemented their opposition to an income tax and have concretized their support for a lottery, but they remain sharply divided on abortion. Remarkable consistency characterizes the latter two issues. No definitive evidence yet exists to indicate whether Tennessee voters will continue a more conservative, Republican drift, and whether this drift will lead to a more conflictual political environment, especially concerning the abortion issue. In terms of the state's political culture, our data suggest that differences among the state's traditional divisions may be disappearing. Indeed, in many ways Tennessee's political culture is increasingly reflective of the nation as a whole. Just as regionalism within the state is becoming less of a factor, regionalism around the country likewise appears to be diminishing. As more and more political communication is nationally based, we would expect these trends to continue.

Part IV
POLICIES

CHAPTER 12

Education in the Volunteer State
—Nancy Keese and James Huffman

INTRODUCTION

For many years, Tennessee state politicians were reluctant to put forward policies regarding the conduct of education in the state, leaving the basic issues of education policy to professional educators, who might be called upon to advise state officials. Recent events in Tennessee's educational arena illustrate the shift to increased political involvement in educational policy making at the local and national levels.

Until the 1960s, governors and legislators, who usually lacked expertise about educational matters, allocated funds for educational programs and institutions as requested by educators.[1] Thus educators, in effect, set educational policy. The 1960s and 1970s brought a dramatic expansion of state government involvement in education. Increased federal aid to all levels of schooling required that state educational agencies distribute funds and supervise the implementation of educational programs. This intrusion of state government into the affairs of education was a concern at all levels but was of special concern in higher education, where it was viewed as a threat to the autonomy of the institutions.[2]

Involvement of state government in the distribution of educational funds continued into the 1980s and 1990s and was expanded to include legislation related to the process and quality of education. Many national reports of the 1980s described the mediocrity of education and initiated an educational reform movement that brought about state legislation aimed at improving school performance.[3] Legislators began to ask for more precise evaluation of the results of schooling before agreeing to financial expenditures. Many states passed bills related to teacher certification and teacher evaluation, which involved state accreditation and licensing requirements aimed at increasing standards for entering the profession. The resulting policies affecting testing and curriculum design narrowed teachers' autonomy in the classroom. Often bills had the effect of restricting teachers' professional judgments in meeting the needs of students.[4] Colleges and universities received instructions to be economical and efficient, to avoid duplication of programs, and to respond to the needs of the public. Thus, in recent years, educational policy has been directed and reshaped, to a striking degree, by governors and legislators of the states rather than by professional educators.[5]

The configurations of educational interest groups also changed between 1960 and 1990 and contributed an additional influence on the new patterns of educational policy making. Expansion of higher education brought about by the implementation of the G I Bill in the 1940s and further student population growth in the 1960s and 1970s contributed to the growth of new constituencies interested in education. A certain fragmentation of distinct groups—like the National Education Association and the American Federation of Teachers, groups specifically focused on the needs of disabled students, and community and business roundtables and cooperative education efforts—competed to draw attention to teacher demands, the needs of students, and community expectations. The divisiveness among a wide variety of viewpoints espoused by different interest groups, combined with the growing expertise of state politicians, allowed state government to emerge as an educational policy maker.[6]

Organizational structure of the executive and legislative branches of Tennessee government from the 1920s to the mid–1960s allowed for total dominance by the governor. In the late 1960s and 1970s reapportioned congressional districts, lengthened senatorial terms, increased staff, and increased legislative funding from less than $500,000 in the late 1950s to $6.7 million in 1980–81 created the foundation for development of a more independent Tennessee legislature.[7] This new independence and professionalism afforded legislators the means to become influential players in state government. Thus, the national shifts of educational policy making also occurred in Tennessee. Some of the most significant and far-reaching educational policy making in Tennessee history occurred between 1960 and 1990. Reorganization of higher education governance, expansion of post-secondary remedial and developmental programs, creation of new funding formulas, implementation of court-ordered desegregation, and passage of reform bills for K–12 education illustrate the heightened involvement of politicians in policy making during this crucial period in the development of Tennessee education.

TENNESSEE HIGHER EDUCATION COMMISSION

Governance of higher education in Tennessee changed dramatically during the 1960s and 1970s. Reports suggesting further change have continued to emerge in the 1990s. The following paragraphs outline the development of the major higher education institutions in Tennessee and provide background for understanding the unique organizational structure of higher education existing in the state.

Prior to the Civil War, the role of higher education was to prepare gentlemen, not to educate the masses. This dominance by the upper class and the lack of a state responsibility for higher education slowed the development of colleges and universities in Tennessee.

Blount College in Knoxville was chartered as a private institution in 1795, was later renamed East Tennessee College, and in 1879 became the University of Tennessee, which is the state's largest public university today. In 1909 the General Assembly passed the important General Education Bill, which provided support for elementary and secondary education and for teacher training.[8] This bill led to the establishment of three normal, or teacher training, schools to prepare white teachers and one normal school to prepare African American teachers. The white schools were located in the three geographic divisions of the state and became East Tennessee State University, Middle Tennessee State University, and The University of Memphis. The African American school, located in Nashville because of the strong support of Nashville African Americans, later became Tennessee State University.[9] The 1915 General Assembly established Tennessee Polytechnic Institute (later Tennessee Technological University), and in 1927 Austin Peay State Normal School (now University) and the University of Tennessee Junior College (now full university status) at Martin were established.

The private higher education institutions of Tennessee, while not governed by the state, contribute to the national reputation of Tennessee. Rhodes College in Memphis and the University of the South at Sewanee are small, religiously affiliated institutions with nationally recognized reputations and rich traditions. Fisk in Nashville, which began in 1867, has been a leader in the education of African-Americans. Davidson Academy was established in 1785, closed and reopened as the University of Nashville, became George Peabody College for Teachers in 1909, and is now Peabody College of Vanderbilt University.[10] A private research institution with professional schools in divinity, education, engineering, law, management, medicine, music, and nursing, Vanderbilt University was endowed in 1873 by Cornelius Vanderbilt. Numerous other private institutions are located across the state and contribute to a strong voice in higher education.

Before World War II, the primary goals of Tennessee higher education were teacher training and agricultural and mechanical training. After the war, increased enrollment, a changing economy, and public demand for curricular diversity brought about expanded programs and facilities at the regional universities to meet the needs of Tennesseans. Additionally, the community college system developed to meet these needs. It continues to provide post-secondary education to large numbers of people in all regions of the state.[11]

Tennessee higher education operated with two types of governance prior to 1967. The University of Tennessee Board of Trustees directed the divisions and junior colleges of the University of Tennessee, while the State Board of Education directed the regional normal schools along with the public schools in the ninety-five counties. Although both boards were appointed by the governor, there was no overall coordination of schooling in Tennessee. In fact, there was overlap of programs, competition for students, and competition for funding between and within the two boards. The governor had the power to make decisions regarding the state budget as well as the political control to pass appropriations bills to fund the budget.

College and university presidents in both systems of higher education met with the governor and the leaders of the legislature to appeal for funds to operate their institutions. The University of Tennessee was a long-established organization that gained support with the Farm Bureau through its agricultural programs and with the public through its football program. Dr. Andrew Holt, president of the University of Tennessee from 1959 to 1970, was very successful in obtaining funds for the university. The State Board of Education operated both 1–12 schools (kindergarten was not a state function until the Comprehensive Education Reform Act of 1984) and the regional universities, creating competition for resources within the agency. Officials with the regional universities complained that elementary and secondary schools, with their larger student population, received more attention from the State Board of Education. In any case, the allocation of resources for education depended on the political influence of the negotiators.[12]

Expansion of programs and facilities at colleges and universities across the state supported the findings of several studies that the regional universities needed more attention and that the two systems of higher education required better coordination. Gov. Buford Ellington attempted to address those needs in 1961 with the establishment of the Coordinating Committee on Higher Education, but this body had no authority and eventually failed. Finally, in his next term, Ellington succeeded in persuading the legislature to pass a bill creating the Tennessee Higher Education Commission (THEC) in 1967.[13] This was no small feat considering the number and influence of people and agencies involved.[14]

Evaluation of THEC in 1971 under Gov. Winfield Dunn was positive. The Governors' Study on Cost Containment found that members of the staff serving THEC were qualified professional personnel and that the commission had made major contributions toward preparation of a master plan of higher education with substantial cost savings. As stated in the *Tennessee Blue Book* (1990–91), the charge to THEC specifically includes private higher education in its assessment and coordination of the higher education needs of Tennesseans. THEC, which is closely monitored by the legislature, is also charged with developing a statewide Master Plan for higher education for use by all policy-making bodies.

TENNESSEE STATE BOARD OF REGENTS

The establishment of THEC did not alter the organization of the State Board of Education, which still had control of 1–12 schools, nine community colleges, three technical institutes, and twenty-five area vocational technical schools along with the six regional universities. Some worried that the regional universities could not receive proper attention and emphasis under this cumbersome structure. In 1968 the University of Tennessee was organized into a system of centers, extension activities, and four major campuses. In 1969 THEC reported the need for a separate board for the regional institutions and a separate board for the community colleges.

In 1970 Winfield Dunn was elected as the first Republican governor in fifty years. Dunn replaced Commissioner of Education J. Howard Warf, who had strong political influence, with Dr. E. C. Stimbert. Dr. Stimbert had less experience than Commissioner Warf and delegated authority to others. This shift in authority caused concern among the regional university and community college presidents, who had worked closely with Warf for many years. Nelson Andrews, a Nashville businessman, was appointed by the governor to chair a committee to recommend needed changes in the governance of Tennessee higher education for effective, efficient management and educational excellence. This committee recommended separate boards for the regional universities and for the community colleges. To overcome the opposition to the two proposed bodies, a coalition of universities and community colleges supported the creation of one body to oversee both of the systems.

The State Board of Regents of the State University and Community College System (SBR) was created in 1972 and became a visible force on the political scene by controlling resources and setting priorities for these schools. Comparable in power to the University of Tennessee Board of Trustees, the SBR became responsible for programs, requirements for degrees, approval of budgets, selection of presidents, and establishing system and operating policies for these schools.[15] In 1983 governance of the state vocational technical institutions was transferred to the SBR. By 1994, according to the *Tennessee Blue Book*, the SBR was operating a system of six state universities, twelve community colleges, two technical institutes, and twenty-six state area vocational technical schools.

FUNDING

The demand for higher education increased from 1965 to 1995, but the funding of education, particularly higher education, has not always been seen as a public responsibility. Establishment of early universities was aided by the sale of public lands, but it was 1881 before any state appropriations were made for higher education in Tennessee. The General Education Act of 1909, which established four normal schools, also provided the first state funding formula for higher education. Through this formula, each of three white schools would receive two-sevenths of the annual normal school appropriation, and an African-American school would receive one-seventh.[16]

THEC was charged with developing policies for the "fair and equitable distribution" of public funds to the state higher education institutions. That charge still applies today.[17] The commission was specifically directed to consider enrollment projections; institution functions, services, and academic programs; and levels of instruction in its distribution of funds. Total expenditure requirements for instruction served as the base of the funding formula. Costs for other functions would be computed as a percentage of this base.[18]

The national trend toward accountability for educational outcomes during the 1970s and 1980s created a dissatisfaction with traditional funding based on enrollment. This dissatisfaction was compounded by a concern for the high attrition rate in colleges and universities. The increased demand for accountability led to a legislative interest in performance funding as a method to assure that constituents were getting their money's worth. The Performance Funding Project, started in 1974 by THEC, explored the possibility of allocating a portion of state funds based on effectiveness rather than on enrollment. Performance indicators included in the study related to student enrollment and test scores, full-time and part-time faculty, research proposals, degrees awarded, and alumni giving.[19] In 1979 the Commission initiated incentives for improvement through performance funding. Beginning in 1984, additional funding of up to 5 percent of the appropriations was allowed based on how well the institution was meeting statewide performance criteria. Representative John Bragg (Dem., Murfreesboro), who was the leading state financial expert, added accountability in the form of "Bragg Marks" to the Comprehensive Education Reform Act (CERA). Bragg Marks required institutions to set goals for the improvement of entrance scores, the number of graduates, National Teacher Examination scores and other standardized test scores for graduates, the number of research and public-service activities, library holdings, and job-placement rates.[20]

Another event that affected higher education funding and that also illustrates the shift in the role of state legislators involved implementation of remedial and developmental studies for under-prepared students at the post-secondary institutions.[21] A 1984 report, *A White Paper,* described the widespread deficiencies in preparation of freshmen entering college level courses. In response to this report, legislators voted to provide funds to colleges and universities for remedial and developmental programs. The mandate provided guidelines for placement of students, defined competencies required for successful completion of the developmental program, and prescribed limited access to college-level work until students had removed academic deficiencies. This legislative action exacerbated the public perception that Tennessee's public schools were failing to educate its children. Because extensive reform was going on in K–12 education, there was an assumption that the enrollment in remedial and developmental courses would steadily decline during the next five years as K–12 education improved. Instead, the enrollment and accompanying expenditures for this program increased, while budgets for higher education in general remained stable or were reduced. The competition for money, loyalty to the mission of the institution, and the belief in reform at the secondary level provided an atmosphere of conflict of interest among the remedial and developmental programs, the college and university programs, and the secondary schools.

GEIER V. BLANTON

Another important issue in Tennessee higher education in the last thirty years, and one that illustrates involvement of the courts and politics in the making of educational policy, is desegregation. A landmark case involving Tennessee State University (TSU) and the University of Tennessee at Nashville (UTN) in the 1960s and 1970s was precedent setting and continues to affect higher education institutions today.[22]

The University of Tennessee (UT) operated a night school extension program in Nashville in the early 1960s. When UT announced plans to build a multimillion dollar facility to house its Nashville extension, Rita Sanders, later Rita Geier, filed a lawsuit. It charged that the expansion of UTN would foster segregation at TSU as the two schools were only three miles apart and competed for the same students. The defendants, including Gov. Buford Ellington, the UT Board of Trustees, and the Tennessee Board of Education maintained that the UTN and TSU missions were so different that they were not in competition for the same students. According to the defendants, TSU was a historically African American land-grant institution whose students were primarily younger, day students, and the UTN night programs attracted part-time adult white and black students who worked full-time. U. S. District Court Judge Frank Gray allowed the UTN facility to be built but ordered the dismantling of the dual higher education system, in effect ordering desegretation of the statewide system. During the ensuing years, plans and reports were filed to monitor progress toward a state desegregation plan with attention to TSU. Judge Gray finally concluded that the groups involved were not going to be successful in developing a constitutionally satisfactory desegregation plan. In January of 1977, after almost nine years under a court order to desegregate higher education, he ordered the merger of Tennessee State University and the University of Tennessee-Nashville under governance of SBR. By 1979 appeals had been exhausted in the lower courts. The U. S. Supreme Court declined to review the case and the merger proceeded on time.

The results of the case were far-reaching and continue to be felt in Tennessee's higher education community today. No court had ruled that any higher education system desegregate prior to Judge Gray's 1968 decision, although some mergers had taken place without court involvement. The people and agencies involved in the case changed through two governors, a new president and new chancellor of the two institutions, and the establishment of THEC and the SBR during the years 1968–1977. TSU remains a predominantly African-American university; but the merging of faculty, students, and programs has provided progress toward desegregation of the higher education system. THEC policies regarding the restriction of duplicative programs, designation of geographic areas in which institutions can offer classes or programs, monitoring of minority enrollment, and hiring of minority faculty and staff are the direct result of the *Geier* case.

K–12 PUBLIC EDUCATION POLICY

The political influence on education since the 1960s has not been limited to higher education. The national reports on the mediocrity of education led to reform that was felt at all levels of education. Legislation was passed in many states that attempted to control who taught, what they taught, and how they taught.

THE COMPREHENSIVE EDUCATION REFORM ACT (CERA)

One of the two most significant and comprehensive educational policy initiatives in Tennessee during the past 30 years was the Comprehensive Education Reform Act, passed by the legislature in 1984. There had been little in the way of policy initiatives affecting K–12 education in the state since the 1950s. By the early 1980s, due to changing social and economic conditions and the educational status of Tennessee in comparison with other states (ranking in the bottom quartile in funding education and below numerous states in student achievement), policy makers believed it was time for an assessment of education in the state to provide a basis for promoting educational improvement. Gov. Lamar Alexander and other policy makers were convinced that the quality of education was critical to the future economic development of the state. The Ninety-Second General Assembly passed a joint resolution providing for the creation of an Education Task Force to conduct a comprehensive study of public education in Tennessee. The study was to examine programs, staff and personnel, organization, finances, and facilities.

An Education Task Force consisting of twenty-seven members was appointed, and the Tennessee Comprehensive Education Study was initiated in 1981. Charged with the responsibility of developing a long-range plan for the system of public education in Tennessee, the Task Force undertook a thorough examination of the system's administrative and organizational structure, an assessment of goals from kindergarten through graduate education, a study of the system's economic and financial prospects, and a review of procedures for distributing funds. The Task Force reviewed pertinent literature, heard testimony from consultants and citizens in open and closed hearings, examined four statewide surveys, and reviewed results of standardized tests. The study was completed and recommendations were made to Governor Alexander in 1983.

The recommendations from the Task Force were used by the Alexander administration to promulgate a ten-point education program that constituted the major plans for the Better Schools Program. Alexander made this program the centerpiece of his second term and promoted the program extensively. It should be noted that the introduction of the Better Schools Program slightly preceded the release of the federal government's much publicized report *A Nation at Risk* in April 1983. The report focused increased national attention on educational reform, and the promotion of the Better Schools Program in Tennessee likely benefited from this attention. Also, many of the recommendations from *A*

Nation at Risk closely paralleled the major planks of the Better Schools Program, resulting in greater national attention on Tennessee's reform effort.[23]

In his State of Education address to the legislature in January 1983, Governor Alexander outlined his ten-point Better Schools Program: basic skills first, computer skills next, kindergarten for every child, more high school math and science, summer schools for gifted juniors and seniors, a redefined vocational education curriculum, better classroom discipline, job-skills training, centers of excellence at universities, and a master teacher program.

After announcing the Better Schools Program, Alexander campaigned for acceptance of the program across Tennessee with the message that better schools would mean better skills, better jobs, and higher income for Tennessee families.[24] The Governor urged citizens throughout the state to encourage their legislators to support the program. He also worked with various professional education groups, such as the Board of Directors of the Tennessee Education Association, the Tennessee School Boards Association, and the Tennessee Organization of School Superintendents in an effort to gain support for the program.[25] A bipartisan Select Committee of fourteen members of the House and Senate was formed to work on the program. Aware that taxpayer support was critical to the success of the program, the Select Committee held hearings throughout the state. Those attending the hearings were generally supportive of the program.

As the Better Schools Program was being promoted and debated across the state, the Master Teacher provision (later to become the Career Ladder Program) emerged as the most controversial part of the program. Teachers were apprehensive about the fairness of making determinations regarding merit in teaching that would lead to differentiation in pay. This apprehension was expressed through the Tennessee Education Association (TEA), which opposed the Master Teacher provision of the program. This constituted the strongest opposition to the Better Schools Program.

A special legislative session of the Tennessee General Assembly was convened in January 1984 to deal exclusively with educational reform legislation. Because of the controversy surrounding the merit pay provision, the Career Ladder bill was a prime topic of debate during the session. Groups such as the TEA and the Select Legislative Committee influenced the final version of the bill, which the Tennessee legislature passed on March 6, 1984, as the Comprehensive Education Reform Act (CERA). An increase of one cent in the sales tax and an increase in certain business taxes were necessary to finance the bill.

A number of reforms were put into place as a result of the CERA legislation. The bill created the Career Ladder Program, allowing for the evaluation of teachers and administrators for the purpose of differentiating pay among those on different levels of the ladder. It created a thirteen-member State Certification Commission responsible for reviewing and recommending applications for advancement submitted by teachers, principals, and supervisors. The Commission was empowered to establish guidelines and minimum standards for evaluating those persons climbing the career ladder.

The CERA legislation set forth a number of requirements for admission to teacher training and for certification by the state: every prospective teacher must attain an acceptable score on the Pre-Professional Skills Test (PPST); all teachers must be graduates of higher education institutions approved by the state in which they are located; teacher education students must spend a significant portion of three academic quarters in classroom observation and teaching; and they must pass a standardized test before they can be certified.[26]

CERA provides for the State Board of Education to review the scores on the state teachers examination for each public and private teacher training institution. If 30 percent or more of an institution's students fail the examination in a given year, the school will be placed on probation; if the condition persists for two consecutive years, certification will be revoked by the State Board of Education. The legislation also calls for all full-time faculty in the field of education to further their professional development by having direct personal involvement in the K–12 public school setting on a periodic basis. CERA also establishes the Tennessee Principal-Administrator Academy to provide training for school leaders and specifies that all administrators attend the Academy at least once every five years. The Tennessee Student Assistance Corporation was established by the act to provide a tuition loan program for students who agree to teach math or science in Tennessee public schools for at least four years.

Another policy change that was viewed as vital to the success of the Better Schools Program was the Public Education Governance Reform Act (PEGRA) of 1984, which was introduced by Lt. Gov. John Wilder. The bill clarified the relationship between the State Board of Education and the State Commissioner of Education and provided for clearer lay governance of public education. The bill stipulated that members of the State Board of Education be lay persons and disallowed professional educators from serving. The Board reports directly to the legislature instead of to the commissioner of education, which had previously been the case. The State Board of Education was provided with its own staff rather than forced to rely on the State Department of Education staff, as done previously. Under the new structure, the State Board of Education is responsible for developing policy for K–12 public education. The State Department of Education, under the direction of the Commissioner of Education, has the responsibility for implementing the policies.[27] The law stipulated that the State Board of Education will consist of a public high school student and a person from each of the state's congressional districts, as well as the director of the Tennessee Higher Education Commission acting as a non-voting ex officio member. Members of the Board are appointed by the governor for nine-year terms subject to confirmation by the Senate and House. The law stipulated that no voting member may be an elected official, an employee of the federal, state, or local government, or an educator. Writing in 1985, Robin Pierce, superintendent of the Athens, Tennessee, City Schools, called the Comprehensive Education Reform Act "the single most important piece of legislation relative to education that has ever been passed in the state of Tennessee." Pierce, whose long experience and widespread reputation make him an excellent sounding board for this landmark legislation, went on to say that "from an educator's point of view, this has to be considered extremely significant because the governor and the General Assembly of the State of Tennessee have declared that education is the top priority for this state."[28]

Pierce noted three profound changes in educational practice resulting from the CERA reform. The first is the way the effectiveness of schools is measured. He stated, "In the past, we have measured schools largely by process; that is, such factors as per pupil expenditures, teacher/pupil ratios, salary schedules, number of library books, number of master's degrees held by staff, etc. CERA will result in schools having their effectiveness measured by outcomes. This means that schools will be measured by the products they send forth, not the process the product goes through."[29] Secondly, Pierce noted the change of paying teachers by performance rather than exclusively by training and experience. He stated that, "the Career Ladder Program mandated in this act is probably the most comprehensive that has been passed by any state to date. In essence, the Career Ladder Program purports to pay teachers who are doing the best job more money than teachers with equal qualifications who are not performing as well."[30] The third change, and the one that Pierce found questionable, is that of having educational policy mandated from the state legislature. He questioned this process, saying "that the changes currently on the horizon are coming from higher up and handed down—in other words, a prescriptive device for improvement from the top down rather than the reverse. The concern I have with this is that much research in recent years indicates that the best run companies in America are using the opposite approach." He went on to say that "current education regulations have not responded to this research, and I feel there is a distinct possibility that top-down decisions will not yield the desired results."[31]

Despite the concerns raised by CERA and the controversy over the Career Ladder provision, there can be no doubt that the Better Schools Program and its accompanying legislation was one of the most significant policy initiatives in education in Tennessee during the past half century. The reform effort pumped considerably more money into public schools, helped impress upon the public the importance of education to the future economic development of the state, and put K–12 education on the "front burner" in terms of public policy in Tennessee. The Better Schools Program and CERA have resulted in a sustained increase in attention on K–12 public education.

STATE BOARD OF EDUCATION MASTER PLAN

The State Board of Education annually develops a master plan for K–12 public education in Tennessee. The master plan that was developed in 1990 was especially significant in terms of guiding educational policy in the state into the next decade. The plan also served as a precursor to the second major education reform bill of the past thirty years, the Education Improvement Act. The Master Plan of 1990 was comprehensive and had as its primary mission to ensure that Tennessee schools were among the best in the nation. At the core of the Master Plan are a number of guiding principles that are reflected through the goals and strategies proposed in the plan. Those guiding principles include: attracting and preparing the best possible school leaders, coupling school-based decision making with accountability for making the decisions, transforming the way children learn through the use of technology and effective teaching strategies, providing all schools with essential resources, giving extra attention to at-risk children, investing in professional development for educators, and establishing the expectation that all children will become educated.[32]

The Master Plan sets forth 17 goals for K–12 education, provides strategies for achieving the goals, and outlines how progress will be measured. Some of the more significant goals pertaining to students include: all children will begin school ready to learn; all children will be able to read, write, and solve mathematical problems by the time they complete the third grade and will demonstrate competency in challenging subject matter by the time they complete the eighth grade; the high school curriculum will be restructured to provide for those students going to college and those going into the world of work (now called the two-path curriculum); and at least 85 percent of all students will complete high school. Included are other goals aimed at the improvement of schools: the teaching profession will attract some of the best and brightest graduates; all leaders of schools will be prepared to demonstrate improved performance of schools; school-based decision making will be emphasized; and the establishment of the Basic Education Program (BEP) will provide adequate and equitable distribution of resources.[33]

The State Board of Education Master Plan of 1990 proposed sweeping reforms and ambitious goals for K–12 education in Tennessee. Implementation of many of the proposed reform initiatives and goals has required legislative action as well as increased funding.

EDUCATION IMPROVEMENT ACT (EIA)

During the 1991 legislative session, the Tennessee legislature dealt with the most sweeping education reform proposals in the history of the state. Senate Bill 1231, introduced by Senator Andy Womack (Dem., Murfreesboro) and House Bill 752, introduced by Rep. Bill Purcell (Dem., Nashville), called for the following major reforms: adequate and equitable funding of K–12 education, less regulation of school systems and schools from the state level, appointment of superintendents by local boards of education, accountability, and increased community involvement at the schools.[34]

While the Senate and House Ethics Committee worked on the bill, various constituencies offered 130 amendments, which kept the Education Improvement Act in committee. Consequently, no action was taken on the bill during the 1991 legislative session. Finally the EIA was passed by the 1992 General Assembly as Public Chapter 535, partially funded by a half-cent sales tax increase.

Numerous significant reforms were implemented by the enactment of EIA. One area of significant change involved the funding of K–12 education. The Education Improvement Act introduced a new funding formula called the Basic Education Program (BEP). This program replaced the Tennessee Foundation Program (TFP), which had been the basis for funding education in Tennessee for decades. While the TFP was based on average daily attendance for funding schools, the BEP is based on average daily membership. The rationale for the change was that a school system has to pay for a student's needs (teacher, desks, materials), regardless of the rate of attendance of the student. The Basic Education Program also differed from the TFP in that it includes capital outlay and cost of operation adjustments. While the Basic Education Program went into effect in July 1992, it was not expected to be fully funded for five to eight years. The Education Improvement Act also established a "Dedicated Education Fund," in which all state education revenues are to be kept separate and can be spent only for K–12 education. Previously, education funds went into the general fund, the money allocated by the legislature on a year-to-year basis. It was stipulated that under the BEP the state is to provide no less than 75 percent of school system funding for classroom components (teachers, materials) and no less that 50 percent of the funding for non-classroom components (capital outlay, transportation). The EIA also waived school activity fees for students qualifying for free or reduced-cost lunches. providing such activities occur during regular school hours.

Another significant change brought about by the Education Improvement Act is a new accountability system for K–12 education. The new system places less emphasis on management and procedures and more emphasis on outcomes. The act directed the commissioner of education to recommend procedures for dealing with student and teacher performance indicators and to urge the state board to adopt the value-added assessment system. These serve as accountability measures based on improvement in student standardized test results. If school systems do not perform adequately in the accountability system, the commissioner of education, with state board approval, is authorized to place systems on probation and to remove the local school board and/or superintendent if improvement is not made. The EIA called for the state board to establish a comprehensive assessment program for students with all high school students required to take an examination to assess their readiness for the workplace or higher education. The EIA also established an Office of Education Accountability within the Comptroller's office, which must submit an annual report to the governor and General Assembly.

The EIA makes some significant changes related to the position of superintendent of schools. It requires that superintendents be appointed by the local school board. Those systems with superintendents elected by the people or appointed by the legislative body were required to decide before the 1994 or 1996 elections whether they wanted to continue the status quo for one additional term.

The Act also gives superintendents final authority for such personnel decisions as employment of teachers, assignment, and tenure recommendations. Previously, the superintendent's recommendation required the approval of the local school board. The law stipulates that the superintendent will employ all principals under written performance-based contracts. It also requires that local school board members be elected by the public.

Related to changes in the area of administration, the EIA allows for the creation of multicounty school systems. If the parties agree, school systems in surrounding counties may combine to provide greater effectiveness and efficiency in operating their schools. The legislation also allows for up to eight school systems to join in operating schools as alternative education programs for students suspended or expelled from grades 7–12 regular classrooms.

In terms of curriculum changes, the EIA stipulates that each school system must operate an approved kindergarten program and that kindergarten attendance be a condition for students to enroll in the first grade. High schools must offer a two-track curriculum (now called paths), one for those entering the work force, the other for those who are college bound. The legislation also allows for ungraded programs in grades K–3 and stipulates that school systems must provide alternative schools for suspended or expelled students.[35]

The Education Improvement Act provided the legislation necessary to implement the reforms and goals set forth in the State Board of Education's Master Plan of 1990. It should be noted that passage of the EIA was greatly aided by the support of Gov. Ned McWherter. Governor McWherter and State Education Commissioner Charles Smith promoted the EIA by presenting the act's proposals for reform in open forums across the state. Improving education in Tennessee was one of McWherter's major goals as governor, and his attention, emphasis, and support resulted in the implementation of some of the most significant educational reforms in Tennessee's history. In the past twenty-five years, Governors McWherter and Alexander, both strongly committed to education improvement and reform, led Tennessee to enact vital policy changes in K–12 education.

THE SCHOOL EQUITY FUNDING CASE

Much of the incentive for the development of the Basic Education Program of the Education Improvement Act of 1992 came from a lawsuit filed against the State of Tennessee in 1988. The lawsuit charged that the Tennessee Foundation Program funding formula resulted in an inequitable distribution of state money to local school systems. Although the state defended the Tennessee Foundation Program in the courts, the legislature recognized, early on, the validity of the plaintiff's case and began to formulate a more equitable funding formula, which resulted in the Basic Education Program.

The Tennessee Foundation Program (TFP) had been established in 1977 for the purpose of equalizing funding for all school systems. The TFP formula allocated state money to local school districts by combining funds for three groups of students: regular academic students, vocational students, and students with disabilities.

A two-year study of the Tennessee Foundation Program, completed in 1979, reported that while the program attempted equalize funding for all school systems, as implemented it did not equalize funding very well. The Tennessee School Finance Equity study found that the TFP had the potential for adequately funding basic education, but only if the base funding was at a much higher level. The Tennessee legislature made no attempt to achieve the much higher level of funding.[36] In 1988 the Tennessee Small School Systems (TSSS) filed a lawsuit against the state, charging that because of inequities in funding the state had failed to provide equal protection of the law to small rural districts and their students and asked the court to declare the Tennessee Foundation Program unconstitutional.[37]

The chancery court concluded that "the statutory funding scheme has produced a great disparity in the revenues available in the different school districts" and went on to say that "the evidence indicates a direct correlation between dollars expended and the quality of education a student receives."[38] The court further determined that the right to a free public education has been "explicitly or implicitly" guaranteed by the Tennessee Constitution of 1835 and stated that "under a uniform system, a child living in a poor district should have the same opportunity to receive substantially the same education as a child living in a rich district."[39]

The state appealed the chancery court decision to the Court of Appeals and was heard by a panel of three judges on April 3, 1992. This came after the Education Improvement Act, which contained the BEP funding reform, had been passed by the legislature. The Appeals Court held that the Tennessee Constitution does not guarantee to every child in every county an education that is exactly equal. The Court pointed out that the current education clause of the Tennessee Constitution was adopted in 1978 and makes no reference to an equal, equitable, or uniform education, and that this present clause had not been taken into account in the chancery court decision. Consequently, the Court of Appeals reversed the trial court by a two-to-one vote.[40] On September 3, 1992, the Tennessee Supreme Court agreed to review the funding case and, after reviewing the record, affirmed the trial court's finding. The Tennessee Supreme Court filed an opinion on March 22, 1993, in which all five justices unanimously endorsed the conclusions of the trial court and remanded the case for the trial judge to draft an order to correct the funding inequity problem.

The chancery court held hearings on July 26, 1993, and considered the BEP funding reforms enacted by the Education Improvement Act. The chancellor concluded that he was impressed with the BEP reforms and resolved that the court would take no further action until the new funding provisions had adequate time to correct the funding inequity problem.[41]

When full funding is achieved, K–12 education in Tennessee will be both adequately and equitably funded for the first time.[42] In terms of providing for quality education in the public schools of Tennessee, the school funding case will certainly be noted as a momentous contribution.

CONCLUSION

The creation of THEC and SBR established a method for coordination and equalization of the higher education systems in Tennessee. A legislative-sponsored 1996 report recommended that the University of Tennessee system and the State Board of Regents system merge under a single board. The report also recommended that the operation of community colleges and vocational schools be coordinated by a different board. In 1996 concerns about political influence on THEC led some to recommend changes and to speculate on the commission's uncertain future.

Reform of K–12 education continues nationally and in Tennessee. New interest groups are emerging and expressing concerns about the education of our children. Incidents of school violence have been increasing in urban areas and are appearing in rural communities. Home schooling is one of the largest growing educational alternatives in Tennessee. Schools are experimenting with providing an extended school day and year. Teachers and parents feel a sense of frustration relating to test scores and accountability. These trends and others will provide an impetus for additional change in the educational policies of the state. The current atmosphere of public distrust of educational systems is not likely to allow educators the sole responsibility for making decisions about school change.

Current state legislators across the country insist on a prominent role in deciding education policy. State legislatures are aggressive and independent bodies and are exerting influence on state higher education boards, state departments of education, educational interest groups, local school boards, and activities of school personnel. In the last thirty years the politics of education has blossomed, and legislators have been "cast in the role of institutional actors in the context of educational policy."[43] Whether educators like it or not, the politicizing of educational policy making has created a need for educators at all levels to communicate with their elected politicians.

CHAPTER 13

The Tennessee Prison System: A Study of Evolving Public Policy in State Corrections

—Richard D. Chesteen

During the 1960s crime more than doubled,[1] and with this rapid growth in crime came a significant increase in the nation's prison population over the next several decades as states reacted with tougher and expanded criminal legislation.[2] From 1970 to 1980 annual prison construction expenditures rose from $74 million to $450 million.[3] By 1982 that amount had doubled again to $946 million;[4] and, by 1995, operating and capital expenses for prisons and jail totaled over $31 billion a year.[5] Yet even with those rapidly increasing expenditures, as late as 1990 forty states were under court mandates to alleviate crowding in their prisons.[6]

TENNESSEE PRISONS UNDER SIEGE

Tennessee's modern prison troubles began in the 1970s as the state's crime rate began to soar. In response the state General Assembly allowed juries to double the minimum sentences on some crimes; took steps to increase sentences for second-degree rape, armed robbery, and kidnapping; and set parole eligibility in life sentences at thirty years. By 1979 the state had adopted Republican Gov. Lamar Alexander's sentencing solution. It imposed minimum mandatory sentences for a category of "class X" crimes that included armed robbery, rape, murder, and certain drug offenses. Plea bargaining was restricted. Three years later the General Assembly passed the Sentencing Reform Act of 1982, which expanded the class X concept to other crimes by setting parole eligibility at 30 percent, with no reduction for good conduct. The result of these enactments was serious prison overcrowding, which, many believe, contributed to the 1985 rioting in the state prison system.

No sooner did state legislators begin to increase penalties for crime than the Tennessee Department of Corrections was charged in state and federal courts with violating the Eighth Amendment prohibition of cruel and unusual punishment. The result was a series of successful prisoner lawsuits that resulted in a state judge taking over jurisdiction of the state prisons; the appointment of a receiver to oversee mandated prison changes; the declaration that the condition of state's ancient main prison in Nashville, with its death row unit, was unconstitutional; and a cap on the state prison population until additional facilities were constructed.[7]

TENNESSEE'S RESPONSE

In response to these court actions, Gov. Lamar Alexander called for a special session of the state General Assembly in November 1985. The special session, realizing the seriousness of the situation for the state, passed a number of acts addressing problems of the corrections system. Among these were actions that provided for: (1) beginning the appropriation and bond issuance process to build six new prisons at a cost of over $300 million to house some 6,000 inmates; (2) enacting the Tennessee Community Corrections Act of 1985 for creation of community based programs as an alternative to incarceration; (3) establishing the Comprehensive Correction Improvement Act of 1985 to allow for the creation of a classification system for state prisoners and to establish "incentive credits" and "contract sentencing" as ways for inmates to reduce their time served; (4) providing state funds, under the Correction Improvement Act, for counties to house state felons with sentences of six years or less in county jails; and (5) creating the Tennessee Sentencing Commission, composed of the commissioner of corrections and fourteen additional members to classify criminal offenses and to develop sentencing guidelines.[8]

THE SENTENCING COMMISSION'S ACTION

For two years the Sentencing Commission worked on the first task of revising the state's antiquated criminal code and developing an equitable sentencing policy. Second, the Sentencing Commission developed a prisoner classification system and a sentencing structure that would not exceed the prison system's operational capacity, which for planning purposes was set at 9,068. This meant the state would have to construct 3,028 beds by July 1997. The Department of Corrections estimated the cost of this plan at $89,005,000 for construction and an increase in annual operating cost of $64,014,000.[9] Third, the commission recommended that convicts receiving a sentence of eight years or less be incarcerated in local jails or workhouses and developed an impact projection analysis of the cost of such a policy for each county in Tennessee, which it provided to the legislators.[10]

EXPANSION

By 1991 the operating budget for adult corrections in Tennessee had more than tripled from $88.2 million in fiscal year 1980–81 to $284.1 million in fiscal year 1991–92,[11] and the state had spent $293.7 million on prison construction and renovation, most of it since 1987. Nearly 6,000 beds had been added to the state prison system. Nevertheless, because the hundred-year old Tennessee State

Prison and the DeBerry Correctional Center were scheduled for closing in 1992, the net increase was only about 4,000 beds. The system capacity by the end of 1992, when six new prisons would be completed and two old ones closed, was predicted at 11,655 beds. Although this represented an increase of almost 8,000 in the system's capacity by 1992, projections indicated a population of 15,200 to 15,400 inmates, making the new capacity short by more than 3,000 beds. These projections led to Department of Corrections Commissioner Jeff Reynolds presenting to the Corrections Oversight Committee a new comprehensive expansion plan that would enable the state to remove all "pen-ready" state inmates from local jails except those being kept under state contracts. The new proposed prison expansion program, according to Reynolds, could be funded for $22.5 million with additional operating costs of only $6.5 million annually.

The legislature voted to fund this expansion plan, but overcrowding continued and even worsened. On December 1, 1992, Christine Bradley took over as the Department of Corrections Commissioner. Bradley soon found that the never-ceasing flood of new convicts was once more threatening to push the state penal system into a crisis. Under then-current state sentencing laws, earlier approval of all the proposed penal expansions would only take care of the space need through 1996. Projections indicated that by June 1997 the state would have 19,462 inmates with only 17,657 bed spaces and 4,900 county jail cells under contract to the state. That meant 1,805 more inmates than places to house them, but the excess would be cut to 205 if developed prison building plans were approved. However, this projection did not take into consideration possible new "get tough on crime" bills or the removal of the 4,000 state prisoners from county jails. To deal with this projected over population, Governor McWherter, in his 1994 budget, asked for and got additional funding for $22 million to make room in state prisons for 978 more prisoners.

Governor McWherter's Tough Sentencing Policy

In line with the growing "get tough" attitude of other state governors, in 1994 Governor McWherter introduced to the General Assembly his new "three strikes and you're out" crime proposal. The State Sentencing Commission's reaction was negative. Commission members argued projecting how many people would be affected by such a law would be impossible because adequate inmate records only went back to 1985. They pointed out that the new bill's proposal that all criminal trials be held within 90 days could not be met, since many state circuit judges handled several counties and visited them only every 120 days. They also noted that the only cost estimate, which was done by the Department of Corrections, did not take into consideration the extra judges, prosecutors, defense attorneys, and court personnel who would be needed. The governor's proposal also did not give judges or district attorneys any leeway in deciding whether a particular offense should be the third strike. The members of the Sentencing Commission concluded that the proposal's unintended end result could be to put more criminals on the street and would eventually burden Tennessee prisons with a large population of elderly convicts no longer posing a threat to society.

State lawmakers also reacted coolly to the governor's new proposal. While the governor's office claimed that the "three strikes" law would cost nothing for the first seven years and then only $20 million over the next thirteen years, Corrections Department officials estimated the proposal to jail career felons for life would cost the state many millions more. Also, in a meeting of the Oversight Committee on Corrections on Monday, November 21, 1994, state correction officials noted that in less than four more years Tennessee would sentence 1,435 more criminals to prison than it had space for—even after it added 1,000 new prison beds funded by the legislature earlier in the year. They warned that proposals to lengthen prison sentences would push the "unmet demand" for prison cells even higher.[12]

GOVERNOR SUNDQUIST'S TOUGH STANCE CONTINUED

When Gov. Don Sundquist took office in January 1995, he introduced his own twenty-one page "get tough" corrections program that he claimed would provide for 500 additional prison beds but only add $2.8 million to the $350 million state prison budget. He said that for fiscal year 1995–96 he would likely recommend building prisons, retrofitting existing ones to house two inmates to a cell, or letting a private company assume construction costs of new beds. Shelby County District Attorney General John Pierotti, who represented state prosecutors in working with Sundquist on the crime package, called his program "ambitious" and predicted it would be welcomed by law enforcement and prosecutors.[13]

In the budget he submitted to the General Assembly, Governor Sundquist included $11.3 million for his crime program. However, after reviewing the plan, the General Assembly's Fiscal Review Committee staff informed the Corrections Oversight Committee that the Sundquist crime plan would cost approximately $22 million in the first year.[14] The committee arrived at this figure by costing out the state law requiring that any bill increasing prison sentences receive enough money during the first year to pay for the most expensive year during the next decade.[15] Members of the Tennessee Sentencing Commission also informed Governor Sundquist that his get-tough-on-crime proposal would be extremely costly, could be unconstitutional, and might result in the state once more facing a federal lawsuit. They voted against recommending the governor's plan to lower the requirement from three offenses to two for a criminal to serve life without parole, noting that the "three-strikes-you're-out law passed the previous year had not yet had time to reveal its impact on population numbers. In addition, the commission rejected the governor's proposal to change the likely sentence given some violent offenders from the minimum to the mid-point of the range, suggesting that the law makers, before adopting any new sentencing guidelines, should first review the Commission's report on truth in sentencing. Only District Attorney Jerry Woodall, newly appointed by Sundquist as Commission chairman, voted to recommend the bill.[16]

A Fourth Expansion

In 1995, Governor Sundquist proposed a new $44 million prison that he contended would satisfy the state's need. The proposed prison would open in July 1997 and hold 1,592 prisoners. However, while these beds, with planned expansions at three other facilities, would add 2,600 beds to the system's current capacity of 12,600, projections showed that when the expansion was complete the state inmate number would have grown by 2,804 according to predictions by Jerry Preston, director of capital projects management for the state. If Preston's projections were accurate, even with the new prison, a deficit of 528 prison beds would exist by 1998. In addition, the projected expansion would not relieve any of the backlog of over 2,000 state felons in county jails sentenced to the state prison system.

A part of Governor Sundquist's prison construction plan included "double-celling" in the new prison and the remodeling of already-built prisons as a way of "cutting expenses in existing facilities." Some prisons had been designed earlier for double-celling and were already at capacity. Other facilities were being enhanced for double celling in the future, but the cost was high—projected at $26.5 million for the state's four largest medium-security prisons. Too, there would be an increased need for utilities, security, and more work programs to keep the inmates active. All told, these needs would add another $14 million every year for additional staff and other expenses.[17]

The Oversight Committee was presented with options other than more prison beds, but the committee rejected all of them, noting that they had all been tried before without great success. One was to house more prisoners at local jails by assessing "excess capacity." According to Tennessee Department of Corrections officials, there were at least 1,200 beds in local lockups that could be made available for state prisoners; but most counties with available space did not want to take state inmates. According to Assistant Corrections Commissioner Bill Dalton, the counties were afraid they would end up with the worst convicts. Shelby County Sheriff A. C. Gilless claimed that few county jails had room for more state prisoners and contended that fewer sheriffs wanted more inmates, in spite of the additional revenue offered by the state. In Gilless's opinion the state needed to build at least two new prisons.[18]

An Expanded Expansion

In early September 1995, the Department of Corrections submitted to the Corrections Oversight Committee a revised plan to increase the number of beds in the state prison system some 35 percent, adding 4,818 beds by the end of 1997. The plan was designed to relieve crowding in county jails across the state and to provide enough additional prison capacity to keep up with projected inmate capacity through 1998. By the year 2000, however, the state would once more be short of prison space since the population increase was projected at 5,000 new prisoners excluding those in the county jails.

One component of the Corrections Department's new plan was the possible shipment of prisoners to another state, particularly Texas, where the construction of new state prisons had left some counties with unused cell capacity as they transferred their inmates to the state system. While at least one state daily newspaper, *The Commercial Appeal,* spoke favorably of out-of-state prisoner placement as a good idea worth exploring, other observers were less enthusiastic. Oversight Committee chairman Senator Jim Kyle (Dem., Memphis) questioned how prisoners in Texas would have parole hearings and how their constitutional right to access Tennessee law books, courts, and lawyers would be handled. Another concern was the liability should a Tennessee prisoner escape in Texas and injure someone. Sen. Bob Rochelle (Dem., Lebanon) said the Texas plan would not work because at some time the prisoners would have to be brought back to Tennessee, leaving the state 1,500 to 3,000 beds short.[19]

Besides the construction expenses of $53 million for the new state prison spaces, the master plan was estimated by the Sundquist administration to require an additional $70 to $80 million annually to operate, maybe less. They estimated costs could be somewhat lowered by moving 900 backlogged state prisoners out of county jails by doubling up prisoners in the few remaining single-occupancy cells and by using an empty Nashville mental health facility until the new prisons were completed, thus reducing the annual corrections budget by $11 million. The adjusted cost would be between $60 and $70 million annually.[20] While the governor's spokespersons did not present any specific funding plan, the governor had stated earlier that he felt his plan could be carried out without a tax increase.

Another part of the master corrections plan included a new prison to be built by Hardeman County, which in turn would lease it to a private company to operate and who, in turn, could contract with the state to take prisoners. While approval of the Oversight Committee was not necessary for Hardeman County to proceed with the plan, the legislature would have to approve at some time the money expenditure needed to house state prisoners there. Tensions grew over the prison issue when the State Building Commission refused to endorse the new state prison proposal or to pay Corrections Corporation of America (CCA) $500,000 more each year to house more inmates at the Wayne County facility it managed. The commission expressed concern with the plan to pay CCA $24.35 a day for the new prisoners added at its facility rather than the $17 a day for those already housed there. The commission did approve the Department of Correction's plan to hire a designer to modify the state's prototype prison design, but members insisted on knowing the proposed site for the new state-owned prison before approving its construction. The commission also approved building a three-hundred-bed minimum security facility at the Wayne County Boot Camp.[21]

As 1995 came to a close and a new fiscal year loomed on the horizon, Governor Sundquist continued to face difficulty with his criminal legislation, its economic impact, and its need for expanded penal facilities. Despite Corrections Commissioner Campbell's assertion that many communities in the state were eager to welcome the proposed new state prison in their county, events contradicted his claim. After an unsuccessful effort to locate the new prison in an east Tennessee county, the Sundquist administration announced that the new 1,676-inmate state prison would be constructed in Lauderdale County in West Tennessee on land already owned by the state and would be constructed within sight of two other already-existing state prisons, the West Tennessee High Security Facility with 679 prisoners and Cold Creek Correctional Facility with 662 inmates. The prison was scheduled for completion by February 1998.[22]

The announcement of the location of the new prison in Lauderdale County immediately met with criticism. When asked about the construction cost, the governor responded that the money had already been allocated in the capital improvements building program, and he stated his confidence that the state could afford the expansions. Too, he noted that he would not consider a tax increase to pay for prison plans. Instead he noted he favored cutting current government services.[23] Another concern had to do with the adequacy of a local labor force available to man the prison. Some noted that the turnover rate for personnel at the other two state prisons in the county was relatively high and that the number of persons claiming to be unemployed in the area—7.6 percent in October 1995 or 710 persons—was not a sufficient number to provide the 429 people who would be needed to staff and operate the proposed new prison.[24] However, Governor Sundquist was not about to alter course. He was facing considerable heat after having five different proposed construction sites rejected for one reason or another, and the opening date for the new prison was slipping farther and farther behind. Also, he was feeling the pressure from those counties demanding relief from the backlog of state prisoners they were holding. Additionally, on the same day that the Sundquist administration made the new prison announcement, the state noted it had resolved some difficulties with the City of Nashville over use of the old Middle Tennessee Mental Health Institute in Nashville. This meant that beginning in January 1996, 250 technical parole violators and about 100 minimum-security female prisoners, who at the time were mainly housed in county jails, would be located there.[25]

As the new year unfolded, political difficulties muddied the waters for the Sundquist plan. In legislative hearings, some members of the Corrections Oversight Committee charged the administration with creating prison tensions by double-celling, shifting wardens without cause, and allowing overtime pay to get out of hand. The committee recommended that the Corrections Department be given only a two-year life extension rather than the normal eight years allowed under the state's sunset review law[26] and ordered the governor to devise a long-range strategic plan, speed up jail construction, devise a better system to forecast prison populations, and improve department management. Corrections Commissioner Campbell retorted that the committee had not been "fair and right" in its criticism and refuted all the points of criticism with a lengthy written response to the committee.

TO BUILD OR NOT TO BUILD: THE OPTIONS

In the ten years after 1985, Tennessee went from having an unconstitutional prison system to having the only fully accredited state prison system in the country. However, with the high level of double celling and other steps being taken to squeeze the state prison capacity, Tennessee is unlikely to retain its fully accredited status. Yet, fear of crime at a high level, the public will not look with favor on those who appear to be reluctant to take a strong stance to punish law violators.[27]

In this state of affairs, what are the state's possible options for either reducing the level of prison sentencing or using alternatives to prison confinement, and which ones should be given serious consideration for adoption or expansion? This question was put to Corrections Commissioner Jeff Reynolds in 1991 by the Corrections Oversight Committee. The committee asked Reynolds to develop an "action plan" to deal with the situation with input from various law enforcement agencies.[28] The following discussion reflects many of the eighteen options that Reynolds put to the panel in response.

PROBATION/PAROLE/EARLY RELEASE

Three-fourths of Tennesseans believe convicted criminals should serve all their prison term and 80 percent believe that the courts are too lenient.[29] When asked specifically if they support allowing persons convicted of certain crimes to serve out their sentences by staying confined in some alternative way in their own communities, 35 percent of the respondents were opposed to any alternative sentencing. Those who were willing to allow such alternatives limited them mainly for shoplifters, marijuana users, and DUI offenders.[30] Despite these views, the fact is that as of 1995 more than nine of every ten criminal defendants in Tennessee were allowed to negotiate deals to plead guilty to reduced criminal charges and thus receive lighter prison sentences.[31] And, once sentenced, convicted criminals only serve about one-third of their sentence behind bars.[32]

As a result of the above noted circumstances, more than two-thirds of the 48,000 convicted felons under state supervision in Tennessee are not serving their sentences behind bars. Statewide, probation and parole grew nearly 50 percent between 1986 and 1994.[33] In 1994 the Department of Corrections supervised 22,000 in regular probation, 2,000 in intensive probation, and another 2,200 in community corrections programs operated by private agencies under contract with the state. Another 12,000 were on parole, after serving part of their sentences behind bars. While supervising probation costs the state about $25 million annually, the alternatives to incarceration save the state about $1.2 billion in construction costs and more than $200 million per year in the cost of operating prisons that have not been built.

When asked if they supported limiting nonviolent offenders to the boundaries of their home rather than placing them in prison, with an electronic method of monitoring the offender, 50 percent of Tennesseans were willing to do so, while 24 percent were not and 23 percent did not know.[34] The program is not flawless and of the over one thousand who were assigned to the system in its first four years of utilization, about 20 percent were sent to prison for violation of their confinement conditions. In most cases they were persons who failed to attend drug treatment or education programs, violated house arrest, or failed drug-screening tests. According to the director of one monitoring program in the state in 1990, it cost the state only $3,745 a year for each such inmate under the Community Corrections Act, while the average cost for penal incarceration was $21,000.[35]

Another means by which prison sentences have been altered is the "safety valve" program enacted by the state legislature in 1985, which allows the governor to declare a "crowding emergency" whenever the number of inmates reaches at least 90 percent of the prison capacity. When this occurs the Board of Paroles is authorized to advance the release dates of inmates by a percentage sufficient to lower the population to a safe level. When it was first instituted, about 900 inmates a year were being released under the system. However, due to prison construction and expansion, the figure in 1993 was down to 345 a year. Under the "safety valve" system, a person sentenced to fifteen years imprisonment could be out in less than three years.[36]

One factor complicating the state parole system was the new criminal classification system carried out by the Tennessee Sentencing Commission. As a result of the changes in the terms of imprisonment, new prisoners coming into the state prison system after 1989 were serving incarceration terms considerably below previously convicted prisoners. This created a serious morale problem among the latter group, who in December 1991 organized some affected prisoners into the Sentencing Equalization Committee (SEC). This group estimated that some 2,500 inmates were affected by what they considered an inequitable sentencing situation. The inmates estimated that if the new guidelines were applied to them, the state would save between $65 to $75 million in incarceration costs.[37] In order to deal with this sentencing inequity, the state, in 1992, created the Parole Eligibility Review Board to assess the sentences of those convicted before 1989. The panel had no power to parole, but it could move up an inmate's parole application date. The state Parole Board then would have to review the inmate's crime and prison behavior and decide whether to release the prisoner. By 1994 that review process had been largely completed; but before it was, many prisoners were released prior to what had been their original possible parole date.

RECIDIVISM AND REHABILITATION
When asked what they thought should be the functions of Tennessee prisons, state residents cited punishment and rehabilitation as the most important. Punishment was chosen most frequently by 42 percent of the respondents, while rehabilitation was selected by 33 percent. However, when asked how good a job they thought the state prisons were doing in preparing prisoners to return to

society, 86 percent gave the prisons only a fair or poor rating. A review of the demogaphics of the state prison population suggests that the respondents' views were accurate. Of some 10,000 admissions into the state penal system a year, about 6,500 are new and about 3,500 are individuals who violate probation or parole guidelines or commit new crimes. The recidivism rate for parolees is about 48 percent.[38]

In September 1995 *The Chattanooga Times* published an in-depth two-part investigative report on crime and punishment in the Chattanooga region. Assistant U.S. Attorney John MacCoon was quoted as saying, "The criminal justice system does not stop crime. It punishes a few and rehabilitates even fewer. But . . . we are not solving problems that cause crime. In the long run, I am afraid that will come back to haunt us."[39]

Judges and lawyers interviewed placed much of the blame for the criminal justice failures on the backs of state politicians who, they claimed, are more interested in reforms that are low-cost, quick fixes but that make them look tough on crime. The judges and lawyers made some specific suggestions for improving the justice system:

- establishing programs to help nonviolent offenders keep from becoming repeat offenders, while giving judges the power to incarcerate for long periods of time unrelenting, unrepenting criminals;
- opening revocation centers for paroled felons who fall subject to substance abuse, which is the most common cause for rearresting parolees;
- improving cooperation between human service and justice-related agencies to identify which criminals can be rehabilitated and the problems of those who can be reformed.

The use of prison "boot camps" for young-adult first-time and non-violent offenders was begun in Georgia and Oklahoma in 1983. By 1993, over half the states were operating boot camps. While the early boot camps emphasized the military atmosphere of rigorous physical training, hard labor, and strong discipline, a movement toward incorporating more education and rehabilitation theory into the programs has gained ground. Those who successfully complete the regimen, which usually runs 90 to 180 days, stand a good chance of being released early.

The Tennessee boot camp program began in Tennessee in 1989 with the opening of a facility in Wayne County. Originally, its inmates were limited to nonviolent offenders under the age of thirty. While the boot camp recidivism rate in Tennessee as of 1994 was, as then Commissioner of Corrections Bradley noted, a relatively good 38 percent, these young inmates had been preselected based on having committed fewer crimes and less serious offenses. An investigation by Leon Alligood of the *Tennessee Banner* of the impact of the state's one boot camp program involved examining the camp's records and interviews with administrators and past and current inmates. The investigation revealed that the program did not keep the boot camp offenders from committing new crimes any better than a conventional prison. The completion rate of inmates assigned to the program was about 75 percent. The remaining fourth were transferred to other prisons in the state.[40] With the cost of operating the Wayne County Bootcamp considerably higher on a per diem basis than the other state prisons, it does not appear that the state is eager to pursue this alternative with enthusiasm. In fact, while the original plan called for up to three hundred inmates, by 1994 the state had raised the maximum incarceration age for offenders to thirty-five and had reduced the number of "boots" to one hundred. The other cells were being occupied by a unit of fifty-five-and-older prisoners who are kept separate from the younger boots.

Use of County Jails

The number of inmates held in the nation's local jails on June 30, 1994, was at a record high.[41] At that time Tennessee, with 12.6 percent of its jail population in county and municipal facilities, was one of eight states with over two hundred local jail inmates per 100,000 citizens.[42] Only Louisiana, Georgia, and Texas had higher rates. If the county and municipal jails of the state had not been willing to house some state felons, the state of Tennessee would have had to build and operate an additional 3,000 to 4,000 bed spaces to maintain the current incarceration level.

In January 1988 the General Assembly Select Oversight Committee on Corrections authorized a staff study of local jail crowding in Tennessee. The study revealed that the state had a long history of housing felons in local jails and that as early as 1933 the state had recognized a responsibility to pay "jailer fees" to counties holding state prisoners and fixed the fee at $.75 a day.[43] The 1981 County Correctional Incentives Act sought to increase state payment for prisoners being held by the counties and to encourage counties to use part of those fees plus state grants to improve their facilities; however, the amount of additional funding came to very little. In 1984 the General Assembly made major revisions in the law and for the first time funds were appropriated to counties for correctional projects.

Few county jails were overcrowded before 1985; however, with the judicial capping of the state prison population, conditions changed rapidly. In a four year period the number of county prisoners went from about 2,000 to 4,500, and the state reimbursement to counties went from $13 million to $50 million. By 1986 Tennessee ranked tenth among all states in terms of the total dollars allocated by the state to local corrections and in terms of spending per capita.

Privatization of Prisons

One of the growth areas in corrections is the privatization of facilities. The current largest company in this field is Corrections Corporation of America, which is home based in Tennessee. CCA was the first company in this activity and now has facilities in several states. A number of major state officials have owned stock in the company at one time or another

CCA has exerted considerable political muscle in Tennessee to gain a major state contract for housing prisoners but has had only limited success, when winning the opportunity to operate one of the new state-constructed facilities for a three-year period, so that its operational costs could then be compared to that of two other state-run prisons opened at about the same time. In 1994 the three-year period was up. The operational-costs reports of the three prisons revealed that there was little difference between those of the CCA run facilities and those operated by the Department of Corrections.[44] However, the CCA run facility did have some internal prisoner control problems that the other two prisons did not experience. But due to the closeness of the figures, the General Assembly decided to extend CCA's contract.

When Governor Sundquist announced that as part of his prison expansion program the state of Tennessee planned to enter into an arrangement with Hardeman County to let the county construct a penal facility itself then contract with a private company to operate it, he ran into a number of problems. First, the governor had arrived at this decision with no input from state officials outside his inner circle. Second, the hand print of CCA was all over the deal. Yet, whenever Hardeman County was to put out the contract bid, all parties interested were to have a chance to bid. The executive officers of CCA readily admitted that they had worked closely with Hardeman County government leaders on the proposal and expected to receive the contract. Third, some of the members of the legislative Oversight Corrections Committee were furious that the governor had not consulted with them on the Hardeman county proposal. Fourth, the Tennessee State Employees Association, which watched carefully over any effort to privatize state operations and which already was at odds with Governor Sundquist over several personnel issues, reacted coolly to the announcement.[45] Fifth, State Comptroller Stan Snodgrass let Governor Sundquist know in no uncertain terms that he had some serious reservations about the legality of the whole operation and was not about to agree to it.[46] Finally, the planned prison was opposed by some of the county citizens. The people of Whitehouse, a small incorporated community in the county, complained that the county's plan placed the new prison too close to their small town. By the end of 1995, CCA and the governor were evidently convinced that the original plan was not going to work, and CCA announced that rather than leasing a facility they intended to build and operate the prison themselves.[47]

Despite the CCA experience in Hardeman County, several bills were introduced in the 1996 session of the state General Assembly to privatize all future prisons. These bills were quickly attacked by the Tennessee State Employees Association as not cost saving in operation, offering employees lower pay and fewer benefits, and not demonstratively capable of doing as good a job as state-run facilities. The bills failed. In 1997 a renewed attempt was made in the General Assembly, but it was revealed that discussions had been underway between CCA officials and certain members of the legislative leadership about a plan for turning all

Tennessee prisons over to a private firm for management. Again TSEA's leaders reacted strongly against such a proposal. CCA countered with an offer of $100 million up-front money to the state for the prisons operaton contract and promised considerable savings. The legislative session ended in 1998 with no significant action being taken in this area. However, skepticism among some legislators and public criticisms led the legislative leaders to promise that nothing would be done before completion of full hearings and a thorough analysis of projected savings. This is where the matter stood at the time this chapter was completed.

EDUCATION

Many convicts did not receive a high school education. Too, many have no marketable skills. Data clearly shows that those persons who do leave prison with some skills that improve their employability are less likely to return. Therefore, states do offer their inmates some type of education or vocational training.

In Tennessee, all state prisoners under the age of twenty-two without a high school diploma are required to take GED classes taught at the prisons. Some prisons also have vocational skills classes. In 1992–93 some 1,200 to 1,400 inmates were enrolled in some seventy prison vocational and academic programs, and 732 inmates received their GED. In the late 1980s and early 1990s Tennessee decided to allow state colleges to offer courses inside the prisons. The tuition costs for these courses and the necessary student study materials were paid for with federal funds through Pell Grants. Some students not only were able to obtain a college degree while in prison but actually were able to find colleges offering graduate degrees by correspondence. However, in 1993 access to the Pell grants for state prisoners was terminated by an act of Congress initiated by Representative Bart Gordon of Tennessee.

Public support for Representative Gordon's action was strong. Many parents of college students who were having to borrow money or reach into limited family income were incredulous that people who had broken the law were getting a "free ride." Yet, as the statistical data showed, the level of recidivism for those who obtained a college degree in prison was far below that of the overall rate of recidivism. Without the Pell Grant funding, however, the college programs were withdrawn from Tennessee prisons.

GETTING TOUGH ON CRIMINALS

In 1994 in Mississippi, Republican Gov. Kirk Fordice pushed the "Clint Eastwood Hang 'em High Bill," as it was called, to get tough on prison inmates. Mississippi legislator Mack McInnis stated, "We want a prisoner to look like a prisoner, to smell like a prisoner."[48] Among other changes, prisoners were once again outfitted in striped uniforms. A number of other states indicated by their actions that they were in agreement with Mississippi, as they banned phones, televisions, basketball, boxing, wrestling, and martial arts in state prisons. For the first time in thirty years Alabama had 160 medium-risk prisoners on chain gangs using sledgehammers to crush limestone rocks into road gravel at the Limestone Correctional Facility. Florida and Arizona followed with their own chain gangs, and Wisconsin and Michigan considered doing so.

Not wanting their state viewed as soft on crime, two Tennessee Senate committees in 1995 voted to get tough on state prisoners. The Senate State and Local Government Committee approved a measure by Sen. Jeff Miller (Rep., Cleveland) that would remove ice cream machines and cable TV and encourage the state officials to build barracks-type facilities instead of traditional prisons that limit prisoners' close contact with each other. Another proposal would have ended the governor's authority to release violent prisoners to relieve overcrowding. Under the bill, no one convicted of first- or second-degree murder, rape or aggravated rape, especially aggravated kidnapping or rape of a child, would have been eligible for early release because of overcrowding. The Senate Judiciary Committee later unanimously approved a measure to amend the state constitution's language requiring the state to have "safe and comfortable prisons." The amendment would take out the word "comfortable."[49] None of these actions were approved by the General Assembly.

State legislators were not the only ones to call for a more rigorous life for prison inmates. Governor Sundquist seemed infatuated with the return of chain gangs in Alabama. On October 18, 1995, he announced that he wanted to use chain gangs in Tennessee if the Alabama program was found to be constitutional.[50] Sundquist said he felt their use was appropriate for certain crimes although he did not mention what those crimes were. The governor had already taken action to remove TVs, radios, and commissary and visitation privileges from inmates who refuse to work and from Riverbend Prison, where those sentenced to execution are located.

LACK OF INCARCERATION: SOLUTION OR PROBLEM?

By 1995 the states were spending $20 billion a year to operate prisons and $2 billion a year to build new ones. The overall operational costs of corrections was roughly 6 percent of state operating budgets, a quantum leap from 1980. Yet, even as the massive building effort in Tennessee and elsewhere is going forth, officials and the general public continue to debate whether the crime problem is moderating. The cost of prison construction has skyrocketed as states have had to build more prisons to keep up with the rapid growth in the prison population. State voters seem willing to spend billions of their tax dollars to do so.[51] Recent state "get tough" legislation ensures that spending on prison construction will continue at a rapid rate.

In a report on truth in sentencing, issued in 1994, the Tennessee Sentencing Commission concluded that to adopt a plan of requiring inmates to serve 85 percent of their sentence would require 6,244 additional bed spaces by the year 2000, at a construction cost of $237 million and cumulative additional annual operating costs of $263 million by then.[52] Finally, in January 1996, Department of Corrections prison projections showed that the state, even with its currently planned prison construction, will have a shortage of 3,620 prison beds in eight years. Only in 1999, when 5,667 new prison beds have been added, will the state, for a short period of time, have enough beds for all its inmates and will not have any inmates backed up in county jails.[53]

According to a Nashville newspaper story, state legislators saw this temporary catching up as giving the state breathing time in which to alter sentencing policy, build more prisons, or do both to try and avoid once more getting into a crisis situation. Senator Kyle, who had earlier stated that the public wanted more prisons built and that the state had better get with the program, altered his view in the face of sobering projections: "This report gives us a window or two to make the serious policy decisions on whether to continue to build or find alternatives to building."[54]

Needless to say, whatever the route the state takes in trying to deal with the criminal element in society, it will not be cheap. Only time will tell whether the hundreds of millions of dollars in brick and mortar will be grotesque monuments to society's failure to deal with its social problems or the only and necessary last bastion to protect the populace from an unredeemable element that refuses to live by the law.

CHAPTER 14

Finances of Tennessee State Government

—Kelly D. Edmiston and Matthew N. Murray

INTRODUCTION

The Tennessee state government budget reflects the level of public service delivery desired by state residents and the revenue requirements to fund these services. By most measures, the Tennessee budget is relatively small in comparison to the budgets of other states. In fiscal year 1992, for example, Tennessee ranked forty-ninth in the nation in state own-source general revenues per capita, trailed only by the state of Mississippi.[1] For some, the relatively small size of state government is one of Tennessee's greatest strengths, reflecting the state's historical legacy of limited government involvement in the economy and in the lives and independent spirit of the state's residents. To others, neglect or poor development of resources for supporting state government are viewed as impediments to providing the services necessary to raise standards of living and promote economic development.

This chapter probes beneath the surface of the Tennessee budget, examining both the sources and uses of state funds. The discussion begins with the revenue side of the budget, including the revenue mix, the role of the federal government in the state's finances, revenue growth and stability, tax capacity and effort, equity, and pressures for tax reform. The focus then turns to the expenditure side, emphasizing the pattern of Tennessee expenditures over time, Tennessee government spending compared with other southeastern states, and the state's financing of capital expenditures.

TENNESSEE STATE GOVERNMENT REVENUES

COMPOSITION OF STATE REVENUES

Tennessee state government obtains revenue from a variety of sources. Taxes administered by the Department of Revenue (DOR) accounted for 52.9 percent of total Tennessee state government revenues in 1995. Federal grants were the second-most important revenue source, accounting for 34.1 percent of total collections. Hence, for every dollar of total revenue received by state government, roughly one-third comes from federal government taxpayers (including Tennesseans). Other sources of Tennessee revenues include interest on state investments (0.4 percent), department services revenue (11.2 percent), and licenses, fees, and permits (1.4 percent). In what follows, the term "tax revenues" refers solely to those revenue sources administered by the DOR.

To place the revenue side of the budget in perspective, figure 14.1 illustrates the composition of total state government revenues for 1995. A significant trend in the last decade has been a slip in the contribution of state tax revenues to total collections, from 59.8 percent in 1986 to 52.6 percent in 1995. Over this same time period, the share of total revenues derived from federal intergovernmental grants rose from 31.7 percent to 34.1 percent.

Tennessee state government imposes a variety of taxes to fund its service delivery needs, the most prominent being the sales, corporate excise, corporate franchise, and gasoline taxes.[2] Together these revenue sources account for approximately 83 percent of DOR tax collections, or about 44 percent of total state government collections. Other taxes include a narrowly based income tax on certain investment income (the Hall income tax), and an assortment of selective sales taxes and user fees applied to specific items and activities (including tobacco, mixed drinks, beer, and diesel fuel sales).

Sales and Use Taxes
The sales tax is imposed on the sale of tangible goods and certain services in Tennessee, while the complementary "use tax" is levied on items imported into the state for consumption or otherwise obtained in the state without payment of a sales tax. For example, if a new car is purchased out of state and no sales tax is paid on the purchase, the buyer is required to pay use tax in Tennessee. While mail order purchases are similarly subject to the use tax, collection from both individual consumers and out-of-state sellers is problematic. The sales tax is the state's most potent revenue producer, accounting for over 60 percent of DOR tax collections.

Figure 14.1

**COMPOSITION OF TOTAL TENNESSEE STATE GOVERNMENT REVENUES
1995**

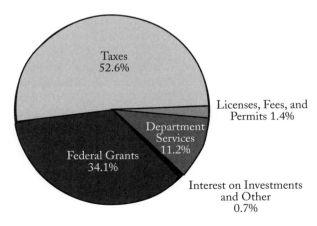

Liability for the sales tax falls on the final consumer, whether the consumer is an individual or a business. However, the burden of collection of the sales tax falls generally on retailers. This administrative structure mandates a more efficient method of collection than if the tax were collected directly from consumers. Because of the sales tax's historical legacy as a tax on "final consumption," a significant portion of the overall sales tax burden is borne by businesses that "consume" various inputs through the production process. Estimates indicate that about 41 percent of sales tax revenues are derived from business firms on their purchases of various inputs.[3] Efforts to alleviate this substantial sales tax burden on businesses have resulted in the statutory exemption of many business purchases from the tax, the most noteworthy being a broad exemption for industrial equipment and machinery.

Corporate Excise and Franchise Taxes
Tennessee taxes incorporate businesses directly via the corporate excise tax and the corporate franchise tax. The corporate excise tax is a 6 percent levy on the net income earned by corporations conducting business in the state, whether the corporation is located in state or not. For corporations doing business in several states, a formula is used to apportion that corporate income deemed to have been earned as a result of activities occurring in Tennessee. Tennessee changed its corporate apportionment formula in 1996 (to a "double-sales weighted" system) in an effort to promote economic development in the state. The corporate franchise tax is levied on the same corporations that pay the corporate excise tax and is currently .25 percent of the apportioned capital stock or of the value of property owned/leased in Tennessee, whichever is greater.

Income Tax
One especially salient characteristic of Tennessee's tax structure is the lack of a broad-based income tax on wage and salary income. The Hall income tax does, however, impose a 6 percent levy on mutual fund earnings, dividend income that Tennessee taxpayers receive from corporations, and interest income earned on bonds issued by corporations and other states. Tennessee is one of only nine states that does not impose a broad-based income tax.

Selective Taxes
In addition to the sales and use tax, Tennessee imposes a variety of other sales-based taxes, including taxes on gasoline and other motor fuels, tobacco, alcohol (liquor, beer, and mixed drinks), and a small group of activities subject to gross receipt taxes. When these selective taxes are considered, over three-fourths of Tennessee's total tax revenues come from sales-based taxes.

Contribution to Total Collections
Table 14.1 provides detail on inflation-adjusted (real) Tennessee state government tax revenues by source for the period 1977–1995. The base year 1977 was chosen because the state economy was at roughly similar points in the business

Table 14.1

TENNESSEE INFLATION-ADJUSTED TAX COLLECTIONS 1977–1985
(millions of 1992 dollars)

TAX SOURCE	1977	1978	1979	1980	1981	1982	1983	1984	1985	1986
Alcoholic Beverage	$ 57.6	$ 56.4	$ 53.4	$ 49.6	$ 46.0	$ 44.4	$ 42.4	$ 41.0	$ 39.4	$ 37.4
Beer	19.9	19.1	18.8	16.1	15.9	17.7	15.3	15.4	15.0	14.8
Business	8.1	8.2	7.8	9.3	8.7	8.7	10.5	10.4	11.2	12.9
Coin Amusement	0.0	0.0	0.0	0.0	0.0	0.0	0.0	5.4	3.6	2.4
Filing Fees	1.4	1.3	1.1	1.2	1.0	1.0	1.0	0.4	0.0	0.0
Excise	348.3	357.1	356.7	342.8	307.9	306.1	286.3	301.8	330.5	334.0
Franchise	72.0	78.9	78.6	76.0	72.1	73.3	79.7	92.7	146.3	178.6
Gasoline	372.7	359.5	342.8	282.8	248.1	297.7	281.3	266.8	249.6	337.7
Gross Receipts	93.7	146.4	139.9	154.7	173.2	187.7	188.7	185.7	188.1	184.0
Income	50.0	51.9	49.9	53.3	56.3	65.8	73.2	73.0	78.8	83.8
Inheritance & Gift	92.1	120.4	71.9	49.0	42.1	42.4	50.9	48.6	42.0	35.8
Mixed Drink	17.7	20.3	21.4	21.3	22.0	23.8	25.0	25.1	24.5	24.8
Motor Fuel	57.6	60.1	60.9	53.9	51.4	72.7	73.5	77.7	77.1	79.5
Motor Vehicle Regist	191.5	176.2	172.3	157.0	141.7	156.3	146.9	149.2	150.3	154.1
Motor Vehicle Title	6.9	6.5	6.2	5.5	4.9	4.7	4.8	4.8	4.6	4.8
Privilege	48.7	54.6	56.1	50.9	46.7	41.5	43.1	53.3	57.3	66.7
Sales & Use	1631.0	1737.4	1799.1	1691.5	1640.8	1646.5	1645.4	1800.4	2216.6	2310.4
Severance	0.0	0.0	0.0	0.4	0.8	3.7	4.8	4.4	3.6	2.9
Special Petroleum	76.4	74.0	69.0	55.5	48.5	44.2	42.5	42.3	41.1	42.0
Tobacco	151.4	147.9	138.1	127.7	121.6	116.1	110.0	102.5	102.2	100.0
SUM	$3296.8	$3475.9	$3443.7	$3198.3	$3049.8	$3154.2	$3125.5	$3301.0	$3781.8	$4006.

TAX SOURCE	1987	1988	1989	1990	1991	1992	1993	1994	1995	Growth Rate*
				1987 – 1995						
Alcoholic Beverage	$ 35.1	$ 33.6	$ 31.6	$ 29.5	$ 28.2	$ 27.0	$ 26.9	$ 26.3	$ 25.7	-4.4
Beer	14.9	14.8	14.2	13.6	13.5	13.3	13.2	13.5	13.2	-2.2
Business	11.4	12.3	12.8	11.9	11.8	11.6	11.5	11.8	11.7	2.1
Coin Amusement	1.7	1.6	1.9	1.1	0.6	0.4	0.3	0.3	0.3	—
Filing Fees	0.0	0.0	0.0	0.0	0.0	0.0	0.0	0.0	0.0	—
Excise	355.8	407.4	414.8	352.0	354.1	295.3	357.6	407.3	454.0	1.5
Franchise	180.2	189.5	193.8	205.3	209.6	227.8	224.2	238.1	248.4	7.1
Gasoline	452.4	440.7	455.6	528.2	501.4	507.0	478.4	504.0	493.7	1.6
Gross Receipts	184.4	186.9	210.5	170.0	167.5	166.0	163.6	161.3	166.6	3.3
Income	81.2	92.2	106.6	109.1	99.4	93.4	92.9	96.6	99.3	3.9
Inheritance & Gift	37.8	38.7	48.7	37.4	45.2	42.4	55.1	42.9	44.9	-3.9
Mixed Drink	24.7	25.0	24.7	24.0	23.4	23.5	23.0	23.3	23.2	1.5
Motor Fuel	90.0	100.6	101.4	99.5	100.1	99.8	103.9	105.7	107.7	3.5
Motor Vehicle Regist	150.0	161.8	161.2	154.6	144.8	147.6	152.3	159.5	161.3	-1.0
Motor Vehicle Title	5.7	5.6	5.5	5.8	5.5	6.4	8.3	9.1	9.2	1.6
Privilege	80.6	69.5	79.7	80.4	71.1	92.2	102.1	122.7	117.3	5.0
Sales & Use	2367.2	2470.2	2488.3	2475.7	2412.8	2505.4	2676.5	2923.9	3239.9	3.9
Severance	1.9	2.1	1.8	1.6	1.5	1.2	1.0	0.9	0.8	—
Special Petroleum	40.6	41.3	40.1	40.3	49.5	49.8	47.0	51.0	49.6	-2.4
Tobacco	97.4	95.2	90.2	83.9	80.3	79.1	77.6	77.4	76.0	-3.8
SUM	$4213.1	$4389.1	$4483.4	$4423.9	$4320.4	$4389.1	$5116.6	$5314.1	$5342.9	2.7

Source: Tennessee Department of Revenue (unadjusted data)
* Compound annual growth rate

cycle in both 1977 and 1995, ensuring greater comparability for both revenues and expenditures. While inflation-adjusted revenues have increased at a compound annual growth rate (CAGR) of 2.7 percent, the state's inflation-adjusted personal income grew at a 2.9 percent (CAGR) pace and the state's population was up 1.1 percent (CAGR) over the same period. Personal income is one broad measure of Tennessee's ability to pay taxes while population is a broad measure of expenditure and service delivery need.

Over the last eighteen years, the sales and use tax, which saw 3.9 percent (CAGR) growth annually, contributed an increasing percentage of total Tennessee state government tax revenues, growing by 3.9 percent (CAGR); only the franchise and privilege taxes grew at a more rapid pace. In 1977, sales and use taxes accounted for 49.5 percent of total Tennessee tax revenues, compared to 60.6 percent in 1995. The percentage of total revenues from selective sales taxes (as defined above) diminished over the same period, falling from 23.2 percent in 1977 to 16.8 percent in 1995. Together, sales-based taxes grew from 72.7 percent of tax revenues in 1977 to 77.4 percent in 1995. Thus, the reliance on sales-based taxes, though very strong, has not seen a tremendous surge over the last eighteen years. Business taxes as a percentage of total Tennessee state government tax revenues also did not change significantly over this period. In 1977, the combination of excise and franchise taxes accounted for 12.8 percent of total revenues, while in 1995 the comparable figure was 13.3 percent. A different pattern emerges if the business share of the sales tax burden is considered. Together, the franchise, excise, and business sales tax burden was 33.1 percent of revenues in 1975, increasing to 38.0 percent in 1995. This consideration highlights the point that the sales tax is the single largest business tax in Tennessee.[4] Income taxes have remained fairly constant over the last twenty years, averaging about 2 percent of total tax collections.

THE ROLE OF FEDERAL GOVERNMENT IN THE TENNESSEE BUDGET
The federal government plays a large role in the state's finances, contributing 34.1 percent of Tennessee's total 1995 state government revenues. Federal grants as a percentage of revenue have not changed significantly over time, ranging between 28 and 36 percent over the last ten years. Federal grants financed 34.9 percent of general fund and education expenditures in 1995, compared with 28.2 percent in 1985 and 27.6 percent in 1977. The federal government also influences state government tax and expenditure policy through "unfunded mandates." For example, under the threat of a loss in federal funds, Tennessee is forced specifically to exempt food stamp purchases from the sales tax. Budget figures indicate that this exemption costs the state about $16.3 million in forgone sales tax revenue per year.[5]

Most federal grants come with strings attached, but over time, states have been given much more discretion over the uses of federal funds. In recent years, Tennessee has been given more control over its use of Medicaid funds via its TennCare waiver and has implemented a new welfare program, Families First. It is argued that states improve the efficiency of service delivery when they are given greater flexibility by the federal government.

Although the trend toward more state discretion in the use of federal funds will likely continue, federal aid to Tennessee is not likely to see much growth. One reason is the prevailing political climate, which favors restrictions on the size and growth of the federal government. Another reason is that some federal aid that Tennessee receives (such as money to support the food stamp program) is based on the state's personal income relative to personal income in other states. As the level of Tennesseans' personal income continues to grow and catch up to the national average, less aid will be forthcoming—the price of economic success. Finally, the block grant system that has supplanted Medicaid and the block grants that accompany welfare reform will likely translate into fewer federal dollars for the state in the longer term.

PERSPECTIVES ON TENNESSEE REVENUE STRUCTURE

A better understanding of Tennessee's tax system can be acquired by examining specific issues and problems. Important among these are Tennessee's fiscal position relative to other states in the Southeast and the implications of Tennessee's tax structure for revenue growth, revenue stability, tax capacity and effort, and equity.

Comparison with the Southeast

A comparison of Tennessee's state government tax structure with neighboring states is provided in table 14.2, which shows per capita revenue collections for the southeastern states in 1994. Tennessee's per capita state government *revenues* of $2,459 were the lowest in the Southeast in 1994. Only Louisiana collected less than Tennessee in per capita *taxes* ($1,016 versus $1,108). Tennessee's intergovernmental aid receipts per capita rank eighth, an indication of the state's relative prosperity within the region.

Table 14.2

PER CAPITA STATE GOVERNMENT REVENUES IN THE SOUTHEAST—1994
(dollars)

REVENUE SOURCE	AL	AR	FL	GA	KY	LA	MS	NC	SC	TN	VA
Total Revenue	2749.32	2800.48	2494.43	2588.89	3064.94	3134.28	2883.80	2977.50	3075.43	2458.94	2639.71
I. General revenue	2373.65	2438.86	2113.09	2201.25	2638.84	2745.43	2475.50	2540.20	2461.84	2113.94	2261.44
A. Intergov revenue	729.34	781.64	530.83	654.01	747.34	1089.90	934.59	749.41	772.42	718.37	471.88
B. Taxes	1129.91	1294.73	1276.30	1245.08	1487.52	1015.69	1245.93	1487.78	1228.65	1107.88	1226.66
1. General sales	303.21	494.01	719.73	463.05	407.65	319.61	594.56	366.20	456.69	595.41	271.76
2. Selective sales	303.57	233.94	251.52	125.39	303.22	209.10	245.59	284.11	177.07	274.47	224.75
3. License taxes	91.67	79.04	93.25	55.42	84.54	100.27	78.80	91.50	101.00	108.76	63.19
4. Individual income	324.16	390.67	0.00	507.54	451.84	226.56	238.90	606.53	417.85	19.15	581.79
5. Corp net income	51.70	75.12	68.10	73.90	70.31	50.80	62.90	104.28	59.78	81.54	46.81
6. Other taxes	55.60	21.95	143.70	19.77	169.96	109.35	25.17	35.17	16.26	28.55	38.37
C. Current charges	361.80	254.07	115.37	177.70	245.79	363.75	213.41	202.43	343.74	199.66	348.28
D. Misc general revenue	152.60	108.42	190.59	124.45	158.19	276.08	81.58	100.58	117.04	88.03	214.62
II. Utility revenue	0.00	0.00	0.39	0.00	0.00	0.00	0.00	0.00	160.89	0.00	0.00
III. Liquor stores revenue	30.80	0.00	0.00	0.00	0.00	0.00	48.46	0.00	0.00	0.00	37.56
IV. Insurance trust revenue	344.86	361.63	380.96	387.65	426.11	388.86	359.84	437.30	452.70	345.00	340.71

Source: Bureau of the Census, *State Government Finances*

Tennessee stands out among southeastern states not only in the modesty of its tax revenues but also in the lack of balance in the composition of revenues. Figure 14.2 shows the composition of Tennessee's tax revenues relative to the Southeast as a whole. Most striking is that Tennessee relies on the sales tax for 53.7 percent of its tax revenues versus 38.4 percent for the Southeast as a whole. Total sales-based taxes made up 78.5 percent of total 1994 Tennessee tax collections, compared with 57.3 percent for the entire Southeast. Much of this discrepancy is due to the absence of a broad-based wage and salary income tax in Tennessee and the resulting need to exploit other sources of revenue to fund state activities. While individual income taxes accounted for 24.7 percent of tax revenues for the Southeast as a whole, Tennessee collected only 1.7 percent of its revenues from this source. Tennessee also taxes corporations (through the excise

Figure 14.2

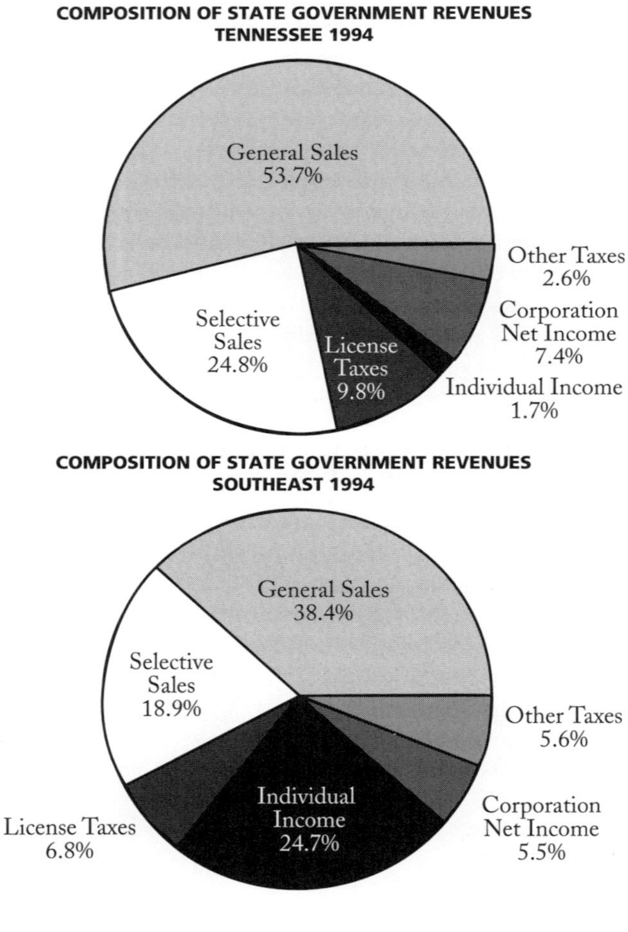

COMPOSITION OF STATE GOVERNMENT REVENUES
TENNESSEE 1994

General Sales
53.7%

Other Taxes
2.6%

Selective
Sales
24.8%

License
Taxes
9.8%

Corporation
Net Income
7.4%

Individual Income
1.7%

COMPOSITION OF STATE GOVERNMENT REVENUES
SOUTHEAST 1994

General Sales
38.4%

Selective
Sales
18.9%

Other Taxes
5.6%

License Taxes
6.8%

Individual
Income
24.7%

Corporation
Net Income
5.5%

and franchise taxes) relatively more intensely than do other southeastern states, with only North Carolina collecting more per capita in corporate taxes than does Tennessee. It should be noted that the primary culprit is the relatively high rate of the Tennessee corporate franchise tax.

Revenue Growth

Although nominal Tennessee tax revenues enjoyed strong 7.8 percent (CAGR) growth over the last eighteen years, growth was much more modest (2.7 percent) once adjusted for inflation. Most of the remaining revenue growth was due to rate changes, which have generally boosted collections. Adjusting for rate changes, the compound annual growth rate for revenues was a mere 0.9 percent, less than the growth in population over the same period. Figure 14.3 shows the trend in real tax collections and collections adjusted for rate changes over the period 1977–1995.

The reason for the very low underlying revenue growth rate in Tennessee is the inelasticity of the state's revenue structure. The concept of tax elasticity provides a measure of the growth of state tax revenues relative to growth in personal income and has been traditionally used as an indicator of the ability of a state's revenue system to grow with the economy and the demand for state-provided services. If the tax structure is inelastic, then tax revenues as a percent of personal income will fall, unless tax rates are continuously increased. Because the demand for government services generally rises with increases in population and personal income, tax rates must rise if the government is to raise sufficient revenues to provide demanded services. figure 14.4 shows that, as a percentage of

Figure 14.3

INFLATION-ADJUSTED STATE GOVERNMENT TAX COLLECTIONS
Tennessee 1977–1995

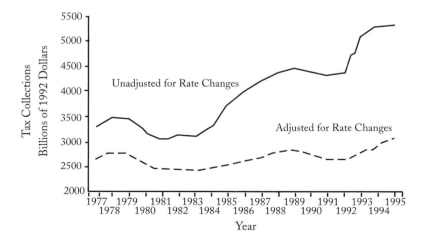

total personal income, real Tennessee rate-adjusted tax revenues have declined since 1977.[6] In contrast, unadjusted (or actual) revenues have maintained a relatively constant share of state personal income. Hence, while the total volume of revenues collected by state government has increased over time, state government's size relative to the size of the economy (as a reflection of personal income level, for instance) has been largely unaltered.

Figure 14.4

TAX COLLECTIONS AS A PERCENTAGE OF PERSONAL INCOME
Tennessee 1977–1995

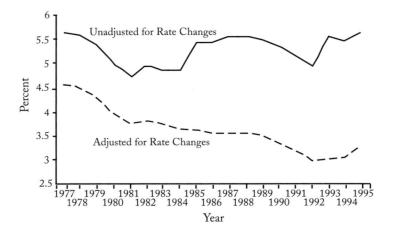

Tennessee's reliance on sales-based taxes is responsible for the inelasticity of its revenue structure. As incomes increase, people tend not only to save more of their income but also to spend more of their income on untaxed services. The growth of the nation's service economy has had a serious negative impact on sales tax collections for all states with a sales tax. Estimates are that general sales tax revenues grow approximately 85 percent as fast as personal income over the long term.[7] Selective sales taxes, such as gasoline taxes and "sin" taxes on tobacco and alcohol, are even more inelastic. Because selective sales taxes are generally imposed per unit rather than *ad valorem* (that is, as a percentage of product price), tax revenues rise only if more tobacco, alcohol, and gasoline are consumed. But as incomes increase, people do not spend appreciably more on these goods, leading to very inelastic revenue growth for selective sales taxes.

Table 14.3 highlights the revenue growth problem for sales-based taxes by showing selected state tax revenues adjusted and unadjusted for rate changes relative to total personal income. Although revenues from Tennessee's sales and use tax as a percentage of total personal income saw solid growth from 1977 to 1995, this growth was clearly and entirely due to changes in tax rates. If not for changes in the sales tax rate, which moved from 3.5 percent to 6.0 percent over the period, sales and use tax revenues would have slipped from 1.87 percent of personal income in 1977 to 1.72 percent of personal income in 1995. Other sales-based tax revenues saw negative growth as a percent of personal income, even with rate increases, illustrating the inelastic nature of these taxes. For example, gasoline tax revenues fell from 0.64 percent to 0.52 percent of personal income, despite an increase in the tax rate from 7 cents to 20 cents per gallon.

Table 14.3

**SELECTED SALES-BASED TAX COLLECTIONS
AS A PERCENT OF TOTAL PERSONAL INCOME
1977–1995**

Tax Source	1977		1985		1995	
	adjusted	unadjusted	adjusted	unadjusted	adjusted	unadjusted
Sales and Use	1.87	2.80	1.74	3.18	1.72	3.44
Gasoline	0.64	0.64	0.28	0.36	0.18	0.52
Tobacco and Alcohol	0.42	0.42	0.26	0.26	0.14	0.15
Gross Receipts	0.16	0.16	0.27	0.27	0.17	0.18
All taxes	4.59	5.66	3.64	5.43	3.31	5.67

Source: Calculated by the Center for Business and Economic Research, University of Tennessee

Revenue Stability

There are two aspects of stability with regard to revenue structure. First, a good tax system will provide a stable stream of income to government so that it can more predictably meet its service delivery obligations. Second, stability means that individuals and businesses face consistent tax rates, tax burdens, and compliance costs.

In general, changes in state tax collections mirror economic expansions and recessions. When the economy is strong, tax bases expand, leading to greater revenue collections. Likewise, when the state economy is in recession, tax collections either contract or grow more slowly. The inherent instability of revenues over the ups and downs of the business cycle has led Tennessee (and many other states) to develop "rainy day" funds to smooth out spending. Although tax revenues will suffer in the face of recession regardless of the tax structure, some tax structures allow for greater stability of revenues than others. Because sales taxes are revenue inelastic—in other words, not very responsive to changes in personal income—strong reliance on sales taxes may make the Tennessee tax structure more stable than would be the case if it relied more on personal income taxes. This is because retail sales generally do not contract as fast as personal income during a recession, nor do sales grow as rapidly as income during boom periods. However, the relative stabilizing influence of a sales tax versus an income tax ultimately depends on the specific structure of the taxes, including the choice of rates, bases, and exemptions.

Another aspect of stability pertains to tax rates and tax bases. Businesses may rank the stability of the tax system as more important than the level of the tax burden, because uncertainty makes it difficult for businesses to plan and to make sound decisions. The recurrent tax rate increases common in Tennessee make the state less attractive to businesses than would be the case if the tax system were more stable.

Tax Capacity and Tax Effort
A state's tax capacity represents its ability to generate revenues, given its tax base. In general, a poorer state has less capacity to generate revenues and fund public services than a richer state. More formally, tax capacity can be defined as the revenue that could be raised if a state were to apply a representative (average) tax rate to its own base. The Advisory Commission on Intergovernmental Relations (ACIR) developed a methodology known as the Representative Tax System that allows comparisons of tax capacity across states.[8]. The ACIR methodology results in an index that measures state tax capacity relative to that of other states. The average state is given an index of 100, and states with an index above (or below) 100 have tax capacities that exceed (or fall short of) the average. A similar index exists to measure tax effort, or the extent to which a state utilizes its available tax capacity. If the tax effort index exceeds (or falls short of) 100, then it is expending greater (or lesser) effort than the average state.

Table 14.4 shows tax capacity and tax effort indices for various state tax bases in Tennessee. Tennessee's rank among all states is also included, with a higher ranking meaning lower capacity and lower effort. By looking at tax capacity in relation to tax effort, one can determine to some extent the degree to which a state overutilizes or underutilizes its available tax bases. Overall, Tennessee's tax capacity index stands at 82, which is below the national average. This value is reflective of per capita personal income in Tennessee, which is low relative to the nation as a whole (ranked thirty-seventh in the country). The index values listed in table 4 indicate that Tennessee taxes general sales and gross receipts, corporation net income and net worth (through the corporate excise and franchise taxes), and motor fuels at rates greater than its capacity to do so. That is, the state's revenue effort for these taxes is relatively high. With regard to general sales and gross receipts taxes, for example, Tennessee collects approximately $3.1 billion from a tax capacity of approximately $2.3 billion. Given Tennessee's negligible individual income tax collections, it is no surprise that the tax effort index for the individual income tax is a mere 6 on the index, placing it forty-fourth among all states. The ACIR estimates that Tennessee had the capacity to raise over $1.7 billion in individual income taxes in 1991. For the most part, Tennessee over taxes general sales and gross receipts, motor fuels, and corporations in an effort to make up for its unused capacity to raise revenues via individual income taxes.

Equity
One of the criteria for a quality tax system is that it be equitable. The tax burden should be distributed across income classes in a fair manner (vertical equity), and

Table 14.4

TAX CAPACITY AND TAX EFFORT INDICES
TENNESSEE STATE GOVERNMENT, 1991
(mean state=100)

| | Tax Capacity | | Tax Effort | |
Tax Source	Index	Rank Across All States	Index	Rank Across All States
All tax bases (RTS)	82	45	82	45
General sales and gross receipts	92	35	133	6
Motor fuels (including gasoline)	114	18	131	6
Corp. net income and net worth*	88	31	131	9
Personal Income	81	35	6	44

Corporate excise and franchise taxes.
Source: *Advisory Commission on Intergovernmental Relations (1993)*

individuals and businesses under similar circumstances should be treated equally under the tax system (horizontal equity).

Tennessee's tax system is inherently inequitable. First, due to its reliance on sales-based taxes, the Tennessee tax system is structurally regressive. Although higher income people tend to pay a greater absolute amount in taxes, they tend to spend a smaller percentage of their incomes on taxable goods and services than do lower income people, which means that lower income people pay a larger share of their income in taxes. Secondly, higher income people generally save a larger percentage of their incomes, and in the absence of an individual income tax, savings are only taxable in Tennessee to the extent that they are held in corporate stocks or bonds. Finally, Tennessee is one of twenty-four states that impose a sales tax on groceries, which makes Tennessee's sales tax especially regressive. (In early 1996, Georgia chose to remove food from its sales tax base.) Conservative estimates put the state tax burden of Tennesseans making less than $15,000 at 8.7 percent of income, compared with 4.6 percent of income for Tennesseans making over $90,000.[9]. If one compares the tax burdens of households earning $25,000 per year and $100,000 per year across all states, Tennessee has the most regressive tax system in the nation.[10]

TAX REFORM OPTIONS

Evaluation of Tennessee's tax structure should to be based on some preestablished criteria. The commonly accepted policy criteria are often referred to as the "requirements for a good tax structure"[11] and inform the following recommendations for structural reform:

- The tax system should be easy to administer and easy to comply with.
- The tax system should be neutral. Taxes should not distort the choices made by businesses (e.g., where they should locate production facilities) or the choices of individuals (e.g., the mix of goods [usually taxable] and services [usually nontaxable] that are purchased).

- Tax revenues should be adequate to fund public service needs, relatively stable over the ups and downs of the business cycle, and elastic (i.e., responsive) in the face of growth in the economy and in the demand for public services over time.
- The tax system should be equitable. Horizontal equity requires that families with similar means should pay similar taxes; vertical equity requires that families with greater means should pay relatively more in taxes.

How does Tennessee's tax structure stack up by these measures? In some respects, the tax system has desirable features. Examples include relatively low tax burdens and relatively low costs of administration and compliance. But the Tennessee tax system has its problems as well. Three of the more serious problems have been noted above. First, Tennessee's tax system is not adequate to fund sufficiently the state's service delivery needs. The state's relatively low tax burdens and low level of tax effort—which are strengths in and of themselves—translate into relatively low levels of state expenditures and state-provided public services. Second, the revenue structure is not very elastic, showing rather anemic growth in response to state-wide economic growth. Accordingly, this has necessitated increases in tax rates over time to maintain the level and quality of public services. Third, the state's heavy reliance on sales-based taxes yields a regressive burden on Tennesseans, a violation of the principle of vertical equity. That is, lower income individuals tend to pay a higher share of their income in taxes than is the case for higher income individuals.

The question is how to address these deficiencies. While there are a number of policy options, each has strengths and weaknesses. First would be the introduction of a state lottery (or more generally, gambling). A lottery would be one step in the direction of addressing the state's revenue adequacy problem. Currently a number of contiguous states—Georgia, Kentucky, Missouri, and Virginia—have state-operated lotteries, which work to drain spending from Tennessee. In 1994, net proceeds from these four lotteries averaged $227.6 million per state, or $40.08 per person. Based on Tennessee's population in 1994 and the region's net lottery proceeds per person, the state might optimistically generate as much as $207.5 million in new government revenues from a lottery. This is 3.6 percent of Department of Revenue collections in fiscal year 1994/95 (about twice the revenues collected from the Hall income tax). This simple estimate likely overstates potential revenues since lotteries in surrounding states are currently buoyed by purchases made by Tennesseans. In addition, if lottery purchases were not subject to sales taxation, sales tax revenue collections would suffer as residents purchased fewer sales taxable items to fund their lottery purchases.

There are two potential economic problems with the lottery. One is that lottery tickets are apparently purchased disproportionately by lower income households.[12] Due to the heavy tax burden implicit in the purchase of a lottery ticket (only about half of the gross proceeds are paid out), this may simply aggravate the existing regressivity of Tennessee's state tax system. A second problem is the erratic growth in lottery revenues that may in turn add a destabilizing influence to the state's overall tax system.

A second reform option would be to expand the sales tax base to include currently nontaxable services, like legal, engineering, education, and contracting services. This reform would address the revenue adequacy problem and help mitigate the elasticity problem as well, since expenditures on services have tended to outstrip the growth in overall consumption spending. William Fox and Matthew Murray[13] estimate that taxation of selected services in Tennessee would increase sales tax collections by nearly 35 percent. Based on sales tax collections for fiscal year 1994/95, this would represent revenues of $1.2 billion (or 20.9 percent of Department of Revenue collections). One problem with base expansion is that businesses are major contributors to the existing sales tax, and base expansion would substantially increase the costs of doing business in Tennessee. A second potential problem is higher tax burdens on low income taxpayers, although the magnitude of this problem would depend on the specific services taxed under base expansion.

A third option is introduction of a state income tax on wage and salary income. Depending on the rate structure and the pattern of exemptions/deductions, an income tax could address the revenue adequacy problem, deal directly with the existing regressivity problem, and yield a tax system that is more responsive to economic growth. In addition, such a tax could accommodate reductions in other taxes that are currently viewed as too high (including the sales tax and the franchise tax). Moreover, an income tax would allow Tennessee to shift part of its tax burden to individuals in other states. Mechanisms include the collection of income tax revenues from out-of-state residents who work in Tennessee and the ability of Tennesseans to deduct state income taxes on their federal tax returns, an option no longer available with the sales tax. Aside from the question of constitutionality, the major problems with an income tax are the perception that it is unduly intrusive and the fear that its introduction will lead to rapid growth in the size and scope of state government.

A fourth option would be to exempt necessities, such as food, from the sales tax base to remedy the regressivity problem. One problem with this policy move is higher administration and compliance costs. For example, it would be necessary to define what constitutes food (e.g., are snacks, fruit drinks, and food supplements food?), and firms would have to separate taxable from nontaxable items at the check-out line. Exempting food would also reduce the adequacy of the tax system, necessitating tax increases elsewhere in the system. The revenue loss problem would be aggravated by the imprecise targeting of the food exemption that benefits middle and high income residents as well as the intended target group, the poor. The extension of the food exemption to all taxpayers increases the revenue cost of the exemption substantially. Finally, removal of food from the base would make the tax system more unstable over the course of business cycle since food consumption patterns are relatively stable over time.

A final option is to do nothing. That is, the state can choose to accept the status quo and existing weaknesses in the tax system. But, as in the past, the need will recur to raise tax rates simply to accommodate the demand for state-provided public services. The likely direction is further increases in the sales tax rate. How much additional revenue can be extracted from the sales tax base remains to be seen.

TENNESSEE STATE GOVERNMENT EXPENDITURES[14]

Total Tennessee government spending amounted to $10.4 billion in 1995, 10.6 percent higher than 1994 expenditures. In real (1992) dollars, total state government expenditures grew 102 percent over the last eighteen years, from approximately $4.8 billion in 1977 to $9.7 billion in 1995. Tennessee spending not only saw great growth over this period, but also a significant change in its structure and composition.

COMPOSITION OF STATE EXPENDITURES[15]

The expenditure side of Tennessee's budget is built around broad functional areas: general government; education; health and social services; law, justice, and public safety; recreation and resources development; regulation of business and professions; and transportation. The purpose of budgeting by functional area is to focus budget development and budget execution on specific activities and services of value to state residents. The intention is that such a focus better serves the citizens of Tennessee than would line item budgeting that concentrates instead on the inputs used to produce state-provided services. Government functions are accounted for via accrual accounting in four governmental funds: the general revenue fund, special revenue funds, debt service, and capital projects.

The general revenue fund is the largest of these funds and is maintained to account for all financial transactions not accounted for in other funds. Expenditures from the general fund in 1995 amounted to approximately $6.3 billion. Almost all of Tennessee's expenditures are financed through the general fund. Of the twelve special revenue funds, the largest are education ($2.3 billion) and transportation ($1.0 billion).

Figure 14.5 shows the composition of state expenditures in 1995. By far the largest expenditure category for Tennessee is health and social services, which accounted for over half of total expenditures in 1995 (versus 39.5 percent in 1977). The bulk of spending in this area is on health (67 percent) and on human services (14 percent). Education accounted for approximately 22 percent of total state spending in 1995. Together, spending on education and health and social services accounted for almost three-fourths of total 1995 Tennessee state government expenditures.

EXPENDITURE GROWTH OVER TIME

Three important institutional provisions restrain state government spending and its growth in Tennessee. First, the governor has line-item veto power that

Figure 14.5

COMPOSITION OF TOTAL TENNESSEE STATE GOVERNMENT EXPENDITURES
1995

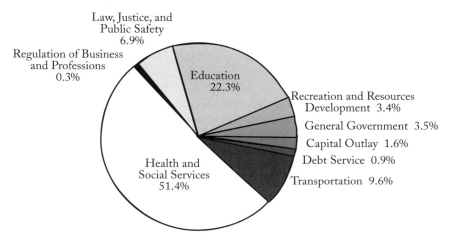

enables reductions or elimination of specific lines of spending, though this power does not extend to changing the language of legislation. Second, the state budget must be in annual balance. Finally, in March 1978 Tennessee became the first state to put constitutional limitations on growth of government expenditures. Specifically, the amendment to the Tennessee Constitution states that the rate of growth in government spending must be limited to the growth rate of the state economy. The state legislature has chosen estimated growth in personal income as the appropriate measure of economic growth.

Nominal government expenditures in Tennessee have seen consistent growth over the last eighteen years, rising 9.1 percent (CAGR). All functional areas of the Tennessee budget saw positive growth over the period, although much of this growth in spending was due to inflation. Once the expenditures are adjusted for inflation, growth rates appear much more modest at 4.0 percent (CAGR). Growth in Tennessee spending was fairly consistent between 1977 and 1990, but spending began to climb more rapidly in the 1990s. Between 1990 and 1995, total Tennessee government expenditures grew 41.7 percent—an increase due almost entirely to rapid growth in spending on health and social services.

Table 14.5 shows real Tennessee government expenditures by function for the years from 1977 to 1995, including compound annual growth rates for each function. The two functional areas with greatest growth over the last eighteen years were health and social services and law, justice, and public safety. Education spending saw weak growth of 0.6 percent (CAGR) while debt service spending has contracted.

Table 14.5

REAL TENNESSEE STATE GOVERNMENT EXPENDITURES BY FUNCTION
1977–1995
(thousands of 1992 dollars)

FUNCTIONAL AREA	1977	1980	1985	1990	1995	Growth Rate*
General Government	$ 292,417	$ 368,285	$ 309,839	$ 305,836	$ 345,192	0.9
Education	1,911,357	2,127,989	1,489,166	1,724,784	2,168,938	0.6
Health and Social Services	1,365,062	2,071,657	2,010,500	2,996,828	5,010,334	7.1
Law, Justice, and Public Safety	222,304	251,649	326,736	520,018	671,532	6.3
Recreation and Resources Development	100,432	111,609	173,763	195,044	332,475	4.6
Regulation of Business and Professions	16,937	23,879	20,300	27,211	32,691	3.7
Transportation /a/	736,480	829,397	773,711	874,188	939,664	1.4
Debt Service /b/	165,985	135,070	106,395	105,576	87,433	(3.5)
Capital Outlay	27,455	154,575	52,548	126,906	153,577	10.0
Total	$4,838,427	$6,074,110	$5,262,957	$6,876,392	$9,741,836	4.0

Notes
/a/ Highway fund 1977
/b/ Sinking fund 1977
Source: *Tennessee Dept of Finance and Administration,* Comprehensive Annual Financial Report, *various years*
* *Compound annual growth rate*

Education

Education spending by Tennessee state government has seen very little growth over the longer term, as reflected in the low growth rate of 0.6 percent over the period 1977–1995. Education spending has accordingly become a much smaller percentage of the state budget, despite recent efforts to extend additional support to elementary and secondary education. In 1977, education accounted for almost 40 percent of total government expenditures in Tennessee. Education's prominence in the Tennessee budget has fallen consistently since then and stood at 22.3 percent in 1995. Relative to other states in the Southeast, only Florida spends less money per capita on education than does Tennessee. One explanation is Florida's relatively large population of senior citizens, which translates into a relatively smaller school-age population. In 1991, 13.8 percent of Florida's population was enrolled in a public elementary or secondary school as opposed to 16.5 percent for Tennessee.

In the 1990s Tennessee began to focus greater attention on its education system. The impetus was a lawsuit brought against the state by the Tennessee Small School Systems in 1988 and national movements to improve education. In 1992 the Education Improvement Act established a new funding formula (Basic Education Program) to improve the quality of education in the state and to eliminate some disparities in education funding across Tennessee school districts. Included in this initiative was a 0.5 cent increase in the sales tax, earmarked for funding education. Additionally, a special revenue fund was established to account for revenues and expenditures involving the Department of Education and Higher Education.[16] By the end of fiscal year 1997/98, this initiative will have injected about $600 million in new funds to support elementary and secondary education.

Health and Social Service

In no functional area has inflation-adjusted Tennessee expenditures seen greater growth over the last two decades than in health and social services, squeezing the state's ability to provide other services. Real spending for health and social services rose 7.1 percent (CAGR) between 1977 and 1995, the culprit being spending on health, which grew at an annual rate of 9.0 percent (CAGR). Health spending has not only grown, but the rate of growth has accelerated as well, especially between 1990 and 1995, when expenditures on health rose almost 67 percent. Tennessee received a waiver from the Health Care Financing Administration, allowing the use of federal Medicaid funds in the implementation of the TennCare program.[17] TennCare was designed to control this growth in state-provided health care delivery costs while providing a standard package of comprehensive benefits to Tennesseans who cannot afford private health insurance. One novel aspect of the program was the extension of benefits to the working poor who previously had no access to Medicaid.

Tennessee is also on the forefront of welfare reform.[18] Tennessee's Families First program, which requires welfare recipients to work after eighteen months of public assistance and imposes a five-year absolute limit on welfare benefits, became effective on September 1, 1996. Over the last eighteen years, health and social services has seen its share of the Tennessee budget increase dramatically from 28.2 percent to 51.4 percent.

Law, Justice, and Public Safety

The second-largest growth rate in real government expenditures over the last eighteen years was for law, justice, and public safety. Growing at an annual rate of 6.3 percent (CAGR), this area saw its share of the Tennessee budget increase from 4.6 percent in 1977 to 6.9 percent in 1995. The largest component of this spending category is corrections, which grew 11.0 percent (CAGR) between 1977 and 1995. An impetus for the increase in corrections expenditures over this period was a court mandate for improvements in Tennessee's prison system, ruled unconstitutional by federal courts in 1981. The state has now met these obligations.

COMPARISON WITH THE SOUTHEAST

Tennessee state government expenditures can be placed in perspective by making comparisons with spending by other states in the Southeast. Table 14.6 provides one illustration, showing per capita state expenditures for the southeastern states in 1994. Tennessee's per capita expenditure of $2,307 was the lowest of the

Table 14.6

PER CAPITA STATE GOVERNMENT EXPENDITURES IN THE SOUTHEAST—1994
(dollars)

REVENUE SOURCE	AL	AR	FL	GA	KY	LA	MS	NC	SC	TN	VA
Total expenditure	2563.46	2477.68	2313.75	2384.53	2754.49	2997.83	2546.40	$2693.04	3059.2	2307.29	2369.16
General expenditure	2351.83	2300.11	2149.46	2217.26	2497.74	2731.42	2314.36	2495.40	2610.03	2163.29	2176.94
Intergov expenditure	556.80	630.78	733.66	634.13	674.53	659.12	775.81	932.11	601.44	579.48	589.43
Direct expenditure	1795.02	1669.34	1415.79	1583.12	1823.21	2072.30	1538.55	1563.29	2008.59	1583.81	1587.52
General expenditure, by function:											
Education	940.81	903.77	733.26	918.91	1004.87	919.61	856.09	1084.90	905.79	751.84	849.34
Public welfare	513.82	565.53	481.98	592.82	657.88	662.85	597.08	509.65	639.73	633.67	388.16
Hospitals	195.12	126.89	34.89	82.50	87.84	250.52	104.19	100.81	168.14	89.92	157.25
Health	115.44	86.31	132.02	77.32	62.64	81.33	68.98	99.12	201.87	90.09	78.57
Highways	209.49	244.09	194.29	138.62	226.56	199.54	209.92	242.36	164.58	212.07	250.19
Police protection	20.58	18.14	15.76	16.60	27.39	28.15	15.74	26.78	28.98	15.13	42.85
Corrections	51.36	53.93	89.34	95.03	54.04	75.71	38.73	101.90	83.88	76.61	104.41
Natural resources	40.06	48.36	77.04	45.53q	62.20	69.42	56.12	47.85	43.25	30.19	26.34
Parks and recreation	2.86	14.61	5.62	21.28	19.66	21.01	22.22	8.76	10.88	14.26	9.32
Gov administration	69.26	61.02	83.01	52.33	96.97	70.31	58.15	76.03	65.91	57.69	92.79
Interest on gen debt	59.41	47.18	61.92	53.24	96.59	148.40	44.95	34.13	54.29	35.78	72.62
Other/unallocable	133.62	130.29	240.33	123.18	101.10	204.56	242.21	163.10	242.73	156.05	106.93
Utility expenditure	0.00	0.00	2.82	0.00	1.25	0.00	0.00	0.00	205.09	0.71	0.47
Liquor stores expenditure	30.83	0.00	0.00	0.00	0.00	0.00	38.95	0.00	0.00	0.00	31.78
Insurance trust expenditure	180.80	177.57	161.48	167.27	255.50	266.41	193.09	197.64	244.11	143.29	159.98

Source: Bureau of the Census, *State Government Finances*

southeastern states. The main explanation for such modest government spending in Tennessee relative to neighboring states is the comparatively low level of per capita tax revenues. Tennessee has long been recognized as one of the most efficiently run states in the country; nevertheless, the relatively low per capita government revenues translate into fewer government services in Tennessee than are provided in surrounding states. Per capita education spending in Tennessee, for example, is 83.9 percent of the Southeast's average, and spending for police protection is only 65.0 percent of the region's average. Tennessee spends considerably more per capita on public welfare (111.6 percent of the average) than do other southeastern states. Other functional areas where Tennessee outspends the Southeast's average are highways, corrections, and parks and recreation.

CAPITAL EXPENDITURES

Acquisitions or construction of major governmental fixed assets are generally financed by long-term bonds, although some revenues from the federal government and department services are available for financing capital projects. Accounting of revenues and expenditures related to capital projects is maintained in a Capital Projects Fund. The balance of this fund can be used to finance capital expenditure in concert with revenues and debt financing. In 1995, for example, 26.9 percent of $164 million in capital projects fund expenditures was financed with revenues from the federal government and department services, 40.9 percent was financed with proceeds from bond issues, and the remainder was financed via a reduction in the capital projects fund balance of approximately $52.7 million. Increments to the fund balance take place in years when revenues and bond proceeds exceed capital expenditures. In 1994, for example, sufficient debt was issued to increase the balance of the capital projects fund by roughly $26.8 million.

Table 5, presented above, shows expenditures for capital outlay over the period 1977–1995. While capital spending in 1995 was much higher than in 1977, there is considerable volatility in spending over time, as capital expenditures are generally incurred as the need for fixed assets arises. Capital expenditures can be allocated across the seven broad functional areas listed in table 6. In 1995 the majority of capital expenditures was for general government (58.7 percent), followed by health and social services (19.0 percent), law, justice, and public safety (11.8 percent), recreation and resources development (9.8 percent), and education (0.7 percent).

CONCLUSION

The Tennessee state budget has witnessed many changes over both the long term and short term. The revenue side of the budget has been buoyed by numerous rate increases, although when adjusted for inflation and the growing income of the state's residents little if any growth has occurred in the size of state government. The expenditure side of the budget has also undergone transformation, including the recent introduction of TennCare, to replace the former Medicaid program, and the new Families First welfare program.

Further challenges to the finances of Tennessee state government most certainly lie ahead. Most prominent will be newly mounted pressures for additional revenues to fund state-provided public services. The likely short-term fix to this revenue problem will be further increases in the state sales tax rate. How far the sales tax rate can be increased without adversely impacting the state's residents and economic development remains to be seen.

State Policy, Global Economy: The Political Economy of Foreign Investment in Tennessee

—Steven G. Livingston

Once among the least internationally oriented of American states, Tennessee has become one of the most reliant upon foreign trade and investment. Over the last twenty years, governors, senators, state economic officials, and business leaders have made innumerable phone calls, presentations, global travels to convince overseas firms to come to Tennessee. Their pursuit has been remarkably successful. What produced this change? What effects have resulted?

Tennessee was not a traditionally favored site for foreign investment. Though the port of Memphis has always attracted some attention, mostly British, few investors were interested in much beyond its cotton trade and the shipping activities it supported. Tennessee developed neither the infrastructure nor the utilities that attracted foreign portfolio investment to many other states in the nineteenth and early twentieth centuries. Similarly, the state was seldom considered by firms looking to open business operations in the U.S. They preferred more accessible and richer northeastern or midwestern locations. As a result, only three foreign owned plants were operating in Tennessee before World War II.[1] As late as 1978, the state could count but thirty-six foreign manufacturing or distribution firms.[2]

Today the picture could hardly be more different. Many foreign firms, including some of the most famous names in the world, have chosen to locate in Tennessee. The handful of foreign manufacturing affiliates active twenty years ago has grown to nearly 420, a 2,100 percent increase. The number of foreign owned firms across all business sectors now exceeds 800, with a combined book value of some $15 billion. This investment has reshaped the state's economy. Today, about a quarter of the value of all products in the state of Tennessee issues from foreign owned firms. More than one in seven manufacturing jobs is in one of these firms. Foreign investments, which can reach many millions of dollars in a single transaction, have become one of the major engines of the state's growth. In addition, through their effects on the development of new industrial sectors, such as the manufacture of automobiles and their components, foreign operations are remolding the composition of the state's economy.

Clearly, things have changed. But explaining *why* is not simple. The explanation involves changes in the global economy, changes in Tennessee's economy, and at least a little bit of "political will" in marrying these changes to an attractive sales pitch to would-be investors.

THE GLOBAL IMPETUS FOR FOREIGN DIRECT INVESTMENT IN THE U.S.

Americans are no strangers to foreign investment; much of this country was built with money from overseas. But after the First World War, America's new wealth and industrial prominence reversed this flow, and America became the world's greatest investor. But the same pressures that had led American firms to globalize their production also began pushing companies in the rapidly growing economies of Japan and Europe to look beyond their own borders.

Events in the mid-1970s gave these companies the incentive to come to America. This time much of the investment was to be in U.S. companies, plants, and equipment (foreign direct investment) rather than the portfolio investment that had dominated in the last century. The collapse of the international regime of fixed exchange rates in 1973 created a tremendous new source of financial instability for firms operating globally. Its end reflected, but also enhanced, the new importance of capital flows in the world economy. Both in response to this trend, and in reaction to the example of the U.S., many governments began deregulating capital controls in their countries. This gave foreign firms vastly increased ability to move their monies overseas and greatly stimulated their interest in foreign investments. Just as importantly, the abandonment of the Bretton Woods regime[3] was accompanied by a marked decline in the value of the dollar, making investment in America much cheaper and even the outright purchase of U.S. firms a real possibility.

These new financial opportunities meshed with a new and rising global imperative. The tremendous trade liberalization in the years after World War II was the foundation on which the post-war world economy had been built. It gave firms the ability, and the incentive, to export. But in the 1970s these rising exports, particularly from Japan, began to fuel a resurgence of political demands in the U.S. for protectionism to save local industries and jobs. Global firms were threatened with the loss of their export markets should these demands succeed. This created a powerful impetus to find a way to evade this protectionism. And what better way than to relocate *within* the potentially protected market, to replace exports with production inside that country?

The fear of protectionism, the advantage of much looser capital regulations, and the opportunity provided by the declining American dollar produced an explosion of foreign direct investment in the American market that began in the late 1970s and accelerated through the early 1980s.[4] That investment continues, waxing and waning as the world economy moves in and out of recession and as the dollar moves up and down in value.

WHERE TO LOCATE?

Recognition of the need to move abroad, however, is only the first step for a would-be global firm. Businesses interested in establishing a presence in the American market face a second decision: where in the U.S. should they locate? The United States offers a vast choice in geography, industrial infrastructures, human capital, and business climates. As importantly, the country's federal structure means deciding from among a myriad of tax structures, business policies, and local regulatory environments. Firms from different countries bring different perspectives to this choice. Canadian and Swedish firms for instance, prefer locating as close to home as possible. Others, such as the Japanese and Germans, pressed by escalating wages at home, are primarily seeking the lowest wage rates. Nevertheless, most foreign investors cite similar factors as critical in choosing where to invest: (1) availability of transportation services, (2) labor attitudes, (3) space for future expansion, (4) nearness to U.S. markets, and (5) availability of suitable plant sites.[5] Investors also prefer a favorable tax structure and regulatory environment.

These criteria favorably situate Tennessee to attract foreign investment. Thanks to the rather recent development of its industrial base, Tennessee's infrastructure (its highways, railroads, communications, and power plants) is relatively new and efficient. The state is crossed by seven interstate highways, an unusually large number, and is served by twenty railroads. In addition, the TVA system provides cheap electrical power.

"Labor attitudes," a euphemism for wage rates and the strength of labor unions, are strikingly favorable to businesses. Tennessee is a "right to work" state, with unionization of its work force far below the national average. In 1984, 15.8 percent of Tennessee's manufacturing work force was unionized while the national average was 27.3 percent; by 1989 Tennessee had fallen to 12.7 percent while the national average was 23.8 percent.[6] Wage rates are similarly low. In 1975, around the time the foreign investment boom began, Tennessee manufacturing workers were earning only about 80 percent of the national hourly rate. By 1995, the state was catching up; workers were earning $10.67 an hour versus the national average of $12.32. Tennessee, however, still ranked fortieth of the fifty states in hourly earnings in the manufacturing sector.[7]

Tennessee's comparative inexperience with large scale industry has not significantly harmed site availability or plant expansions. Indeed, in the early 1980s Japanese businesses approvingly commented upon "Tennessee's relative state of underdevelopment."[8] The state is almost ideally positioned for access to the U.S. market: about three quarters of the U.S. population lives within six hundred miles of Tennessee's borders. The combination of its central location and the number of interstates gives businesses, in the Nashville area in particular, very favorable trucking costs. Last, but not least, the state is lightly taxed. In 1990 it had the lowest combined state and local taxes as a percentage of income of any state in the country, and it has several favorable tax credits for business.[9]

Tennessee, then, *ought* to be attracting foreign direct investment simply due to its economic fundamentals. A 1976 study placed Tennessee among the top four states in attractiveness to new plants.[10] But statistical advantages do not deliver the investment on their own. And economic fundamentals still allow wide latitude in the relative scale of the investment a state might receive. Thus rather than simply wait for it to appear, many county, city, and state governments have actively sought foreign investment.

TENNESSEE'S PURSUIT OF FOREIGN INVESTMENT

Tennessee was not among the first states to develop an aggressive strategy to attract foreign investment. Consistent with its history of small international involvement, the state was not even tracking its incoming foreign investment as late as 1974.[11] The state first noticed foreign investment in 1972, when the Department of Economic and Community Development (ECD) was reorganized, but the agency was partially dismantled during the mid-1970s, and a 1976 survey accused it of "uneven performance" in its ability to attract new businesses.[12]

As of May 1974, Tennessee's total budget for international promotion was only $45,200; this placed it twenty-second among the states, a number of whose budgets were already exceeding $1 million.[13] In 1975 the ECD finally established a separate Division of International Marketing, thus formalizing efforts to attract foreign investment. In fact, Tennessee was likely first involved in the foreign investment "race" through its association with other, more active southeastern states. Georgia Gov. George Busbee, as part of his efforts for that state, organized the Southeast US/Japan Association in 1975 on the premise that, given their common features, a regional sell might be more effective than a series of individual state efforts.[14] The Association still hosts an annual three-day conference promoting southeastern states as investment sites. Businesses were also often ahead of the state. *U.S. News and World Report* credited a Tennessee businessman, Toshiba's Bob Traeger, not the state, with beginning the promotional drumbeat that first aroused interest from Japanese investors in Tennessee as a production site. Traeger, hired by Toshiba to establish a new television assembly plant, located the operation in Lebanon, in Middle Tennessee, and then encouraged other Japanese firms to follow suit.[15]

But any laxity in Tennessee's pursuit of foreign investment ended with the 1970s. Two events combined to push the state into the forefront of the scramble for overseas firms. The precipitating event was undoubtedly the discovery, in early 1978, that Nissan was including Tennessee locations in its search for a site to build its North American truck plant (later to become its auto plant as well). The desirability of securing this plum was obvious, and the state, along with local Chambers of Commerce and business associations, responded aggressively. To gain the plant Tennessee had to compete with thirty-nine other states. Lamar Alexander, the new governor, was only one of fifteen governors who went to Japan to argue their case.

The election of Alexander in 1978 was the second important event. Alexander claimed that raising personal incomes throughout the state would be the primary aim of his administration. He believed attracting new businesses to Tennessee would be critical to achieving this goal. His initial thinking was probably in domestic terms, but the Nissan plant suggested the potential in looking overseas. Alexander moved to increase the state's efforts in that direction. The defining moment was perhaps his initial trip to Japan in October 1979 (he would make eight more while in office), a visit that cemented the "state's new focus on attracting" foreign direct investment.[16] Thirty Tennessee businessmen traveled with the Governor as he called on some eighty Japanese firms. The trip reversed a decision by the previous administration to end high level overseas trade missions.[17]

The upsurge in interest in foreign investment across America, along with Nissan's expression of interest, were already rousing the state government. Following Alexander's first trip, which truly began Tennessee's determined pursuit of foreign investment, the ECD's international budget rose to $350,000 by fiscal year 1978–1979, a nearly 700 percent increase from five years earlier.[18] The Department of Economic and Community Development strengthened its international activities, creating regional foci under a director of international investment. Frequent trade missions were developed, high level politicos became personally involved, and the state's sales message was honed.

The state's efforts were rewarded on October 30, 1980, when Nissan announced its decision to locate a new factory near Smyrna, Tennessee. State and local communities together developed a package of incentives valued at $66 million to gain the plant. The package included job training, infrastructure improvements, local property tax abatements, and company payments in lieu of taxes.[19] This package contained all of the carrots that would compose the substance of the state's future offers in luring overseas businesses to Tennessee. The Nissan deal remains the biggest single foreign direct investment in Tennessee. By 1995 the automobile company had invested $1.38 billion in the state, more than one eighth of all Tennessee foreign manufacturing investment.

Before Nissan, the state had actually been focusing its international efforts on Canada and Germany.[20] But, following the Nissan announcement, Tennessee explicitly shifted its target to Japan. Three weeks after the decision, Alexander told industry recruiters to make Japanese industries their "most important targets" and forecast large increases in Tennessee investments from that country's firms.[21] The sales pitch was to be "sunshine and cheap labor." Everyone got into the act. Particularly important was Republican Senator Howard Baker. In 1980–1981 he spent a full month promoting the state to Japanese firms. Not only was he in the same political party as Alexander, but he was the United States Senate majority leader, an estimable advantage when competing to recruit firms concerned about congressionally imposed protectionist measures.[22]

The focus on Japan paid off. Japanese investment in Tennessee has increased massively, and it has become the state's largest source of foreign investment.

However, funds from other areas also flooded into the state. In the 1980s, communities mobilized throughout the state to pursue that investment. Soon after the Nissan deal, both Memphis and Nashville developed Foreign Trade Zones, special U.S. customs zones favorable for reexporting, a staple activity of many foreign firm operations, to attract more foreign businesses.[23] They were among the first inland American cities to do so. It was indicative of a state quickly moving from the back row to the front ranks in the dedication and sophistication with which international business was pursued.

Though it was the Alexander administration that recognized and responded to the possibilities for foreign investment, support was bipartisan. Ten years into the policy, Jim Neely, the President of the Tennessee Labor Council, hardly a traditional fan of "pro-business" programs, continued to give it his endorsement. Alexander's major 1980 initiative to eliminate the 1 percent sales tax and corporate excise taxes on industrial machinery, specifically offered to assist the state in competing for investments, received support on both sides of the aisle.[24] And in 1982 when Alexander was succeeded by Democrat Ned McWherter, the new Governor made it clear foreign investment would remain a priority.

Some fine tuning did occur. The ECD refocused its activities on the industrial sectors the state believed to be its strengths: automotive-compatible industries, industrial instruments, food processing, and chemicals.[25] Few results were obtained in the food processing industry, but the other three targeted sectors did gain the lion's share of incoming investment. Also, by the late 1980s the state was slowly shifting its efforts from Japan to Europe. McWherter undertook trips to Europe almost every year in search of more investment from that quarter.[26] The state organized, in partnership with some 250 major Tennessee business executives, the Tennessee-European Economic Alliance to pursue more effectively that investment. To some extent this reemphasis resulted from a feeling that the relationship with the Japan was secure, that more effort should placed in building stronger ties with other investor countries. But a more immediate cause was the deepening and enlargement of the European Union, which attracted great publicity and suggested a new economic dynamism in Europe.

As yet, Europe has not come close to supplanting Japan as the state's major source of foreign investment. The European connection has not generated the excitement of the earlier ties with Japan. Indeed, in the 1990s, the novelty of foreign investment generally has declined. Though Tennessee routinely announces major new overseas investments in the state, they no longer obtain much media coverage or interest.

Even at its height Tennessee did not devote unusually large resources to attracting foreign direct investment. In 1979 the Department of Economic and Community Development's international arm consisted of four staffers. In the early 1980s the Department's entire international budget never much exceeded $500,000 a year.[27] Its efforts paled besides those of Georgia, North Carolina, or South Carolina, the Southeast's most active states.[28] By the early 1990s the state had significantly reduced the visibility of its efforts. There is a sense that a successful policy has reached its plateau. The ECD has blended its international investment activities into its Marketing and Industrial Development Division. The state instead began to emphasize its export promotion activities. No longer is there a director of international investment, but in 1994 a director for export trade was appointed. Clearly, Tennessee is following a national trend.[29] In 1995 the incoming Sundquist administration initiated a further shift, targeting state efforts at assisting the expansion of existing firms rather than attracting new ones. ECD officials spoke of the "Governor's priority of taking care of what the state already has."[30] A policy cycle appears to have been completed. At least in the state's own eyes, the policy of focusing on obtaining foreign investment has reached its fruition. Though efforts to obtain more have not ended, the emphasis is now on consolidation.

THE RESULTS: A SURVEY OF FOREIGN
INVESTMENT IN TENNESSEE

Both the state and local Tennessee communities have aggressively courted foreign investment for nearly twenty years. During that time, foreign firms have made twelve to fifteen new multimillion dollar investments a year in Tennessee. The book value of the state's foreign investment has grown from about $736 million in 1974 to over $15 billion in 1994.[31] Many of the individual transactions are very large indeed (eight have been over $100 million) and have a tremendous impact on the local economy.

Figure 15.1

**THE BOOK VALUE OF FOREIGN-OWNED PROPERTY,
PLANT, AND EQUIPMENT IN TENNESSEE**

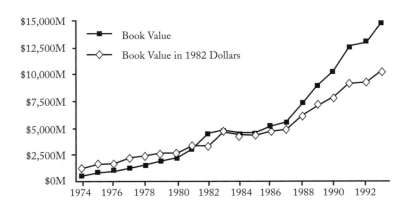

Where Has It Come From?

As already made clear, Japan has been, for most of this period, the prime target of the state's effort to attract investors. While firms from more than twenty other countries have invested nearly $10 billion in assets in Tennessee, holding 79 percent of all foreign owned establishments and 63 percent of the book value of the state's foreign investment, they get only a fraction of the publicity given Japan. In fact the first significant investors came from Canada and the countries of the European Union. Britain led the way; indeed, there were more British owned firms in Tennessee than firms owned by any other country right up until 1992. British investments are worth more than $2 billion. The size of their investment is exceeded only by those of Japan and Canada. Canadian activity is quieter than that of the other big investing countries, with only about 20 percent in the manufacturing sector, but it is large, nearing $2.5 billion in total book value. Major continental European economies have also been interested in Tennessee. Germany in particular merits some attention, having recently become the fourth country with over a billion dollars in Tennessee investments (and the third with over a billion in manufacturing investment). However, Tennessee attracts not only wealthier, more developed countries. Developing countries now have over $600 million in investments here, surprising perhaps, but an indication of the extent of world economic integration and of the attractiveness of Tennessee as a locale in which to do business.

Certainly, Tennessee has attracted a variety of countries to invest their operations within the state, but the special role Japan has played in Tennessee's explosion of foreign investment is unique. Japanese firms are the largest, the fastest growing, and most the significant investors in Tennessee. With nearly two hundred firms operating in the state, together worth well over $5 billion, Japan is today the largest investor in Tennessee. Its investment has skyrocketed. Japanese investment grew an astounding 23,000 percent between 1977 and 1993. Japanese manufacturing investment reached $1 billion in 1987 and has not look backed, growing almost 400 percent more by 1995.[32] In 1977 Japanese investment was about 2 percent of all the state's foreign investment; today it is nearly 40 percent, and this, if anything, understates its impact. Almost all Japanese investment is in manufacturing. By 1995, almost half of all foreign investment in manufacturing came from Japan. Perhaps most importantly, Japanese investments were critical in establishing the state's automotive industry, now one of the most vital parts of the Tennessee economy. One can plausibly assert that Japanese investment decisions of the past two decades have as much impact on the state economy as any decision made inside the state.

Where Is It Going?

Where has this enormous investment been located in Tennessee? As it turns out, foreign investment flows to all parts of the state. Sixty-five counties are home to one or more foreign owned manufacturer. But, to be sure, the state's large cities attract the bulk of it.

Figure 15.2

GROSS BOOK VALUE OF FOREIGN DIRECT INVESTMENT BY COUNTRY

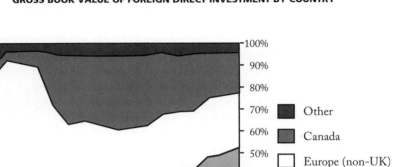

Memphis has long been the single favorite site of foreign investors. It was home-away-from-home for the most foreign owned firms in the first 1974 survey, and still is today. Together Shelby (Memphis) and Davidson (Nashville) counties contain over a third of all the foreign affiliates operating in the state, and their respective metropolitan areas include an even larger fraction of total investment. A second clustering of firms occurs along Tennessee's interstate highways, especially I-75, America's so-called "Automotive Highway."

Most Tennesseans would probably respond "automobiles" if asked to name the manufacturing sector with the largest foreign presence, but they would be wrong. While the book value of investments in the two industries is close, the chemical industry (this includes the manufacture of plastics) has the most foreign owned firms of any industrial sector, the highest percentage of foreign owned firms (about 20 percent of all chemical firms are foreign owned), and the most employment by foreign owned firms (over 9000 workers). The value added to Tennessee's economy by foreign owned chemical industry manufacture is half again as large as that in the transportation sector. Generally, the sectors where foreign activity is largest are the state's largest industries. The exception is the food processing industry, Tennessee's second largest as measured by value added by manufacture. This is still overwhelmingly domestic. But chemicals, the transportation (automotive) sector, and industrial machinery, the first, third, and fourth largest manufacturing sectors in the state, are also the three where foreign owned firms have the biggest presence.

Another way to look at where foreign investment is going is to ask which of the state's industries are most dominated by foreign owned firms. As can be seen in Figure 15.3, close to a third of the value added by manufacture comes from

Figure 15.3

THE ECONOMIC IMPORTANCE OF FOREIGN DIRECT INVESTMENT TO TENNESSEE
(Industrial Sectors Ranked by the Percent of Industry Value
Added by Manufacture Attributable to Foreign-Owned Firms)

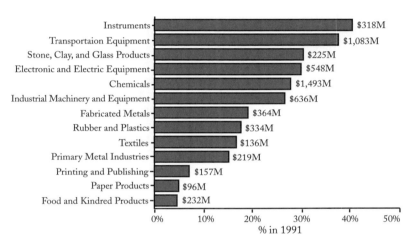

foreign owned firms in a number of Tennessee industries. Here the transportation sector does show a greater foreign presence than the chemical industry, but neither turns out to be as reliant on foreign investment as is the production of scientific and medical instruments, where 40 percent of the value added by manufacture is accounted for by foreign owned firms. Although more than 20 percent of workers are employed in a foreign owned firm in six of the thirteen sectors shown on the graph, this is only half the rate in instrument manufacture, where 45 percent of the work force is accounted for by foreign owned firms.

What is the Economic Impact?

Quantifying the impact of this enormous investment is not always easy, but several figures give us a clue as to its magnitude. By any measure—employment, value added, or value of shipments—foreign investment accounts for about one-fifth of Tennessee's total manufacturing sector. If "foreign owned" were thought of as a separate economic sector, it would be Tennessee's largest industry. And it is growing. Even ten years ago, foreign investment accounted for a little over a tenth of the state's manufacture. Twenty years ago it was virtually nil. By 1995, as foreign owned manufacturing employment alone reached the 100,000 jobs mark, the number of workers in the state who earned their pay in foreign owned firms had grown 600 percent since 1974. These figures suggest the important role foreign investment has had in Tennessee's economic growth over the past few years.

In fact, foreign investment has been more important for Tennessee's economic health than for most other states, or for the national economy. Whether measured by employment, value added by manufacture, or value of shipments, Tennessee's economy is the seventh most reliant on foreign owned firms of the fifty states. (Interestingly, three of the six states more reliant are nearby: North Carolina, West Virginia, and Georgia.) The size of the foreign owned impact on Tennessee is almost a third again as large as it is for the U.S. economy as a whole.

TENNESSEE IN COMPARATIVE PERSPECTIVE

Demonstrating the size and economic impact of the foreign investment that has flowed into the state is simple enough. But how does Tennessee's experience compare to the other states? Tennessee's economy has become one of the most reliant on foreign investment, but has Tennessee been *unusually* successful in this regard? From 1977 to 1993 Tennessee has significantly exceeded the national average in its rate of growth in new foreign firms. It has also more modestly exceeded the U.S. in its growth in foreign owned firm book value and employment. But the state's profile looks remarkably similar to that of its sister states in the Southeast. Another way to examine the state's relative success is to look at its share of all American foreign firm activity. Is this share growing, thereby indicating that Tennessee's foreign investment is exceeding that of other states? Except for the book value of manufacturing investment, the answer is yes, but only slightly. In this respect its record also closely matches that of the other southeastern states, although on most measures Tennessee does mildly surpass them.

Table 15.1

FOREIGN INVESTMENT 1977–1993

Growth Rate

	Number of Firms	Book Value	Employment
Tennessee	430%	366%	371%
Southeast States	378%	347%	357%
U.S. Total	196%	342%	287%

National Share

	Number of Firms		Book Value		Employment	
	1977	1993	1977	1993	1977	1993
Tennessee	4.1%	5.8%	2%	2.1%	2.2%	2.6%
Southeast States (average)	4.8%	6.4%	2%	2%	1.8%	2.1%

These figures are highly aggregated. A more discerning analysis might locate greater differences between Tennessee, the rest of the Southeast, and the nation. One especially important consideration is the degree to which a state's investment goes to creating entirely new plants, rather than merely acquiring existing operations. Some evidence shows that Tennessee's investment in this regard is more favorable than the investment of most other states. Between 1979–1986 Tennessee well exceeded the national average in new foreign plants and expansions, ranking eighth among the states in the number of total new foreign plants and expansion and ninth in the rate of growth in that category.[33] Meanwhile it lagged in the amount of its foreign merger and acquisition activity (thirty-sixth, and nineteenth respectively). The disproportionate amount attracted in the form of new plants and expansion may be a more finely tuned sign that Tennessee has been more successful in its pursuit of foreign investment than most states, but this is offset by the fact that the rest of the states in the Southeast compiled figures that average almost exactly equal to those of Tennessee's.

These statistics, together, indicate that the state has done well in attracting foreign investment, but its performance has been roughly in line with other southeastern states. It is thus very hard to tell whether this is primarily because of the state's location, climate, and economic conditions or because of the policy so actively pursued. The similarity in the foreign investment histories of Tennessee's neighbors hints that location and general economic factors may overwhelm state policies in determining the flow of foreign investment.

On the one hand, many are skeptical of the importance of incentives, or state actions generally, in garnering foreign investment. They argue that larger economic factors outweigh anything a state can do. Glickman and Woodward flatly claim, "States and Cities cannot influence [foreign investors] in the short-run."[34] Nissan has said that it was location and ease of transportation, not anything the state did, which led it to choose its site in Smyrna.[35] Others note that all governments have roughly the same tools and that few differences exist that can distinguish one state importantly from others with respect to foreign investment policies and incentives.[36] Indeed, a 1984 survey showed Tennessee to be the eighth ranked U.S. state in *domestic* new plant location and expansion, suggesting that foreign activity was simply one aspect of a larger picture.[37]

On the other hand, in a KPMG Peat Marwick survey of two hundred foreign owned firms in Tennessee, a little over a quarter of the interviewees cited state or local officials as important sources of assistance in choosing where to locate.[38] And wasn't state policy particularly important in developing the ties with Japan? An earlier survey found that Japanese firms were impressed with the state's recruiting efforts, having a much higher regard for the state's abilities than firms from other countries indicated.[39] But here one should note that most states ultimately "specialize" in attracting investment from one or a few countries. The typical pattern is based on a country's earlier, fortuitous decision to invest in a given state. South Carolina's relationship with Germany is a good example.

In sum, the extent to which state policies supplemented Tennessee's "natural" advantages is ultimately hard to determine.[40] The role of policy may have been at the margins. What cannot be in dispute is that the state and foreign firms, in their mutual pursuit of economic advantage, have worked in tandem to alter fundamentally the state's economy.

FOREIGN INVESTMENT: A THREAT?

Many people worry, for a variety of reasons, about foreign owned firms. A 1988 poll found 89 percent of Americans were "somewhat" or "very concerned" about foreign businesses investing heavily in the U.S, and in a second poll a year later 70 percent of Americans thought foreign investment was a "bad thing."[41] But are foreign firms really different? Are they worse (or better) than locally or nationally owned ones? Unfortunately, this question is almost impossible to answer. We can say that foreign owned firms tend to be bigger. About 4 percent of all manufacturing establishments in Tennessee are foreign owned, but about a quarter of those firms that employ one thousand or more workers are foreign owned. In nonmanufacturing sectors, foreign owned firms tend to be the department store chain or the large apartment complex rather than smaller enterprises.

Casual observation suggests that foreign firms offer higher pay, but the Bureau of Economic Analysis has concluded "differences between the hourly wage rates of foreign owned and U.S. owned establishments do not appear to be the result of foreign ownership per se."[42] Studies have found little statistical differences in wage rates between foreign owned and domestic firms, once the different industry and occupational mixes of foreign firms are accounted for. Foreign owned firms tend to have somewhat higher labor productivity and capital intensity than other firms, but this again is probably due more to their larger size and the type of industries in which they operate than to any effect of foreign ownership itself. By most measures it is hard to conclude that foreign owned firms operate much differently from domestic ones. Nor is there any evidence that foreign firms eliminate or depress their domestic competitors. In fact, foreign owned firms are often merely substituting local production for the products they once exported into the U.S.

Against this is balanced the "giveaways" or incentives offered to attract foreign businesses. This is an often emotional issue. The costs of these incentives prove extremely difficult to analyze. Job training programs are almost universally hailed as cost effective and positive for the development of the state in the long run. The effects of tax incentives and subsidy packages, which receive most of the criticism, are almost hopelessly ambiguous.[43] Do they lead to harmful competition between political units, or do they improve economic efficiency? Equally difficult to analyze is the value of infrastructure costs.

Yet having foreign owned firms in a state's economy does offer some clear benefits: they are sources of new production techniques, new labor management practices, and an industrial dynamism from which all firms can draw. Combining the value of the jobs they provide and the money they pump into the state economy leaves little room to doubt that Tennessee's foreign investment has been a positive force in the state's economy.

CONCLUSION

Will foreign investment in Tennessee continue? The inexorable globalization of the world economy, combined with the state's advantages as a place from which to do business, suggests foreign investment will continue to grow, even if not at the explosive rate of the 1980s. The state's location and infrastructure, its economic growth, its advantageous labor situation, and a history of successful investments in the state continue to make Tennessee attractive. The likely outcome is for continuing, sizable foreign investments in Tennessee. It seems certain that Tennessee's economy will be ever more intertwined with that investment. Tennessee today is very much a part of a global economy, and that economy will play a critical role in the state's future development.

Appendix

Although the essay by Lewis Laska in this book (chapter 2) suggests that the roots of Tennessee's commitment to constitutionalism date even earlier, its first constitution was established in 1796, concomitant with Tennessee's admission as a state. Two new constitutions, both proposed by conventions, were ratified during the Jacksonian era in 1835 and during the Reconstruction period in 1870. This Constitution of 1870, printed below, was unchanged until a limited constitutional convention was held in 1953. Subsequent conventions—all limited—have been held in 1959, 1965, 1971, and 1977. The last constitutional amendment, dealing with tax relief for elderly citizens, was adopted by two successive general assemblies and subsequently approved by the voters in 1982. Amendments to the Tennessee Constitution are incorporated in the text rather than, as in the case of the U.S. Constitution, being appended to the end of the document.

CONSTITUTION OF THE STATE OF TENNESSEE

PREAMBLE AND DECLARATION OF RIGHTS

Whereas, The people of the territory of the United States south of the river Ohio, having the right of admission into the general government as a member state thereof, consistent with the Constitution of the United States, and the act of cession of the state of North Carolina, recognizing the ordinance for the government of—the territory of the United States north west of the Ohio River, by their delegates and representatives in convention assembled, did on the sixth day of February, in the year of our Lord one thousand seven hundred and ninety-six, ordain and establish a Constitution, or form of government, and mutually agreed with each other to form themselves into a free and independent state by the name of the state of Tennessee, and,

Whereas, The General Assembly of the said state of Tennessee, (pursuant to the third section of the tenth article of the Constitution,) by an act passed on the Twenty-seventh day of November, in the year of our Lord one thousand eight hundred and thirty-three, entitles, "An Act" to provide for the calling of a convention, passed in obedience to the declared will of the voters of the state, as expressed at the general election of August, in the year of our Lord one thousand eight hundred and thirty-three, did authorize and provide for the election

217

by the people of delegates and representatives, to meet at Nashville, in Davidson County, on the third Monday in May, in the year of our Lord one thousand eight hundred and thirty-four, for the purpose of revising and amending, or changing, the Constitution, and said convention did accordingly meet and form a Constitution which was submitted to the people, and was ratified by them, on the first Friday in March, in the year of our Lord one thousand eight hundred and thirty-five, and,

Whereas, The General Assembly of said state of Tennessee, under and in virtue of the first section of the first article of the Declaration of Rights, contained in and forming a part of the existing Constitution of the state, by an act passed on the fifteenth day of November, in the year of our Lord one thousand eight hundred and sixty-nine, did provide for the calling of a convention by the people of the state, to meet at Nashville, on the second Monday in January, in the year of our Lord one thousand eight hundred and seventy, and for the election of delegates for the purpose of amending or revising the present Constitution, or forming and making a new Constitution; and,

Whereas, The people of the state, in the mode provided by said Act, have called said convention, and elected delegates to represent them therein; now therefore,

We, the delegates and representatives of the people of the state of Tennessee, duly elected, and in convention assembled, in pursuance of said act of Assembly have ordained and established the following Constitution and form of government for this state, which we recommend to the people of Tennessee for their ratification: That is to say

ARTICLE I — DECLARATION OF RIGHTS

All Power Inherent in the People — Government under Their Control
Section 1. That all power is inherent in the people, and all free governments are founded on their authority, and instituted for their peace, safety, and happiness; for the advancement of those ends they have at all times, an unalienable and indefeasible right to alter, reform, or abolish the government in such manner as they may think proper.

Doctrine of Nonresistance Condemned
Section 2. That government being instituted for the common benefit, the doctrine of nonresistance against arbitrary power and oppression is absurd, slavish, and destructive of the good and happiness of mankind.

Freedom of Worship

Section 3. That all men have a natural and indefeasible right to worship Almighty God according to the dictates of their own conscience; that no man can of right be compelled to attend, erect, or support any place of worship, or to maintain any minister against his consent; that no human authority can, in any case whatever, control or interfere with the rights of conscience; and that no preference shall ever be given, by law, to any religious establishment or mode of worship.

No Religious or Political Test

Section 4. That no political or religious test, other than an oath to support the Constitution of the United States and of this state, shall ever be required as a qualification to any office or public trust under this state.

Election to Be Free and Equal — Right of Suffrage

Section 5. The elections shall be free and equal, and the right of suffrage, as hereinafter declared, shall never be denied to any person entitled thereto, except upon a conviction by a jury of some infamous crime, previously ascertained and declared by law, and judgment thereon by court of competent jurisdiction

Trial by Jury — Qualifications of Jurors

Section 6. That the right of trial by jury shall remain inviolate, and no religious or political test shall ever be required as a qualification for jurors.

Unreasonable Searches and Seizures — General Warrants

Section 7. That the people shall be secure in their persons, houses, papers and possessions, from unreasonable searches and seizures; and that general warrants, whereby an officer may be commanded to search suspected places, without evidence of the fact committed, or to seize any person or persons not named, whose offences are not particularly described and supported by evidence, are dangerous to liberty and ought not be granted.

No Man to Be Disturbed but by Law

Section 8. That no man shall be taken or imprisoned, or disseized of his freehold, liberties or privileges, or outlawed, or exiled, or in any manner destroyed or deprived of his life, liberty or property, but by the judgment of his peers, or the law of the land.

Right of the Accused in Criminal Prosecutions

Section 9. That in all criminal prosecutions, the accused hath the right to be heard by himself and his counsel; to demand the nature and cause of the accusation against him, and to have a copy thereof, to meet the witnesses face to face, to have compulsory process for obtaining witnesses in his favor, and in prosecutions by indictment or presentment, a speedy public trial, by an impartial jury of the county in which the crime shall have been committed, and shall not be compelled to give evidence against himself.

Double Jeopardy Prohibited
Section 10. That no person shall, for the same offence, be twice put in jeopardy of life or limb.

No Ex Post Facto Laws
Section 11. That laws made for the punishment of acts committed previous to the existence of such laws, and by them only declared criminal, are contrary to the principles of a free government; wherefore no ex post facto law shall be made.

No Corruption of Blood or Forfeiture of Estates.
Section 12. That no conviction shall work corruption of blood or forfeiture of estate. The estate of such persons as shall destroy their own lives shall descend or vest as in case of natural death. If any person be killed by casualty, there shall be no forfeiture in consequence thereof.

Treatment after Arrest
Section 13. That no person arrested and confined in jail shall be treated with unnecessary rigor.

Prerequisites to Criminal Charge
Section 14. That no person shall be put to answer any criminal charge but by presentment, indictment or impeachment.

Bailable Offenses — Habeas Corpus
Section 15. That all prisoners shall be bailable by sufficient sureties, unless for capital offences, when the proof is evident, or the presumption great. And the privilege of the writ of Habeas Corpus shall not be suspended, unless when in case of rebellion or invasion, the General Assembly shall declare the public safety requires it.

Restrictions on Bail, Fines, and Punishment
Section 16. That excessive bail shall not be required, nor excessive fines imposed, nor cruel and unusual punishments inflicted.

Open Courts — Redress of Injuries — Suits against the State
Section 17. That all courts shall be open; and every man, for an injury done him in his lands, goods, person or reputation, shall have remedy by due course of law, and right and justice administered without sale, denial, or delay. Suits may be brought against the state in such manner and in such courts as the Legislature may by law direct.

No Imprisonment for Debt

Section 18. The Legislature shall pass no law authorizing imprisonment for debt in civil cases.

Freedom of Speech and Press

Section 19. That the printing press shall be free to every person to examine the proceedings of the Legislature; or of any branch or officer of the government, and no law shall ever be made to restrain the right thereof. The free communication of thoughts and opinions, is one of the invaluable rights of man and every citizen may freely speak, write, and print on any subject, being responsible for the abuse of that liberty. But in prosecutions for the publication of papers investigating the official conduct of officers, or men in public capacity, the truth thereof may be given in evidence; and in all indictments for libel, the jury shall have a right to determine the law and the facts, under the direction of the court, as in other criminal cases.

No Retrospective Laws

Section 20. That no retrospective law, or law impairing the obligations of contracts, shall be made.

No Man's Services or Property Taken without Consent or Compensation

Section 21. That no man's particular services shall be demanded, or property taken, or applied to public use, without the consent of his representatives, or without just compensation being made therefore.

No Perpetuities or Monopolies

Section 22. That perpetuities and monopolies are contrary to the genius of a free state, and shall not be allowed.

Right of Assembly

Section 23. That the citizens have a right, in a peaceable manner, to assemble together for their common good, to instruct their representatives, and to apply to those invested with the powers of government for redress of grievances, or other proper purposes, by address of remonstrance.

Militia — Civil Authority

Section 24. That the sure and certain defense of a free people, is a well regulated militia; and, as standing armies in time of peace are dangerous to freedom, they ought to be avoided as far as the circumstances and safety of the community will admit; and that in all cases the military shall be kept in strict subordination to the civil authority.

Martial Law — Punishment

Section 25. That no citizen of this state, except such as are employed in the army of the United States, or militia in actual service, shall be subjected to punishment under the martial or military law. That martial law, in the sense of the unrestricted power of military officers, or others, to dispose of the persons, liberties or property of the citizen, is inconsistent with the principles of free government, and is not confided to any department of the government of this state.

Right to Bear Arms — Regulations
Section 26. That the citizens of this state have a right to keep and to bear arms for their common defense; but the Legislature shall have power, by law, to regulate the wearing of arms with a view to prevent crime.

Quartering Soldiers
Section 27. That no soldier shall, in time of peace, be quartered in any house without the consent of the owner; nor in time of war, but in a manner prescribed by law.

No One Compelled to Bear Arms
Section 28. That no citizen of this state shall be compelled to bear arms, provided he will pay an equivalent, to be ascertained by law.

Navigation of the Mississippi
Section 29. That an equal participation in the free navigation of the Mississippi, is one of the inherent rights of the citizens of this state; it cannot, therefore, be conceded to any prince, potentate, power, person or persons whatever.

No Hereditary Honors
Section 30. That no hereditary emoluments, privileges, or honors, shall ever be granted or conferred in this state.

Boundaries of the State
Section 31. That the limits and boundaries of this state be ascertained, it is declared they are as hereafter mentioned, that is to say: Beginning on the extreme height of the Stone Mountain, at the place where the line of Virginia intersects it, in latitude thirty-six degrees and thirty minutes north; running thence along the extreme height of the said mountain, to the place where Watauga river breaks through it; thence a direct course to the top of the Yellow Mountain, where Bright's road crosses the same; thence along the ridge of said mountain, between the waters of Doe river and the waters of Rock creek, to the place where the road crosses the Iron Mountain; from thence along the extreme height of said mountain, to the place where Nolichucky river runs through the same; thence to the top of the Bald Mountain; thence along the extreme height of said mountain to the Painted Rock on French Broad river; thence along the highest ridge of said mountain, to the place where it is called the Great Iron or

Smoky Mountain; thence along the extreme height of said mountain to the place where it is called Unicoi or Unaka Mountain, between the Indian towns of Cowee and Old Chota; thence along the main ridge of the said mountain to the southern boundary of this state, as described in the act of cession of North Carolina to the United States of America; and that all the territory, lands and waters lying west of said line, as before mentioned, and contained within the chartered limits of the state of North Carolina, are within the boundaries and limits of this state, over which the people have the right of exercising sovereignty, and the right of soil, so far as is consistent with the Constitution of the United States, recognizing the Articles of Confederation, the Bill of Rights and Constitution of North Carolina, the cession act of the said state, and the ordinance of Congress for the government of the territory north west of Ohio; Provided, nothing herein contained shall extend to affect the claim or claims of individuals to any part of the soil which is recognized to them by the aforesaid cession act; And provided also, that the limits and jurisdiction of this state shall extend to any other land and territory now acquired, or that may hereafter be acquired, by compact or agreement with other states, or otherwise, although such land and territory are not included within the boundaries herein before designated.

PRISONS AND PRISONERS
Section 32. That the erection of safe and comfortable prisons, the inspection of prisons, and the humane treatment of prisoners, shall be provided for.

SLAVERY PROHIBITED
Section 33. That slavery and involuntary servitude, except as a punishment for crime, whereof the party shall have been duly convicted, are forever prohibited in this state.

RIGHT OF PROPERTY IN MAN
Section 34. The General Assembly shall make no law recognizing the right of property in man.

ARTICLE II — DISTRIBUTION OF POWERS

DIVISION OF POWERS
Section 1. The powers of the government shall be divided into three distinct departments: legislative, executive, and judicial.

LIMITATION OF POWERS
Section 2. No person or persons belonging to one of these departments shall exercise any of the powers properly belonging to either of the others, except in the cases herein directed or permitted.

LEGISLATIVE DEPARTMENT

LEGISLATIVE AUTHORITY — TERM OF OFFICE

Section 3. The legislative authority of this state shall be vested in a General Assembly, which shall consist of a Senate and House of Representatives, both dependent on the people. Representatives shall hold office for two years and senators for four years from the day of the general election, except that the speaker of the Senate and the speaker of the House of Representatives each shall hold his office as speaker for two years or until his successor is elected and qualified provided however, that in the first general election after adoption of this amendment senators elected in districts designated by even numbers shall be elected for four years and those elected in districts designated by odd numbers shall be elected for two years. In a county having more than one senatorial district, the districts shall be numbered consecutively.

CENSUS

Section 4. The apportionment of senators and representatives shall be substantially according to population. After each decennial census made by the Bureau of Census of the United States is available the General Assembly shall establish senatorial and representative districts. Nothing in this Section nor in this Article II shall deny to the General Assembly the right at any time to apportion one House of the General Assembly using geography, political subdivisions, substantially equal population and other criteria as factors; provided such apportionment when effective shall comply with the Constitution of the United States as then amended or authoritatively interpreted. If the Constitution of the United States shall require that legislative apportionment not based entirely on population be approved by vote of the electorate, the General Assembly shall provide for such vote in the apportionment act.

APPORTIONMENT OF REPRESENTATIVES

Section 5. The number of representatives shall be ninety-nine and shall be apportioned by the General Assembly among the several counties or districts as shall be provided by law. Counties having two or more representatives shall be divided into separate districts. In a district composed of two or more counties each county shall adjoin at least one other county of such district; and no county shall be divided in forming such a district.

Section 5a. Each district shall be represented by a qualified voter of that district.

APPORTIONMENT OF SENATORS

Section 6. The number of senators shall be apportioned by the General Assembly among the several counties or districts substantially according to population, and shall not exceed one-third the number of representatives. Counties having two or more senators shall be divided into separate districts. In a district composed of two or more counties, each county shall adjoin at least one other county of such district; and no county shall be divided in forming such a district.

Section 6a. Each district shall be represented by a qualified voter of that district.

TIMES OF ELECTIONS
Section 7. The first election for senators and representatives shall be held on the second Tuesday in November, one thousand eight hundred and seventy; and forever thereafter, elections for members of the General Assembly shall be held once in two years, on the first Tuesday after the first Monday in November. Said elections shall terminate the same day.

LEGISLATIVE SESSIONS — GOVERNOR'S INAUGURATION
Section 8. The General Assembly shall meet in organizational session on the second Tuesday in January next succeeding the election of the members of the House of Representatives, at which session, if in order, the governor shall be inaugurated. The General Assembly shall remain in session for organizational purposes not longer than fifteen consecutive calendar days, during which session no legislation shall be passed on third and final consideration. Thereafter, the General Assembly shall meet on the first Tuesday next following the conclusion of the organizational session unless the General Assembly by joint resolution of both houses sets an earlier date.

The General Assembly may by joint resolution recess or adjourn until such time or times as it shall determine. It shall be convened at other times by the governor as provided in Article III, Section 9, or by the presiding officers of both Houses at the written request of two-thirds of the members of each House.

QUALIFICATIONS OF REPRESENTATIVES
Section 9. No person shall be a representative unless he shall be a citizen of the United States, of the age of twenty-one years, and shall have been a citizen of this state for three years, and a resident in the county he represents one year, immediately preceding the election.

SENATORS — QUALIFICATIONS
Section 10. No person shall be a senator unless he shall be a citizen of the United States, of the age of thirty years, and shall have resided three years in this state, and one year in the county or district, immediately preceding the election. No senator or representative shall, during the time for which he was elected, be eligible to any office or place of trust, the appointment to which is vested in the executive or the General Assembly, except to the office of trustee of a literary institution.

Election of Officers — Quorum — Adjournments

Section 11. The Senate and House of Representatives, when assembled shall each choose a speaker and its other officers; be judges of the qualifications and election of its members, and sit upon its own adjournments from day to day. Not less than two-thirds of all the members to which each house shall be entitled shall constitute a quorum to do business; but a smaller number may adjourn from day to day, and may be authorized, by law, to compel the attendance of absent members.

Each House Has to Make Its Own Rules

Section 12. Each house may determine the rules of its proceedings, punish its members for disorderly behavior, and, with the concurrence of two-thirds, expel a member, but not a second time for the same offence, and shall have all other powers necessary for a branch of the Legislature of a free state.

Privilege of Members

Section 13. Senators and representatives shall, in all cases, except treason, felony, or breach of the peace, be privileged from arrest during the session of the General Assembly, and in going to and returning from the same; and for any speech or debate in either House, they shall not be questioned in any other place.

Power to Punish Other Than Members

Section 14. Each House may punish, by imprisonment, during its session, any person not a member, who shall be guilty of disrespect to the House, by any disorderly or any contemptuous behavior in its presence.

Vacancies

Section 15. Vacancies. When the seat of any member of either House becomes vacant, the vacancy shall be filled as follows:

(a) When twelve months or more remain prior to the next general election for legislators, a successor shall be elected by the qualified voters of the district represented, and such successor shall serve the remainder of the original terms. The election shall be held within such time as provided by law. The legislative body of the replaced legislator's county of residence at the time of his or her election may elect an interim successor to serve until the election.

(b) When less than twelve months remain prior to the next general election for legislators, a successor shall be elected by the legislative body of the replaced legislator's county of residence at the time of his or her election. The term of any senator so elected shall expire at the next general election for legislators, at which election a successor shall be elected.

(c) Only a qualified voter of the district represented shall be eligible to succeed to the vacant seat.

Limitation Upon Power of Adjournment

Section 16. Neither house shall, during its session, adjourn without the consent of the other for more than three days, nor to any other place than that in which the two Houses shall be sitting.

Origin and Frame of Bills

Section 17. Bills may originate in either House; but may be amended, altered or rejected by the other. No bill shall become a law which embraces more than one subject, that subject to be expressed in the title. All acts which repeal, revive or amend former laws, shall recite in their caption, or otherwise, the title or substance of the law repealed, revived or amended.

Passage of Bills

Section 18. A bill shall become law when it has been considered and passed on three different days in each House and on third and final consideration has received the assent of a majority of all the members to which each House is entitled under this Constitution, when the respective speakers have signed the bill with the date of such signing appearing in the journal, and when the bill has been approved by the governor or otherwise passed under the provisions of this Constitution.

Rejection of a Bill

Section 19. After a bill has been rejected, no bill containing the same substance shall be passed into a law during the same session.

Style of Laws — Effective Date

Section 20. The style of the laws of this state shall be, "Be it enacted by the General Assembly of the state of Tennessee. " No law of a general nature shall take effect until forty days after its passage unless the same or the caption thereof shall state that the public welfare requires that it should take effect sooner.

Journal of Proceedings

Section 21. Each House shall keep a journal of its proceedings, and publish it, except such parts as the welfare of the state may require to be kept secret; the ayes and noes shall be taken in each House upon the final passage of every bill of a general character, and bills making appropriations of public moneys; and the ayes and noes of the members on any question, shall, at the request of any five of them, be entered on the journal.

Open Sessions and Meetings — Exception

Section 22. The doors of each House and of committees of the whole shall be kept open, unless when the business shall be such as ought to be kept secret.

Compensation of Members of General Assembly

Section 23. Each member of the General Assembly shall receive an annual salary of $1,800.00 per year payable in equal monthly installments from the date of his election, and in addition, such other allowances for expenses in attending sessions or committee meetings as may be provided by law. The senators, when sitting as a Court of Impeachment, shall receive the same allowances for expenses as have been provided by law for the members of the General Assembly. The compensation and expenses of the members of the General Assembly may from time to time be reduced or increased by laws enacted by the General Assembly; however, no increase or decrease in the amount thereof shall take effect until the next general election for representatives to the General Assembly. Provided, further, that the first General Assembly meeting after adoption of this amendment shall be allowed to set its own expenses. However, no member shall be paid expenses, nor travel allowances for more than ninety Legislative days of a regular session, excluding the organization session, nor for more than thirty Legislative days of any extraordinary session.

This amendment shall take effect immediately upon adoption so that any member of the General Assembly elected at a general election wherein this amendment is approved shall be entitled to the compensation set herein.

APPROPRIATIONS OF PUBLIC MONEYS
Section 24. No public money shall be expended except pursuant to appropriations made by law. Expenditures for any fiscal year shall not exceed the state's revenues and reserves, including the proceeds of any debt obligation, for that year. No debt obligation, except as shall be repaid within the fiscal year of issuance, shall be authorized for the current operation of any state service or program, nor shall the proceeds of any debt obligation be expended for a purpose other than that for which it was authorized.

In no year shall the rate of growth of appropriations from state tax revenues exceed the estimated rate of growth of the state's economy as determined by law. No appropriation in excess of this limitation shall be made unless the General Assembly shall, by law containing no other subject matter, set forth the dollar amount and the rate by which the limit will be exceeded.

Any law requiring the expenditure of state funds shall be null and void unless, during the session in which the act receives final passage, an appropriation is made for the estimated first year's funding.

No law of general application shall impose increased expenditure requirements on cities or counties unless the General Assembly shall provide that the state share in the cost.

An accurate financial statement of the state's fiscal condition shall be published annually.

DEFAULTERS INELIGIBLE
Section 25. No person who heretofore hath been, or may hereafter be, a collector or holder of public moneys, shall have a seat in either House of the General Assembly, or hold any other office under the state government, until such per-

son shall have accounted for, and paid into the Treasury, all sums for which he may be accountable or liable.

INELIGIBILTY — LUCRATIVE OFFICES

Section 26. No judge of any court of law or equity, secretary of state, attorney general, register, clerk of any Court of Record, or person holding any office under the authority of the United States, shall have a seat in the General Assembly; nor shall any person in this state hold more than one lucrative office at the same time; provided, that no appointment in the Militia, or to the Office of Justice of the Peace, shall be considered a lucrative office, or operative as a disqualification to a seat in either House of the General Assembly.

RIGHT TO PROTEST

Section 27. Any member of either House of the General Assembly shall have liberty to dissent from and protest against, any act or resolve which he may think injurious to the public or to any individual, and to have the reasons for his dissent entered on the journals.

TAXABLE PROPERTY — VALUATION — RATES

Section 28. In accordance with the following provisions, all property real, personal or mixed shall be subject to taxation, but the Legislature may except such as may be held by the state, by counties, cities or towns, and used exclusively for public or corporation purposes, and such as may be held and used for purposes purely religious, charitable, scientific, literary or educational, and shall except the direct product of the soil in the hands of the producer, and his immediate vendee, and the entire amount of money deposited in an individual's personal or family checking or savings accounts. For purposes of taxation, property shall be classified into three classes, to wit: Real property, tangible personal property and intangible personal property.

Real property shall be classified into four (4) subclassifications and assessed as follows:

(a) Public utility property, to be assessed at fifty-five (55%) percent of its value;

(b) industrial and commercial property, to be assessed at forty (40%) percent of its value

(c) residential property, to be assessed at twenty five (25%) percent of its value; provided that residential property containing two (2) or more rental units is hereby defined as industrial and commercial property; and

(d) farm property, to be assessed at twenty-five (25%) percent of its value. House trailers, mobile homes, and all other similar movable structures used for commercial, industrial, or residential purposes shall be assessed as real property as an improvement to the land where located.

The Legislature shall provide, in such a manner as it deems appropriate, tax relief to elderly, low-income taxpayers through payments by the state to reimburse all or part of the taxes paid by such persons on owner-occupied residential property, but such reimbursement shall not be an obligation imposed, directly or indirectly, upon counties, cities or towns.

The Legislature may provide tax relief to home owners totally and permanently disabled, irrespective of age, as provided herein for the elderly.

Tangible personal property shall be classified into three (3) subclassifications and assessed as follows:

(a) Public utility property, to be assessed at fifty-five (55%) percent of its value;

(b) industrial and commercial property, to be assessed at thirty (30%) percent of its value; and

(c) all other tangible personal property, to be assessed at five (5%) percent of its value; provided, however, that the Legislature shall exempt seven thousand five hundred ($7,500) dollars worth of such tangible personal property which shall cover personal household goods and furnishings, wearing apparel and other such tangible property in the hands of a taxpayer.

The Legislature shall have power to classify intangible personal property into subclassifications and to establish a ratio of assessment to value in each class or subclass, and shall provide fair and equitable methods of apportionment of the value of same to this state for purposes of taxation. Banks, insurance companies, loan and investment companies, savings and loan associations, and all similar financial institutions, shall be assessed and taxed in such manner as the Legislature shall direct; provided that for the year 1973, or until such time as the Legislature may provide otherwise, the ratio of assessment to value of property presently taxed shall remain the same as provided by law for the year 1972; provided further that the taxes imposed upon such financial institutions, and paid by them, shall be in lieu of all taxes on the redeemable or cash value of all of their outstanding shares of capital stock, policies of insurance, customer savings and checking accounts, certificates of deposit, and certificates of investment, by whatever name called, including other intangible corporate property of such financial institutions.

The ratio of assessment to value of property in each class or subclass shall be equal and uniform throughout the state, the value and definition of property in each class or subclass to be ascertained in such manner as the Legislature shall direct. Each respective taxing authority shall apply the same tax rate to all property within its jurisdiction.

The Legislature shall have power to tax merchants, peddlers, and privileges, in such manner as they may from time to time direct, and the Legislature may levy a gross receipts tax on merchants and businesses in lieu of ad valorem taxes on the inventories of merchandise held by such merchants and businesses for sale or exchange. The portion of a merchant's capital used in the purchase of merchandise sold by him to nonresidents and sent beyond the state, shall not be taxed at a rate higher than the ad valorem tax on property. The Legislature shall have power to levy a tax upon incomes derived from stocks and bonds that are not taxed ad valorem.

This amendment shall take effect on the first day of January, 1973.

COUNTIES AND TOWNS — POWER TO TAX — CREDIT

Section 29. The General Assembly shall have power to authorize the several counties and incorporated towns in this state, to impose taxes for county and corporation purposes respectively, in such manner as shall be prescribed by law; and all property shall be taxed according to its value, upon the principles established in regard to state taxation. But the credit of no county, city or town shall be given or loaned to or in aid of any person, company, association or corporation, except upon an election to be first held by the qualified voters of such county, city or town, and the assent of three-fourths of the votes cast at said election. Nor shall any county, city or town become a stockholder with others in any company, association or corporation except upon a like election, and the assent of a like majority. But the counties of Grainger, Hawkins, Hancock, Union, Campbell, Scott, Morgan, Grundy, Sumner, Smith, Fentress, Van Buren, and the new county herein authorized to be established out of fractions of Sumner, Macon and Smith Counties, White, Putnam, Overton, Jackson, Cumberland, Anderson, Henderson, Wayne, Cocke, Coffee, Macon, Marshall, and Roane shall be excepted out of the provisions of this section so far that the assent of a majority of the qualified voters of either of said counties voting on the question shall be sufficient when the credit of such county is given or loaned to any person, association or corporation; provided, that the exception of the counties above named shall not be in force beyond the year one thousand eight hundred and eighty: and after that period they shall be subject to the three-fourths majority applicable to the other counties of the state.

ARTICLES NOT TAXABLE — INSPECTION FEES

Section 30. No article manufactured of the produce of this state, shall be taxed otherwise than to pay inspection fees.

ACTS FORBIDDEN THE STATE

Section 31. The credit of this state shall not be hereafter loaned or given to or in aid of any person, association, company, corporation or municipality; nor shall the state become the owner in whole or in part of any bank or a stockholder with others in any association, company, corporation or municipality.

AMENDMENTS TO CONSTITUTION OF UNITED STATES

Section 32. No convention or general assembly of this state shall act upon any amendment of the Constitution of the United States proposed by Congress to the several states; unless such convention or general assembly shall have been elected after such amendment is submitted.

No State Bonds to Defaulting Railroads

Section 33. No bonds of the state shall be issued to any rail road company which at the time of its application for the same shall be in default in paying the interest upon the state bonds previously loaned to it or that shall hereafter and before such application sell or absolutely dispose of any state bonds loaned to it for less than par.

ARTICLE III — EXECUTIVE DEPARTMENT

Governor's Executive Power

Section 1. The supreme executive power of this state shall be vested in a governor.

Election of Governor

Section 2. The governor shall be chosen by the electors of the members of the General Assembly, at the time and places where they shall respectively vote for the members thereof. The returns of every election for governor shall be sealed up, and transmitted to the seat of government, by the returning officers, directed to the speaker of the Senate, who shall open and publish them in the presence of a majority of the members of each House of the General Assembly. The person having the highest number of votes shall be governor; but if two or more shall be equal and highest in votes, one of them shall be chosen governor by joint vote of both Houses of the General Assembly. Contested elections for governor shall be determined by both Houses of the General Assembly, in such manner as shall be prescribed by law.

Governor's Qualifications

Section 3. He shall be at least thirty years of age, shall be a citizen of the United States, and shall have been a citizen of this state seven years next before his election.

Governor's Term of Service

Section 4. The governor shall be elected to hold office for four years and until a successor is elected and qualified. A person may be eligible to succeed in office for additional four year terms, provided that no person presently serving or elected hereafter shall be eligible for election to more than two terms consecutively, including an election to a partial term.

One succeeding to the office vacated during the first eighteen calendar months of the term shall hold office until a successor is elected for the remainder of the term at the next election of members of the General Assembly and qualified pursuant to this Constitution. One succeeding to the office vacated after the first eighteen calendar months of the term shall continue to hold office for the remainder of the full term.

GOVERNOR AS COMMANDER-IN-CHIEF — CALLING OUT MILITIA
Section 5. He shall be commander-in-chief of the Army and Navy of this state, and of the Militia, except when they shall be called into the service of the United States. But the Militia shall not be called into service except in case of rebellion or invasion, and then only when the General Assembly shall declare, by law, that the public safety requires it.

PARDONS AND REPRIEVES
Section 6. He shall have power to grant reprieves and pardons, after conviction, except in cases of impeachment.

GOVERNOR'S COMPENSATION
Section 7. He shall, at stated times, receive a compensation for his services, which shall not be increased or diminished during the period for which he shall have been elected.

GOVERNOR MAY REQUIRE INFORMATION
Section 8. He may require information in writing, from the officers in the executive department, upon any subject relating to the duties of their respective offices.

GOVERNOR MAY CONVENE THE LEGISLATURE
Section 9. He may, on extraordinary occasions, convene the General Assembly by proclamation, in which he shall state specifically the purposes for which they are to convene; but they shall enter on no legislative business except that for which they were specifically called together.

GOVERNOR TO EXECUTE LAWS
Section 10. He shall take care that the laws be faithfully executed.

GOVERNOR TO GIVE INFORMATION TO THE LEGISLATURE
Section 11. He shall, from time to time, give to the General Assembly information of the state of the government, and recommend for their consideration such measures as he shall judge expedient.

VACANCY IN OFFICE OF GOVERNOR
Section 12. In case of the removal of the governor from office, or of his death, or resignation, the powers and duties of the office shall devolve on the speaker of the Senate; and in case of the death, removal from office, or resignation of the speaker of the Senate, the powers and duties of the office shall devolve on the speaker of the House of Representatives.

Ineligibility for Governorship

Section 13. No member of Congress, or person holding any office under the United States, or this state, shall execute the office of governor.

Governor to Make Temporary Appointments

Section 14. When any officer, the right of whose appointment is by this Constitution vested in the General Assembly, shall, during the recess, die, or the office, by the expiration of the term, or by other means, become vacant, the governor shall have the power to fill such vacancy by granting a temporary commission, which shall expire at the end of the next session of the Legislature.

Seal of State

Section 15. There shall be a seal of this state, which shall be kept by the governor, and used by him officially, and shall be called the Great Seal of the State of Tennessee.

Grants and Commissions to be Sealed and Signed by the Governor

Section 16. All grants and commissions shall be in the name and by the authority of the state of Tennessee, be sealed with the State Seal, and signed by the governor.

Secretary of State

Section 17. A secretary of state shall be appointed by joint vote of the General Assembly, and commissioned during the term of four years; he shall keep a fair register of all the official acts and proceedings of the governor; and shall, when required lay the same, and all papers, minutes and vouchers relative thereto, before the General Assembly; and shall perform such other duties as shall be enjoined by law.

Bills to Be Approved by the Governor — Governor's Veto — Bills Passed over Governor's Veto

Section 18. Every bill which may pass both Houses of the General Assembly shall, before it becomes a law, be presented to the governor for his signature. If he approve, he shall sign it, and the same shall become a law; but if he refuse, to sign it, he shall return it with his objections thereto, in writing, to the house in which it originated; and said House shall cause said objections to be entered at large upon its journal, and proceed to reconsider the bill. If after such reconsideration, a majority of all the members elected to that House shall agree to pass the bill, notwithstanding the objections of the executive, it shall be sent, with said objections, to the other House, by which it shall be likewise reconsidered. If approved by a majority of the whole number elected to that House, it shall become a law. The votes of both Houses shall be determined by yeas and nays, and the names of all the members voting for or against the bill shall be entered upon the journals of their respective Houses.

If the governor shall fail to return any bill with his objections in writing within ten calendar days (Sundays excepted) after it shall have been presented to him, the same shall become a law without his signature. If the General Assembly by its adjournment prevents the return of any bill within said ten-day period, the bill shall become a law, unless disapproved by the governor and filed by him with his objections in writing in the office of the secretary of state within said ten-day period.

Every joint resolution or order (except on question of adjournment and proposals of specific amendments to the Constitution) shall likewise be presented to the governor for his signature, and on being disapproved by him shall in like manner, be returned with his objections; and the same before it shall take effect shall be repassed by a majority of all the members elected to both houses in the manner and according to the rules prescribed in case of a bill.

The governor may reduce or disapprove the sum of money appropriated by any one or more items or parts of items in any bill appropriating money, while approving other portions of the bill. The portions so approved shall become law, and the items or parts of items disapproved or reduced shall be void to the extent that they have been disapproved or reduced unless repassed as hereinafter provided. The governor, within ten calendar days (Sundays excepted) after the bill shall have been presented to him, shall report the items or parts of items disapproved or reduced with his objections in writing to the House in which the bill originated, or if the General Assembly shall have adjourned, to the office of the secretary of state. Any such items or parts of items so disapproved or reduced shall be restored to the bill in the original amount and become law if repassed by the General Assembly according to the rules and limitations prescribed for the passage of other bills over the executive veto.

ARTICLE IV — ELECTIONS

RIGHT TO VOTE — ELECTION PRECINCTS — MILITARY DUTY

Section 1. Every person, being eighteen years of age, being a citizen of the United States, being a resident of the state for a period of time as prescribed by the General Assembly, and being duly registered in the county of residence for a period of time prior to the day of any election as prescribed by the General Assembly, shall be entitled to vote in all federal, state, and local elections held in the county or district in which such person resides. All such requirements shall be equal and uniform across the state, and there shall be no other qualification attached to the right of suffrage.

The General Assembly shall have power to enact laws requiring voters to vote in the election precincts in which they may reside, and laws to secure the freedom of elections and the purity of the ballot box.

All male citizens of this state shall be subject to the performance of military duty, as may be prescribed by law.

RIGHT OF SUFFRAGE MAY BE EXCLUDED FOR CRIME
Section 2. Laws may be passed excluding from the right of suffrage persons who may be convicted of infamous crimes.

PRIVILEGES OF VOTERS
Section 3. Electors shall, in all cases, except treason, felony, or breach of the peace, be privileged from arrest or summons, during their attendance at elections and in going to and returning from them.

MODE OF VOTING
Section 4. In all elections to be made by the General Assembly, the members thereof shall vote viva voce, and their votes shall be entered on the journal. All other elections shall be by ballot.

ARTICLE V — IMPEACHMENTS

IMPEACHMENT
Section 1. The House of Representatives shall have the sole power of impeachment.

TRIAL OF IMPEACHMENTS
Section 2. All impeachments shall be tried by the Senate. When sitting for that purpose the senators shall be upon oath or affirmation, and the chief justice of the Supreme Court, or if he be on trial, the senior associate judge, shall preside over them. No person shall be convicted without the concurrence of two-thirds of the senators sworn to try the officer impeached.

HOW PROSECUTED
Section 3. The House of Representatives shall elect from their own body three members, whose duty it shall be to prosecute impeachments. No impeachment shall be tried until the Legislature shall have adjourned sine die, when the Senate shall proceed to try such impeachment.

WHO MAY BE IMPEACHED
Section 4. The governor, judges of the Supreme Court, judges of the inferior courts, chancellors, attorneys for the state, treasurer, comptroller, and secretary of state, shall be liable to impeachment, whenever they may, in the opinion of the House of Representatives, commit any crime in their official capacity which may require disqualification but judgment shall only extend to removal from office, and disqualification to fill any office thereafter. The party shall, nevertheless, be liable to indictment, trial, judgment and punishment according to law. The Legislature now has, and shall continue to have, power to relieve from the

penalties imposed, any person disqualified from holding office by the judgment of a Court of Impeachment.

Officers Liable to Indictment and Removal from Office
Section 5. Justices of the peace, and other civil officers not herein before mentioned, for crimes or misdemeanors in office, shall be liable to indictment in such courts as the Legislature may direct; and upon conviction, shall be removed from office by said court, as if found guilty on impeachment; and shall be subject to such other punishment as may be prescribed by law.

ARTICLE VI — JUDICIAL DEPARTMENT
Judicial Power
Section 1. The judicial power of this state shall be vested in one Supreme Court and in such Circuit, Chancery and other Inferior Courts as the Legislature shall from time to time, ordain and establish; in the judges thereof, and in justices of the peace. The Legislature may also vest such jurisdiction in Corporation Courts as may be deemed necessary. Courts to be holden by justices of the peace may also be established.

Supreme Court
Section 2. The Supreme Court shall consist of five judges, of whom not more than two shall reside in any one of the grand divisions of the state. The judges shall designate one of their own number who shall preside as chief justice. The concurrence of three of the judges shall in every case be necessary to a decision. The jurisdiction of this court shall be appellate only, under such restrictions and regulations as may from time to time be prescribed by law; but it may possess such other jurisdiction as is now conferred by law on the present Supreme Court. Said court shall be held at Knoxville, Nashville and Jackson.

Supreme Court Judges
Section 3. The judges of the Supreme Court shall be elected by the qualified voters of the state. The Legislature shall have power to prescribe such rules as may be necessary to carry out the provisions of section two of this article. Every judge of the Supreme Court shall be thirty-five years of age, and shall before his election have been a resident of the state for five years. His term of service shall be eight years.

Judges of Inferior Courts
Section 4. The Judges of the Circuit and Chancery Courts, and of other Inferior Courts, shall be elected by the qualified voters of the district or circuit to which they are to be assigned. Every judge of such courts shall be thirty years of age, and shall before his election, have been a resident of the state for five years, and of the circuit or district one year. His term of service shall be eight years.

ATTORNEY-GENERAL AND REPORTER

Section 5. An attorney general and reporter for the state, shall be appointed by the judges of the Supreme Court and shall hold his office for a term of eight years. An attorney for the state for any circuit or district, for which a judge having criminal jurisdiction shall be provided by law, shall be elected by the qualified voters of such circuit or district, and shall hold his office for a term of eight years, and shall have been a resident of the state five years, and of the circuit or district one year. In all cases where the attorney for any district fails or refuses to attend and prosecute according to law, the court shall have power to appoint an attorney pro tempore.

REMOVAL OF JUDGES AND ATTORNEYS

Section 6. Judges and attorneys for the state may be removed from office by a concurrent vote of both Houses of the General Assembly, each House voting separately; but two-thirds of the members to which each House may be entitled must concur in such vote. The vote shall be determined by ayes and noes, and the names of the members voting for or against the judge or attorney for the state together with the cause or causes of removal, shall be entered on the journals of each House respectively. The judge or attorney for the state, against whom the Legislature may be about to proceed, shall receive notice thereof accompanied with a copy of the causes alleged for his removal, at least ten days before the day on which either House of the General Assembly shall act thereupon.

COMPENSATION OF JUDGES

Section 7. The judges of the Supreme or Inferior Courts, shall, at stated times, receive a compensation for their services, to be ascertained by law, which shall not be increased or diminished during the time for which they are elected. They shall not be allowed any fees or perquisites of office nor hold any other office of trust or profit under this state or the United States.

JURISDICTION OF INFERIOR COURTS

Section 8. The jurisdiction of the Circuit, Chancery and other Inferior Courts, shall be as now established by law, until changed by the Legislature.

JUDGE'S CHARGE

Section 9. The judges shall not charge juries with respect to matters of fact, but may state the testimony and declare the law.

CERTIORARI

Section 10. The judges or justices of the Inferior Courts of Law and Equity, shall have power in all civil cases, to issue writs of certiorari to remove any cause or the transcript of the record thereof, from any inferior jurisdiction, into such court of law, on sufficient cause, supported by oath or affirmation.

INCOMPETENCY OF JUDGES — SPECIAL JUDGES

Section 11. No judge of the Supreme or Inferior Courts shall preside on the trial of any cause in the event of which he may be interested, or where either of the parties shall be connected with him by affinity or consanguinity, within such degrees as may be prescribed by law, or in which he may have been of counsel, or in which he may have presided in any Inferior Court, except by consent of all the parties. In case all or any of the judges of the Supreme Court shall thus be disqualified from presiding on the trial of any cause or causes, the court or the judges thereof, shall certify the same to the governor of the state, and he shall forthwith specially commission the requisite number of men, of law knowledge, for the trial and determination thereof. The Legislature may by general laws make provision that special judges may be appointed, to hold any courts the judge of which shall be unable or fail to attend or sit; or to hear any cause in which the judge may be incompetent.

REQUISITES OF WRITS AND PROCESS

Section 12. All writs and other process shall run in the name of the state of Tennessee and bear test and be signed by the respective clerks. Indictments shall conclude, "against the peace and dignity of the state."

CLERKS OF COURTS

Section 13. Judges of the Supreme Court shall appoint their clerks who shall hold their offices for six years. Chancellors shall appoint their clerks and masters, who shall hold their offices for six years. Clerks of the Inferior Courts holden in the respective counties or districts, shall be elected by the qualified voters thereof for the term of four years. Any clerk may be removed from office for malfeasance, incompetency or neglect of duty, in such manner as may be prescribed by law.

FINES EXCEEDING FIFTY DOLLARS TO BE ASSESSED BY JURY

Section 14. No fine shall be laid on any citizen of this state that shall exceed fifty dollars, unless it shall be assessed by a jury of his peers, who shall assess the fine at the time they find the fact, if they think the fine should be more than fifty dollars.

ARTICLE VII — STATE AND COUNTY OFFICERS

COUNTY OFFICERS — THEIR ELECTION — TERMS — REMOVAL

Section 1. The qualified voters of each county shall elect for terms of four years a legislative body, a county executive, a sheriff, a trustee, a register, a county clerk and an assessor of property. Their qualifications and duties shall be prescribed by the General Assembly. Any officer shall be removed for malfeasance or neglect of duty as prescribed by the General Assembly.

The legislative body shall be composed of representatives from districts in the county as drawn by the county legislative body pursuant to statutes enacted by the General Assembly. Districts shall be reapportioned at least every ten years based upon the most recent federal census. The legislative body shall not exceed twenty-five members, and no more than three representatives shall be elected from a district. Any county organized under the consolidated government provisions of Article XI, Section 9, of this Constitution shall be exempt from having a county executive and a county legislative body as described in this paragraph.

The General Assembly may provide alternate forms of county government including the right to charter and the manner by which a referendum may be called. The new form of government shall replace the existing form if approved by a majority of the voters in the referendum.

No officeholder's current term shall be diminished by the ratification of this article.

Vacancies — How Filled
Section 2. Vacancies in county offices shall be filled by the county legislative body, and any person so appointed shall serve until a successor is elected at the next election occurring after the vacancy is qualified.

Treasurer and Comptroller
Section 3. There shall be a treasurer or treasurers and a comptroller of the treasury appointed for the state, by the joint vote of both Houses of the General Assembly, who shall hold their offices for two years.

Other Elections and Vacancies
Section 4. The election of officers, and the filling of all vacancies not otherwise directed or provided by this Constitution, shall be made in such manner as the Legislature shall direct.

Civil Officers — Election — Vacancies
Section 5. Elections for judicial and other civil officers shall be held on the first Thursday in August, one thousand eight hundred and seventy, and forever thereafter on the first Thursday in August next preceding the expiration of their respective terms of service. The term of each officer so elected shall be computed from the first day of September next succeeding his election. The term of office of the governor and other executive officers shall be computed from the fifteenth of January next after the election of the governor. No appointment or election to fill a vacancy shall be made for a period extending beyond the unexpired term. Every officer shall hold his office until his successor is elected or appointed, and qualified. No special election shall be held to fill a vacancy in the office of judge or district attorney, but a the time herein fixed for the biennial election of civil officers, and such vacancy shall be filled at the next biennial election recurring more than thirty days after the vacancy occurs.

ARTICLE VIII — MILITIA

MILITIA OFFICERS TO BE ELECTED

Section 1. All militia officers shall be elected by persons subject to military duty, within the bounds of their several companies, battalions, regiments, brigades and divisions, under such rules and regulations as the Legislature may from time to time direct and establish.

STAFF OFFICERS TO BE APPOINTED

Section 2. The governor shall appoint the adjutant-general and his other staff officers; the major generals, brigadier-generals, and commanding officers of regiments, shall respectively appoint their staff officers.

EXEMPTIONS FROM ATTENDING MUSTERS

Section 3. The Legislature shall pass laws exempting citizens belonging to any sect or denomination of religion, the tenets of which are known to be opposed to the bearing of arms, from attending private and general musters.

ARTICLE IX — DISQUALIFICATIONS

INELIGIBILITY OF MINISTERS AND PRIESTS TO SEATS IN LEGISLATURE

Section 1. Whereas ministers of the Gospel are by their profession, dedicated to God and the care of souls, and ought not to be diverted from the great duties of their functions; therefore, no minister of the Gospel, or priest of any denomination whatever, shall be eligible to a seat in either House of the Legislature.

NO ATHEIST SHALL HOLD A CIVIL OFFICE

Section 2. No person who denies the being of God, or a future state of rewards and punishments, shall hold any office in the civil department of this state.

DUELISTS SHALL HOLD NO OFFICE

Section 3. Any person who shall, after the adoption of this Constitution, fight a duel, or knowingly be the bearer of a challenge to fight a duel, or send or accept a challenge for that purpose, or be an aider or abettor in fighting a duel, shall be deprived of the right to hold any office of honor or profit in this state, and shall be punished otherwise, in such manner as the Legislature may prescribe.

ARTICLE X — OATHS, BRIBERY OF ELECTORS, NEW COUNTIES

OATH OF OFFICE

Section 1. Every person who shall be chosen or appointed to any office of trust or profit under this Constitution, or any law made in pursuance thereof, shall, before entering on the duties thereof, take an oath to support the Constitution of this state, and of the United States, and an oath of office.

OATH OF MEMBERS OF THE GENERAL ASSEMBLY

Section 2. Each member of the Senate and House of Representatives, shall before they proceed to business take an oath or affirmation to support the Constitution of this state, and of the United States and also the following oath: I _____do solemnly swear (or affirm) that as a member of this General Assembly, I will, in all appointments, vote without favor, affection, partiality, or prejudice; and that I will not propose or assent to any bill, vote or resolution, which shall appear to me injurious to the people, or consent to any act or thing, whatever, that shall have a tendency to lessen or abridge their rights and privileges, as declared by the Constitution of this state.

PUNISHMENT OF ELECTORS AND CANDIDATES FOR BRIBERY

Section 3. Any elector who shall receive any gift or reward for his vote, in meat, drink, money or otherwise, shall suffer such punishment as the laws shall direct. And any person who shall directly or indirectly give, promise or bestow any such reward to be elected, shall thereby be rendered incapable, for six years, to serve in the office for which he was elected, and be subject to such further punishment as the Legislature shall direct.

NEW COUNTIES — APPROACH OF COUNTY LINES TO COURTHOUSE — LIMIT TO REDUCTION OF COUNTIES — EXCEPTIONS — VOTE NECESSARY TO DETACH FRACTIONS FOR FORMATION OF NEW COUNTIES OR TO REMOVE A COUNTY SEAT — LIABILITY FOR EXISTING DEBT

Section 4. New Counties may be established by the Legislature to consist of not less than two hundred and seventy five square miles, and which shall contain a population of seven hundred qualified voters; no line of such county shall approach the court house of any old county from which it may be taken nearer than eleven miles, nor shall such old county be reduced to less than five hundred square miles. But the following exceptions are made to the foregoing provisions viz: New counties may be established by the present or any succeeding Legislature out of the following territory to wit: Out of that portion of Obion County which lies west of the low water mark of Reel Foot Lake: Out of fractions of Sumner, Macon and Smith Counties; but no line of such new county shall approach the court house of Sumner or of Smith Counties nearer than ten miles, nor include any part of Macon County lying within nine and a half miles of the court house of said County nor shall more than twenty square miles of Macon County nor any part of Sumner County lying due west of the western boundary of Macon County, be taken in the formation of said new county: Out of fractions of Grainger and Jefferson Counties but no line of such new county shall include any part of Grainger County north of the Holston River; nor shall any line thereof approach the court house of Jefferson County nearer than eleven miles. Such new county may include any other territory which is not excluded by any general provision of this Constitution: Out of fractions of

Jackson and Overton Counties but no line of such new county shall approach the court house of Jackson or Overton Counties nearer than ten miles, nor shall such county contain less that four hundred qualified voters, nor shall the area of either of the old counties be reduced below four hundred and fifty square miles: Out of fractions of Roane, Monroe, and Blount Counties, around the town of Loudon; but no line of such new county shall ever approach the towns of Maryville, Kingston, or Madisonville, nearer than eleven miles, except that on the south side of the Tennessee River, said lines may approach as near as ten miles to the court house of Roane County.

The counties of Lewis, Cheatham, and Sequatchie, as now established by Legislative enactments are hereby declared to be constitutional counties. No part of Bledsoe County shall be taken to form a new county or a part thereof or be attached to any adjoining county. That portion of Marion County included within the following boundaries, beginning on the Grundy and Marion County line at the Nickajack trace and running about six hundred yards west of Ben Poseys, to where the Tennessee Coal Rail Road crosses the line, running thence southeast through the Pocket near William Summers crossing the Battle Creek Gulf at the corner of Thomas Wootons field, thence running across the Little Gizzard Gulf at Raven Point, thence in a direct line to the bridge crossing the Big Fiery Gizzard, thence in a direct line to the mouth of Holy Water Creek, thence up said Creek to the Grundy County line, and thence with said line to the beginning; is hereby detached from Marion County, and attached to the county of Grundy. No part of a county shall be taken off to form a new county or a part thereof without the consent of two-thirds of the qualified voters in such part taken off; and where an old county is reduced for the purpose of forming a new one, the seat of justice in said old county shall not be removed without the concurrence of two-thirds in both branches of the Legislature, nor shall the seat of justice of any county be removed without the concurrence of two-thirds of the qualified voters of the county. But the foregoing provision requiring a two-thirds majority of the voters of a county to remove its county seat shall not apply to the counties of Obion and Cocke. The fractions taken from old counties to form new counties or taken from one county and added to another shall continue liable for their pro rata of all debts contracted by their respective counties prior to the separation, and be entitled to their proportion of any stocks or credits belonging to such old counties.

To Vote with Old County
Section 5. The citizens who may be included in any new county shall vote with the county or counties from which they may have been stricken off, for members of Congress, for governor and for members of the General Assembly until the next apportionment of members to the General Assembly after the establishment of such new county.

ARTICLE XI — MISCELLANEOUS PROVISIONS

Existing Laws Not Affected by This Constitution

Section 1. All laws and ordinances now in force and use in this state, not inconsistent with this Constitution, shall continue in force and use until they shall expire, be altered or repealed by the Legislature; but ordinances contained in any former Constitution or schedule thereto are hereby abrogated.

No Impairment of Rights

Section 2. Nothing contained in this Constitution shall impair the validity of any debts or contracts, or affect any rights of property or any suits, actions, rights of action or other proceedings in Courts of Justice.

Amendments to Constitution

Section 3. Any amendment or amendments to this Constitution may be proposed in the Senate or House of Representatives, and if the same shall be agreed to by a majority of all the members elected to each of the two houses, such proposed amendment or amendments shall be entered on their journals with the yeas and nays thereon, and referred to the General Assembly then next to be chosen; and shall be published six months previous to the time of making such choice; and if in the General Assembly then next chosen as aforesaid, such proposed amendment or amendments shall be agreed to by two-thirds of all the members elected to each house, then it shall be the duty of the General Assembly to submit such proposed amendment or amendments to the people at the next general election in which a governor is to be chosen. And if the people shall approve and ratify such amendment or amendments by a majority of all the citizens of the state voting for governor, voting in their favor, such amendment or amendments shall become a part of this Constitution. When any amendment or amendments to the Constitution shall be proposed in pursuance of the foregoing provisions the same shall at each of said sessions be read three times on three several days in each house. The Legislature shall have the right by law to submit to the people, at any general election, the question of calling a convention to alter, reform, or abolish this Constitution, or to alter, reform or abolish any specified part or parts of it; and when, upon such submission, a majority of all the voters voting upon the proposal submitted shall approve the proposal to call a convention, the delegates to such convention shall be chosen at the next general election and the convention shall assemble for the consideration of such proposals as shall have received a favorable vote in said election, in such mode and manner as shall be prescribed. No change in, or amendment to, this Constitution proposed by such convention shall become effective, unless within the limitations of the call of the convention, and unless approved and ratified by a majority of the qualified voters voting separately on such change or amendment at an election to be held in such manner and on such date as may be fixed by the convention. No such convention shall be held oftener than once in six years.

POWER TO GRANT DIVORCE
Section 4. The Legislature shall have no power to grant divorces; but may authorize the Courts of Justice to grant them for such causes as may be specified by law; but such laws shall be general and uniform in their operation throughout the state.

LOTTERIES
Section 5. The Legislature shall have no power to authorize lotteries for any purpose, and shall pass laws to prohibit the sale of lottery tickets in this state.

CHANGING NAMES — ADOPTION — LEGITIMATION
Section 6. The Legislature shall have no power to change the names of persons, or to pass acts adopting or legitimatizing persons, but shall, by general laws, confer this power on the courts.

INTEREST RATES
Section 7. The General Assembly shall define and regulate interest, and set maximum effective rates thereof.

If no applicable statute is hereafter enacted, the effective rate of interest collected shall not exceed ten (10%) percent per annum.

All provisions of existing statutes regulating rates of interest and other charges on loans shall remain in full force and effect until July 1, 1980, unless earlier amended or repealed.

GENERAL LAWS ONLY TO BE PASSED
Section 8. The Legislature shall have no power to suspend any general law for the benefit of any particular individual, nor to pass any law for the benefit of individuals inconsistent with the general laws of the land; nor to pass any law granting to any individual or individuals, rights, privileges, immunities, or exemptions other than such as may be, by the same law extended to any member of the community, who may be able to bring himself within the provisions of such law. No corporation shall be created or its powers increased or diminished by special laws but the General Assembly shall provide by general laws for the organization of all corporations, hereafter created, which laws may, at any time, be altered or repealed, and no such alteration or repeal shall interfere with or divest rights which have become vested.

POWER OVER LOCAL AFFAIRS — HOME RULE FOR
CITIES AND COUNTIES — CONSOLIDATION OF FUNCTIONS
Section 9. The Legislature shall have the right to vest such powers in the Courts of Justice, with regard to private and local affairs, as may be expedient.

The General Assembly shall have no power to pass a special, local or private act having the effect of removing the incumbent from any municipal or county office or abridging the term or altering the salary prior to the end of the term for which such public officer was selected, and any act of the General Assembly private or local in form or effect applicable to a particular county or municipality either in its governmental or its proprietary capacity shall be void and of no effect unless the act by its terms either requires the approval of a two-thirds vote of the local legislative body of the municipality or county, or requires approval in an election by a majority of those voting in said election in the municipality or county affected.

Any municipality may by ordinance submit to its qualified voters in a general or special election the question: "Shall this municipality adopt home rule?"

In the event of an affirmative vote by a majority of the qualified voters voting thereon, and until the repeal thereof by the same procedure, such municipality shall be a home rule municipality, and the General Assembly shall act with respect to such home rule municipality only by laws which are general in terms and effect.

Any municipality after adopting home rule may continue to operate under its existing charter, or amend the same, or adopt and thereafter amend a new charter to provide for its governmental and proprietary powers, duties and functions, and for the form, structure, personnel and organization of its government, provided that no charter provision except with respect to compensation of municipal personnel shall be effective if inconsistent with any general act of the General Assembly and provided further that the power of taxation of such municipality shall not be enlarged or increased except by general act of the General Assembly. The General Assembly shall by general law provide the exclusive methods by which municipalities may be created, merged, consolidated and dissolved and by which municipal boundaries may be altered.

A charter or amendment may be proposed by ordinance of any home rule municipality, by a charter commission provided for by act of the General Assembly and elected by the qualified voters of a home rule municipality voting thereon or, in the absence of such act of the General Assembly, by a charter commission of seven (7) members, chosen at large not more often than once in two (2) years, in a municipal election pursuant to petition for such election signed by qualified voters of a home rule municipality not less in number than ten (10%) percent of those voting in the then most recent general municipal election.

It shall be the duty of the legislative body of such municipality to publish any proposal so made and to submit the same to its qualified voters at the first general state election which shall be held at least sixty (60) days after such publication and such proposal shall become effective sixty (60) days after approval by a majority of the qualified voters voting thereon. The General Assembly shall not authorize any municipality to tax incomes, estates, or inheritances, or to impose any other tax not authorized by Sections 28 or 29 of Article II of this Constitution. Nothing herein shall be construed as invalidating the provisions of any municipal charter in existence at the time of the adoption of this amendment.

The General Assembly may provide for the consolidation of any or all of the governmental and corporate functions now or hereafter vested in municipal corporations with the governmental and corporate functions now or hereafter vested in the counties in which such municipal corporations are located; provided, such consolidations shall not become effective until submitted to the qualified voters residing within the municipal corporation and in the county outside thereof, and approved by a majority of those voting within the municipal corporation and by a majority of those voting in the county outside the municipal corporation.

Internal Improvements to Be Encouraged
Section 10. A well regulated system of internal improvement is calculated to develop, the resources of the state, and promote the happiness and prosperity of her citizens, therefore it ought to be encouraged by the General Assembly.

Homestead Exemption
Section 11. There shall be a homestead exemption from execution in an amount of five thousand dollars or such greater amount as the General Assembly may establish. The General Assembly shall also establish personal property exemptions. The definition and application of the homestead and personal property exemptions and the manner in which they may be waived shall be as prescribed by law.

Education to Be Cherished — Common School Fund
Section 12. The state of Tennessee recognizes the inherent value of education and encourages its support. The General Assembly shall provide for the maintenance, support and eligibility standards of a system of free public schools. The General Assembly may establish and support such post-secondary educational institutions, including public institutions of higher learning, as it determines.

Game and Fish
Section 13. The General Assembly shall have power to enact laws for the protection and preservation of game and fish, within the state, and such laws may be enacted for and applied and enforced in particular counties or geographical districts, designated by the General Assembly.

Intermarriage between Whites and Negroes
Section 14. The intermarriage of white persons with negroes, mullattos, or persons of mixed blood, descended from a negro to the third generation inclusive or their living together as a man and wife in this State is prohibited. The legislature shall enforce this section by appropriate legislation. [This provision was repealed in 1977.]

Religious Holidays

Section 15. No person shall in time of peace be required to perform any service to the public on any day set apart by his religion as a day of rest.

Bill of Rights to Remain Inviolate

Section 16. The declaration of rights hereto prefixed is declared to be a part of the Constitution of the state, and shall never be violated on any pretense whatever. And to guard against transgression of the high powers we have delegated, we declare that everything in the bill of rights contained, is excepted out of the general powers of the government, and shall forever remain inviolate.

County Offices

Section 17. No county office created by the Legislature shall be filled otherwise than by the people or the County Court.

SCHEDULE

Terms of Public Officers — Appointments — Exceptions

Section 1. That no inconvenience may arise from a change of the Constitution, it is declared that the governor of the state, the members of the General Assembly and all officers elected at or after the general election of March one thousand eight hundred and seventy, shall hold their offices for the terms prescribed in this Constitution.

Officers appointed by the courts shall be filled by appointment, to be made and to take effect during the first term of the court held by judges elected under this Constitution.

All other officers shall vacate their places thirty days after the day fixed for the election of their successors under this Constitution.

The secretary of state, comptroller and treasurer shall hold their offices until the first session of the present General Assembly occurring after the ratification of this Constitution and until their successors are elected and qualified.

The officers then elected shall hold their offices until the fifteenth day of January one thousand eight hundred and seventy three.

Supreme Court Judges — Vacancies —
Attorney-General and Reporter

Section 2. At the first election of judges under this Constitution there shall be elected six judges of the Supreme Court, two from each grand division of the state, who shall hold their offices for the term herein prescribed.

In the event any vacancy shall occur in the office of either of said judges at any time after the first day of January one thousand eight hundred seventy three; it shall remain unfilled and the court shall from that time be constituted of five judges. While the court shall consist of six judges they may sit in two sections, and may hear and determine causes in each at the same time, but not in different grand divisions at the same time.

When so sitting the concurrence of two judges shall be necessary to a decision.

The attorney general and reporter for the state shall be appointed after the election and qualification of the judges of the Supreme Court herein provided for.

OATH OF OFFICE MANDATORY

Section 3. Every judge and every officer of the executive department of this state, and every sheriff holding over under this Constitution, shall, within twenty days after the ratification of this Constitution is proclaimed, take an oath to support the same, and the failure of any officer to take such oath shall vacate his office.

STATUTE OF LIMITATIONS

Section 4. The time which has elapsed from the sixth day of May one thousand eight hundred and sixty one until the first day of January one thousand eight hundred and sixty seven shall not be computed, in any cases affected by the statutes of limitation, nor shall any writ of error be affected by such lapse of time.

Notes

Introduction

1. Alexander Hamilton, John Jay, and James Madison, *The Federalist* (New York: Robert B. Luce, 1976), 102–3.

2. *The Volunteer State: Readings in Tennessee Politics,* ed., Dorothy F. Olshfski and T. McN. Simpson III (Nashville: Tennessee Political Science Association, 1985).

3. Lewis Laska, in chapter 2, notes that, although this phrase is often attributed to Thomas Jefferson in secondary sources, he has been unable to trace it to an original source.

Chapter 1. Tennessee's Postbellum Political History

1. V. O. Key, Jr., *Southern Politics* (New York: Vantage Books, 1949), 78–79.

2. Joseph A. Califano, "Tough Talk for Democrats," *New York Times Magazine,* 8 January 1989, 28.

3. John C. Kuzenski and Michael K. Corbello, "Racial and Economic Explanations for Republican Growth in the South: A Case Study of Attitudinal Voting in Louisiana," *American Review of Politics* 10 (Summer 1996): 130.

4. Merle Black and Earl Black, *Politics and Society in the South* (Cambridge: Harvard University Press, 1987), 196.

Chapter 2. The Tennessee Constitution

1. For a discussion of the history of constitutional development in Tennessee, see Lewis L. Laska, "A Legal and Constitutional History of Tennessee, 1772–1972," 6 *Memphis State University Law Review* (1976) 563–672. For a narrative description of the provisions and interpretation of the Constitution, see Lewis L. Laska, *The Tennessee State Constitution: A Reference Guide* (Westport, Conn.: Greenwood, 1990).

2. Theodore Roosevelt, *The Winning of the West,* 6 vols. The Sagamore Series, vols. 8–13 (New York: Putnam, 1900; repr., New York: Current Literature, 1905), 1:231.

3. John Phillip Reid, *A Law of Blood: Primitive Law of the Cherokee Nation* (New York: New York University Press, 1970).

4. The romantic story of the "lost" State of Franklin was best told by jurist-historian Williams in 1924. See Samuel Cole Williams, *History of the Lost State of Franklin* (1924); see also William R. Garrett, ed., "The Provisional Constitution of Frankland," 1 *American Historical Magazine* (1896): 48–63; see also Albert V. Goodpasture, "Constitution of the State of Franklin," 9 *American Historical Magazine* (1904): 399–408.

5. Technically, it is the Constitution of 1835 because it was approved and proclaimed on March 27, 1835, but common usage has been to call it the Constitution

of 1834, the year of the convention. The courts tend to use both dates. State v. Keller, 813 S.W.2d 146 (Tenn. Crim. App. 1991).

6. James G. M. Ramsey, The Annals of Tennessee to the End of the Eighteenth Century (1853; reprint, 1967, 1972), 657. Commentators uniformly cite Ramsey as authority for Jefferson's observation, but Ramsey does not document the quotation, and this author has been unable to verify it independently.

7. Nat Turner's slave rebellion in Virginia in 1831, which killed fifty-five whites, was still in the public mind. Several anti-black laws were passed in the 1830s. For example, in 1831 a state law provided that emancipated slaves had to leave the state, and none could migrate into Tennessee. See H. M. Henry, "The Slave Laws of Tennessee," 2 *Tennessee Historical Magazine* (1916): 175–203; William L. Imes, "The Legal Status of the Free Negroes and Slaves in Tennessee," 4 *Journal of Negro History* (1919): 254–272; see also Chase C. Mooney, "The Question of Slavery and the Free Negro in the Tennessee Constitutional Convention of 1834," 12 *Journal of Southern History* (1946): 487–509.

8. *Journal of the Convention of the State of Tennessee, Convened for the Purpose of Revising and Amending the Constitution Thereof* (Nashville, W. H. Hunt, 1834), 93.

9. The fund was a casualty of the Civil War, but for decades thereafter the state pretended that it still existed, dutifully "paying" (appropriating) 6 percent interest on the phantom fund to support education. Robert H. White, *Development of the Tennessee State Educational Organization, 1796–1929* (Kingsport: Southern Publishers, 1929), 203.

10. Naturally, a provision of the new 1870 Constitution reversed the "null and void" language and said laws passed by the secession legislature were valid until declared unconstitutional on a case by case basis. Article 2, Section 1. Pace v. Strouse, 74 Tenn. 1 (1865); Frierson v. General Assembly of Presbyterian Church, 54 Tenn. 683 (1872).

11. Joshua W. Caldwell, *Studies in the Constitutional History of Tennessee*, 2d ed. (Cincinnati: Robert Clarke, 1907), 300.

12. The 1870 requirement was racially motivated but was supported by the argument that blacks should financially support the government, especially now that they could vote. The tax was fifty cents in 1870 and one dollar in 1883 but was irregularly collected. The law began to be enforced in 1890 (when Jim Crow took hold in Tennessee) and within two decades had effectively precluded meaningful black participation in all but the most intense local politics. See James E. Thorogood, *A Financial History of Tennessee Since 1870* (Nashville,: Tennessee Industrial School, 1949).

13. Baker v. Carr, 369 U.S. 186, 82 S. Ct. 691, 7 L.Ed.2d 663 (1963).

14. Snow v. City of Memphis, 527 S.W.2d 55 (1975).

15. Lewis L. Laska, "The 1977 Limited Constitutional Convention," 61 *Tennessee Law Review* (1994): 485–572.

16. Merchants Bank v. State Wildlife Resources Agency, 567 W.W. 2d 476 (Tenn. App. 1978); State ex rel. Anglin v. Mitchell, 596 S.W. 2d 779 (Tenn. 1980); Leech v. American Booksellers Association, 582 S.W. 2d 738 (1979); State v. Deuter, 839 S.W. 2d 391 (1992); State v. Middlebrooks, 840 S.W. 1d 317 (1992);

Tennesee Small School Systems v. McWherter, 851 S.W 2d 139 (1993). See Frederic S. LeClerc, "The Process of Selecting Constitutional Standards: Some Incongruities of Tennessee Practice," 61 *Tennessee Law Review* (1994): 573; Otis H. Stephens, Jr, "The Tennessee Constitution and the Dynamics of American Federalism," 61 *Tennessee Law Review* (1994): 707.

17. Illinois v. Gates, 462 U.S. 213 (1983); Aguilar v. Texas, 378 U.S. 108 (1964); Spinelli v. United States, 393 U.S. 410 (1969).

18. State v. Jacumin, 778 S.W. 2d 430 (1989). The court found the "totality of circumstances" test to be "inadequate as a test of probable cause" and observed that Article I, Section 7 of the Tennessee Constitution bars warrants "without evidence of the fact committed." Such language does not appear in the Fourth Amendment. See also State v. Valentine, 911 S.W. 2d 328 (1995).

19. State v. Marshall, 659 S.W. 1d 289 (1993); Davis-Kidd Booksellers, Inc. v. McWherter, 866 S.W. 2d. 520 (1993); Southern Living, Inc. v. Calauro, 890 S.W.2d 251 (1990).

20. State v. Creasy, 885 S.W. 2d 829 (Tenn. Crim. App. 1994).

21. Abernathy v. Whitley, 838 S.W. 2d 829 (Tenn. App. 1992). The right is statutory under the open records act. See T.C.A. 10-7-503.

22. Cannon v. Bristol Board of Education, 19 TAM 50–11 (Court of Appeals, November 11, 1994), appeal denied, March 17, 1995; Watts v. Civil Service Board, 606 S.W. 2d 274 (1980); Croushorn v. Board of Trustees, 518 F. Supp. 9 (M.D. Tenn. 1980); Anderson v. Evans, 660 F. 2d 153 (6th Cir. 1981); Garvie v. Jackson, 845 F. 2d 647 (6th Cir. 1988).

23. Smith v. University of Tennessee, 300 F. Supp. 777 (M.D. Tenn. 1990) (Civil rights activist Dick Gregory and LSD-use advocate Dr. Timothy Leary denied right to speak.)

24. Norton v. Discipline Committee of East Tennessee State University, 419 F.2d 195 (6th Cir. 1969). Jones v. State Board of Education, 279 F. Supp. 190 (M.D. Tenn. 1968), affirmed, 407 F.2d 834 (6th Cir. 1969).

25. Student Coalition for Gay Rights v. Austin Peay State University, 477 F.Supp. 1267 (M.D. Tenn. 1979); Knights of KKK v. Martin Luther King, Jr. Worshippers, 735 F. Supp. 745 (M.D. Tenn 1990).

26. Caldwell v. Craighead, 432 F.2d 213 (6th Cir. 1970).

27. State ex rel. Swann v. Pack, 527 S.W. 2d 99 (1975).

28. State v. Loudon, 857 S.W.2d 878 (Tenn. App. 1993). (Defendant insisted it was the "mark of the beast" mentioned in Revelation 13: 16–18.)

29. Martin v. Beer Board for Dickson, 908 S.W.2d 941 (Tenn. App. 1995). ("While Sunday was originally a day of religious observance, passage of time has converted it into a secular day for many citizens and has freed it from its exclusively religious origins.")

30. Goodwin v. Metropolitan Board of Health, 656 S.W.2d 383 (Tenn. App. 1983); State v. Anderson, 20 TAM 41–24 (Court of Criminal Appeals, September 20, 1995), appeal denied.

31. State ex rel. Anglin v. Mitchell, 596 S.W.2d 779, 786 (1980).

32. Rule 13, Tennessee Supreme Court Rules (July 1, 1997).

33. Gregg v. Lawson, 732 F.Supp. 849 (E.D.Tenn. 1989).

34. Miller v. State, 584 S.W.2d 758 (1979).

35. Mays's last words were, "I am as innocent as the sun that shines." See "Maurice Mays and the Knoxville Riot of 1919," in John Egerton, *Shades of Gray: Dispatches from the Modern South* (Baton Rouge: Louisiana State University Press, 1991), 164–187.

36. Forbes v. State, 559 S.W. 2d 318, 329 (1977).

37. Dwight Lewis," Smiling Forbes Leaves Sentence Behind," (Nashville) *Tennessean*, November 25, 1980, pp. 1, 10.

38. Welch v. State, 289 S.W.510 (1926); State v. Lakin, 588 S.W.2d544 (1969); State v. Jennette, 706 S.W.2d 614 (1986).

39. Cole v. State, 858 S.W.2d 915 (Crim. App. 1993).

40. Compare, State v. Perier, 752 S.W.1d 667 (1987) with United States v. Dunn, 107 S.Ct. 1134 (1987).

41. State v. Downey, 945 S.W.2d 102 (Tenn. 1997).

42. State v. Pendergrass, 20 TAM 14–27 (Court of Criminal Appeals, March 9, 1995); reversed on procedural grounds, State v. Pendergrass, 937 S.W.2d 834 (Tenn. 1996). Conversations must not be recorded. T.C.A. 39-13-604.

43. State v. Black, 814 S.W. 2d 166 (1991). See Penny J.. White, "A Survey of Tennessee Supreme Court Death Penalty Cases in the 1990s," 61 *Tennessee Law Review* (1994): 733.

44. Groseclose v. Dutton, 609 F.Supp. 1432 (M.D. Tenn. 1985). After this opinion was issued, the Tennessee Department of Corrections remodeled "Old Sparky," the state's electric chair.

45. State v. McKee, 803 S.W.2d 705 (Tenn. Crimin. App. 1990); Hancock v. Avery, 301 F. Supp. 786 (M.D. Tenn. 1969).

46. Dunn v. Palermo, 522 S.W.2d 679 (1975); Hanover v. Ruch, 809 S.W.2d 893 (1991); Dupuis v. Hand, 814 S.W. 2d 340 (1991).

47. Nale v. Robertson, 871 S.W.2d 674 (1994).

48. Cape v. Tennessee Secondary School Athletic Association, 563 F.2d 793 (6th Cir. 1977). (Girls' teams had six players and played to mid-court only.)

49. Davis v. Davis, 842 S.W.2d 588 (1992); Philip J. Prygoski, "The Implications of Davis v. Davis for Reproductive Right Analysis," 61 *Tennessee Law Review* (1994): 609.

50. Hawk v. Hawk, 855 S.W.2d 573 (1993). (The Court cited Article I, Section 8, freedom of speech. The grandparent visitation statute is T.C.A. 36-6-301).

51. Morrison v. Hamilton County Board of Education, 494 S.W.2d 770 (1973).

52. Campbell v. Sundquist, 926 S.W.2d. 250 (Tenn. App. 1996) app. denied.

53. Harrison v. Schrader, 569 S.W.2d 822 (1978); McDaniel v. Baptist Memorial Hospital, 352 F.Supp. 690 (W.D. Tenn. 1971), affirmed, 469 F.2d 230 (6th Cir. 1972).

54. Stutts v. Ford Motor Company, 574 F.Supp. 100) (M.D. Tenn. 1983). See William C. Koch, Jr., "Reopening Tennessee's Open Courts Clause: A Historical Reconsideration of Article 1, Section 17 of the Tennessee Constitution," 27 *University of Memphis Law Review* (1997): 333.

55. Grubbs v. Bradley, 552 F.Supp. 1052 (M.D. Tenn. 1982).

56. State v. Wilburn, 66 Tenn. 57 (1872); Kandall v. State, 118 Tenn. 156 (1906) ("Army or Navy pistol carried openly in the hand.") See Glenn Harlan Reynolds, "The Right to Keep and Bear Arms Under the Tennessee Constitution: A Case Study in Civic Republican Thought," 61 *Tennessee Law Review* (1994): 647.

57. Lee v. Ladd, 834 S.W.2d 323 (Tenn. App. 1992); See Lewis L. Laska, "A General Practitioner's Guide to Handling Claims Against the State of Tennessee," 23 *Tennessee Bar Journal* (July/August 1987): 26–31. An exception to the doctrine of sovereign immunity is the provision that persons who own land taken by the state for public projects may sue the state for "just compensation" if they are unhappy with the amount of money the state offers.

58. Church v. Church, 19 TAM 8-6 (Court of Appeals, February 3, 1994), no appeal taken.

59. State v. Superior Oil, Inc., 875 S.W.2d 658 (1994).

60. Ball v. Lawson, 19 TAM 37–21 (Court of Appeals, February 3, 1994), no appeal taken. See Lewis L. Laska and Brian Holmgren, "Forfeitures under the Tennessee Drug Control Act," 16 *Memphis State University Law Review* (1986): 431–530.

61. State v. Cumberland Club, 188 S.W.583 (1916).

62. Vincent v. State, 21 TAM 20-16 (Court of Appeals, 1996), appeal dismissed.

63. Lewis L. Laska, "The 1977 Limited Constitutional Convention," 61 *Tennessee Law Review* 485, 531 (1994).

64. Ibid. 532–44.

65. Walter P. Armstrong, Jr., "Constitutional Limitations on Income Taxes in Tennessee," 27 *Vanderbilt Law Review* (1974): 475; Lewis R. Donelson, "Tax Reform in Tennessee," 4 *Memphis State University Law Review* (1975): 201; John J. Harrington, Comment, "A Review of the Struggle for Tennessee Tax Reform," 60 *Tennessee Law Review* (1993): 431; Lewis L. Laska, "A Legal and Constitutional History of Tennessee, 1772–1972," 6 *Memphis State University Law Review* (1976): 563, 646–652.

66. Tennessee Constitution, Article II, Section 22.

67. James Eugene Lewis, "The Tennessee Gubernatorial Campaign and Election of 1894" (master's thesis, Emory University, 1948).

68. Belmont v. Board of Law Examiners, 511 S.W.2d 461 (1974).

69. Lewis L. Laska, "The 1977 Limited Constitutional Convention," 61 *Tennessee Law Review* 486 (1994): 546–49.

70. Tennessee Constitution, Article VI, Section 12.

71. City of Gatlinburg v. Goans, 600 S.W. 2ds 735 (Tenn. App.. 1980); City of Jackson v. Bledsoe, 830 S.W.2d 71 (Tenn. App. 1991).

72. State v. Mahoney, 874 S.W.2d 627 (Tenn. Crim. App. 1993).

73. Scopes v. State, 289 S.W. 363 (1927).

74. Crawford v. Buckner, 839 S.W.2d 754 (1992).

75. State v. Tester, 879 S.W.2d 823 (1994).

76. Stalcup v. City of Gatlinburg, 577 S.W.2d 439 (1978). Civil Service Merit Board v. Burson, 816 S.W. 2d 725 (1991) (Nashville is now largely immune from these laws).

77. Patty v. McDaniel, 547 S.W.2d 896 (1977), rev'd 435 U.S. 618, 998 S. Ct. 1322, 55 L.Ed. 2d 593 (1978).

78. Tennessee Constitution, Article XI, Section 3.

79. Cited in State ex rel. Anglin v. Mitchell, 596 S.W. 2d 779, 785 (1980).

Chapter 3. The Institutionalization of the Tennessee Legislature, 1968–1997

1. Malcolm Jewell, "The Neglected World of State Politics," *Journal of Politics* 44 (1982): 638–657.

2. Ibid., 654.

3. Nelson Polsby, "The Institutionalization of the U.S. House of Representatives," *American Political Science Review* 62 (1968): 144–68.

4. Roger H. Davidson, *The Role of the Congressman* (New York: Pegasus, 1969); Peverill Squire, "The Theory of Legislative Institutionalization and the California Assembly," *Journal of Politics* 54 (1992): 1026–1054; Barbara Sinclair, *Legislators, Leaders, and Lawmaking* (Baltimore: Johns Hopkins University Press, 1990); Joseph Cooper, "Congress in Organizational Perspective," in *Congress Reconsidered*, ed. Lawrence C. Dodd and Bruce C. Oppenheimer (New York: Praeger, 1977); Douglas Chafee, "The Institutionalization of State Legislatures: A Comparative Study," *Western Political Quarterly* 18 (1970): 180–196.

5. Davidson, 43.

6. Malcolm Jewell and Samuel C Patterson, *The Legislative Process in the United States*, 4th ed. (New York: Random House, 1986); Alan Rosenthal, *Legislative Life: Process and Performance in the States* (New York: Harper & Row, 1981).

7. Rosenthal, 58.

8. Lee S. Greene, David H. Grubbs, and Victor C. Hobday, *Government in Tennessee* (Knoxville: University of Tennessee Press, 1982), 115–17.

9. Bruce Mallard, "Executive-Legislative Relations in Tennessee: A Historical Perspective," in *The Volunteer State: Readings in Tennessee Politics*, ed. Dorothy F. Olshfski and T. McN. Simpson III (Nashville: Tennessee Political Science Association, 1985).

10. Paul C. Hain, "The Tennessee Legislature: An Historical Perspective," unpublished paper presented at the annual meeting of the Southern Political Science Association, 1979; Hyrum Plass Mallard, and Charles A. Zuzak, *The Budgetary System in Tennessee*, 2d ed. (Knoxville: University of Tennessee, Bureau of Public Administration, 1977).

11. Greene, Grubbs, and Hobday, 325–327.

12. Coleman McGinnis, "The Tennessee General Assembly: A Choice, an Echo or a Deafening Silence," in *The Volunteer State: Readings in Tennessee Politics*.

13. Edward Carmines, "The Mediating Influence of State Legislatures: The Linkage Between Interparty Competition and Welfare Policies," *American Political Science Review* 68 (1974): 1118–24; Lance LeLoup, "Reassessing the Mediating Impact of Legislative Capability," *American Political Science Review* 72 (1978): 616–21; Albert Karnig and Lee Sigelman, "State Legislative Reform and Public Policy: Another Look," *Western Political Quarterly* 30 (1975): 548–52.

14. McGinnis, 104.

15. V. O. Key, *Southern Politics in State and Nation* (New York: Knopf, 1949).

16. J. Leiper Freeman, *Political Change in Tennessee, 1948–1978: Party Politics*

Trickles Down (Knoxville: University of Tennessee, Bureau of Public Administration, 1980).

17. Robert H. Swansbrough, "The Tennessee Voter," in *The Volunteer State: Readings in Tennessee Politics.*

18. McGinnis, 195.

19. Austin Ranney, "Parties in State Politics," in *Politics in the American States,* ed. Herbert Jacob and Kenneth Vines, 3d ed. (Boston: Little, Brown, 1976).

20. Morris P. Fiorina, *Congress: Keystone of the Washington Establishment* (New Haven: Yale University Press, 1977).

21. We have used figures that reflect approximately one-half the total number of bills in both categories because the normal practice has been to introduce companion bills in the two houses.

22. John C. Wahlke, Heinz Eulau, William Buchanan, and Leroy C. Ferguson, *The Legislative System: Explanations in Legislative Behavior* (New York: John Wiley & Sons, 1962), 376.

23. Thomas R. Dye, *Politics in States and Communities*, 8th ed. (Englewood Cliffs, N.J.: Prentice Hall, 1994), 146–49; Jewell, 52–54; Hugh L. LeBlanc, "Voting in State Senates: Party and Constituency Influences," *Midwest Journal of Political Science* 13 (1969): 33–57.

24. Dye, 165.

25. Charles Mahtesian, "The Sick Legislature Syndrome and How to Avoid It," *Governing* (February 1997): 16–20.

26. Mahtesian uses the National Conference of State Legislatures listing of "professional" legislatures. The ten legislatures in this category are characterized as having a large full-time staff, relatively high pay, and stable membership.

Chapter 4. The Governorship

1. Leslie Lipson, *The American Governor: From Figurehead to Leader* (Chicago: University of Chicago Press, 1949).

2. See Coleman B. Ransone, *The Office of the Governor in the South* (Birmingham: University of Alabama Press, 1951), 5–7, and Larry Sabato, *Goodbye to Good-Time Charlie*, 2d ed. (Washington, D.C.: Congressional Quarterly Press, 1983), 2–5.

3. Bruce Mallard, "Executive-Legislative Relations in Tennessee: A Historical Perspective," in *The Volunteer State: Readings in Tennessee Politics*, ed. Dorothy F. Olshfski and T. McN. Simpson (Nashville: Tennessee Political Science Association, 1985), 176.

4. On the governors of the Civil War period, see William R. Majors, *Change and Continuity: Tennessee Politics Since the Civil War* (Macon: Mercer University Press, 1986), 1–13.

5. On the administrative reforms, see A. E. Buck, *The Reorganization of State Governments in the United States* (New York: National Municipal League and Columbia University press, 1938); Joseph MacPherson, "Democratic Progressivism in Tennessee: The Administration of Governor Austin Peay" (Ph.D. diss., Vanderbilt University, 1969); and David D. Lee, *Tennessee in Turmoil: Politics in the Volunteer State, 1920–1932* (Memphis: Memphis State University Press, 1979).

6. Robert E. Corlew, *Tennessee: A Short History*, 2d ed., (Knoxville: University of Tennessee Press, 1981), 456; see also Lee, *Tennessee in Turmoil.*

7. On Peay's policy agenda, see Margaret I. Phillips, *The Governors of Tennessee* (Grenta: Pelican, 1978), 140–41; and Corlew, *Tennessee*, 456–58.

8. See Lee Seifert Greene, David H. Grubbs, and Victor C. Hobday, *Government in Tennessee*, 4th ed. (Knoxville: University of Tennessee Press, 1982), 119, and Mallard, "Executive-Legislative Relations," 178.

9. Greene, et. al., *Government in Tennessee*, 100–101.

10. See Mallard, "Executive-Legislative Relations," 177–80.

11. Greene, et. al., *Government in Tennessee*, 106.

12. Ibid., 102, 110; and Mallard, "Executive-Legislative Relations," 180–188.

13. See Sabato, *Good-Time Charlie*, 20–32.

14. See Greene, et. al., *Government in Tennessee*, 114–15.

15. See, for instance, Joseph A. Schlesinger, "The Politics of the Executive," in *Politics in the American States: A Comparative Analysis*, ed. Herbert Jacob and Kenneth Vines (Boston: Little, Brown, 1965), 207–37; Nelson C. Dometrius, "Measuring Gubernatorial Power," *Journal of Politics* 41 (1979): 589–610; and Thad L. Beyle, "Governors," in *Politics in the American States: A Comparative Analysis*, 5th ed., ed. Virginia Gray, Herbert Jacob, and Kenneth Vines (Boston: Little, Brown, 1983), 180–221, 454–59.

16. Sabato, *Good-Time Charlie*, 57.

17. Beyle, "Governors," 201.

18. Lamar Alexander, "What Do Governors Do?" in *Governors on Governing* (Washington, D.C.: National Governors Association and University Press of America, 1991), 42.

19. See Coleman B. Ransone, *The American Governorship* (Westport, Conn.: Greenwood, 1982), 87–101.

20. See Greene, et. al., *Government in Tennessee*, 104.

21. See Edward Flentje, "Governor as Manager," *State Government* 54, no. 3 (1981): 76–81.

22. Greene, et. al., *Government in Tennessee*, 122.

23. See Lynn Muchmore, "The Governor as Manager," *State Government* 54, no. 3 (1981): 71–75.

24. See Beyle, "Governors," 459.

25. See Greene, et. al., *Government in Tennessee*, 126–131.

26. See, for instance, Charles Mahtesian, "The Sick Legislature Syndrome Aand How to Avoid It," *Governing* (February 1997): 16–21.

27. Thad L.Beyle, "Governors: The Middlemen and Women in Our Political System," in *Politics in the American States: A Comparative Analysis*, 6th ed., ed. Virginia Gray and Herbert Jacob (Washington, D.C.: Congressional Quarterly Press, 1996), 228–38.

28. See, for instance, Ann O'M. Bowman and Richard C. Kearney, *The Resurgence of the States* (Englewood Cliffs, N.J.: Prentice Hall, 1986); and David Osborne, *Laboratories of Democracy* (Boston: Harvard Business School Press, 1988).

29. See Thad L. Beyle, "The Governor as Innovator in the Federal System," *Publius* 18 (Summer 1988): 131–52.

Chapter 5. The Changing Court System

1. *Proceedings of the Conference for Delegates to the 1977 Tennessee Constitutional Convention*, ed. Bobby Corcoran and David H. Grubbs (Murfreesboro, Tenn.: Middle Tennessee State University, 1977), 103.

2. Speech by Joseph W. Henry before the Tennessee Municipal Attorneys Association, Nashville, Tennessee (Jan. 6, 1978) as reported in Lewis L. Laska, "The 1977 Limited Constitutional Convention" *Tennessee Law Review* 61, no. 2 (Winter 1994): 551.

3. *Higgins v. Dunn*, 496 S.W.2d 480, Tenn. 1973.

4. *McCulley v. State*, 102 Tenn. 509, 53 S.W. 134, 1899.

5. Ibid., 81.

6. *Halsey v. Gaines*, 70 Tenn. 316, 1879.

7. Lee S. Greene, *Lead Me On: Frank Goad Clement and Tennessee Politics* (Knoxville: University of Tennessee Press, 1982), 242–272.

8. Ibid., 272.

9. S.W.2d 509 (Tenn. 1987).

10. Joe G. Riley, "Ethical Obligations of Judges," *Memphis State Law Review* 23 (1993): 508–9.

11. *Murphy, In re*, 726 S.W.2d 509, Tenn. 1987.

12. U.S. 335, 1963.

13. *Argersinger v. Hamlin*, 407 U.S. 25, 1972.

14. Robertson, Suzanne C. "TBA's State-Wide Public Defender Bill Priority Number One," *Tennessee Bar Journal* 25 (1989): 18.

15. Effective July 1, 1995, T.C.A. 8-14-207.

16. S.W.2d 480, Tenn. 1973.

17. Le Clercq, Frederic S. "Merit Selection Outs Politics," (Nashville) *Tennessean*, Oct. 30, 1977, B3.

18. *Proceedings of the Conference for Delegates*, 82.

19. Charles L. Fontenay, "Judicial Reform Battle Brings out Big Guns," *Tennessean*, Oct. 6, 1977, pp. 1,4.

20. Laska, Lewis L. "The 1977 Limited Constitutional Convention," *Tennessee Law Review* 61, no. 2 (Winter 1994).

21. Tennessee Municipal League, *Town and Country*, July 17, 1995.

22. TCA 17-4-1-1.

23. 127-4-102.

24. Brian J. Ostrom et al., *State Court Caseload Statistics: Annual Report 1992* (Williamsburg, Va.: National Center for State Courts, 1994, 165–166.

25. Provided by the Administrative Office of the Courts, *Annual Report of the Tennessee Judiciary*, Fiscal Year 1995–96, 8.

26. *Ex rel. Anglin v. Mitchell*, 596 S.W.2d, Tenn. 1980. See also Le Clercq, "The Constitutional Policy That Judges Be Learned in the Law," *Tennessee Law Review* 47 (1980,): 689–741.

27. Brian J. Ostrom et al., 11 and 31.

28. Brian J. Ostrom and Neal B. Kauder, *Examining the Work of State Courts*, 1993. A National Perspective from the Court Statistics Project (Williamsburg, Va.: National Center for State Courts, 1995), 13.

29. Tennessee Supreme Court, *Annual Report of the Tennessee Judiciary 1993–94* (Nashville: Administrative Office of the Courts, 1994).

30. Lewis L. Laska, "The 1977 Limited Constitutional Convention," *Tennessee Law Review* 61, no. 2 (Winter 1994): 584–85.

31. Administrative Office of the Courts of Tennessee, *To Serve All People* (Nashville: Administrative Office of the Courts of Tennessee).

32. Aug. 2, 1996, 1.

33. *State v. Odom*, delivered June 3, 1996.

34. *Tenneesean*, Aug. 2, 1996, 1.

35. See several articles on "Judicial Independence" in the Jan.-Feb. 1997 issue of *Judicature*, including "An Introduction," 155; Stephen B. Bright, "Political Attacks on the Judiciary," 165–73; Penny J. White, "An America without Judicial Independence," 174–77.

Chapter 6. Local Government and Politics

1. The U.S. Census Bureau only recognizes ninety-three because the two metropolitan governments are not counted among the ninety-five counties. Also, only the fourteen special school districts are counted as independent governmental units. There are, though, actually 140 school districts in Tennessee. See U.S. Department of Commerce, Bureau of the Census, *Census of Governments* (Washington, D.C.: Government Printing Office, 1992), A-228.

2. The maps have been produced by James McCluskey, Associate Professor, Department of Geology and Geography, Austin Peay State University.

3. Department of Commerce, *Census of Governments*, A-228.

4. Department of Commerce, Bureau of the Census, *City County Data Book* (Washington, D.C.: Government Printing Office, 1992), 508.

5. Richard D. Bingham, *State and Local Government in an Urban Society* (New York: Random House, 1986), 55.

6. Vincent L. Marando and Mavis Mann Reeves, "County Government Structural Reform: Influence of State, Region, and Urbanization," *Publius: Journal of Federalism* 23 (Winter 1993): 44.

7. Department of Commerce, Bureau of the Census, *County and City Data Book*, (Washington, D.C.: Government Printing Office, 1994), 507, 521.

8. Department of Commerce, *Census of Governments*, A-228.

9. Compiled from The University of Tennessee, Municipal Technical Advisory Service, *Directory of Tennessee Municipal Officials* (Knoxville, University of Tennessee, 1995), 1–239.

10. International City/County Management Association, *Municipal Year Book 1995* (Washington, D.C.: International City/County Management Association, 1995), xii.

11. Ibid.

12. Department of Commerce, *Census of Governments*, 16.

13. Bingham, 58.

14. The University of Tennessee, Center for Business and Economic Research, College of Business Administration, *Tennessee Statistical Abstract* (Knoxville: University of Tennessee, 1994), 651–53.

15. See, for example, Tennessee. *Private Acts* (1961), chapt. 24, 60–64 and Tennessee. *Private Acts* (1991), chapt. 138, 355–56.

16. Tennessee. *Codes Annotated*, Supplement (1995), 9: 49-2-201, 29–30.

17. Department of Commerce, *County and City Data Book*, 498, 512.

18. Ibid., 20–21.

19. Ibid., 21

20. *1996 City and County Extra: Annual Metro., City, and County Data Book*, ed. Courtenay M. Slater and George E. Hall (Lanham, Md.: Bernan, 1996), 966.

21. The University of Tennessee, Municipal Technical Advisory Service, 271–274.

22. See David Kanervo, "Problems, Attractions, and Chief Executive Priorities in Small Towns," *Southeastern Political Review* 18, no. 1, (Spring 1990): 145–172, for an elaboration of the discussion that follows.

23. John A. Kuehn and Lloyd D. Bender, "Non-metropolitan Economic Bases and Their Policy Implications," *Growth and Change* 16 (January 1985): 24–29.

24. Ibid.

25. Terry N. Clark, "Urban Policy Analysis," *Annual Review of Sociology* 11 (1985): 452.

26. See Ronald K. Vogel and Bert E. Swanson, "The Growth Machine Versus the Antigrowth Coalition: The Battle for Our Communities," *Urban Affairs Quarterly* 25, no. 1 (September 1989): 63–85.

27. See, for example, H. Molotch, "The City as Growth Machine: Toward a Political Economy of Place," *American Journal of Sociology* 82 (September 1976): 309–332; and Vogel and Swanson.

28. Department of Commerce, *County and City Data Book*, 818.

29. Ibid.

30. John V. Moeser and Christopher Silver, "Race, Social Stratification, and Politics: The Case of Atlanta, Memphis, and Richmond," *Virginia Magazine of History and Biography* 102, no. 4 (October 1994): 531.

31. Department of Commerce, *County and City Data Book*, 818

32. See John J. Harrigan, *Political Change in the Metropolis*, 6th ed. (New York: HarperCollins, 1993), 281; and Bernard H. Ross et al., *Urban Politics: Power in Metropolitan America*, 4th ed. (Itasca, Ill.: F. E. Peacock, 1991), 234–235.

33. Department of Commerce, *Census of Governments*, xxx.

34. William P. Barrett, "The Bluff City: Sidney Schlenker and the Pyramid in Memphis," *Forbes*, September 30, 1991, 66–68.

35. Moeser and Silver, "Race, Social Stratification, and Politics," 532.

36. Ibid., 534.

37. Ibid., 547.

38. Department of Commerce, *County and City Data Book*, 497, 511.

39. Ibid., 548.

40. *Department of Commerce, 1997 Statistical Abstract of U.S.* (Washington, D.C.: Government Printing Office, 1997), 46.

41. Department of Commerce, *Resident Population and Change for Metropolitan Areas in the United States by Population Rank: July 1, 1994* (Washington, D.C.: Government Printing Office, 1995), http://www.census.gov, 14.

42. Department of Commerce, *Census of Governments*, xxx.

43. Ibid., xxxii.

44. William Stern, "Health Care City, U.S.A.," *Forbes*, May 10, 1993, 92–93.

45. See John J. Harrigan, *Political Change in the Metropolis*, 5th ed. (New York: HarperCollins, 1993), 195.

46. Dennis R. Judd and Todd Swanstrom, *City Politics: Private Power and Public Policy* (New York: HarperCollins, 1994), 365.

47. See Lawrence Tabak, "Wild About Convention Centers," in *Urban Society*, 7th ed., Annual Editions, ed. Fred Siegel (Guilford, CT.: The Dushkin Publishing Group, 1995), 41.

48. Department of Commerce, *Census of Governments*, xxix.

49. *1996 City and County Extra,* 966.

50. Department of Commerce, *County and City Data Book*, 818.

51. Patrick Rains, "Politics with Bite," *American City and County* 109, no. 7, 63.

52. Ibid., 64.

53. George Poague, "City 109th Best Place to Live," *The Leaf-Chronicle*, August 17, 1995, A-1.

54. Rains, "Politics with Bite," 63.

55. Rains, "Politics with Bite," 64.

56. *1996 City and County Extra,* 966.

57. Department of Commerce, *County and City Data Book*, 818.

58. Jay Walljasper, "Chattanooga Chooses: The Revitalization of this Once Dying City Shows Urban Decline is not Inevitable," *Utne Reader* (March-April 1994): 15–16.

59. Ibid., 16.

60. Ibid.

61. Ibid.

62. Ibid.

63. *1996 City and County Extra,* 966.

64. Ibid.

65. Montgomery County, where Clarksville is located, has the highest percentage of foreign born residents (3.1 percent) of any county in the state (Department of Commerce, *County and City Data Book*, xxi).

66. Ibid.

67. *Clarksville-Montgomery County Chamber Journal* (September 1995): 7.

68. Carla Fried, "Best Places to Live in America," *Money* (July 1996): 72.

Chapter 7. Turnout and Partisanship in Tennessee Elections

1. V. O. Key, *Southern Politics* (New York: Knopf, 1949), 75.

2. For a discussion of how American turnout compares to other nations of the world, see G. Bingham Powell, Jr., "American Voter Turnout in Comparative Perspective," *American Political Science Review* 80 (March 1986): 17–43.

3. For explanations of why Americans do not vote, see Raymond E. Wolfinger and Steven J. Rosenstone, *Who Votes?* (New Haven, Conn.: Yale University Press, 1980); and Ruy A. Teixeira, *The Disappearing American Voter* (Washington, D.C.: Brookings, 1992).

4. For discussions of legal barriers to participation, see Frances F. Piven and Richard A. Cloward, *Why Americans Don't Vote*, (New York: Pantheon, 1988); and *Quiet Revolution in the South: The Impact of the Voting Rights Act 1965–1990*, ed. Chandler Davidson and Bernard Grofman (Princeton, N.J.: Princeton, 1994).

5. See Lee Seifert Greene, David H. Grubbs, and Victor C. Hobday, *Government in Tennessee*, 3d ed. (Knoxville: University of Tennessee Press, 1975) for a discussion of voting laws in Tennessee prior to the 1970s.

6. See Steven J. Rosenstone and Raymond E. Wolfinger, "The Effect of Registration Laws on Voter Turnout," *American Political Science Review* 72 (1978): 22–45; and Robert S. Erikson, "Why Do People Vote? Because They Are Registered," *American Politics Quarterly* 9 (1981): 259–276.

7. See Richard M. Scammon and Alice V. McGillivray, *America Votes 20* (Washington D.C.: Congressional Quarterly, 1993).

8. We operationalize "South" by using the Census Bureau definition (i.e., AL, AR, DE, FL, GA, KY, LA, MD, MS, NC, OK, SC, TN, TX, VA, WV). While this definition includes states outside of the Confederacy, this provides for a more conservative comparison between Tennessee, the South, and the nation.

9. Key, 59.

10. We calculate the Democratic percentage of the vote using only the votes cast for the two major parties.

Chapter 8. Women in Tennessee Politics

1. Conversation with Representative Mike Williams, June 1996.

2. Kimberly Hadley, "War of the Roses," *Nashville Banner*, Aug., 17, 1995: 1.

3. Mary Frances Berry, *Why ERA Failed: Politics, Women's Rights, and the Amending Process of the Constitution* (Bloomington: Indiana University Press, 1986), 67.

4. See A. Elizabeth Taylor, "Tennessee: The Thirty-Sixth State," in Marjorie Spruill Wheeler, ed., *Votes for Women! The Woman Suffrage Movement in Tennessee, the South, and the Nation* (Knoxville: The University of Tennessee Press, 1995), 53–70; and Ellen J. Weed and Thomas M. Pickney, Jr., "Women's Rights in Tennessee," in *The Volunteer State: Readings in Tennessee Politics*, ed. Dorothy F. Olshfski and T. McN. Simpson III (Tennessee Political Science Association, 1985), 129–45.

5. See the "Letter of Transmittal" submitted by Gloria H. Rawls, Chairperson in *Women in Tennessee: Report of the Governor's Commission on the Status of Women in Tennessee* (Nashville, 1964).

6. Weed and Pickney, 132–33.

7. Lee Seifert et al., *Government in Tennessee*, 4th ed.. (Knoxville: University of Tennessee Press, 1982), 125.

8. *Women in Tennessee.*

9. 404 U.S. 71.

10. 411 U.S. 677.

11. 410 U.S. 113.

12. Weed and Pickney, 134–138.

13. See Wheeler for an account of Tennessee woman in the suffrage movement.

14. Ilene J. Cornwell, Linda T. Wynn, and Thura Mack, comps., "Selected Thematic Bibliography and Resources," in *Shaping a State; The Legacy of Tennessee Women–A Symposium* (Nashville: Margaret Cuninggim Women's Center, Vanderbilt University, 1995), 54.

15. U.S. 186.

16. *Time Magazine,* Aug. 26, 1995, 25. The highest ranking state was Washington State with 39.5 percent; the lowest was Alabama with only 3.6 percent. According to an article in the *New York Times,* Pennsylvania, Alaska, Tennessee, Kentucky, South Carolina, Mississippi, Louisiana, Oklahoma, and Alabama all have low representation of women in the state legislatures with 14 percent or less. The states with the highest representation of women in the legislature (35 percent–39 percent) are Arizona, Colorado, and Washington. See Drummond Ayres, Jr., "Women in Washington Statehouse Lead U.S. Tide," *New York Times,* April 14, 1997, A-1.

17. Lynne E. Ford and Kathleen Dolan, "Contemporary Women State Legislators: A Diverse Group with Diverse Agendas," in *Women in Politics: Outsider or Insider?* ed. Lois Lovelace Duke, 2d ed. (Upper Saddle River, N.J.: Prentice Hall, 1996), 158.

18. Senator Harper and Representatives DeBerry, Bowers, Brooks, Brown, Langster, and Pruitt represent two minority constituencies: women and African Americans.

19. Implicit in this statement is the assumption that women have a different political agenda than men as represented by the "Gender Gap," which has played a role in several national elections including the 1996 vote. Whether this holds for the more conservative Southern states is yet to be proven. Poll data for Tennessee show that women are more likely to identify themselves as Democrats (36 percent) than men (28 percent) and less likely to identify themselves as Republican (women 27 percent, men 30 percent) or independent (women 37 percent, men 42 percent). Concomitantly, women are more likely to identify their ideology as liberal (women 17 percent, men 14 percent) or moderate (women 49 percent, men 47 percent), while men are more likely to identify themselves as ideologically conservative (women 35 percent, men 39 percent). This difference is probably ameliorated by conservative religious views. According to poll data, women are less likely to favor a state lottery and are more likely to support stronger anti-abortion legislation than men. A third issue, state income tax, seems to reflect better the party and ideological differences based on gender. Roughly the same percentage of both genders favor a state income tax, but only 57 percent of the women polled oppose such a tax, compared to 62 percent of their male counterparts. Most significantly, while only 7 percent of the men polled were unsure of their opinion on a state income tax, 13 percent of the women in the poll fell into this category. See chapter 11 in this volume.

20. Ruth Mandel and Debra Dodson, "Do Women Officeholders Make a Difference?" in *The American Woman,* ed. Sara E. Rix (New York: Norton, 1992); Sue Thomas and Susan Welch, "The Impact of Gender on Activities and Priorities of State Legislators," *Western Political Quarterly,* 44 (1991): 445–56.

21. Nancy E. McGlen and Karen O'Conner, *Women, Politics, and American Society* (Englewood Cliffs, N.J.: Prentice-Hall, 1995), 89.

22. Sue Thomas, *How Women Legislate* (New York: Oxford University Press, 1994); Rosabeth Kantor, "Some Effects of Proportion on Group Life: Skewed Sex Ratios and Response to Token Women," *American Journal of Sociology*, 82 (1971): 965–90.

23. Ford and Dolan, 135.

24. Duren Cheek, "Women Happy, GOP Not with Committee Postings," *Tennessean*, Jan. 17, 1997: 4-B; and Larry Daughtrey, "Speaker Unveils Newest Committee," *Tennessean*, Jan.14, 1997: 1-B.

25. *Tennessee Blue Book, 1991–1994* (Nashville: Tennessee Secretary of State).

26. Cornwell et al.

27. Like their counterparts on the national level, Tennessee women seem to be more likely to identify themselves as Democrats while men are more likely to identify themselves as Republicans. According to the *New York Times*, women have been more likely than men to identify themselves as Democrats for at least two decades. In 1996, 50 percent of the women polled identified themselves and Democrats while only 37 percent of the men did. Conversely, 47 percent of the men polled identified themselves as Republican while only 37 percent identified themselves as democrats. See Robin Toner, "With G.O.P. Congress the Issue, 'Gender Gap' Is Growing Wider," *New York Times*, April 21, 1996, 1. For comparable Tennessee data, see chapter 11 in this volume.

28. Ibid.

29. See *Tennessee Blue Book 1995–1996: Bicentennial Edition (1796–1996)* (Nashville: Secretary of State).

30. Ann Betts, "The Unsung Heroines of Tennessee History," *Tennessean*, March 31, 1996: 3-D.

31. One example would be Wilson County Sheriff Laura Mason, who was named to succeed her husband after his death in 1926 and elected to a four-year term in 1928. Ibid.

32. Institute for Women's Policy Research, *The Status of Women in the States* (Washington: Institute for Women's Policy Research, 1996). Rankings are based on data from the 1992 and 1994 elections.

33. Ibid., 7.

Chapter 9. African Americans in Tennessee

1. For analysis of African American politics in Tennessee as a whole, see, for example, C. Perry Patterson, *The Negro in Tennessee*, 1790–1865 (Westport, Conn.: Negro Universities Press, 1968); Joseph Cartwright, *The Triumph of Jim Crow: Tennessee Race Relations in the 1880s* (Knoxville: University of Tennessee Press, 1976); Lester Lamon, *Blacks in Tennessee, 1791–1970* (Knoxville: University of Tennessee Press, 1981). Also see David Halberstam, *The Children* (New York: Random House, 1998).

2. U.S. Department of Commerce, Bureau of the Census, *Census of the Population, 1940* (Washington, D.C.: Government Printing Office, 1941); U.S.

Department of Commerce, Bureau of the Census, *Statistical Abstracts of the United States, 1996* (Washington, D.C.: Government Printing Office, 1996).

3. See Charles Crawford, *Yesterday's Memphis* (Miami: Seemann, 1976); John Hope Franklin, *From Slavery to Freedom* (New York: Knopf, 1980).

4. Sandra Vaughn, "Memphis: Heart of the Mid-South," in *In Search of the New South: The Black Urban Experience in the 1970s and 1980s,* ed. Robert Bullard (Tuscaloosa: University of Alabama Press, 1989), 99.

5. See Shields McIlwaine, *Memphis Down in Dixie* (New York: Dutton, 1948).

6. Crawford, *Yesterday's Memphis;* Blaine Brownell and David Goldfield, *The City in Southern History* (Port Washington, N.Y.: Kennikat, 1977), 16.

7. George Lee, *Beale Street* (New York: R. O. Ballou, 1934), 13.

8. John Ellis, "Disease and the Destiny of a City: The 1878 Yellow Fever Epidemic in Memphis," *West Tennessee Historical Papers* 28 (1974): 76.

9. Ibid., 82.

10. Ibid., 82, 87.

11. For example, see ibid., 75–89. And for a more general account of rural influence on urban politics in the South, see David Goldfield, *Cotton Fields and Skyscrapers* (Baltimore: Johns Hopkins University Press, 1989); Earl Black and Merle Black, *Politics and Society in the South* (Cambridge, Mass.: Harvard University Press, 1987).

12. Goldfield, *Cotton Fields and Skyscrapers*, 94.

13. Roger Biles, *Memphis in the Great Depression* (Knoxville: University of Tennessee Press, 1986), 6. Also see Rayford Logan, *The Betrayal of the Negro* (London: Collier & McMillan, 1965), 300.

14. Gerald Capers, *The Biography of a River Town* (New York: Vanguard, 1966), 216.

15. For example, see the (Memphis) *Commercial Appeal*, February 17, 1991, B-1; Memphis and Shelby County Planning Commission, *Annexation: A Must for a Growing Memphis* (September 1967).

16. Yung Wei and H. R. Mahood, "Racial Attitudes and the Wallace Vote," *Polity* 3 (Summer 1971): 532–49.

17. As for out-migration, see Vaughn, "Memphis: Heart of the Mid-South," 102; Jimmie Covington, "Jobs in '80s Revamped Population of County: Young Blacks Left and Whites Arrived," *Commercial Appeal*, May 26, 1992, A-11.

18. For example, see Paul Lewinsohn, *Race, Class and Party: A History of Negro Suffrage and White Politics in the South* (New York: Russell & Russell, 1963), 139; Denoral Davis, "Against the Odds"(Ph.D. diss., SUNY-Binghamton, 1987), 211; Vaughn, "Memphis: Heart of the Mid-South," 99–115; Ira Berlin, *Slaves Without Masters* (New York: Pantheon, 1974).

19. See Lee, *Beale Street*, 13.

20. W. E. B. DuBois, *The Souls of Black Folks* (Chicago: McClung, 1903).

21. (Memphis) *Press-Scimitar*, April 19, 1952, 1. Also see Annette Church and Roberta Church, *The Robert R. Churches* (Ann Arbor: University of Michigan Press, 1974).

22. See Vaughn, "Memphis: Heart of the Mid-South," 100; Lewinsohn, *Race, Class and Party*, 139.

23. See Vaughn, "Memphis: Heart of the Mid-South," 113–15.

24. *Commercial Appeal*, July 18, 1993, 46. Also see Cindy Wolff, "Distribution Jobs Are a Boon to Area; Experts Also Want Manufacturing," *Commercial Appeal*, July 3, 1994.

25. Davis, "Against the Odds," 223. Also, see Kenneth Wald, "The Electoral Base of Political Machines," *Urban Affairs Quarterly* 16 (September 1980): 6.

26. See William Cohen, "Negro Involuntary Servitude in the South, 1865–1940," *Journal of Southern History* 42 (February 1976): 39.

27. Davis, "Against the Odds," 50–55.

28. Ibid., 292–296. Also see Jalenak, "Beale Street Politics" (honors thesis, Yale University, 1961), 32, 163–66.

29. See Vaughn, "Memphis: Heart of the Mid-South," 112.

30. Goldfield, *Cotton Fields and Skyscrapers*, 166.

31. Ibid., 191.

32. F. Ray Marshall and Arvil Van Adams, "Negro Employment in Memphis," *Industrial Relations* 9 (May 1970): 308–323. Also see *Commercial Appeal*, June 20, 1986.

33. U. S. Department of Commerce, Bureau of the Census, *Census of the Population, 1990* (Washington, D.C.: Government Printing Office, 1991). It also should be noted that the three zip codes overlapped the six census tracts.

34. Lester Lamon, *Black Tennesseans* (Knoxville: University of Tennessee Press, 1977).

35. *Chicago Defender*, April 24, 1915, 1.

36. *Commercial Appeal*, August 14, 1916, 5.

37. Ibid., October 22, 1916, 1. And similarly, see *Chicago Defender*, May 28, 1918, 5.

38. *Commercial Appeal*, December 4, 1916, 7.

39. See John Dollard, *Caste and Class in a Southern Town* (New Haven, Conn.: Yale University Press, 1938), 290.

40. Howard Rabinowitz, *Race Relations in the South, 1865–1890* (New York: Oxford University Press, 1978), 336. Specifically, see *Commercial Appeal*, November 11, 1916, 6; October 29, 1916, 20; August 6, 1916, 1; *Chicago Defender*, March 2, 1918, 1. Also see Gloria Brown Melton, "Blacks in Memphis, Tennessee, 1920–1955" (Ph.D. diss., Washington State University, 1982), 202.

41. Harry Holloway, *The Politics of the Southern Negro* (New York: Random House, 1969), 287.

42. For example, see Gloria Melton, "Blacks in Memphis, Tennessee, 1920–1955," (Ph.D. diss., Washington State University, 1982), 363–364; Vaughn, "Memphis: Heart of the Mid-South," 107; Holloway, *The Politics of the Southern Negro*, 287. As for the 1968 sanitation strike, see Joan Beifuss, *At The River I Stand* (Memphis: B & W Books, 1985); David Tucker, *Memphis Since Crump* (Knoxville: University of Tennessee Press, 1980), chaps. 3 and 9; Robert Bailey, "The 1968 Memphis Sanitation Strike" (master's thesis, Memphis State University, 1974).

43. For example, see Michael Honey, *Southern Labor and Black Civil Rights* (Champaign: University of Illinois Press, 1993); *Memphis World*, August 8 and

August 25, 1944; *Chicago Defender*, September 22, 1917, 1; May 1, 1920, 1; Tucker, *Memphis Since Crump*, chap. 3.

44. *Memphis World*, August 8 and 25, 1944.

45. See Beifuss, *By the River We Stand*; Bailey, "The 1968 Memphis Sanitation Strike"; Tucker, *Memphis Since Crump*, chap. 9.

46. Tucker, *Memphis Since Crump*, 161.

47. See Melton, "Blacks in Memphis, Tennessee," 14.

48. See Margaret Price, *The Negro Vote in the South* (Atlanta: Southern Regional Council, 1957), 68.

49. For example, see Melton, "Blacks in Memphis, Tennessee," 363–64; Vaughn, "Memphis: Heart of the Mid-South," 107.

50. See Melton, "Blacks in Memphis, Tennessee," 253.

51. Tucker, *Memphis Since Crump*, 142.

52. *Commercial Appeal*, September 20, 1982, A-7.

53. Attorney John Ryder, former Republican County Chairman, quoted in Jackson Baker, "Election Aftermath as Simple as Black and White?" *Memphis Flyer*, August 13–19, 1992.

54. For example, see Walter Adkins, "Beale Street Goes to the Polls" (master's thesis, Ohio State University, 1935), 6. Also note, however, that Tennessee had one of the smallest African American populations in the South; e.g., see V. O. Key, *Southern Politics in State and Nation* (New York: Knopf, 1949), 10.

55. For example, see David Tucker, *Lieutenant Lee of Beale Street* (Nashville: Vanderbilt University Press, 1971), chap. 1; A. A. Taylor, *The Negro in Tennessee* (New York: Associated Publishers, 1941), 155, 233, and 249.

56. For example, see Nate Hobbs, "Can Shelby GOP attract blacks to the party?" *Commercial Appeal*, February 27, 194, B-5.

57. See Lynette Wren, "Commission Government in the Gilded Age," *Tennessee Historical Quarterly*, 47 (Winter 1988): 216–26.

58. The Tennessee Supreme Court upheld the constitutionality of the poll tax in *Biggs v. Beeler* 180 Tenn 198.

59. For example, Robert Church, Jr., was chosen as a delegate to the Republican national convention in 1896 and to each of the conventions from 1912 through 1940. His daughter, Roberta, was elected to the executive committee of the Tennessee Republican Party in 1952. Her father had been the only black on that committee earlier in the century. See *The Colored American*, March 24, 1900; *Press Scimitar*, August 20, 1952.

60. For example, see *Commercial Appeal*, October 21, 1916. Also see Church and Church, *The Robert R. Churches*; Roger Biles, "Robert R. Church Jr. of Memphis," *Tennessee Historical Quarterly* 42 (Winter 1983): 362–383.

61. See Melton, "Blacks in Memphis, Tennessee," 41–42; Lamon, *Black Tennesseans*; Biles, "Robert R. Church Jr. of Memphis."

62. Jalenak, " Beale Street Politics," 114.

63. Holloway, *The Politics of the Southern Negro*, 272, 346. Also see James Jalenak, "Beale Street Politics" (honors thesis, Yale University, 1961), chaps. 7 and 9.

64. *Memphis World*, August 3, 1960, 1.

65. For example, see Jalenak, "Beale Street Politics," chap. 2; Jonathan Daniels, "He Suits Memphis," *Saturday Evening Post*, June 10, 1939; Randolph Meade Walker, "The Role of the Black Clergy in Memphis During the Crump Era," *West Tennessee Historical Papers* 33 (October 1979): 33.

66. Lewinsohn, *Race, Class and Party*, 162. Also see Holloway, *The Politics of the Southern Negro*, 280; Price, *The Negro Vote in the South*, 31; Gunnar Mydral, *The American Dilemma* (New York: Harper & Brothers), 486; Jalenak, "Beale Street Politics," chap. 2.

67. Lewinsohn, *Race, Class and Party*, 120, 138, and 162.

68. For example, see Biles, "Robert R. Church Jr. of Memphis," 362–82; Adkins, "Beale Street Goes to the Polls," 59; Lewinsohn, *Race, Class and Party*, 139–141; Tucker, *Memphis Since Crump*, 18–19 and 133; Vaughn, "Memphis: Heart of the Mid-South," 116.

69. See William Wright, *Memphis Politics: An Example of Racial Bloc Voting* (New York: McGraw-Hill, 1962); Jalenak, "Beale Street Politics," 27. As for declining rewards, see Ralph Bunche, *The Political Status of the Negro in the Age of FDR* (Chicago: University of Chicago Press, 1973), 493–502.

70. Holloway, *The Politics of the Southern Negro*, 291. Also, see Tucker, *Memphis Since Crump*.

71. For example, see Melton, "Blacks in Memphis, Tennessee," 330–32.

72. See David Matthews and James Prothro, *Negroes and the New Southern Politics* (New York: Harcourt, Brace & World), 148–62.

73. See Jack Bass and Walter DeVries, *The Transformation of Southern Politics* (New York: Basic, 1976); Holloway, *The Politics of the Southern Negro*, 327 and 335–36; Key, *Southern Politics in State and Nation*, 648.

74. See David Tucker, *Black Pastors and Leaders, 1819–1972* (Memphis: Memphis State University Press, 1975); Walker, "The Role of the Black Clergy in Memphis . . . ," 38–43; Rabinowitz, *Race Relations in the Urban South*, chap. 2.

75. See Tucker, *Black Pastors and Leaders*; Walker, "The Role of the Black Clergy in Memphis . . . ," 29–47; Lewinsohn, *Race, Class and Party*, 140–41; Jalenak, "Beale Street Politics."

76. See Wright, *Memphis Politics*, 8.

77. *Memphis World*, November 11, 1955, article described in Melton, "Blacks in Memphis, Tennessee," 346–47.

78. See Jalenak, "Beale Street Politics," 82; Vaughn, "Memphis: Heart of the Mid-South," 117; Holloway, *The Politics of the Southern Negro*, 291.

79. For example, if you may vote for as many as five people to fill five vacancies in a multimember district, you cast a vote for only your most preferred candidate so that your votes for the others do not decrease your most preferred candidate's chances of election. For white reaction to this practice, see *Commercial Appeal*, September 17 and 18, 1958.

80. For example, see Jalenak, "Beale Street Politics," 66 and 69; *Memphis World*, July 4, 1959, 1.

81. Ibid.; *Commercial Appeal* June 17, 1959, 21.

82. *Commercial Appeal*, August 2, 1959, A-1.

83. Wright, *Memphis Politics*, 31.

84. See Holloway, *The Politics of the Southern Negro*, 286.

85. *Press-Scimitar*, October 18, 1963, 28. Also see October 12, 1963, 12; October 16, 1963, 3; November 4, 1963, 21.

86. *Commercial Appeal*, February 6, 1966.

87. For example, see Holloway, *The Politics of the Southern Negro*, 298–99.

88. Ibid., 293.

89. See Tucker, *Memphis Since Crump*, 141.

90. For detailed analysis, see *Press-Scimitar*, February 12, 1976.

91. For example, see *Commercial Appeal*, September 20, 1982, A-7; Williams, "Two Black Communities in Memphis, Tennessee," 103–6; Jalenak, "Beale Street Politics," 120–21.

92. For good general reference on blacks in Memphis and in Tennessee, see Taylor, *The Negro in Tennessee*.

93. *Press-Scimitar*, February 12, 1976. Also see the *Commercial Appeal*, September 22, 1976; October 11, 1976.

94. There was a runoff election in both 1975 and 1979.

95. Williams, "Two Black Communities in Memphis, Tennessee," 101–2.

96. For example, see Kay Pittman Black, "Whites Financing Higgs, Ford says," *Press-Scimitar*, August 10, 1983.

97. See Terry Keeter, "John Ford Endorses Gibbons in Mayor Race," *Commercial Appeal*, September 9, 1987, A-1.

98. *Commercial Appeal*, October 25, 1987, A-3.

99. Racial polarization refers to the percentage of votes cast by all the voters of a racial group for the various candidates of that race (e.g., black votes for any of the black candidates).

Chapter 11. Trends in Public Opinion, 1989–1996

1. For a good discussion of public opinion in both empirical political science and normative political theory, see Jerry L. Yeric and John R. Todd, *Public Opinion: The Visible Politics*, 2d ed. (Itasca, Ill.: Peacock, 1989), chapter 1.

2. See, for instance, William Lyons and John M. Scheb II, "Ideology and Candidate Evaluation in the 1984 and 1988 Presidential Elections," *Journal of Politics* 54 (May 1992): 573–84.

3. The literature on party identification and ideology is voluminous, but two fundamental works are Angus Campbell, Philip E. Converse, Warren E. Miller, and Donald Stokes, *The American Voter* (Chicago: University of Chicago Press, 1960); and Norman H. Nie, Sidney Verba, and John R. Petrocik, *The Changing American Voter* (Cambridge: Harvard University Press, 1976).

4. The margin of error for each edition of the Tennessee Poll is approximately three and one-half percentage points at the 95 percent confidence level, although the editions with sample sizes slightly under seven hundred (1994 and Fall 1996) are closer to four percentage points.

5. V. O. Key, Jr., *Southern Politics in State and Nation* (New York: Vintage, 1949), 78.

6. Robert H. Swansborough, "The Tennessee Voter," in *The Volunteer State:*

Readings in Tennessee Politics, ed. Dorothy F. Olshfski and T. McN. Simpson III (Nashville: Tennessee Political Science Association, 1985), 43. Based on a 1981 statewide survey, Swansborough estimated the distribution of party identification as approximately 42 percent Democrat, 33 percent independent, and 25 percent Republican. Using the 1980 National Election Study, Swansborough estimated the level of Republican identification throughout the South at approximately 17 percent.

7. For the sake of simplicity, we have collapsed the Tennessee Poll's seven-point party identification measure (see chapter appendix for question wording) into a trichotomy in which the categories are "Democrat," "Independent" and "Republican."

8. There is a lively ongoing debate over the proper conceptualization of ideology in American politics. See, for examples, William S. Maddox and Stuart A. Lilie, *Beyond Liberal and Conservative: Reassessing the Political Spectrum* (Washington, D.C.: Cato Institute, 1984); and Herbert McClosky and John Zaller, *The American Ethos* (Cambridge, Mass.: Harvard University Press, 1984). It is fair to say that while ideological labeling is tricky at best, the standard liberal-conservative continuum does hold reasonable utility in explaining and predicting voting behavior. See, e.g., John D. Holm and John D. Robinson, "Ideological Identification and the American Voter," *Public Opinion Quarterly* 42 (1978): 235–46; and Theresa Levitin and Warren Miller, "Ideological Interpretations of Presidential Elections," *American Political Science Review* 73 (1979): 751–71.

9. As with party identification, we have collapsed the seven-point ideological identification scale used in the Tennessee Poll (see chapter appendix for question wording) into a trichotomy in which the three categories are "liberal," "moderate" and "conservative."

10. Lee Seifert Greene, David H. Grubbs, and Victor C. Hobday, *Government in Tennessee*, 3d ed. (Knoxville: University of Tennessee Press, 1975), 66.

11. Ibid.

12. The same question was included in the Spring and Fall 1996 editions of the Tennessee Poll with similar results.

Chapter 12. Education in the Volunteer State

1. S. H. Fuhrman, "Education Policy: A New Context for Governance," *Publius*, 17 (1987): 131–43.

2. Lois A. Fisher,"State Legislatures and the Autonomy of Colleges and Universities: A Comparative Study of Legislation in Four States, 1900–1979," *Journal of Higher Education* 59 (March/April 1988): 132–61.

3. Such reports include: *A Nation at Risk*, National Commission of Excellence in Education (Washington, D.C.: Government Printing Office, 1983).

4. L. Darling-Hammond and B. Barry, "The Evolution of Teacher Policy," Joint Report of the Center for Policy Research in Education and Center for the Study of the Teaching Profession, 1988.

5. Michael W. Kirst, "Who Should Control our Schools: Reassessing Current Policy," paper prepared for Breckenridge Forum for the Enhancement of Teaching (San Antonio, Trinity University, August 1987).

6. T. Mazzoni, Barry Sullivan, and Beth Sullivan, "Legislative Lobbying for Education," *Planning and Changing* 14 (1983): 226–33.

7. Frank Essex and T. B. Ungs, "The Institutionalization of the Tennessee Legislature," paper presented at the meeting of the Southwestern Political Science Association, (Ft. Worth, March 1990).

8. Yvonne Wood, "The Importance and Impact of Three Significant Political Decisions upon Higher Education in Tennessee" (Nashville: Tennessee Higher Education Commission, 1983).

9. Samuel H. Shannon, "Land-Grant College Legislation and Black Tennesseans: A Case Study in the Politics of Education," *History of Education Quarterly* (Summer 1982): 139–57.

10. John F. Ohles and Shirley M. Ohles, *Private Colleges and Universities*, 2 vols. (Greenwood, 1982), 2:1315–18.

11. Lee S. Green, David H. Grubbs, and Victor C. Hobday, *Government in Tennessee*, (Knoxville: University of Tennessee Press, 1975).

12. Wood, 1983.

13. Ibid.

14. Commissioner of Education Warf, a powerful commissioner and politician, was not in favor of a coordinating body. Governor Ellington presented Commissioner Warf with a choice of two bills. One bill established a coordinating body but left the structure of the State Board of Education and the University of Tennessee Board of Trustees unchanged. The second bill created a separate body and put the regional universities under its direction removing them from the State Board of Education. Commissioner Warf supported the bill establishing the creation of the coordinating body. Support of the legislature for the coordinating body followed after compromise regarding charge and duties of the new body, consideration of numerous special interest groups, and influence of regional institution presidents and faculty.

15. Wood, 1983; and Fisher, 1988.

16. Greene, Grubb, and Hobday, 1975; and Shannon, 1988.

17. Tennessee Code Annotated, 1990, vol. 9, part 2: 384.

18. Francis M. Gross, "A Comparative Analysis of the Existing Budget Formulas Used for Justifing Budget Requests or Allocating Funds for the Operating Expenses of State-Supported Colleges and Universities" (Ph.D. diss., University of Tennessee, 1973).

19. Grady E. Bogue and William E. Trout, "Allocation of State Funds on a Performance Criterion: Acting on the Possible While Awaiting Perfection," paper presented at the Association for Institutional Research Forum (1977).

20. Ted Marchese, "Let's Reward Quality: Tennessee's Bold Experiment," *Change* 17 (November/December 1985): 37–45.

21. Information summarized from George H. Van Allen and Valerie S. Belew, "Mandatory Remediation in Tennessee: Strategy for Promoting Excellence While Serving the Underprepared," ERIC document ED353015 (1992).

22. Material relating to *Geier v. Blanton* is summarized from the following newspaper accounts and study:

"Judge Gray Orders Merger of UTN, TSU," (Nashville) *Tennessean*, February 1, 1977.

"Tennessee's Long-Running Desegregation Drama," *The Chronicle of Higher Education*, April 4, 1977.

"Merger Order for 2 Tennessee Campuses Is Upheld," *New York Times*, April, 14. 1979.

"High Court Rejects Review of Merger," *Nashville Banner*, October 1, 1979.

James F. Blumstein, "Legal Issues in the Desegregation of Postsecondary Education. The Postsecondary Desegregation Project, Report II" (Nashville: Vanderbilt University, 1981).

23. Material on the background of the Comprehensive Reform Act is based on George M. Drew, "The Comprehensive Education Reform Act of 1984 (CERA)," *Education* 108, no. 4 (Summer 1988).

24. C. B. Furtwengler, "Career Ladders: Summative Evaluation of Teachers: The Political Perspective," paper given at Symposium conducted at the meeting of the American Educational Research Association, (Washington, D.C., April 1987).

25. Furtwengler, 1987.

26. Material explaining the provisions of the Comphrehensive Education Reform Act is based on George M. Drew, "The Comprehensive Education Reform Act of 1988 (CERA)," *Education* 108, no 4 (Summer 1988).

27. Furtwengler, 1987.

28. Robin L. Pierce, "The Comprehensive Education Reform Act of 1984: A Superintendent's View," *Tennessee Education* 15, nos. 1-2 (Fall 1985).

29. Pierce, 1985.

30. Ibid.

31. Ibid.

32. Don McAlister, "The Master Plan for Reform," *Tennessee School Boards Journal* 8, no. 2 (Winter 1991).

33. Ibid.

34. Don McAlister, "Education Legislation," *Tennessee School Boards Journal* 8, no. 4 (Summer 1991).

35. Material explaining the provisions of the Education Improvement Act is based on Beth Garfrerick et al., "Rebuilding Education: The Point of Reform," *Tennessee School Boards Journal* 9, no. 2 (Spring 1992).

36. Theodore J. Meyers, Thomas C. Valesky, and Marilyn A. Hirth, "K–12 Education Funding in Tennessee: Equity Now—Adequacy Coming," *Journal of Education Finance* 20, (Spring 1995).

37. *Tennessee Small School Systems v. McWherter*, Chancery Court, 20th Judicial District, Davidson County, part 2. case no. 88-1812-II, 1988.

38. *TSSS v. McWherter*, 1988.

39. *TSSS v. McWherter*, 1988.

40. *Tennessee Small School Systems v. McWherter*, Court of Appeals of Tennessee, Middle Section, at Nashville. Appeal no. 01-A-01–9111-CH-00433, 1991.

41. *Tennessee Small School Systems v. McWherter*, Chancery Court, 20th Judicial District, Davidson County, part 2. case no. 88-1812-II, on remand from the Tennessee Supreme Court, 1993.

42. Meyers, 1995.

43. R. Lehne and A. Rosenthal, Research Perspectives on State Legislatures

and Education Policy, Report No. BBB06621, (Washington, D. C.: National Institute of Education, 1980).

Chapter 13. The Tennessee Prison System

1. U.S. Department of Justice, Bureau of Justice Statistics, *Sourcebook of Criminal Justice Statistics, –1994*, ed. Kathleen Maguire and Ann L. Pastore (Washington, D.C.: Government Printing Office, 1995), table 6.19, p. 540.

2. Whereas between 1960 and 1970 the number of persons serving prison time dropped from 119 per 100,000 population to 97 per 100,000, by 1994, the proportion had more than trebled to 387 per 100,000. By the end of 1994, the United States had the second highest prison population of any nation in the world at 1,053,738. And this figure did not include inmates in local jails, 490,000. In 1994 alone, sixteen states had prison population increases of 10 percent or more. In Tennessee it was up 12.9 percent.

3. Gloria Danziger, "Prison Crowding," *Editorial Research Reports*, August 7, 1987.

4. Ibid.

5. Barbara Neal, "Putting a Lock on Prison Costs," *American City & County* (January 1995): 26.

6. Paul Cohan, "Between a Rock and a Hard Place, *American City & County* (June 1993): 56–63.

7. The filing of lawsuits by state prisoners has become a common practice. In 1993 more than 1,000 lawsuits were filed in Tennessee by state prisoners. While only a few gain a full hearing, as is noted in this article, they can have major consequences for a state justice system.

8. The commission members consisted of state trial and appellate court judges, general session judges, district attorneys general, the state attorney general, defense attorneys, law enforcement officials, legislators, clerks of court association, corrections commissioner, parole board chairman, and code commission chairman. Additionally, professors of law from Vanderbilt University Law School and the University of Tennessee Law School assisted the commission. The chair was appointed by the governor.

9. In its report to the legislature, the commission developed three additional sentencing structures, Two of these would have met the 95 percent mandate by drastically cutting the sentence lengths. The other one, which closely resembled the sentencing structure then in place, would have required the construction of 6,896 beds at an estimated cost of $220,280,000 and required an annual increased operating cost of $150,667,000.

10. At that time the state was paying about $50 million to local governments to house prisoners. Of this amount about $10 million was for pretrial detainees and the remaining $40 million was for locally held convicted felons. Of the latter about half had been sentenced to local jails to complete their sentence and about half were state inmates waiting for room in a state-run prison.

11. In 1984 the General Assembly enacted Public Chapter 408, generally referred to as the Jail Removal Bill, which prohibited the placement of juveniles in

adult jails after January 1, 1985. Without such action, Tennessee stood to lose federal funding through the federal Juvenile Justice and Delinquency Prevention Act. In 1989 the Juvenile Corrections program was separated from the Department of Corrections. Its budget too had grown considerably since 1980—from $20 million to $61.7 million in 1991.

12. Richard Locker, "Prison Study Warns 'Get Tough' Means 'Get Money,'" (Memphis) *Commercial Appeal*, November 11, 1994.

13. Reed Branson, "Sundquist Details Crime Battle Plan," *Commercial Appeal*, February 16, 1995.

14. Paula Wade, "Sundquist's Crime Package Estimate Short by $10 Million," *Commercial Appeal*, April 4, 1995.

15. The General Assembly's Fiscal Review Committee concluded that the Sundquist plan to lock away repeat violent criminals with no opportunity for parole would cost the state $9.5 million alone in housing, with an additional $1.3 million in court costs. Charles Ferrell, administrative director for the Tennessee Supreme Court, noted that the extra court costs would likely come because many persons, who under the then current plan agreed to plea bargain their case rather than go to trial, would not do so under the new no parole guidelines, which would require them to serve 85 percent of their time rather that the normal one-third. For the indigent who decided to go to trial, the state would have to provide criminal defense. The Fiscal Review Committee also informed the Oversight Committee that if the governor had not deleted some of the criminal offenses he originally intended to include in his "no parole" bill, the cost to the state would have been $60 million (*The Daily Herald*, March 17,1995).

16. *Report on Truth in Sentencing* (Nashville: Tennessee Sentencing Commission, January 1995).

17. Among new beds to be constructed by the state were additions planned for the Lois DeBerry Special Needs Facility in Nashville, the Turney Center Industrial Prison and Farm in Hickman County, and 192 at the Tennessee Prison for Women. At that time 198 female state prisoners were backed up in county jails. Senator Kyle, chairman of the Select Oversight Committee on Corrections, reacted to this announcement by noting that the state had not yet presented a future plan for the growing number of state women prisoners and was opening itself up to a possible law suits because of $350 million in new prison construction, nothing has been spent on women's-prison expansion (Reed Branson, "Cramming Prisons Would Be Costly, Officials Warn," *Commercial Appeal*, November 23,1994).

18. Wade, "Prison Growth."

19. *Union City Daily Messenger*, August 9, 1995. Adding to the two senators' concerns was the Saturday, October 28, 1995, inmate uprising at the West Tennessee Detention Facility in Mason, a small community in Tipton County. The facility was owned by Corrections Corporation of America (CCA). Inmates involved in the confrontation were at the prison on contract from the North Carolina Department of Corrections, which was paying CCA $55 a day to house them. The inmates were serving terms of from five to forty years. This event raised several questions, in addition to those mentioned by Senators Kyle and Rochelle.

First, if CCA operates facilities in Tennessee, should the state insist that beds be made available to the state first if needed? Second, should the state prescribe the kind of convict (the degree of offense) that can be brought into this system? While none of those involved in the incident at Mason were murderers, would that necessarily be the case in the future? Third, how will people in the communities where such out of state prisoners are housed react to the plan if those prisoners, separated by a great distance from family members, are more prone to escape attempts?

20. Under the Sundquist administration plan, the only cells that would not be subject to double celling would be those judged to be dangerous to themselves or others, including prison "sexual predators."

21. Paula Wade, "Building Commission Rejects Sundquist's Proposals on Prisons," *Commercial Appeal*, September 15, 1995.

22. Richard Locker, "$48 Million Megaprison Planned in Lauderdale," *Commercial Appeal*, December 15, 1995.

23. State Senator Rochelle responded to the governor's plans by stating, "I don't want to waste any more money. It has all the earmarks of something that was thrown together at the last minute. Really, I don't know where you're going to get the money to do much more without some modification of a campaign promise made a year or so ago," ("Corrections," *Co-Worker* 12, no, 9 [September 1995]).

24. Department of Corrections figures noted that 9,351 unemployed Tennesseans with high school degrees lived within a fifty-mile radius of Ripley, located jut north of the proposed prison site. Of that number, 8,468 would accept full-time employment. It further estimated that of all of those persons eligible to take the necessary examination for employment, only 38 percent would actually show up to take it. Of those, 72 percent would pass. About 62 percent of those who passed the exam would be hired. Of that total, 63 percent would complete the 6 month probation period. The best case scenario showed that of people hired, 905 would still be working at one of the three prisons after six months. That scenario would result in 326 vacancies in the facilities (*Union City Daily Messenger*, December 16, 1995).

25. Paula Wade, "Keeping Prisoners in Mental Facility Approved," *Commercial Appeal*, December 15, 1995.

26. Committee member Sen. Bob Rochelle had two weeks before proposing that the state create an independent board to govern the state prisons.

27. For an insight into the attitude of Tennessee citizens on crime and justice issues, see *Crime and Justice Survey Results: Tennessee 1992* (Nashville: Tennessee Bureau of Investigation, Tennessee Statistical Analysis Center, 1992).

28. *Commercial Appeal*, August 29,1991.

29. *Crime and Justice*.

30. Ibid.

31. According to the Tennessee Sentencing Commission in 1993, of 13,032 defendants convicted of felonies, only 457 were convicted by jury. This was due to the large number entering into a plea bargain (*Report on Truth in Sentencing*, 12).

32. According to the State Sentencing Commission, 34.3 percent of the 10,694 felony convictions reported to it between January and November 1994 resulted in

incarceration in a state prison. Other sentences were: 24.3 percent to local jails, 21.9 percent to some sort of probation, 10 percent to confinement in conjunction with probation, 6.4 percent to a community corrections center, 2.2 percent to confinement in conjunction with a community corrections center (*Commercial Appeal*, January 30,1995).

33. Marc Perrusquia, "Early Release of Prisoners Fuels Anger, Frustration," *Commercial Appeal*, November 21, 1994.

34. *Crime and Justice.*

35. James Chisum, "Nonprison Sentences a Growing Alternative for Courts," *Commercial Appeal*. March 5, 1990.

36. The percentage was originally set at 20 percent. By 1995 that percentage was up to 45 percent for offenders convicted as habitual criminals. In 1988 Governor McWherter issued a directive excluding from "safety valve" coverage any inmate who committed one of several crimes while incarcerated. In 1990 he extended exclusion to all sex offenders, and in 1993 he extended it to any inmate convicted of a homicide offense.

37. Fiona Soltes, "Inmates: Free Us, Free Up Funds," *The Tennessean*, December 8, 1991.

38. In 1991, 45 percent of state prisoners nationwide were persons who, at the time they committed their offenses, were under conditional supervision in the community either on parole or on probation. Roby L. Cohen, *Probation and Parole Violators in State Prison, 1991* (Washington, D.C.: U.S. Department of Justice, Office of Justice Programs, Bureau of Justice Statistics, August 1995), 1.

39. Curriden, "The Crime Problem," *The Chattanooga Times*, September 25, 1995; and Curriden, Katrina Beets, and Mary Rebyansky, "Felons Escape Hard Time," *The Chattanooga Times*, September 25, 1992.

40. Leon Alligood, "Sir!Yes Sir!," *The Nashville Banner*, n.d.

41. Craig Perkins, James J.Stephens, and Allen J. Beck, *Jails and Jail Inmates 1993–94.* (Washington,DC: U.S. Department of Justice, Office of Justice Programs, Bureau of Justice Statistics), p.1.

42. Perkins, Stephens, and Beck.

43. *State and Local Corrections: A Coordinated Strategy for Tennessee.* (Nashville: Tennessee General Assembly Select Oversight Committee on Corrections, 1988).

44. The two state-run facilities were Northwest Corrections Center and Northeast Corrections Center. Their daily cost per prisoner was $35.76 . The cost for Central Correctional Center, CCA's run facility was $35.38. These figures compared to about $55 a day for the seventeen other state-run facilities (Karen Miller, "Private Prison Gains Good Marks," *Commercial Appeal*, February 6, 1995.)

45. Linda McCarty , President of the Tennessee State Employees Association, reacted negatively to both the proposed CCA prison and the additional double-celling of prison inmates. In her view, "Double-celling is a practice that dramatically increases prison tensions and therefore endangers the lives of the state employees who work in these facilities. They already face danger each day, but this is beyond reason. And, giving another prison to CCA directly violates state law. It also smacks of a conflict of interest for Gov. Sundquist" ("Corrections," *Co-Worker*).

46. Paula Wade, "Private Prison Plan Questioned," *Commercial Appeal*, October 24, 1995. Snodgrass, who was a member of the State Building Commission, claimed the plan could not go forth without his approval. One concern Snodgrass had was that Hardeman County wanted to build the new prison with prototype plans developed by the State Department of Corrections for prisons so as to cut down construction costs. Yet, the state would have no say in whether or not the construction was or was not sufficiently in line with the state's plans.

47. In an article in T*he Commercial Appeal*, Nashville reporter Paula Wade did a column on Governor Sundquist backing away from the CCA proposal as first laid out. Her comment was, "Frankly put, the deal smelled to high heaven." Wade went on to note the various connections and potential ethical conflicts involving money and CCA personnel and Nashville political leaders of both parties (Paula Wade, "Don't Fence Me In," *Commercial Appeal*, November 19, 1995). According to CCA chairman Doctor Crants, the private firm abandoned the idea of Hardeman County building the prison because "it seemed at every turn the comptroller (Snodgrass) was going to find a way to throw rocks at the project" (Paula Wade, "CCA Plans Prison Without Using State Aid," *Commercial Appeal*, November 14, 1995).

48. Larry Reibstein, Ginny Carroll and Carroll Bogert, "Back to the Chain Gang," *Newsweek*, October 17, 1994, 87–88.

49. Paula Wade, "Senators Seek to Cut Prison Cable, Ice Cream Machines, Early Release," *Commercial Appeal*, May 10, 1995. The words "safe and comfortable" were added to the Tennessee Constitution at the state's 1870 constitutional convention at the suggestion of Knox County delegate John Baxter, as a response to Civil war veterans' treatment in Union prison camps (Karen Miller, "Lawmakers Propose Tougher Time for Inmates," *Commercial Appeal*, March 3, 1995). In several states, legislators in 1994 and 1995 introduced bills calling for caning or paddling as punishment for certain misdemeanors. In Tennessee in 1995 three Republican legislators introduced a bill that would allow public caning on courthouse steps for vandals, flag-burners, cemetery desecrators, and others. John Beifuss, "Criminal-Weary States Wave the Whip, Noose; 'Old Ideas,' Critics Say," *Commercial Appeal*, February 15, 1992.

50. While the governor's talk of considering using chain gangs in Tennessee was vigorously attacked by the Tennessee ACLU in Nashville as nothing but politics, the executive director of the Tennessee Sheriff's Association and sixteen Tennessee sheriffs who visited Alabama came back stating they saw nothing cruel or inappropriate about it (*Jackson Sun*, October 19, 1995). In December Cheathamn County Sheriff Pat Chandler, with the approval of the County Commission, initiated the first chain gang in Tennessee in about three decades when he instituted an "inmates-at-work program." Prior to this the county had only used minimum-security inmates to work outside; however, the chained inmates would be maximum-security inmates and would include convicted sex-offenders (*Commercial Appeal*, December 7, 1995).

51. When asked in 1992 which of several tax options they would support in Tennessee in order to build more jails and prisons, 25 percent of those polled said they would not support any tax increase. A tax on alcohol was preferred by 57 percent

and a tax on tobacco by 50 percent. The least popular tax increase was the sales tax, which was the only one of the current state taxes likely to be adequate enough to raise the funds needed. High enough taxes on tobacco and alcohol would generate tremendous resistance from members of those economic elements.

52. *Report on Truth in Sentencing*.

53. Richard Locker, "Prison Report Shows Time to Catch Up," *Commercial Appeal*, November 9, 1995.

54. Ibid. In Mississippi , where the state legislature in 1994 passed a truth in sentencing law requiring all convicts to serve 85 percent of their sentences, the states's Correction Commissioner Steve Puckett said the law, which applies to all crimes, was causing the state serious financial problems. Puckett's department estimated that by the year 2005 the state's inmate population would increase from 12,294 to 31,031, a 152 percent increase (*Commercial Appeal*, January 18, 1996).

Chapter 14. Finances of Tennessee State Government

The authors would like to thank Stan Chervin, Pat Price, and Hyrum Plaas for useful comments and suggestions. The views expressed here are those of the authors.

1. U.S. Data on Demand, Inc. and State Policy Research, Inc., *States In Profile: The State Policy Reference Book 1995* (McConnellsburg, Penn.: 1995), table C-8. Own-source general revenues are taxes and fees levied by Tennessee state government on economic activity in the state. The state derives additional funds from other sources, including intergovernmental aid from the federal government.

2. See Bradford N. Forrister, Bill Buechler, and Marlin Womack, *1994 Tennessee Tax Guide: A Comprehensive Survey of Major Tennessee State and Local Taxes* (Nashville: M. Lee Smith, 1994) for a more detailed discussion of individual Tennessee state taxes.

3. See Raymond J. Ring, Jr., "The Proportion of Consumers' and Producers' Goods in the General Sales Tax," *National Tax Journal* 42 (1989): 167-80.

4. The business share of the sales tax, as used here, relies on Ring's estimates that 41 percent of total sales and use tax collections are derived from business purchases of goods and services.

5. See Tennessee, *The Budget: 1994–1995*. (Nashville: Department of Finance and Administration).

6. The base year for adjusting tax revenues for changes in tax rates is 197′ which explains the difference between adjusted and unadjusted tax revenues 1977.

7. William F. Fox, *Tennessee's Revenue Structure: A 20-Year Forecast* (Kn′ Center for Business and Economic Research, University of Tennessee, 1989′

8. See Advisory Commission on Intergovernmental Relations, *RTS 1 Revenue Capacity and Effort*. Information Report M-187 (Washing′ Advisory Commission on Intergovernmental Relations, 1993).

9. Tennesseans for Fair Taxation, *Taxation in Tennessee: There* ′ (Nashville: Tennesseans for Fair Taxation, 1996).

10. Hal Hovey, *State Fact Finder* (Washington, D.C.: Congressional Quarterly, 1996).

11. See Richard A. Musgrave and Peggy B. Musgrave, *Public Finance in Theory and Practice*, 5th edition (New York: McGraw-Hill, 1989), 216.

12. Mary O.Borg, Paul M. Mason, and Stephen L. Shapiro, *The Economic Consequences of State Lotteries* (New York: Praeger, 1991).

13. William F. Fox and Matthew N. Murray, "Economic Aspects of Taxing Services" *National Tax Journal* 41 (1988): 19–36.

14. Expenditures as described here include spending by Tennessee state government from all revenue sources, including federal grants.

15. See Russell Dabbs and Matthew N. Murray, "Expenditures in the Tennessee Budget: 1980–1990," in *An Economic Report to the Governor of the State of Tennessee*, chapter 4 (Knoxville: Center for Business and Economic Research, University of Tennessee, 1992) for additional background.

16. See Tennessee Advisory Commission on Intergovernmental Relations, *Funding Tennessee Schools: From Reform to Restructuring* (Nashville, 1995) for a more thorough treatment of Tennessee's education reform efforts.

17. For background on the former Medicaid program and pressures for its replacement, see Russell Dabbs, "Medicaid in Tennessee: Trends and Prospects," in *An Economic Report to the Governor of the State of Tennessee*, chapter 4 (Knoxville: Center for Business and Economic Research, The University of Tennessee, 1993).

18. See Kelly D. Edmiston, "Welfare Reform: Issues and Consequences for Tennessee and the Nation" in *An Economic Report to the Governor of the State of Tennessee*, chapter 4 (Knoxville: Center for Business and Economic Research, University of Tennessee, 1996).

Chapter 15. State Policy, Global Economy: The Political Economy of Foreign Investment in Tennessee

1. Steven D. Williams and William J. Brinker, "A Survey of Foreign Firms Recently Locating in Tennessee," *Growth and Change* 16, no. 3(1985): 56.

2. Tennessee Department of Economic and Community Development, *Foreign Investment, 1994: Tennessee*, 2.

3. At the end of World War II, a new international monetary system was established through a set of rules negotiated on an estate in Bretton Woods, New Hampshire. One key rule was fixing the value of the dollar at $35 to an ounce of gold, from which it was not allowed to deviate. This rule was abandoned in the early 1970s.

4. Edward John Ray, *The Determinants of Foreign Direct Investment in the United States: 1979–1985* (Cambridge Mass.: National Bureau of Economic Research, 1988).

5. Hsin-Min Tong and C. K. Walter, "An Empirical Study of Plant Location Decisions of Foreign Manufacturing Investors in the United States," *Columbia Journal of World Business*, 15, no. 1 (1980): 66–73.

6. *Statistical Abstract of the United States, 1993*, 435.

7. Ibid., 402; and U.S. Bureau of Labor Statistics, Department of Labor,

Employment and Earnings from its LABSTAT on-line bulletin board (ftp://ftp.bls.gov/gov/pub/time.series/).

8. Edwardo Lachica, "Tennessee's 'Hustle' Is Attracting Japanese Industries," *Nashville Banner*, March 4, 1981, 15 (reprint from *The Asian Wall Street Journal*).

9. KPMG Peat Marwick, *Tennessee: 1994 Inbound Investment Survey* and Nashville Area Chamber of Commerce information.

10. "Industrial Development," *Tennessee Journal,* October 11, 1976, 2. The evaluator was Fantus, Inc., an international business consulting firm.

11. Materials in U.S. Department of Commerce, *Foreign Direct Investment in the United States*, Report of the Secretary of Commerce to the Congress in Compliance with the Foreign Investment Study Act of 1974 (April 1976).

12. "Industrial Development."

13. James Harwell, "The States' Growing International Role," *State Government* 48, no. 1 (1975): 2–5.

14. David Griesen, "Busbee Key Man in US-Japanese Business," *Nashville Banner*, September 17, 1982: C-3.

15. "How Japan is Winning Dixie: The Tennessee Story," *U.S. News and World Report,* May 9, 1988, 43–59.

16. "Alexander to Visit Taiwan, Japan on Trade Mission," *Tennessee Journal*, October 15, 1979, 2.

17. Spero C. Pappas, "A Comparative Study of Promotional Activities to Attract Foreign Investment: An Application of Marketing Theory to the Efforts of the Southeastern States" (Ph.D. diss., Georgia State University, 1979), 142.

18. Ibid., 139; and Harwell.

19. Glickman and Woodward, 230. See also William F. Fox, "Japanese Investment in Tennessee: The Economic Effects of Nissan's Location in Smyrna," in *The Politics of Industrial Recruitment: Japanese Automobile Investment and Economic Development in the American States,* ed. Ernest J. Yanarella and William C. Green (New York: Greenwood, 1990), 175–87.

20. Pappas, 142.

21. "Tennessee Business Highlights," *Tennessee Journal,* November 24, 1980, 5.

22. Baker's assistance is described in Lachica. For his influence, see Shelley Liles, "State Continues to Snare Industrial Prizes," (Nashville) *Tennessean*, May 30, 1988, E-2.

23. Reexporting involves bringing in products from outside the country, enhancing the products in some way, and then exporting them back out to other markets.

24. "General Assembly Resumes Work . . . Receives Alexander Proposals," *Tennessee Journal,* January 7, 1980, 1.

25. Liles.

26. Beth Fortune, "Governor Will Woo European Investors," *Nashville Banner*, June 22, 1989, B-1.

27. John M. Kline, *State Government Influence in U.S. International Economic Policy* (Lexington, Mass.: Lexington, 1983).

28. See Steven M. Neuse, "State Activities in International Trade," *State Government* 45, no. 2 (1982), 57–64. Tennessee ranked sixth of the twelve south-

eastern states and not among America's top ten states in Neuse's spending survey. However, where Tennessee did differ was in its concentration on investment rather than trade. In 1980 the state ranked twenty-fifth in spending on export promotion but twelfth on attracting foreign investment; sixty percent of its international budget was devoted to foreign investment (see Kline).

29. Peter Eisinger, *The Rise of the Entrepreneurial State: State and Local Development Policy in the United States* (Madison: University of Wisconsin Press, 1988), 293ff.

30. "Administration Highlights Include Strong 1st Quarter Growth," *Tennessee Business and Industry Review* 50, no. 2 (July 1995): 1.

31. These figures, and those cited in the paragraphs below, are from the Department of Commerce, Bureau of Economic Analysis, *Foreign Direct Investment in the United States, Operations of U.S. Affiliates of Foreign Countries, Revised Estimates* (annual).

32. These figures, and the manufacturing figures cited below, are from the joint publication of the Department of Commerce, Bureau of Economic Analysis and the Bureau of the Census, *Foreign Direct Investment in the United States, Establishment Data for Manufacturing*, various years, and the Tennessee Department of Economic and Community Development, *Tennessee Total Foreign Direct Investment and Employment by Country, Current Through January 1995*.

33. Glickman and Woodward, 326–28.

34. Ibid., 228.

35. "Ripple Effect of Datsun Truck Plant to Boost Midstate Economy," *Tennessee Journal*, November 3, 1980, 5.

36. Jeffrey S. Arpan has noted this is particularly true when examining the southeastern states where even the basic sales pitch (low cost labor, low taxes, a nice climate, and a probusiness environment) is the same. Arpan, "The Impact of State Incentives on Foreign Investor's Site Selection," *Economic Review* (The Federal Reserve Bank of Atlanta) (December 1981): 36–42.

37. Eisinger, 60.

38. KPMG Peat Marwick, 13.

39. Williams and Brinker.

40. The answer also depends upon what one means by "state policies." Research affirming the importance of state policies on investment decisions often focuses on broad policies such as right-to-work laws, histories of policy activism, and levels of state spending, rather than specifically on investment-attracting activities. See, for instance, Sharon E. Fox and Jeong-Hwa Lee, "Determinants of Foreign Firm Locations in the United States 1985–1990: Implications for State Economic Development Policies," *American Politics Quarterly* 24, no. 1 (1996): 81–104. However, Cletus Cloughlin, Joseph V. Terza, and Vachira Arromdee, "State Characteristics and the Location of Foreign Direct Investment within the United States," *Review of Economics and Statistics* 73, no. 4 (1991): 675–83, did find a direct relationship between promotional spending and success in attracting investments in the early 1980s.

41. Rosita Thomas, "American Public Opinion towards Foreign Investment," in *Foreign Direct Investment: Effects on the United States*, Report by the

Subcommittee on Economic Stabilization of the House Committee on Banking, Finance, and Urban Affairs, 101st Congress, first session (July 1989), 176–77.

42. Ned G. Howenstine and William J. Zeile, "Characteristics of Foreign-Owned U.S. Manufacturing Establishments," in Department of Commerce, Economics and Statistics Administration, Office of the Chief Economist, *Foreign Direct Investment in the United States: An Update* (January 1995).

43. Joe Mattey and Mark Spiegel, "Is State and Local Competition for Firms Harmful?" *FRBSF Weekly Letter* (Federal Reserve Bank of San Francisco) August 4, 1995.

Selected Bibliography

Armstrong, Walter P., Jr. "Constitutional Limitations on Income Taxes in Tennessee." *Vanderbilt Law Review* 27 (1974): 475–89.

Black, Earl, and Merle Black. *The Vital South: How Presidents are Elected.* Cambridge: Harvard University Press, 1992.

———. *Politics and Society in the South.* Cambridge: Harvard University Press, 1987.

The Book of the States, 1996–1997. Lexington, Ky.: Council of State Governments, 1996.

Bullock, Charles S. III, and Mark J. Rozell, eds. *The New Politics of the Old South.* Landham, Md.: Rowman & Littlefield, 1998.

Caldwell, Joshua W. *Studies in the Constitutional History of Tennessee.* 2d ed. Cincinnati: Robert Clarke, 1907.

Capers, Gerald. *The Biography of a River Town.* New York: Vanguard, 1966.

Corbello, Michael K., and John C. Kuzenski. "Racial and Economic Explanations for Republican Growth in the South: A Case Study of Attitudinal Voting in Louisiana." *American Review of Politics* 10 (Summer 1996).

Corcoran, Bobby, and David H. Grubbs, eds. *Proceedings of the Conference for Delegates to the 1977 Tennessee Constitutional Convention.* Murfreesboro, Tenn.: Middle Tennessee State University, May 20–21, 1977.

Corlew, Robert E. *Tennessee: A Short History.* 2d ed. Knoxville: University of Tennessee Press, 1981.

Crawford, Charles. *Yesterday's Memphis.* Miami: Seemann, 1976.

Darnell, Riley C. *Tennessee Blue Book, 1995–1996: Bicentennial Edition (1796–1996).* Nashville: Tennessee Secretary of State, 1996.

Davidson, Chandler, and Bernard Grofman, eds. *Quiet Revolution in the South: The Impact of the Voting Rights Act 1965–1990.* Princeton: Princeton University Press, 1994.

Donelson, Lewis R. "Tax Reform in Tennessee." *Memphis State University Law Review* 4 (1975): 201–20.

Dunning, Natilee, ed. *Shaping a State; The Legacy of Tennessee Women—A Symposium.* Nashville: Margaret Cuninggim Women's Center, Vanderbilt University, October 28, 1995.

Dye, Thomas R. *Politics in States and Communities.* 8th ed. Englewood Cliffs, N.J.: Prentice Hall, 1994.

Forrister, Bradford N., Bill Buechler, and Marlin Womack. *1994 Tennessee Tax Guide: A Comprehensive Survey of Major Tennessee State and Local Taxes.* Nashville: M. Lee Smith Publishers and Printers, 1994.

Fox, William F., and Matthew N. Murray. "Economic Aspects of Taxing Services." *National Tax Journal* 41 (1988): 19–36.

Freeman, J. Leiper. *Political Change in Tennessee, 1948–1978: Party Politics Trickles Down.* Knoxville: University of Tennessee, Bureau of Public Administration, 1980.

Funding Tennessee Schools: From Reform to Restructuring. Nashville: Tennessee Advisory Commission on Intergovernmental Relations, 1995.

Glaser, James M. *Race, Campaign Politics, and the Realignment in the South.* New Haven: Yale University Press, 1996.

Goldfield, David. *Cotton Fields and Skyscrapers.* Baltimore: Johns Hopkins University Press, 1989.

Goodman, William. *Inherited Domain: Political Parties in Tennessee.* Knoxville: Bureau of Public Administration, 1954.

Grantham, Dewey W. *The Life and Death of the Solid South.* Lexington: University Press of Kentucky, 1988.

Gray, Virginia, and Herbert Jacob, eds. *Politics in the American States: A Comparative Analysis.* 6th ed. Washington, D.C.: Congressional Quarterly Press, 1996.

Greene, Lee S., David H. Grubbs, and, Victor C. Hobday. *Government in Tennessee.* Knoxville: University of Tennessee Press, 1982.

Greene, Lee S. *Lead Me On: Frank Goad Clement and Tennessee Politics.* Knoxville: University of Tennessee Press, 1982.

Halberstam, David. *The Children.* New York: Random House, 1998.

Harrigan, John J. *Political Change in the Metropolis.* 6th ed. New York: HarperCollins College Publishers, 1993.

Harrington, John J. "A Review of the Struggle for Tennessee Tax Reform." *Tennessee Law Review* 60 (1993): 431–47.

Hirth, Marilyn A., Theodore J. Meyers, and Thomas C. Valesky. "K–12 Education Funding in Tennessee: Equity Now—Adequacy Coming." *Journal of Education Finance* 20 (Spring 1995).

Holloway, Harry. *The Politics of the Southern Negro.* New York: Random House, 1969.

Kanervo, David. "Problems, Attractions, and Chief Executive Priorities in Small Towns." *Southeastern Political Review* 1 (Spring 1990): 145–172.

Key, V. O., Jr. *Southern Politics in State and Nation.* New York: Alfred A. Knopf, 1949.

Lamon, Lester. *Blacks in Tennessee, 1791–1970.* Knoxville: University of Tennessee Press, 1981.

———. *Black Tennesseans.* Knoxville: University of Tennessee Press, 1977.

Laska, Lewis L. "The 1997 Limited Constitutional Convention." *Tennessee Law Review* 61 (1994): 485–572.

———. *The Tennessee State Constitution: A Reference Guide.* (Westport, Conn.: Greenwood, 1990.

———. "A Legal and Constitutional History of Tennessee, 1772–1972." *Memphis State University Law Review* 6 (1976): 563–672.

Lee, David D. *Tennessee in Turmoil: Politics in the Volunteer State, 1920–1932.* Memphis: Memphis State University Press, 1979.

Mahtesian, Charles. "The Sick Legislature Syndrome and How to Avoid It." *Governing* (February 1997): 16–20.

Majors, William R. *Change and Continuity: Tennessee Politics Since the Civil War.* Macon, Georgia: Mercer University Press, 1986.

McIlwaine, Shields. *Memphis Down in Dixie*. New York: Dutton, 1948.

Memphis in the Great Depression. Knoxville: University of Tennessee Press, 1986.

Moreland, Lawrence W., and Tod A. Baker. *The Disappearing South? Studies in Regional Change and Continuity*. Tuscaloosa: University of Alabama Press, 1990.

Olshfski, F. Dorothy, and T. McN. Simpson. *The Volunteer State: Readings in Tennessee Politics*. Nashville: Tennessee Political Science Association, 1985.

Patterson, Perry C. *The Negro in Tennessee*, 1790–1865. Westport, Conn.: Negro Universities Press, 1968.

Phillips, Margaret I. *The Governors of Tennessee*. Gretna, La.: Pelican, 1978.

Pierce, Robin L. "The Comprehensive Education Reform Act of 1984: A Superintendent's View." *Tennessee Education* 15 (Fall 1985): 20–23.

Plaas, Hyrum, and Charles A. Zuzak. *The Budgetary System in Tennessee*. 2d ed. Knoxville: Bureau of Public Administration, University of Tennessee, 1977.

Rosenthal, Alan. *The Decline of Representative Democracy: Process, Participation, and Power in State Legislatures*. Washington, D.C.: CQ, 1998.

Ross, Bernard H., et al. *Urban Politics: Power in Metropolitan America*. 4th ed. Itasca, Ill.: F. E. Peacock, 1991.

Sabato, Larry. *Goodbye to Good-Time Charlie*. 2d ed. Washington, D.C.: CQ, 1983.

Scher, Richard K. *Politics in the New South: Republicanism, Race and Leadership in the Twentieth Century*. 2d ed. Armark, N.Y.: M. E. Sharpe, 1997.

Squires, James D. *The Secrets of the Hopewell Box: Stolen Elections, Southern Politics, and a City's Coming of Age*. New York: Times Books, 1996.

Steed, Robert P., John A. Clark, Lewis Bowman, and Charles D. Hadley, eds. *Party Organization and Activism in the American South*. Tuscaloosa: University of Alabama Press, 1998.

Steed, Robert P., Laurence W. Moreland, and Todd A. Baker, eds. *Southern Parties and Elections: Studies in Regional Political Change*. Tuscaloosa: University of Alabama Press, 1997.

Stephens, Otis H., Jr. "The Tennessee Constitution and the Dynamics of American Federalism." *Tennessee Law Review* 61 (1994): 707–31.

Swansborough, Robert H., and David M. Brodsky, eds. *The South's New Politics: Realignment and Dealignment*. Columbia: University of South Carolina Press, 1988.

Taxation in Tennessee: There Is a Better Way. Nashville, Tennesseans for Fair Taxation, 1996.

Tennessee County Government Handbook. 5th ed. Knoxville: University of Tennessee County Technical Assistance Service, 1996.

Tennessee Statistical Abstract. Knoxville: Center for Business and Economic Research, University of Tennessee, 1997.

Tindall, George. *The Disruption of the Solid South*. Athens: University of Georgia Press, 1972.

———. *The Emergence of the New South, 1913–1945*. Baton Rouge: Louisiana State University Press, 1967.

Tucker, David. *Memphis Since Crump*. Knoxville: University of Tennessee Press, 1980.

West, Carroll Van. *Tennessee History: The Land, the People, and the Culture* (Knoxville: University of Tennessee Press, 1998).

West, Carroll Van, ed. *Tennessee Encyclopedia of History and Culture*. Nashville: Tennessee Historical Society, 1998.

Wheeler, Marjorie Spruill, ed. *Votes for Women! The Woman Suffrage Movement in Tennessee, the South, and the Nation*. Knoxville: University of Tennessee Press, 1995.

Williams, Samuel Cole. *History of the Lost State of Franklin*. Johnson City, Tenn.: Watauga, 1924.

Yanarella, Ernest J., and William G. Green. *The Politics of Industrial Recruitment: Japanese Automobile Investment and Economic Development in the American States*. New York: Greenwood, 1990.

Contributors

MARK BYRNES (Ph.D., Vanderbilt University) is an associate professor of political science at Middle Tennessee State University. He is the author of *Politics and Space* (Praeger, 1994) and has contributed to the *Congressional Quarterly's Guide to the Presidency*, Oxford's *Historical Guide to American Government* and to a number of other books and journals.

DAVID CARLETON (Ph.D., Purdue University) teaches political science at Middle Tennessee State University, where he specializes in state and local government. He has published articles in several journals, including the *Journal of Politics*, *Human Rights Quarterly*, and the *Journal of Peace Research*.

RICHARD D. CHESTEEN (Ph.D., University of Mississippi) teaches at the University of Tennessee, Martin, where he serves as chair of the Department of History and Political Science. He is active in county government and in 1994 ran for the Democratic nomination for governor of Tennessee. He has published essays in the *Journal of Mississippi History*, the *Journal of Negro History*, and *Presidential Studies Quarterly*.

JIM COOPER (M.A., Oxford University; J.D., Harvard University) practiced law before being elected to Congress from Tennessee's fourth district. During his twelve year tenure in the House, he served on the Budget Committee and the Energy and Commerce Committee. Cooper ran unsuccessfully for the U.S. Senate in 1994 and now works in Nashville with the Equitable Securities Company.

KELLY D. EDMISTON (finishing Ph.D. at the University of Tennessee) has accepted an assistant professorship of economics at the Policy Research Center, Georgia State University. His research focuses on state and local tax issues and economic development, and he has published articles and reports on a variety of public finance issues, including " User Charge Financing of Urban Public Services in Africa" (with William F. Fox), *African Urban Quarterly*, 1996; and "The Long-term Outlook for Tennessee. An Economic Report to the Governor of the State of Tennessee," 1995 and 1998.

FRANK ESSEX (Ph.D., Vanderbilt University) is a professor emeritus of political science at Middle Tennessee State University. He is a past president of the Tennessee Political Science Association.

JAMES HUFFMAN (Ed.D., University of Tennessee) is a professor of educational leadership at Middle Tennessee State University. He has published a number of articles and coauthored books on instructional supervision, putting research into practice, and the role of accreditation, including *Helping Teachers Use Research Findings: The Consumer-Validation Process* (with Robert E. Eaker) (Institute for Research on Teaching, Michigan State University, 1980).

DAVID W. KANERVO (Ph.D., University of Wisconsin, Madison) is a professor of political science at Austin Peay State University. He has published articles in the *Southeastern Political Review*, *Journalism Quarterly*, and *Newspaper Research*. Kanervo has served as president of the Tennessee Political Science Association.

NANCY KEESE (Ed.D., University of Tennessee) is an associate professor and chair of the Department of Educational Leadership at Middle Tennessee State University. Her research interests include alternative scheduling, assessment, cooperative learning, and gender differences relevant to teaching and learning.

LEWIS L. LASKA (J.D., Vanderbilt University; Ph.D., George Peabody College) is a professor of business law at Tennessee State University. He has published numerous articles in a variety of professional journals and a number of books, including *The Tennessee Manual of Complaints* (M. Lee Smith, 1988) and *The Tennessee State Constitution: A Reference Guide* (Greenwood, 1990).

STEVEN G. LIVINGSTON (Ph.D., Harvard University) is an associate professor of political science at Middle Tennessee State University and editor of the quarterly *Global Commerce: Tennessee and the International Economy*. His articles on international political economy and American foreign economic policy have appeared in *International Studies Quarterly*, *Polity*, and *Pacific Focus*, among other journals.

WILLIAM LYONS (Ph.D., University of Oklahoma) has taught political science at the University of Tennessee, Knoxville, since 1975. He has had extensive experience in public opinion polling and has worked as a consultant to numerous public agencies, private companies, and political candidates. He has published articles in many journals, including the *Journal of Politics*, the *American Journal of Political Science*, *American Politics Quarterly*, *Social Science Quarterly*, and *Public Administration Review*. He is coauthor of *American Government: Politics and Political Culture* (West, 1995).

MATTHEW N. MURRAY (Ph.D., University of Northern Iowa) is an associate professor of economics at the University of Tennessee, Knoxville. He has published chapters in a variety of books and in such journals as *Applied Economics*, *Southern Economic Journal*, *Review of Economics and Statistics*, and *National Tax Journal*. He is coauthor of *Sales Tax in the 21st Century* (Greenwood, forthcoming). Murray has testified before Tennessee legislative committees.

GRANT W. NEELEY (Ph.D., University of Tennessee, Knoxville) is an assistant professor of political science at Texas Tech University. He has published articles in *Political Science Quarterly*, *Social Science Quarterly*, *State and Local Government Review*, *Evaluation Review*, and other journals.

MARCUS D. POHLMANN (Ph.D., Columbia University) teaches political science at Rhodes College. A Fulbright Senior Lecturer in the Soviet Union, his writings have appeared in numerous journals, including the *Journal of Politics*, *Political Science Quarterly*, and *Presidential Studies Quarterly*. He has published four books, including *Racial Politics at the Crossroads* (University of Tennessee Press, 1996).

LILLIARD E. RICHARDSON, JR. (Ph.D., University of Texas) is an associate professor of political science at the University of Tennessee, Knoxville. He is the coauthor of *American Government: Politics and Political Culture* (West, 1995) and has written articles for *Political Research Quarterly*, *Social Science Quarterly*, *Legislative Studies Quarterly*, and numerous other journals.

JOHN M. SCHEB II (Ph.D., University of Florida) is a member of the political science faculty and director of the Social Science Research Institute at the University of Tennessee, Knoxville. He has published articles in a variety of journals, including the *Journal of Politics*, *American Politics Quarterly*, and *Social Science Quarterly*. He is coauthor of *American Government: Politics and Political Culture* (West, 1995), *Criminal Law and Procedure*, 2d. ed. (West, 1994), and *American Constitutional Law* (West, 1993).

ANNE SLOAN (Ph.D., Ohio State University) teaches political science at Middle Tennessee State University, where she is a member of the Women's Studies faculty and director of the Global Studies program. Her publications include chapters in several books, including *Public Sector Management*, ed. Marcia Lynn Whicker and Todd W. Areson (Praeger, 1990).

M. LEE SMITH (J.D., Vanderbilt University) is the publisher of M. Lee Smith Publishers LLC, a company that publishes over ninety legal newsletters, three directories, and the *Tennessee Journal*, a weekly newsletter on Tennessee government and politics. Smith, who previously worked as a legislative assistant to Senator Howard Baker and as an executive assistant to Governor Winfield Dunn, is also a political analyst for WTVF-TV in Nashville.

THOMAS D. UNGS (Ph.D., University of Iowa) recently retired as a professor of political science at the University of Tennessee, Knoxville. His articles have appeared in a variety of professional journals, and his books include *American Political Patterns: Conflict and Consensus* (with Dan Nimmo) (Little, Brown, 1973).

THOMAS R. VAN DERVORT (Ph.D., University of Tennessee, Knoxville) is a professor of political science at Middle Tennessee State University. In addition to a number of articles and reviews, he is the author of *Law and Organization in an Interdependent World* (Sage, 1997) and *Equal Justice Under the Law* (West, 1995). He has also served as president of the Tennessee Political Science Association.

JOHN R. VILE (Ph.D., University of Virginia) is a professor in and chair of the Department of Political Science at Middle Tennessee State University. In addition to numerous articles, reviews, and chapters in books, Vile has written and edited eight previous books. These include *The United States Constitution: Questions and Answers* (Greenwood, 1998); *A Companion to the United States Constitution*, 2d. ed. (Praeger, 1997); and *An Encyclopedia of Amendments, Proposed Amendments, and Amending Issues, 1787–1995* (ABC-CLIO, 1996). Vile served as the 1995–96 president of the Tennessee Political Science Association.

Index

TENNESSEE GOVERNMENT AND POLITICS

was composed electronically using
Adobe Caslon types, with displays in
Latino Elongated, Frutiger Bold, and Frutiger Black.
The book was printed on 60# Natural Smooth paper.
The hardback copy was Smyth sewn and cased in Pearl Linen cloth
and the paperback was notch perfect bound
by Braun-Brumfield, Inc.
The dust jacket and cover were printed in three colors by
Vanderbilt University Printing Services.
Book, dust jacket, and cover designs are the work of Deborah Hightower.
Published by Vanderbilt University Press
Nashville, Tennessee 37235